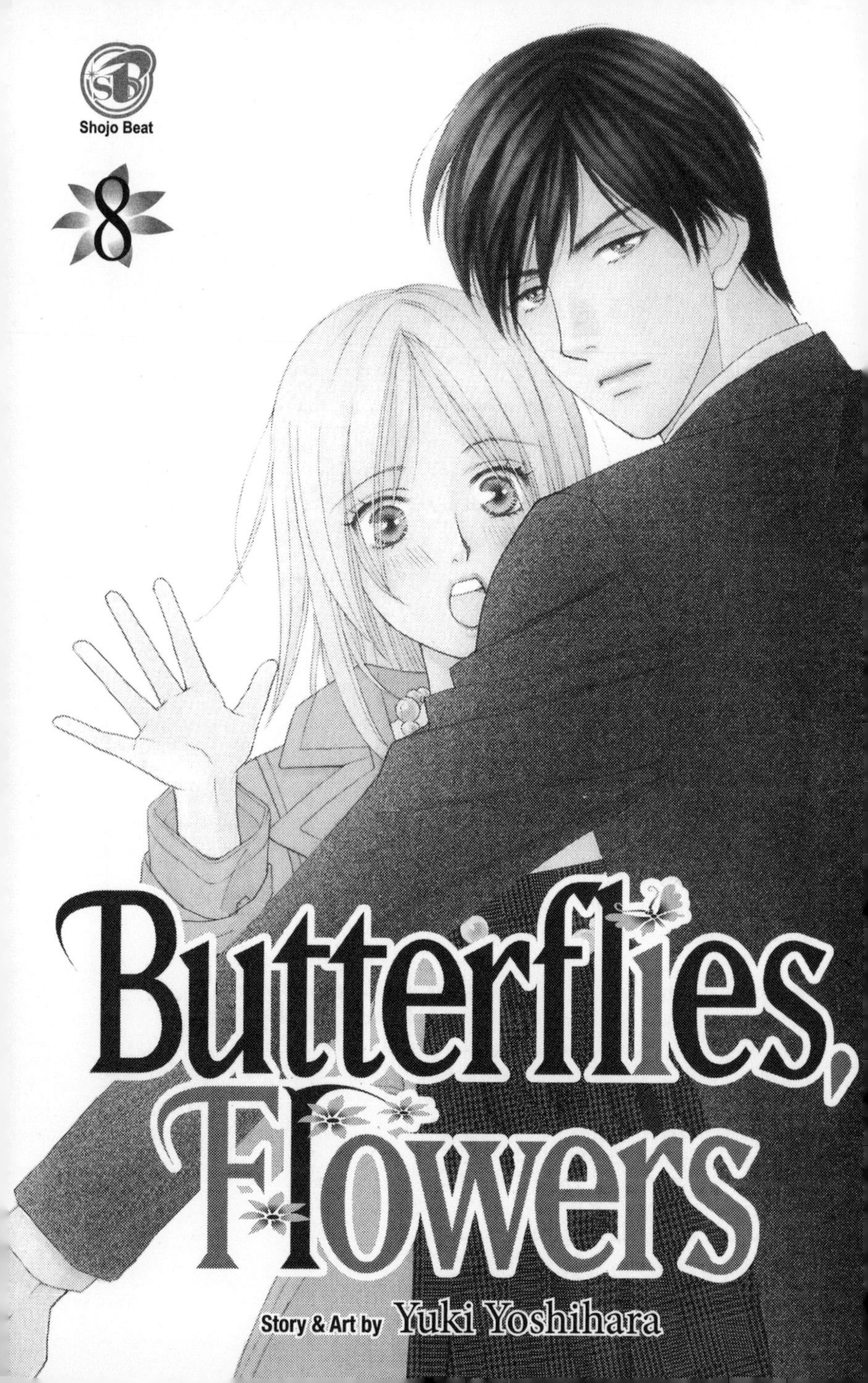

Shojo Beat

8

Butterflies, Flowers

Story & Art by Yuki Yoshihara

Butterflies, Flowers 8

Characters

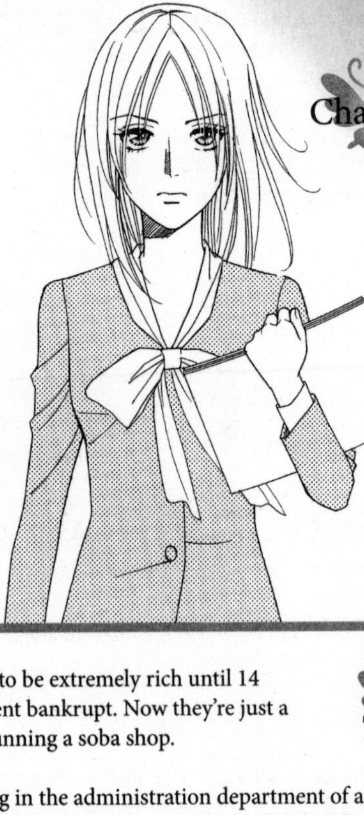

◆Choko Kuze
She's an office worker from an upper-class family who used to be rich. Domoto usually gets the better of her, but at times, she brings out her "aristocratic girl's resolve."

Story Thus Far

◆Choko's family used to be extremely rich until 14 years ago when they went bankrupt. Now they're just a working-class family running a soba shop.

◆Choko starts working in the administration department of a real estate company. But being unskilled, Choko finds herself being pushed around by the senior staff and the mean Director Domoto...

◆Domoto's father used to be a servant who worked for the Kuze family. The director is actually "Cha-chan," the boy who looked after Choko when she was small!

◆Masayuki Domoto

The Director whom Choko loves. He's the son of a former servant to the Kuze family. He is a rather high-handed supervisor, but he supports Choko in her private life. Her childhood nickname for him is "Cha-chan."

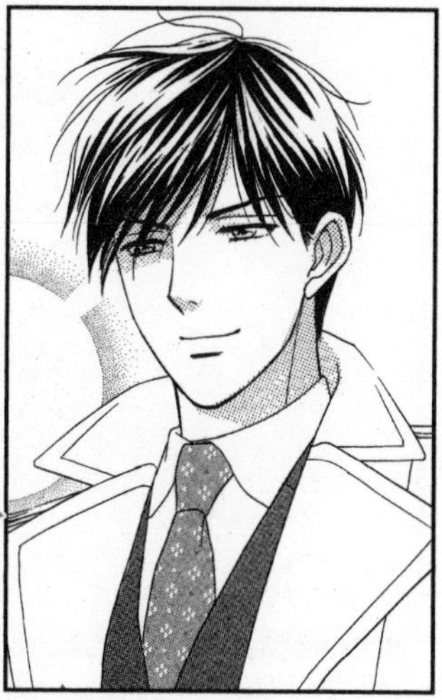

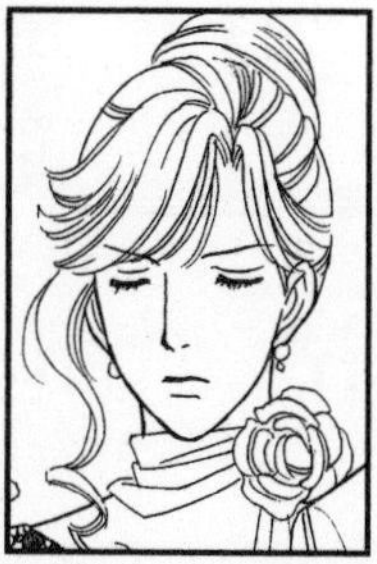

◆Genzaburo Suou

He's a veteran office worker in the Administration Department and a good friend of Domoto. He's a guy, but he usually cross-dresses.

◆Domoto tells Choko that he will protect her with his life. Choko finds out what it's like to be in love, and they make love.♡

◆Kaori, Domoto's ex-girlfriend, approaches Choko and tries to get her to break up with him. Branch Manager Otaki from Shanghai falls in love with Choko and starts courting her... But Choko and Domoto succeed in overcoming these obstacles and are back together as a loving couple once again.

◆After developing a better understanding of each other, the two are closer than ever...?!

Butterflies, Flowers

Contents

Chapter 36
My Lover, My Servant and I

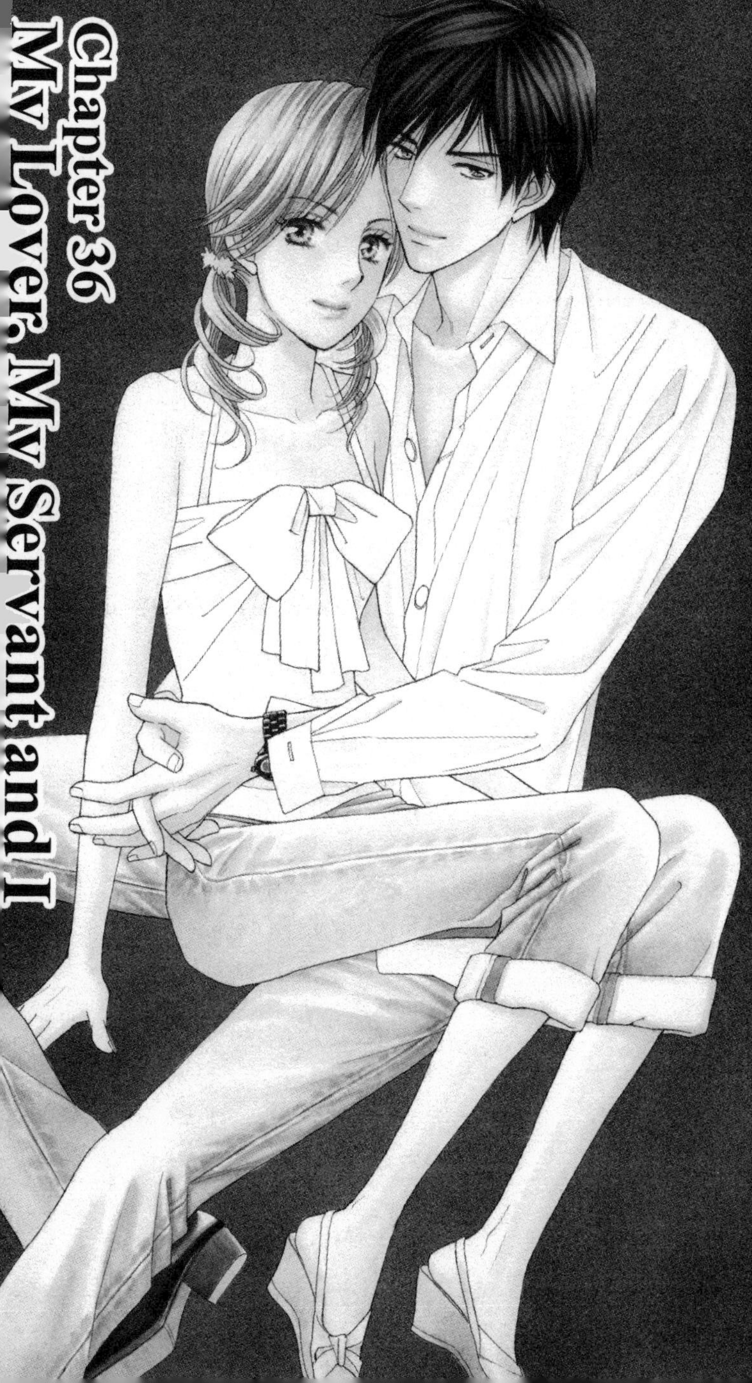

MASA-YUKI'S FIRST AND LAST COSPLAY

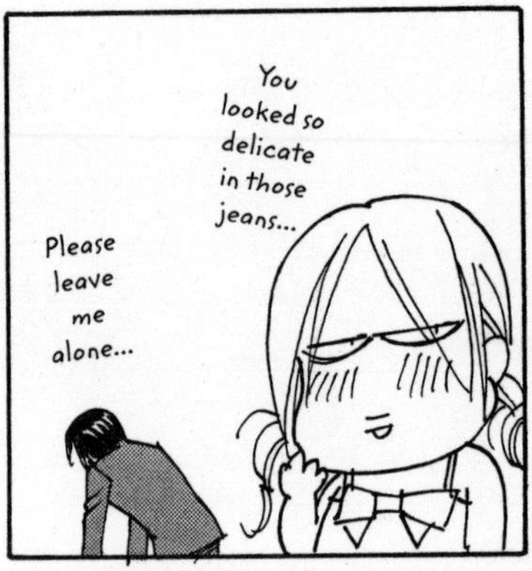
You looked so delicate in those jeans...
Please leave me alone...

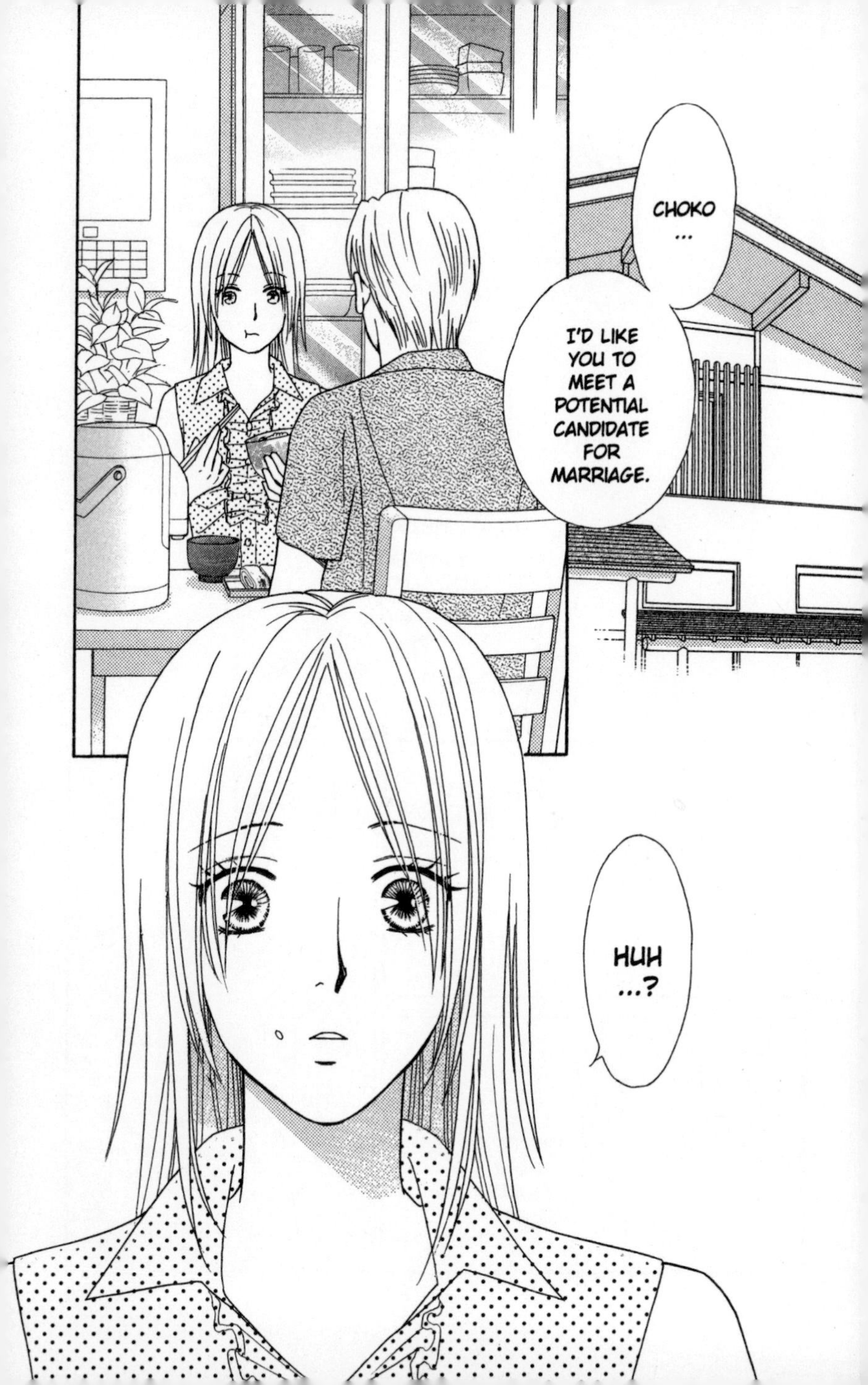
CHOKO ...
I'D LIKE YOU TO MEET A POTENTIAL CANDIDATE FOR MARRIAGE.
HUH ...?

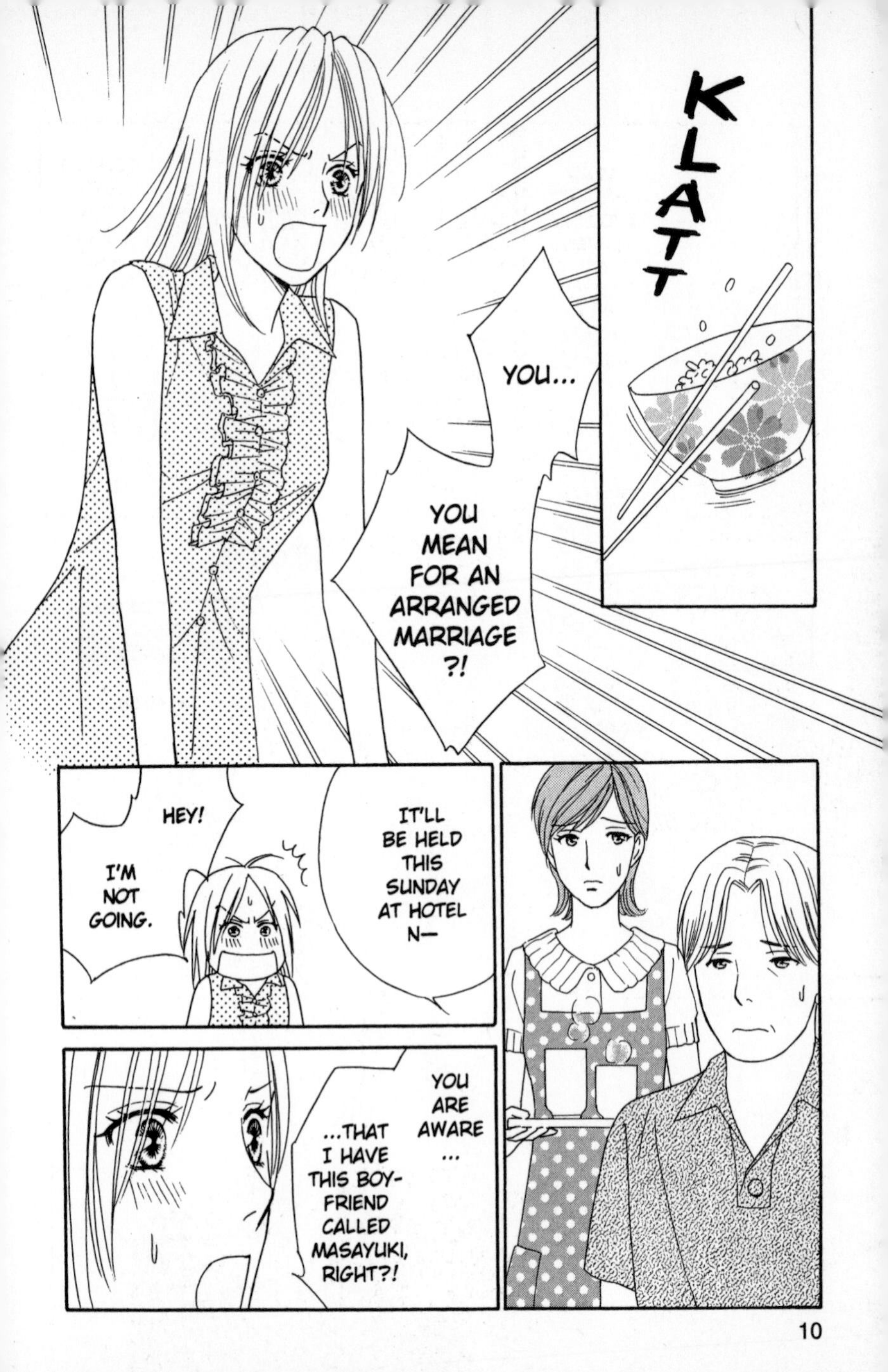
KLATT
YOU...
YOU MEAN FOR AN ARRANGED MARRIAGE ?!
IT'LL BE HELD THIS SUNDAY AT HOTEL N—
HEY!
I'M NOT GOING.
YOU ARE AWARE ...
...THAT I HAVE THIS BOY-FRIEND CALLED MASAYUKI, RIGHT?!

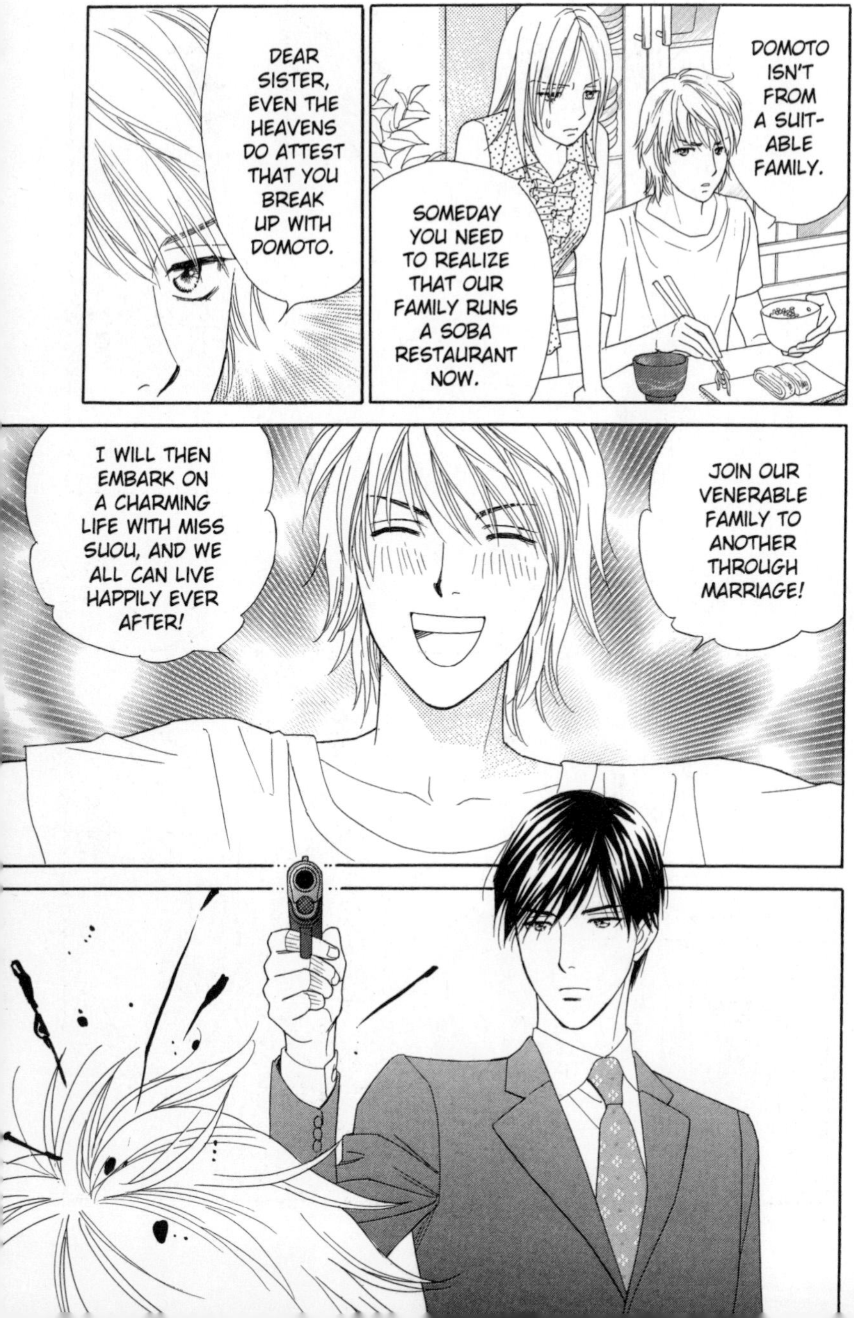
DOMOTO ISN'T FROM A SUIT-ABLE FAMILY.
SOMEDAY YOU NEED TO REALIZE THAT OUR FAMILY RUNS A SOBA RESTAURANT NOW.
DEAR SISTER, EVEN THE HEAVENS DO ATTEST THAT YOU BREAK UP WITH DOMOTO.
JOIN OUR VENERABLE FAMILY TO ANOTHER THROUGH MARRIAGE!
I WILL THEN EMBARK ON A CHARMING LIFE WITH MISS SUOU, AND WE ALL CAN LIVE HAPPILY EVER AFTER!

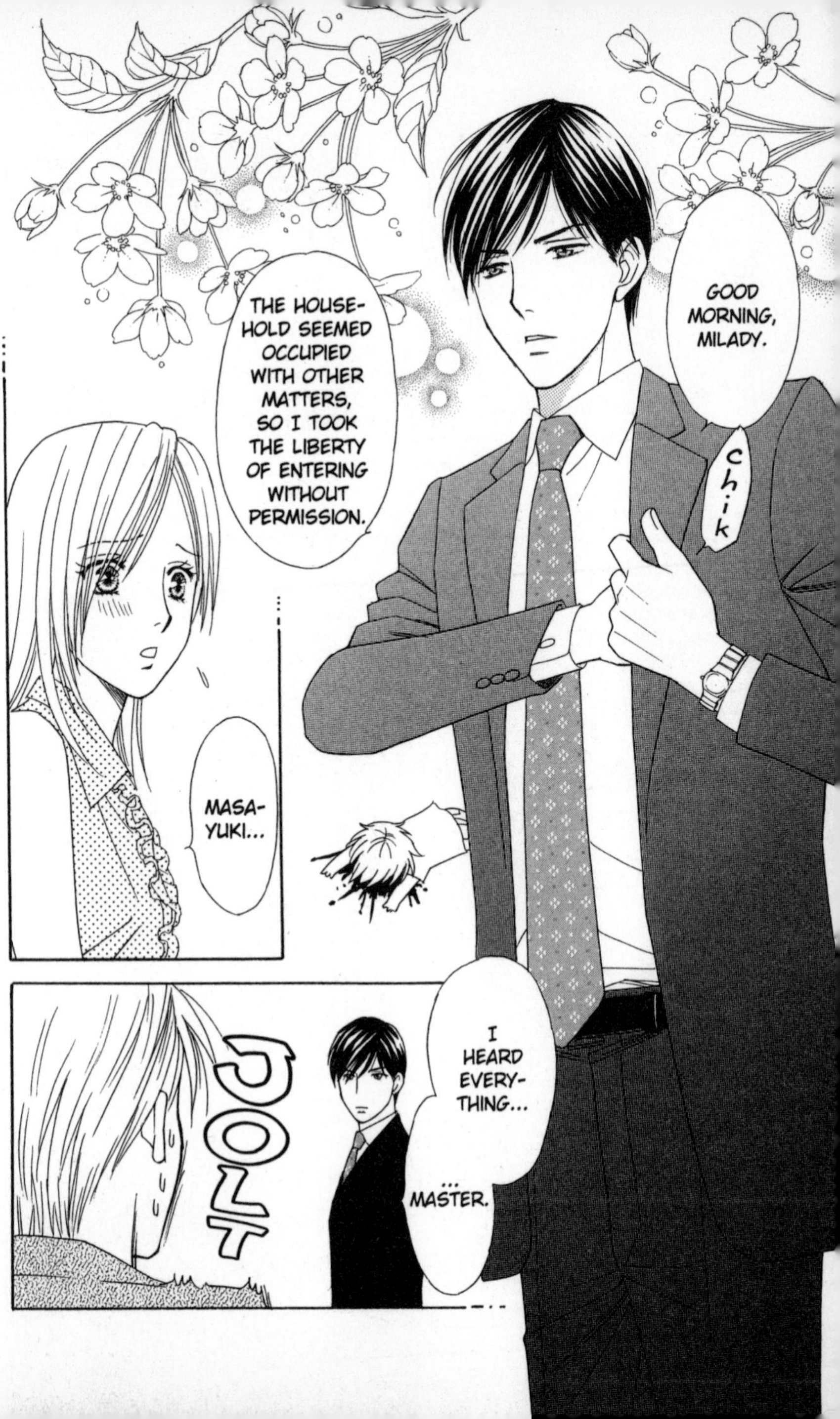
GOOD MORNING, MILADY.
chik
THE HOUSE-HOLD SEEMED OCCUPIED WITH OTHER MATTERS, SO I TOOK THE LIBERTY OF ENTERING WITHOUT PERMISSION.
MASA-YUKI...
I HEARD EVERY-THING...
...MASTER.
JOLT

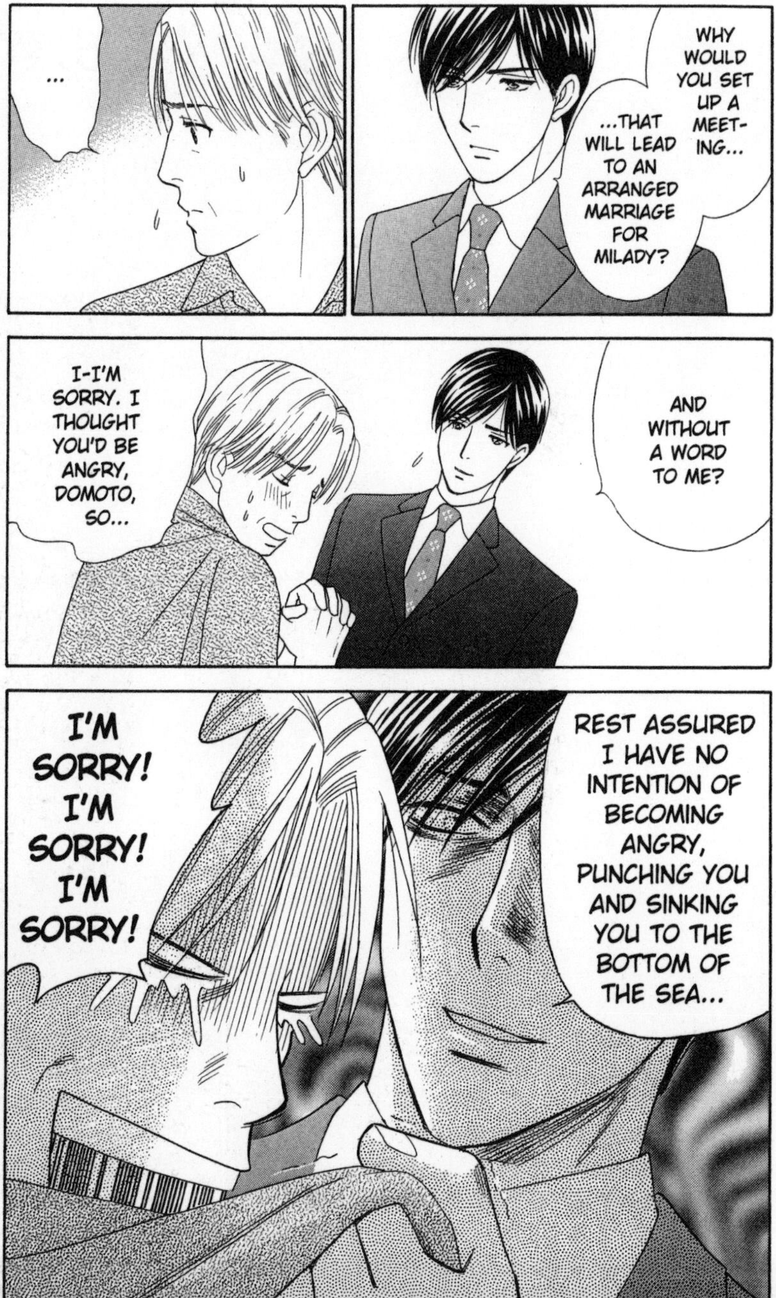
WHY WOULD YOU SET UP A MEET-ING...
...THAT WILL LEAD TO AN ARRANGED MARRIAGE FOR MILADY?
...
AND WITHOUT A WORD TO ME?
I-I'M SORRY. I THOUGHT YOU'D BE ANGRY, DOMOTO, SO...
REST ASSURED I HAVE NO INTENTION OF BECOMING ANGRY, PUNCHING YOU AND SINKING YOU TO THE BOTTOM OF THE SEA...
I'M SORRY! I'M SORRY! I'M SORRY!

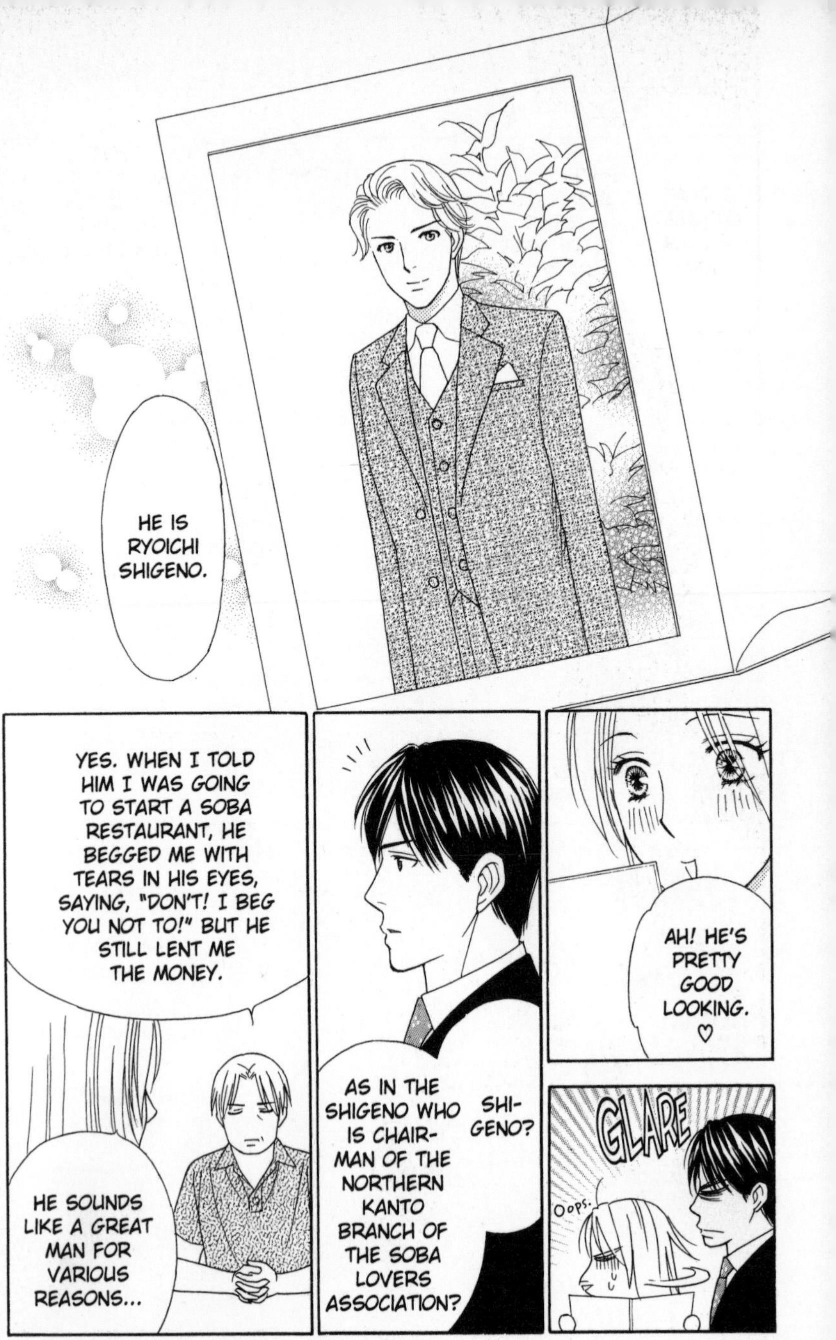
HE IS RYOICHI SHIGENO.
AH! HE'S PRETTY GOOD LOOKING. ♡
GLARE
OOPS.
SHI-GENO?
AS IN THE SHIGENO WHO IS CHAIR-MAN OF THE NORTHERN KANTO BRANCH OF THE SOBA LOVERS ASSOCIATION?
YES. WHEN I TOLD HIM I WAS GOING TO START A SOBA RESTAURANT, HE BEGGED ME WITH TEARS IN HIS EYES, SAYING, "DON'T! I BEG YOU NOT TO!" BUT HE STILL LENT ME THE MONEY.
HE SOUNDS LIKE A GREAT MAN FOR VARIOUS REASONS...

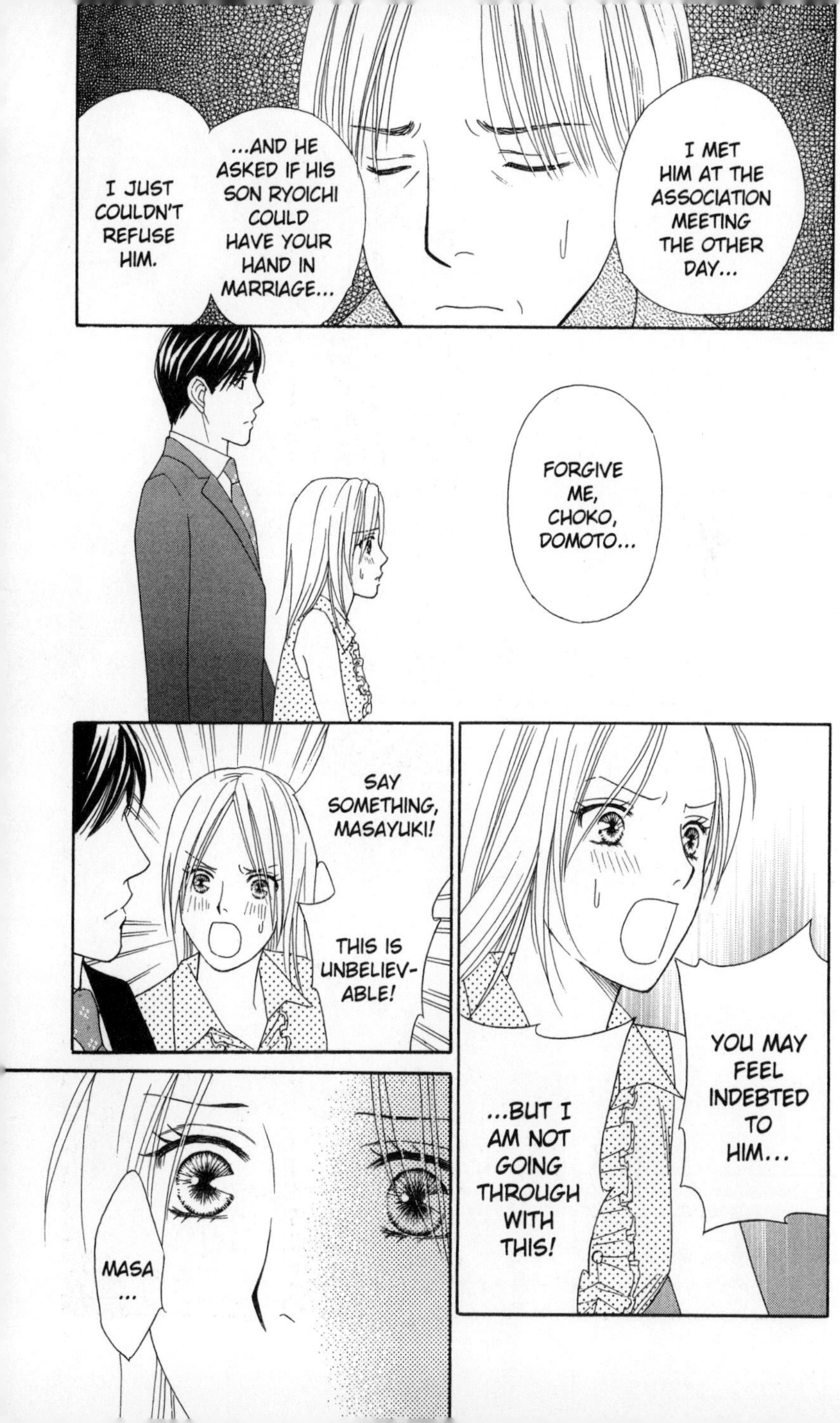
I MET HIM AT THE ASSOCIATION MEETING THE OTHER DAY...
...AND HE ASKED IF HIS SON RYOICHI COULD HAVE YOUR HAND IN MARRIAGE...
I JUST COULDN'T REFUSE HIM.
FORGIVE ME, CHOKO, DOMOTO...
YOU MAY FEEL INDEBTED TO HIM...
...BUT I AM NOT GOING THROUGH WITH THIS!
SAY SOMETHING, MASAYUKI!
THIS IS UNBELIEV-ABLE!
MASA...

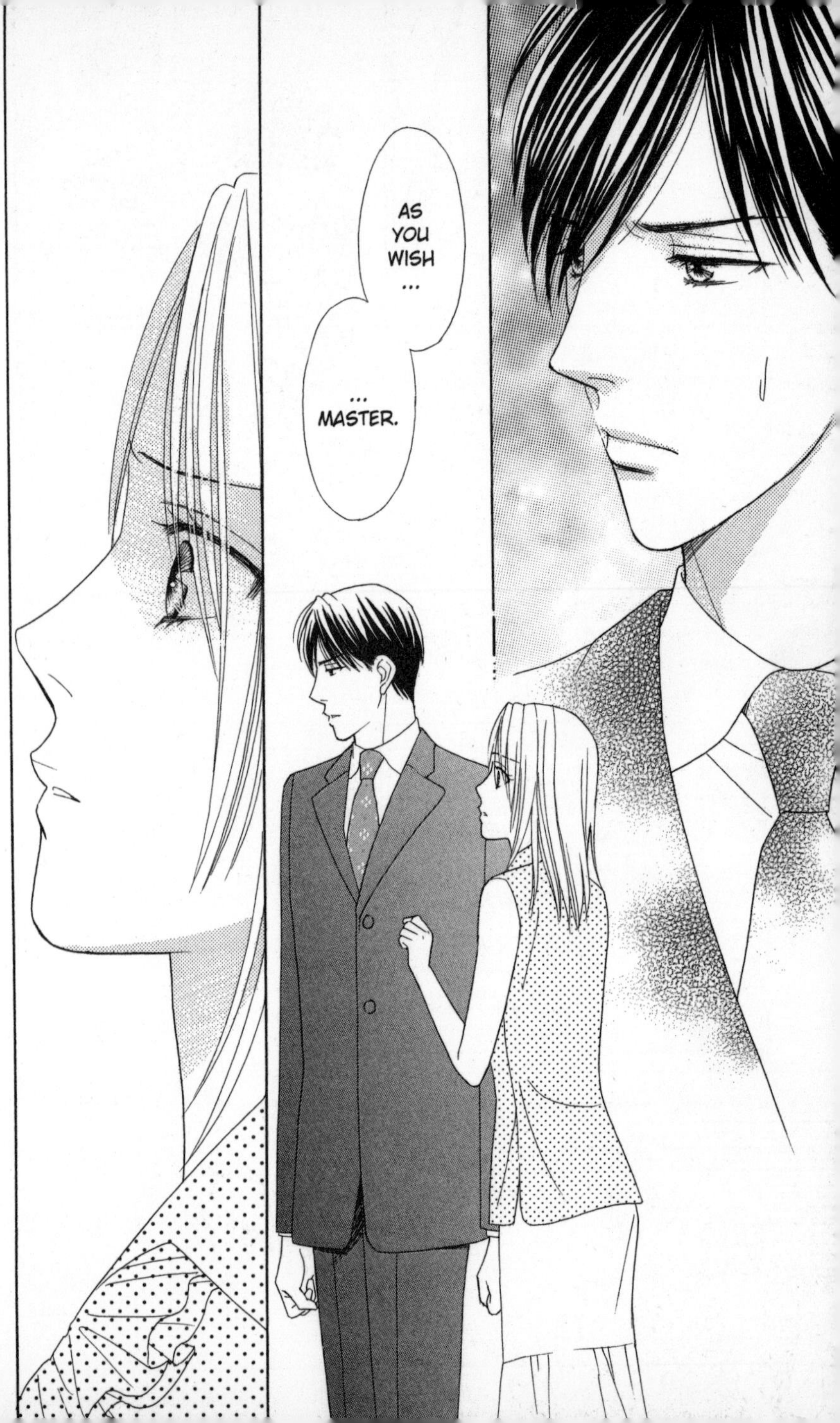

AS YOU WISH ...
... MASTER.

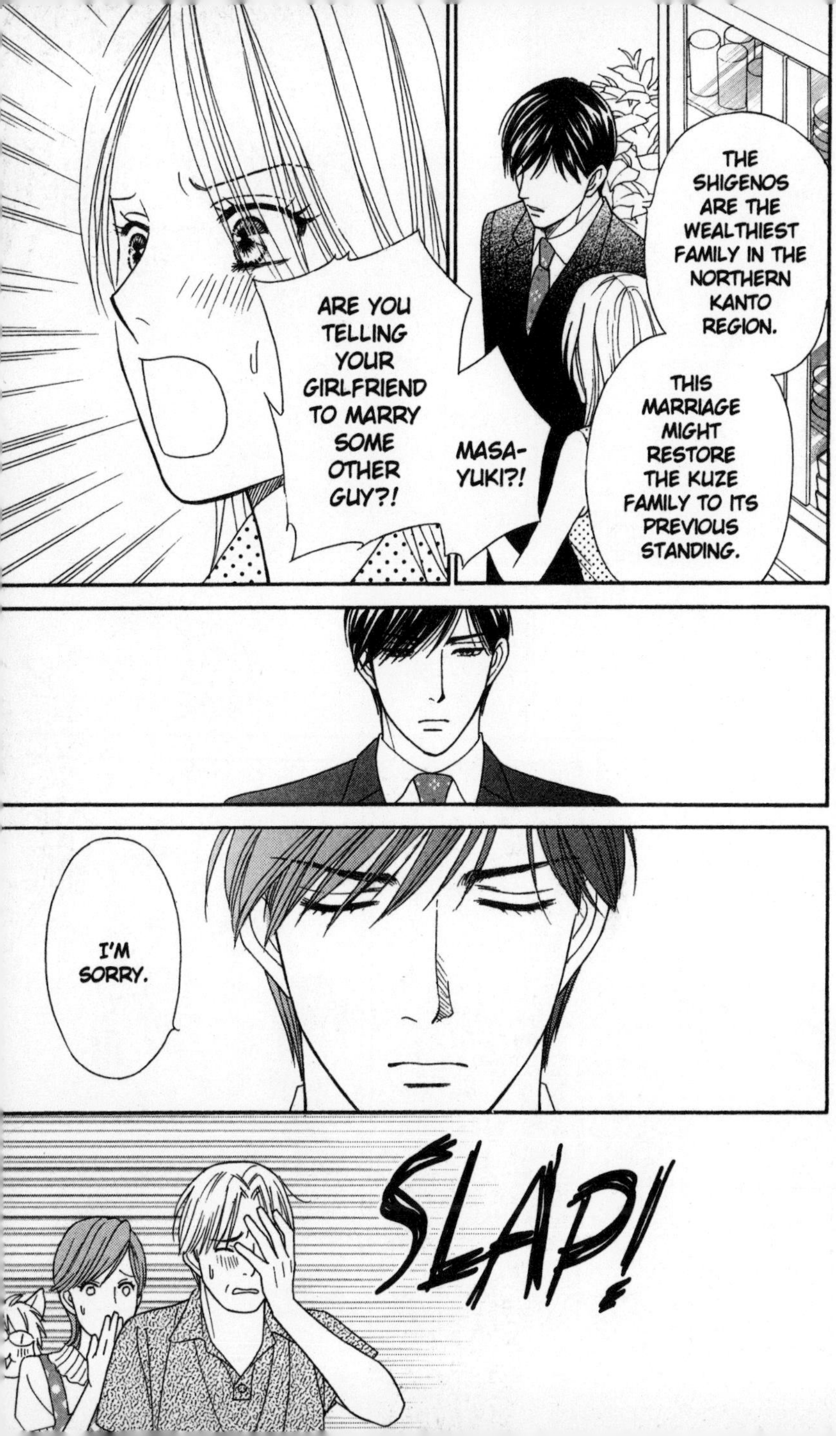
THE SHIGENOS ARE THE WEALTHIEST FAMILY IN THE NORTHERN KANTO REGION.
THIS MARRIAGE MIGHT RESTORE THE KUZE FAMILY TO ITS PREVIOUS STANDING.
MASA-YUKI?!
ARE YOU TELLING YOUR GIRLFRIEND TO MARRY SOME OTHER GUY?!
I'M SORRY.
SLAP!

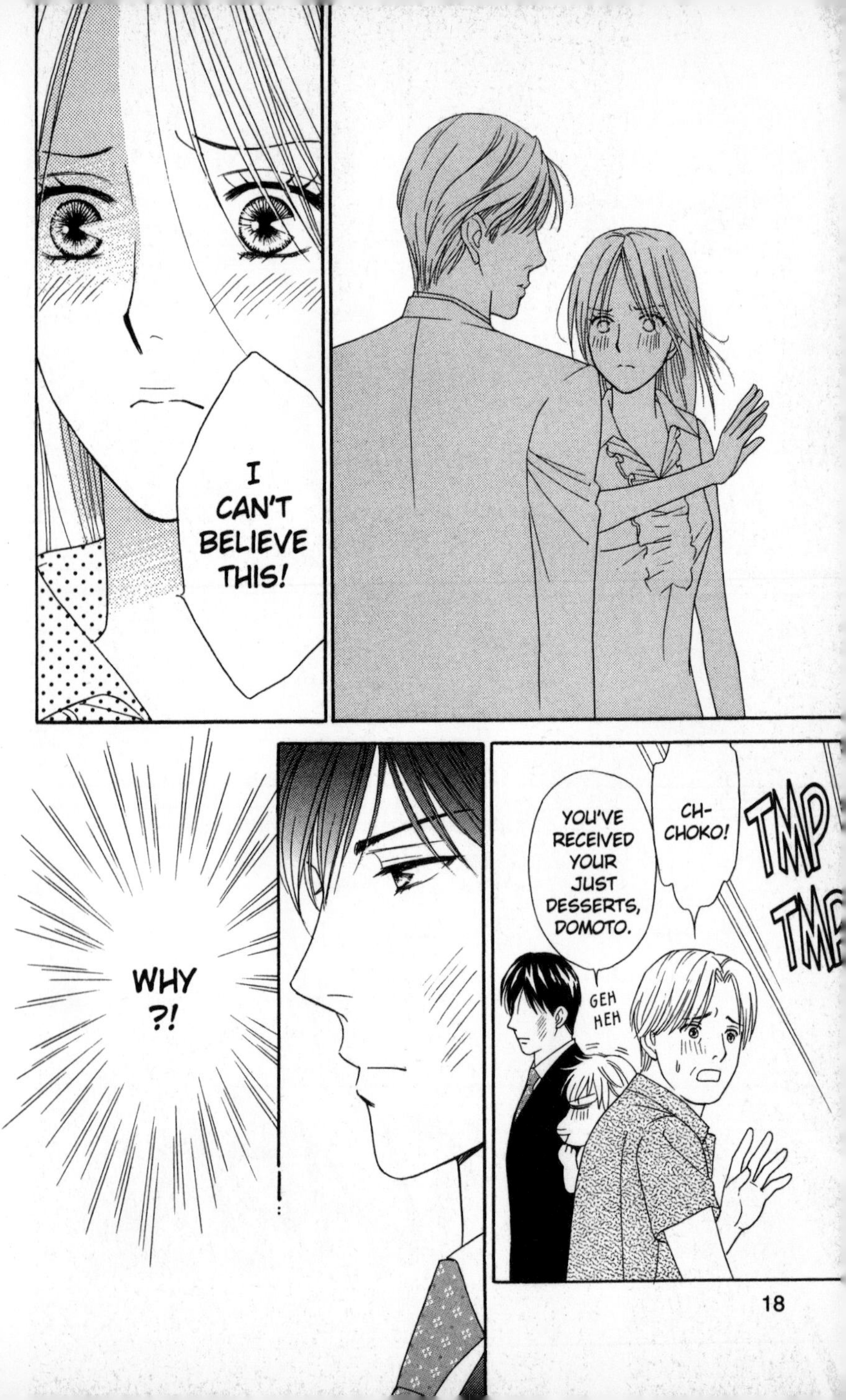
I CAN'T BELIEVE THIS!
CH-CHOKO!
YOU'VE RECEIVED YOUR JUST DESSERTS, DOMOTO.
GEH HEH
TMP
WHY ?!

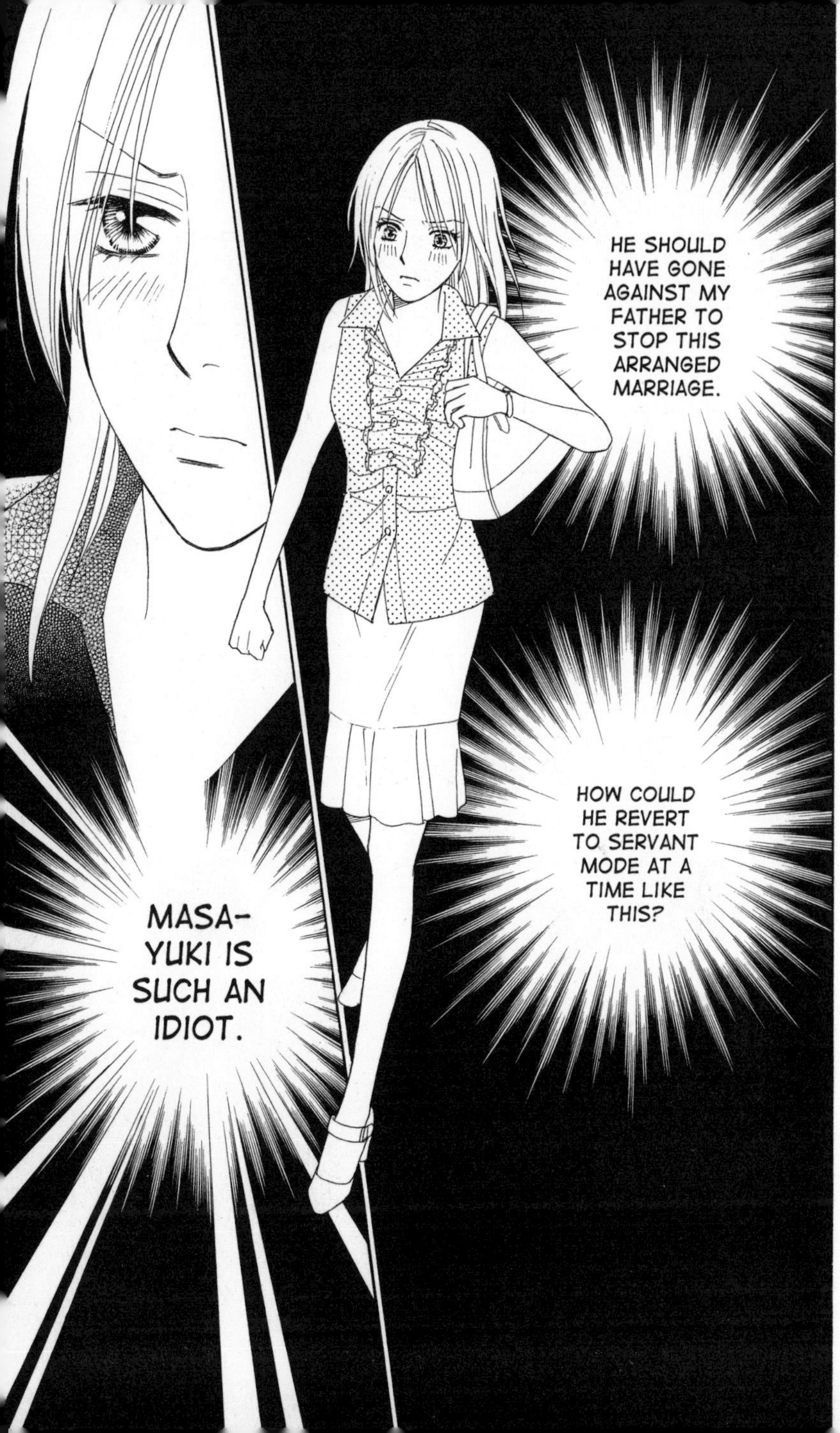
HE SHOULD HAVE GONE AGAINST MY FATHER TO STOP THIS ARRANGED MARRIAGE.
HOW COULD HE REVERT TO SERVANT MODE AT A TIME LIKE THIS?
MASA-YUKI IS SUCH AN IDIOT.

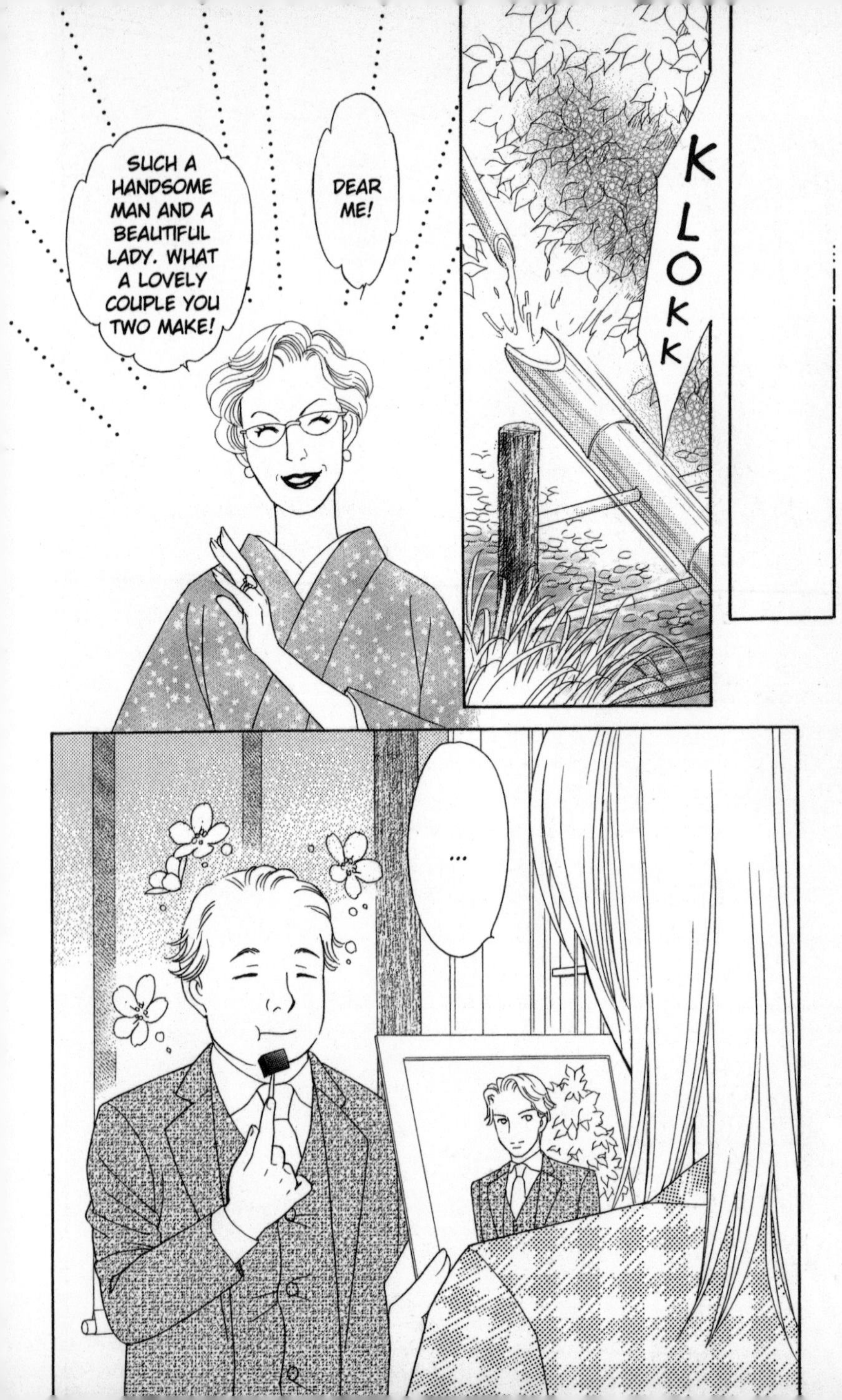
KLOKK
DEAR ME!
SUCH A HANDSOME MAN AND A BEAUTIFUL LADY. WHAT A LOVELY COUPLE YOU TWO MAKE!
...

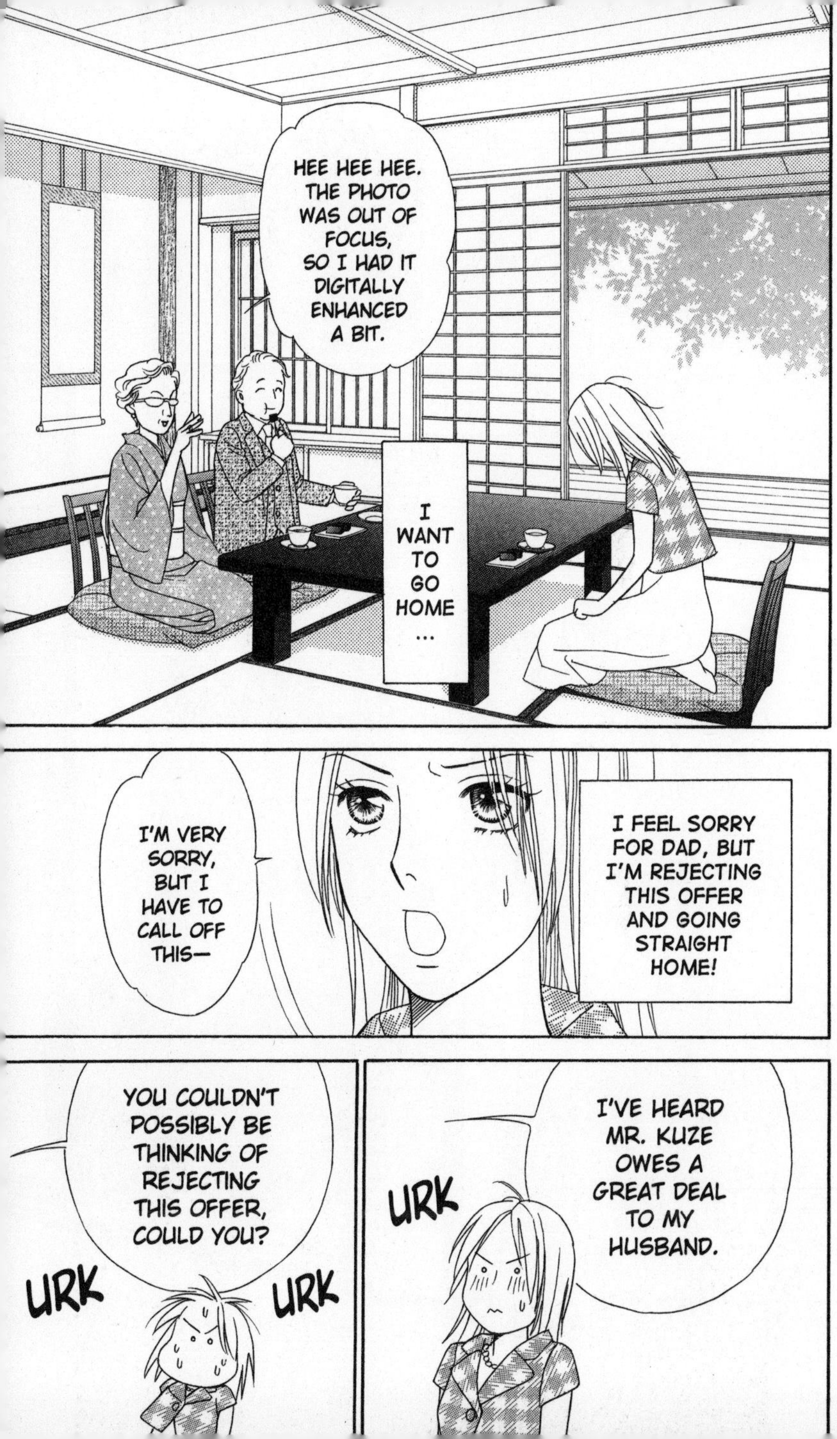
HEE HEE HEE. THE PHOTO WAS OUT OF FOCUS, SO I HAD IT DIGITALLY ENHANCED A BIT.
I WANT TO GO HOME...
I FEEL SORRY FOR DAD, BUT I'M REJECTING THIS OFFER AND GOING STRAIGHT HOME!
I'M VERY SORRY, BUT I HAVE TO CALL OFF THIS—
I'VE HEARD MR. KUZE OWES A GREAT DEAL TO MY HUSBAND.
URK
YOU COULDN'T POSSIBLY BE THINKING OF REJECTING THIS OFFER, COULD YOU?
URK
URK

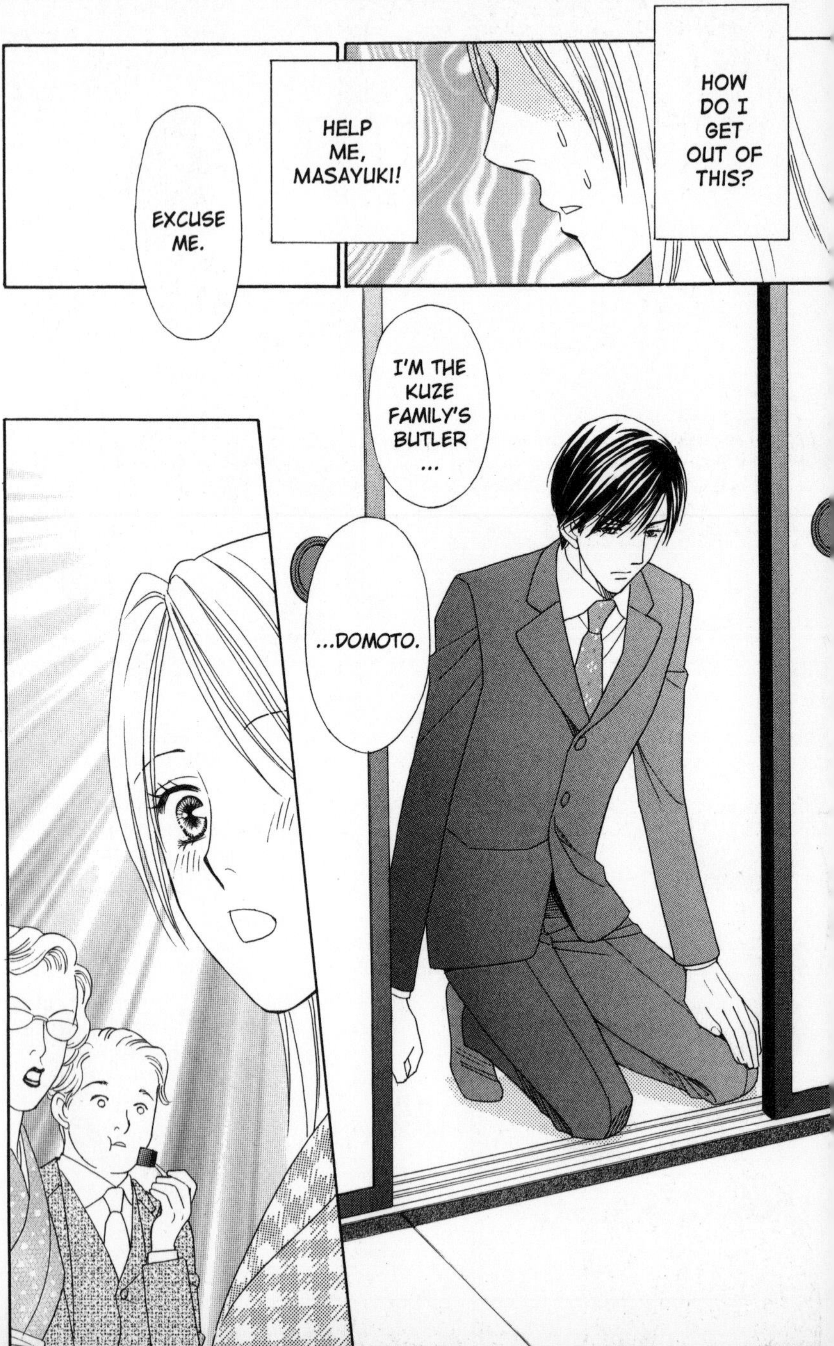
HOW DO I GET OUT OF THIS?
HELP ME, MASAYUKI!
EXCUSE ME.
I'M THE KUZE FAMILY'S BUTLER ...
...DOMOTO.

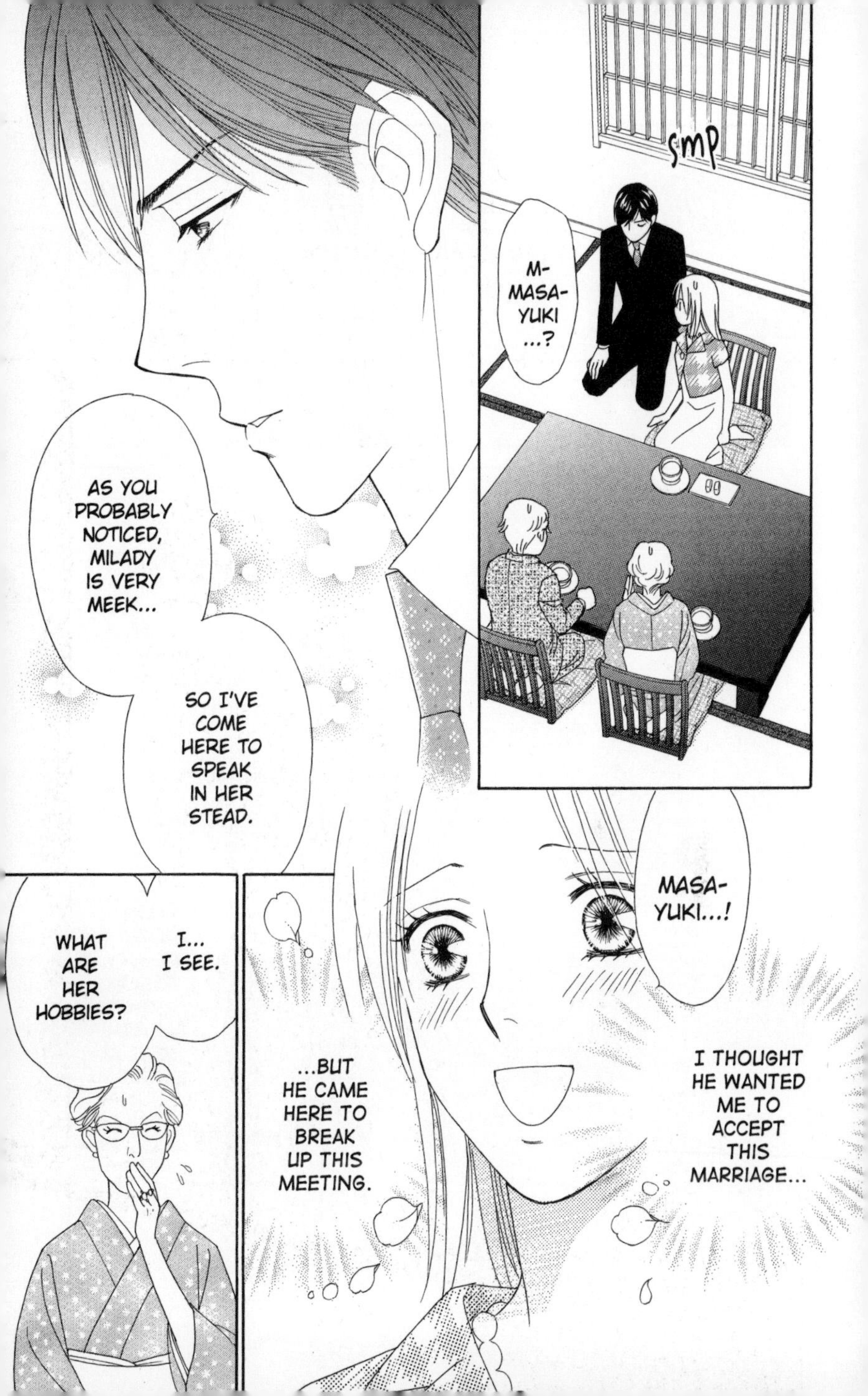
SMP
M-MASAYUKI...?
AS YOU PROBABLY NOTICED, MILADY IS VERY MEEK...
SO I'VE COME HERE TO SPEAK IN HER STEAD.
MASAYUKI...!
I THOUGHT HE WANTED ME TO ACCEPT THIS MARRIAGE...
...BUT HE CAME HERE TO BREAK UP THIS MEETING.
I... I SEE.
WHAT ARE HER HOBBIES?

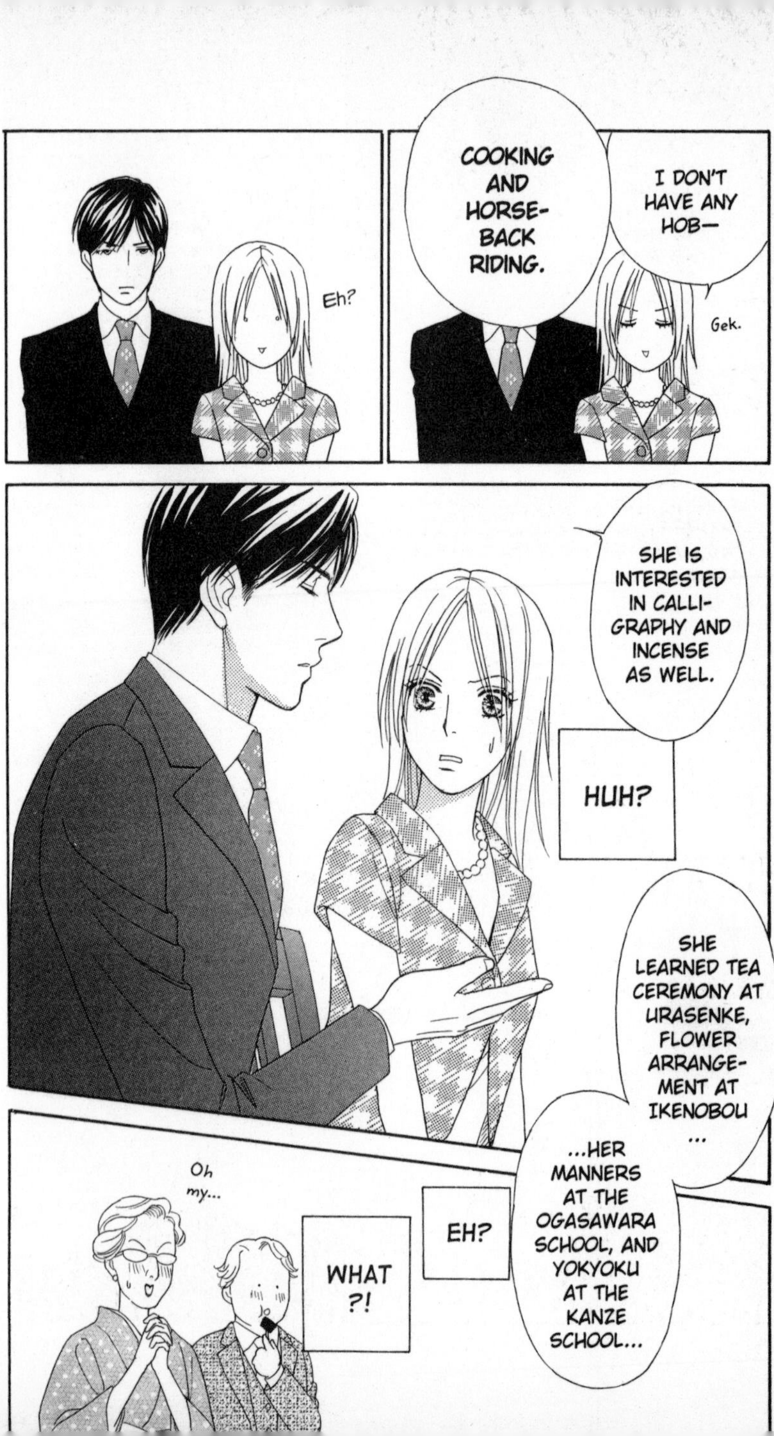
I DON'T HAVE ANY HOB—
COOKING AND HORSE-BACK RIDING.
Gek.
Eh?
SHE IS INTERESTED IN CALLI-GRAPHY AND INCENSE AS WELL.
HUH?
SHE LEARNED TEA CEREMONY AT URASENKE, FLOWER ARRANGE-MENT AT IKENOBOU ...
...HER MANNERS AT THE OGASAWARA SCHOOL, AND YOKYOKU AT THE KANZE SCHOOL...
EH?
WHAT ?!
Oh my...

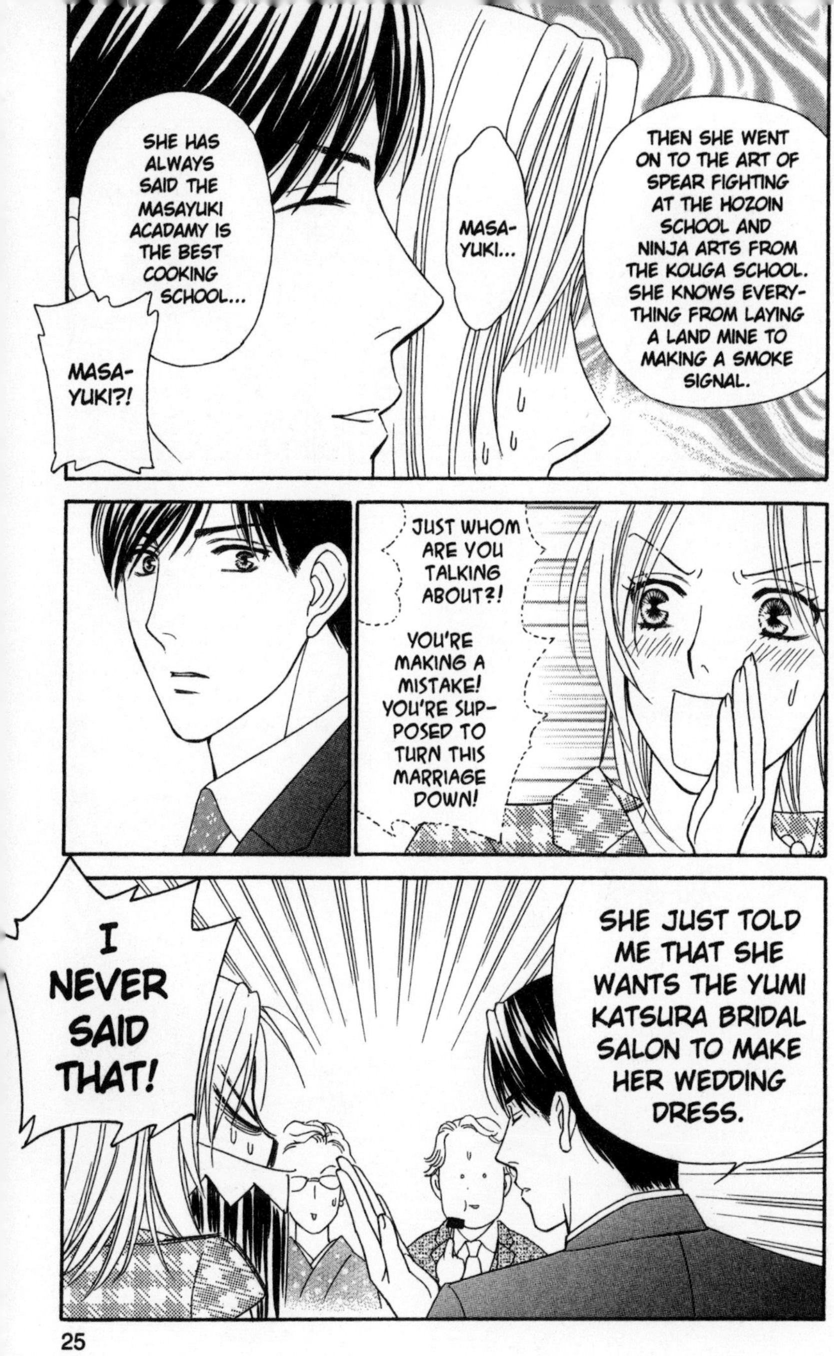
THEN SHE WENT ON TO THE ART OF SPEAR FIGHTING AT THE HOZOIN SCHOOL AND NINJA ARTS FROM THE KOUGA SCHOOL. SHE KNOWS EVERY-THING FROM LAYING A LAND MINE TO MAKING A SMOKE SIGNAL.
MASA-YUKI...
SHE HAS ALWAYS SAID THE MASAYUKI ACADAMY IS THE BEST COOKING SCHOOL...
MASA-YUKI?!
JUST WHOM ARE YOU TALKING ABOUT?!
YOU'RE MAKING A MISTAKE! YOU'RE SUP-POSED TO TURN THIS MARRIAGE DOWN!
SHE JUST TOLD ME THAT SHE WANTS THE YUMI KATSURA BRIDAL SALON TO MAKE HER WEDDING DRESS.
I NEVER SAID THAT!

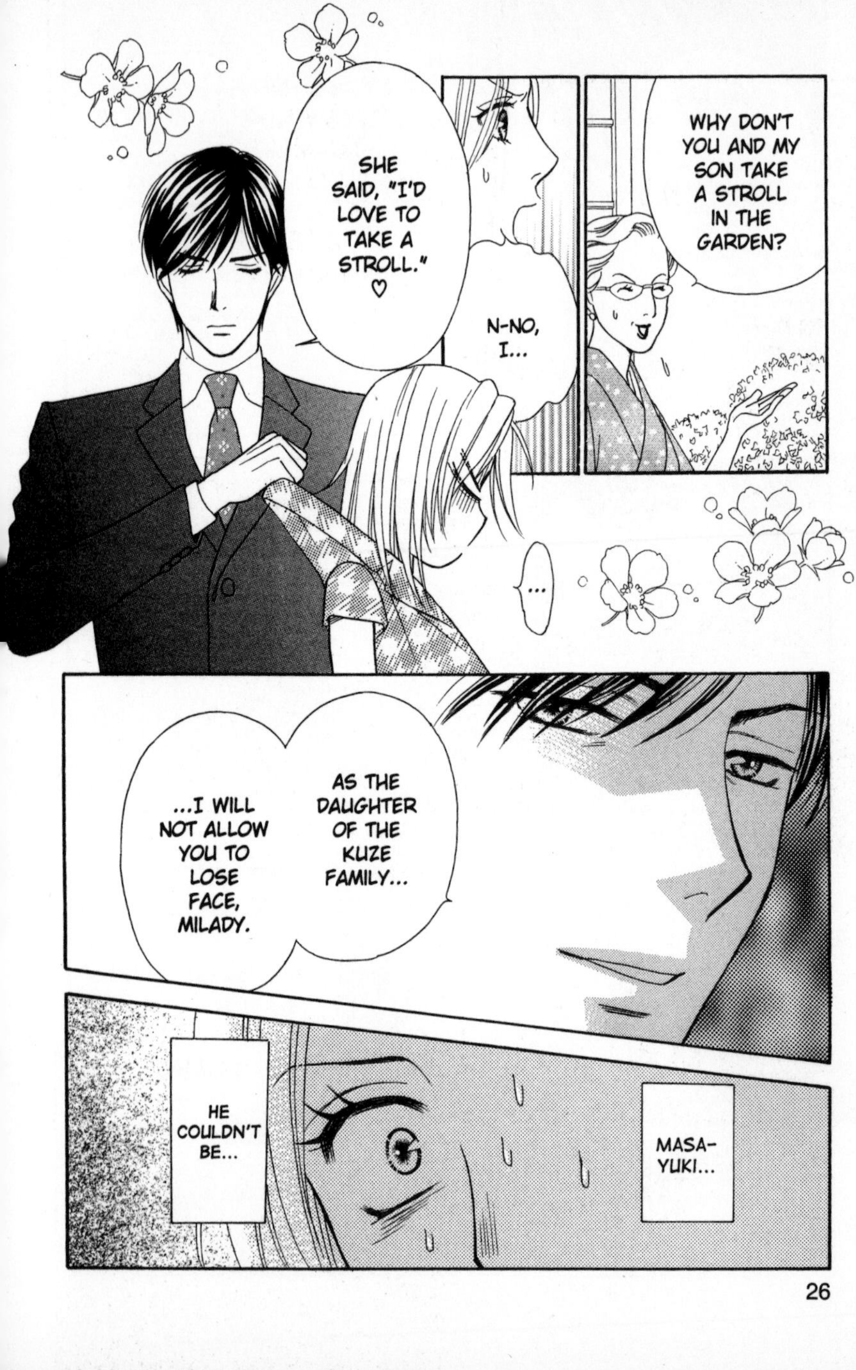
WHY DON'T YOU AND MY SON TAKE A STROLL IN THE GARDEN?
N-NO, I...
SHE SAID, "I'D LOVE TO TAKE A STROLL." ♡
...
AS THE DAUGHTER OF THE KUZE FAMILY...
...I WILL NOT ALLOW YOU TO LOSE FACE, MILADY.
MASA-YUKI...
HE COULDN'T BE...

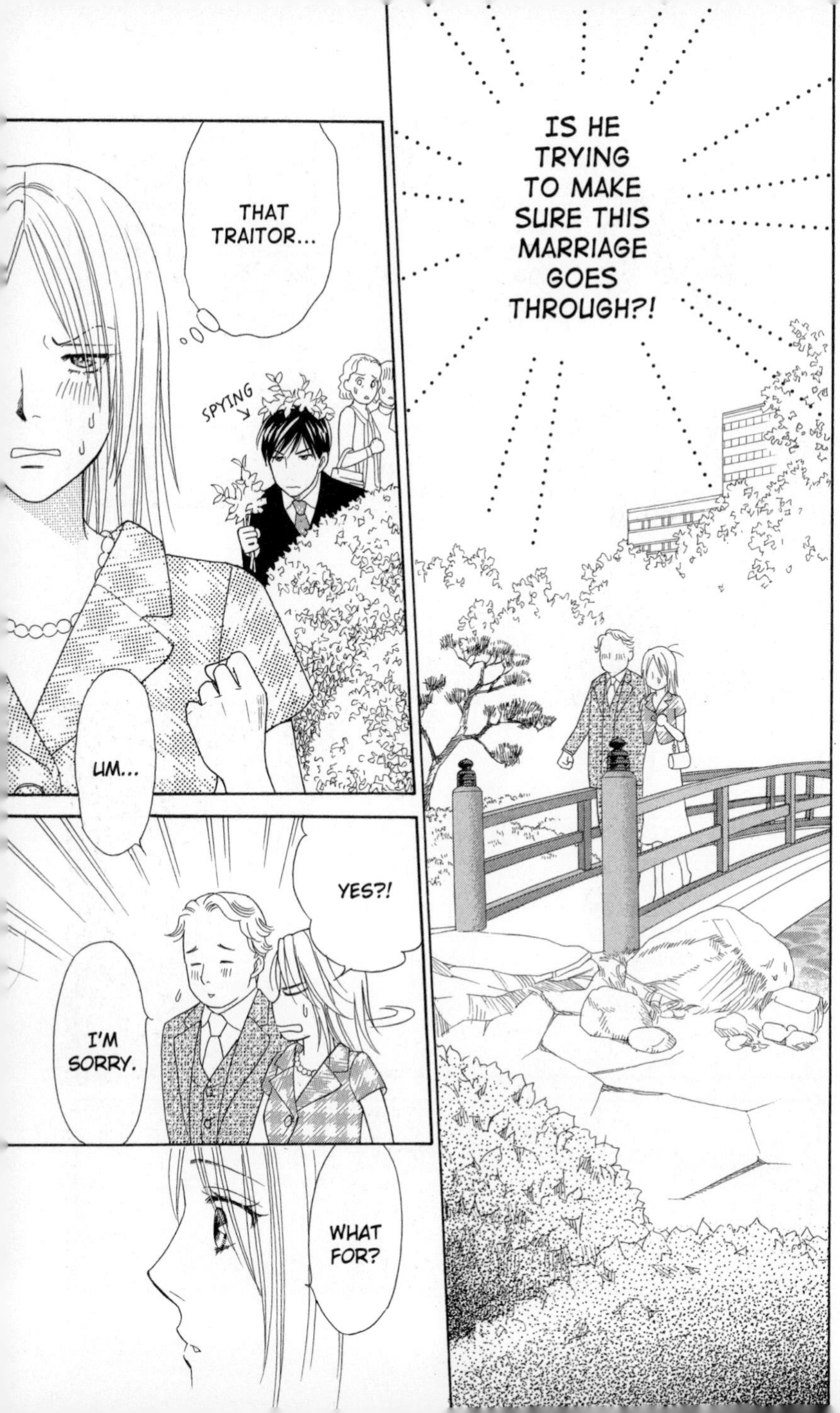
IS HE TRYING TO MAKE SURE THIS MARRIAGE GOES THROUGH?!
THAT TRAITOR...
SPYING
UM...
YES?!
I'M SORRY.
WHAT FOR?

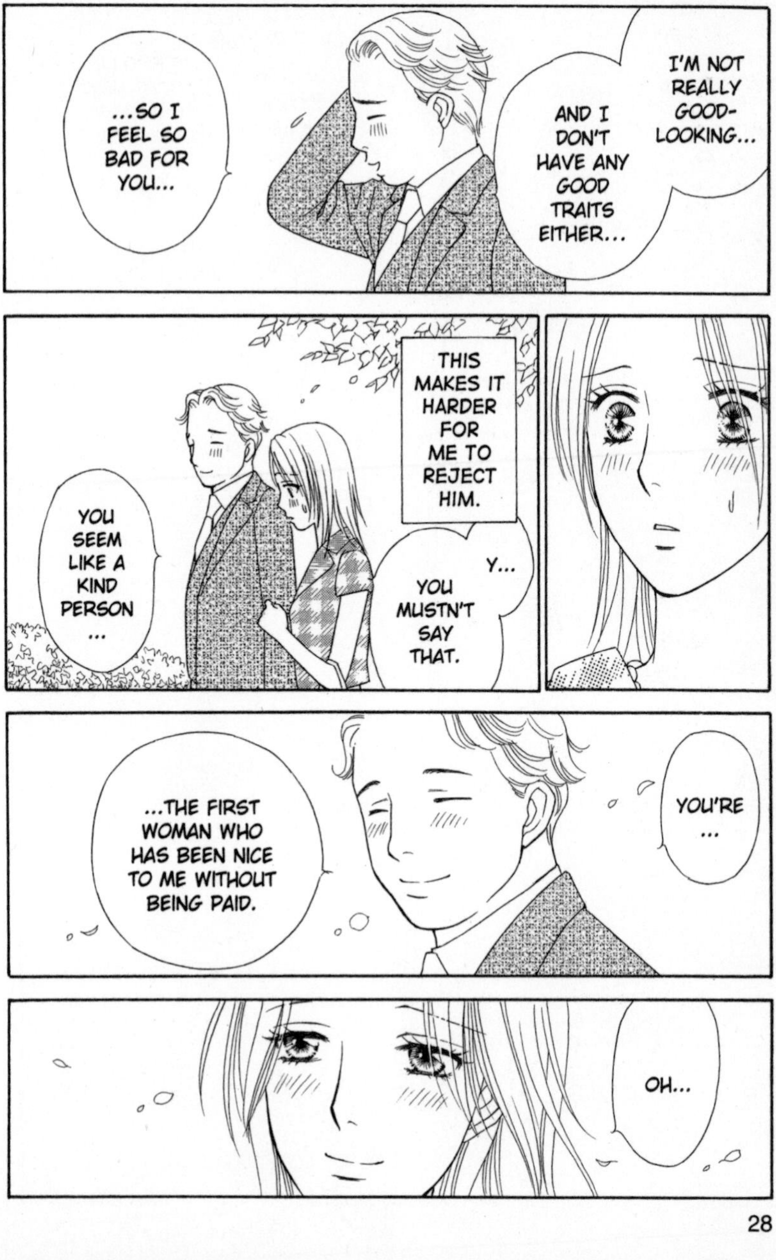
I'M NOT REALLY GOOD-LOOKING...
AND I DON'T HAVE ANY GOOD TRAITS EITHER...
...SO I FEEL SO BAD FOR YOU...
THIS MAKES IT HARDER FOR ME TO REJECT HIM.
Y... YOU MUSTN'T SAY THAT.
YOU SEEM LIKE A KIND PERSON ...
YOU'RE ...
...THE FIRST WOMAN WHO HAS BEEN NICE TO ME WITHOUT BEING PAID.
OH...

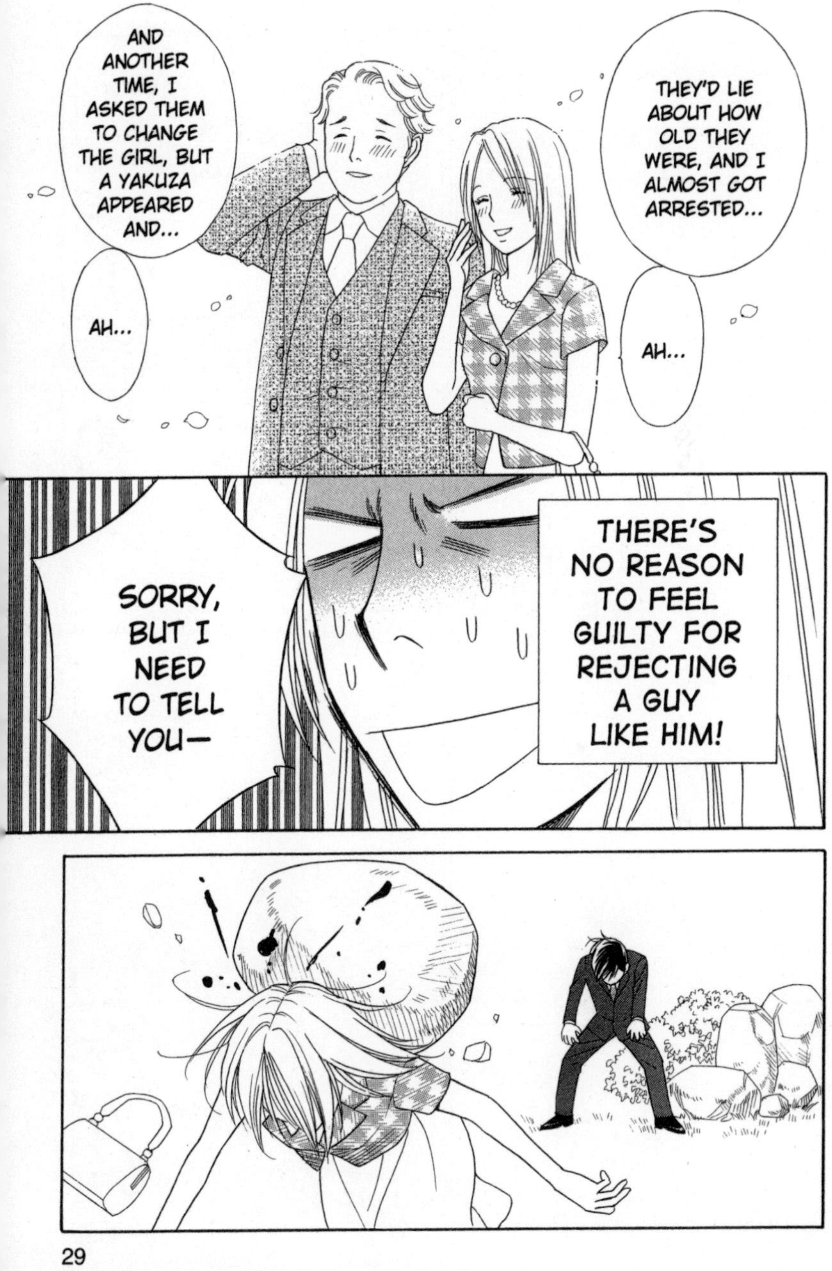
THEY'D LIE ABOUT HOW OLD THEY WERE, AND I ALMOST GOT ARRESTED...
AND ANOTHER TIME, I ASKED THEM TO CHANGE THE GIRL, BUT A YAKUZA APPEARED AND...
AH...
AH...
THERE'S NO REASON TO FEEL GUILTY FOR REJECTING A GUY LIKE HIM!
SORRY, BUT I NEED TO TELL YOU—

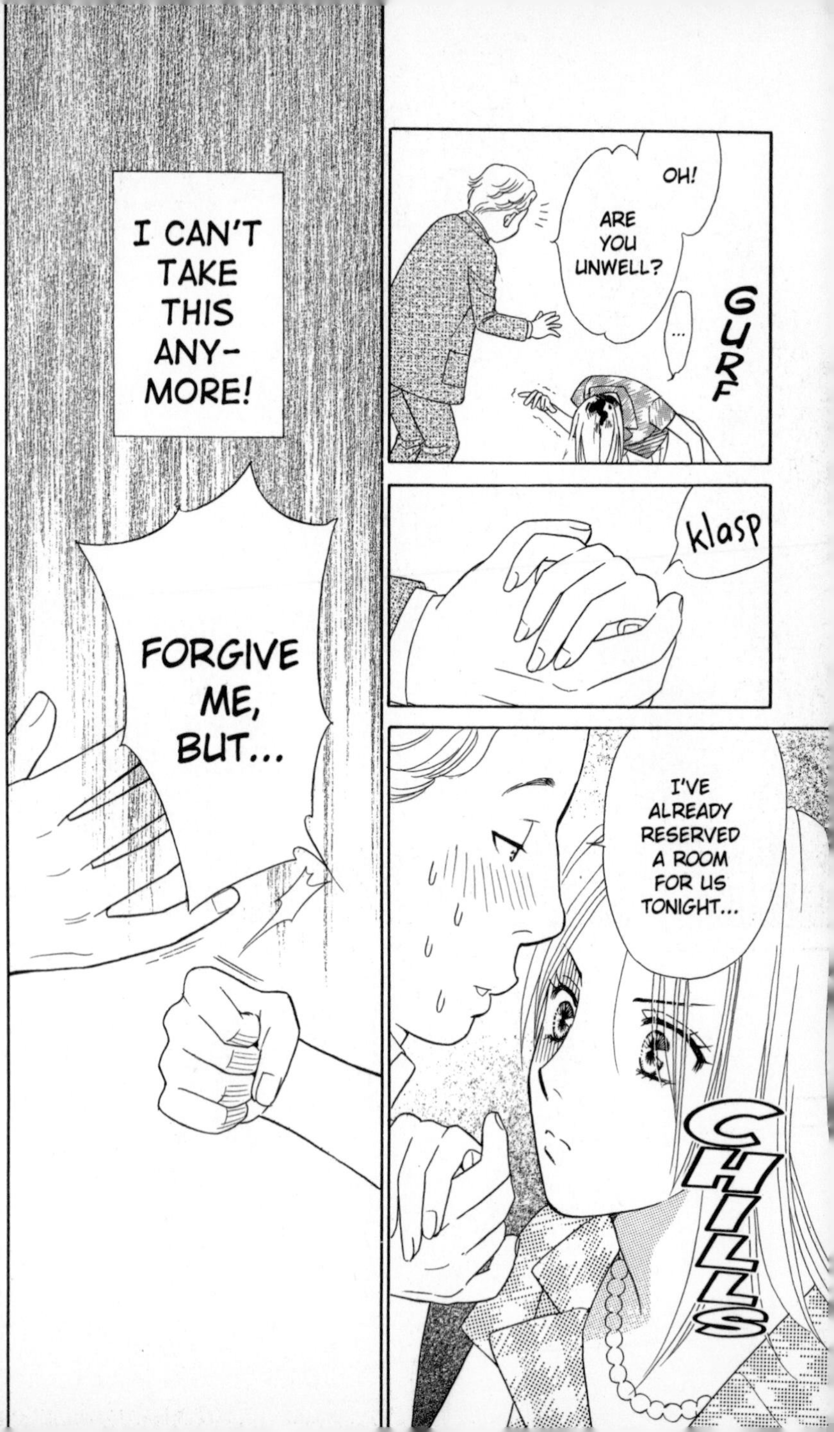
OH!
ARE YOU UNWELL?
...
GURF
klasp
I'VE ALREADY RESERVED A ROOM FOR US TONIGHT...
CHILLS
I CAN'T TAKE THIS ANY-MORE!
FORGIVE ME, BUT...

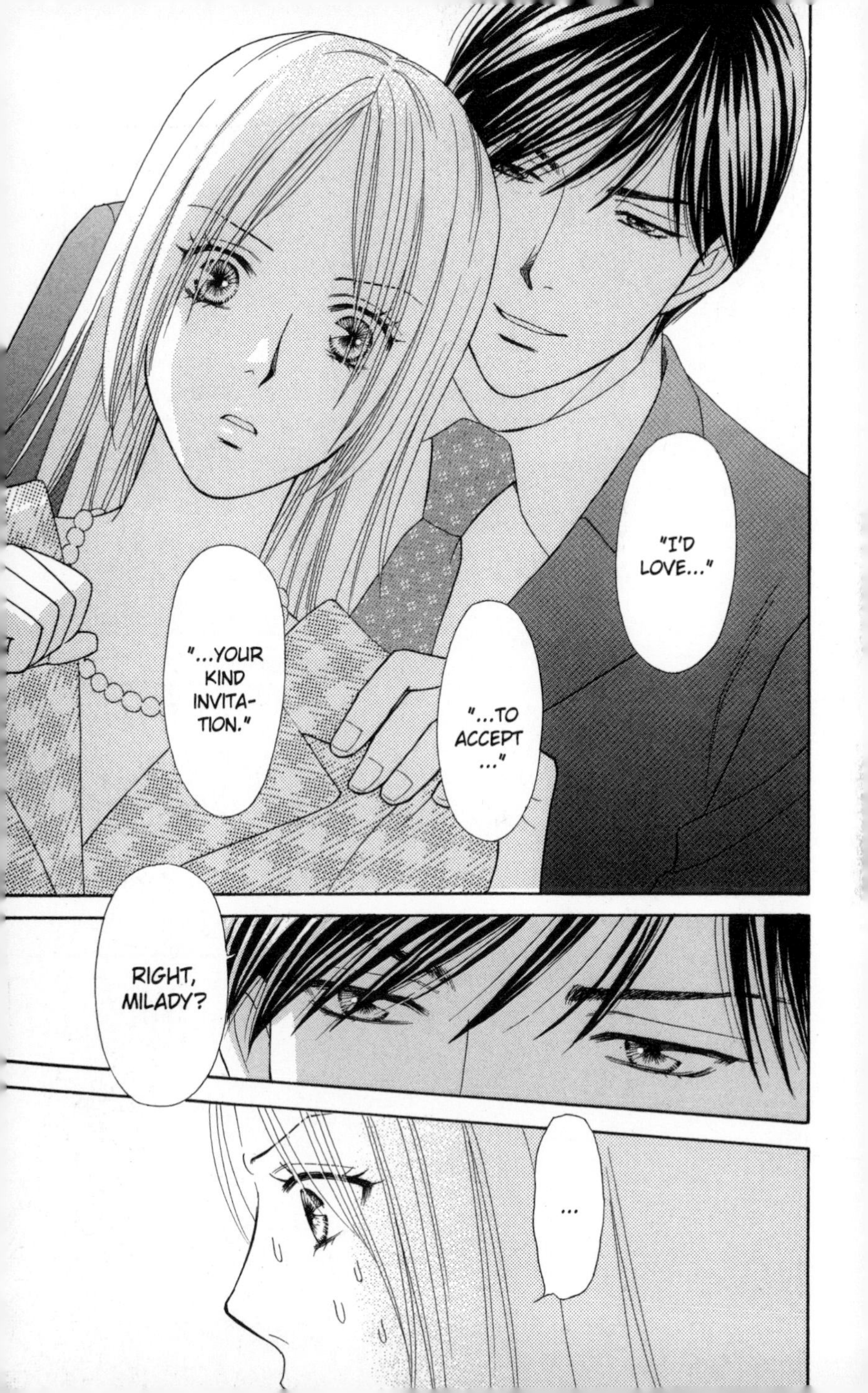
"I'D LOVE..."
"...TO ACCEPT ..."
"...YOUR KIND INVITA-TION."
RIGHT, MILADY?
...

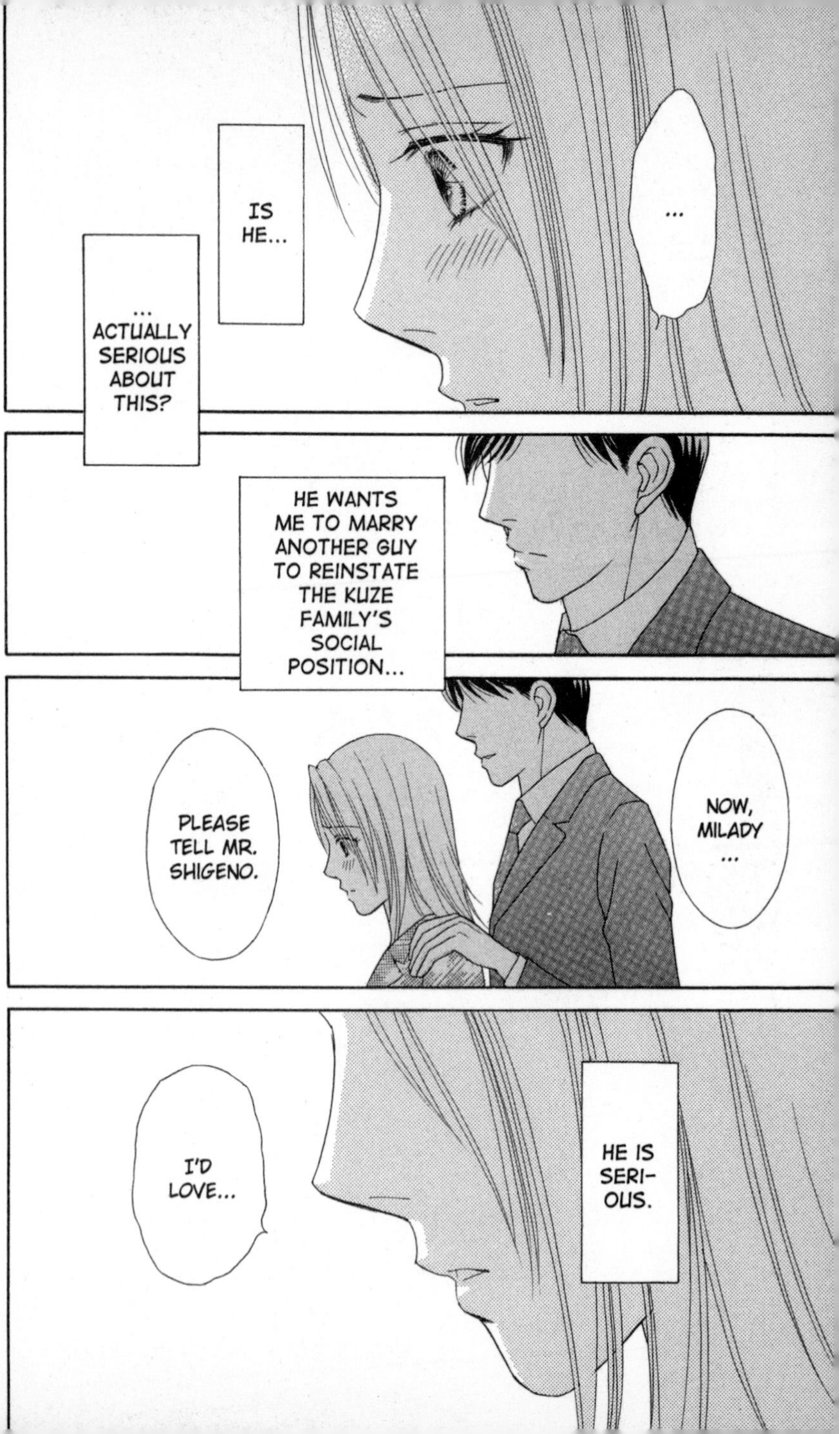
...
IS HE...
...ACTUALLY SERIOUS ABOUT THIS?
HE WANTS ME TO MARRY ANOTHER GUY TO REINSTATE THE KUZE FAMILY'S SOCIAL POSITION...
NOW, MILADY...
PLEASE TELL MR. SHIGENO.
HE IS SERI-OUS.
I'D LOVE...

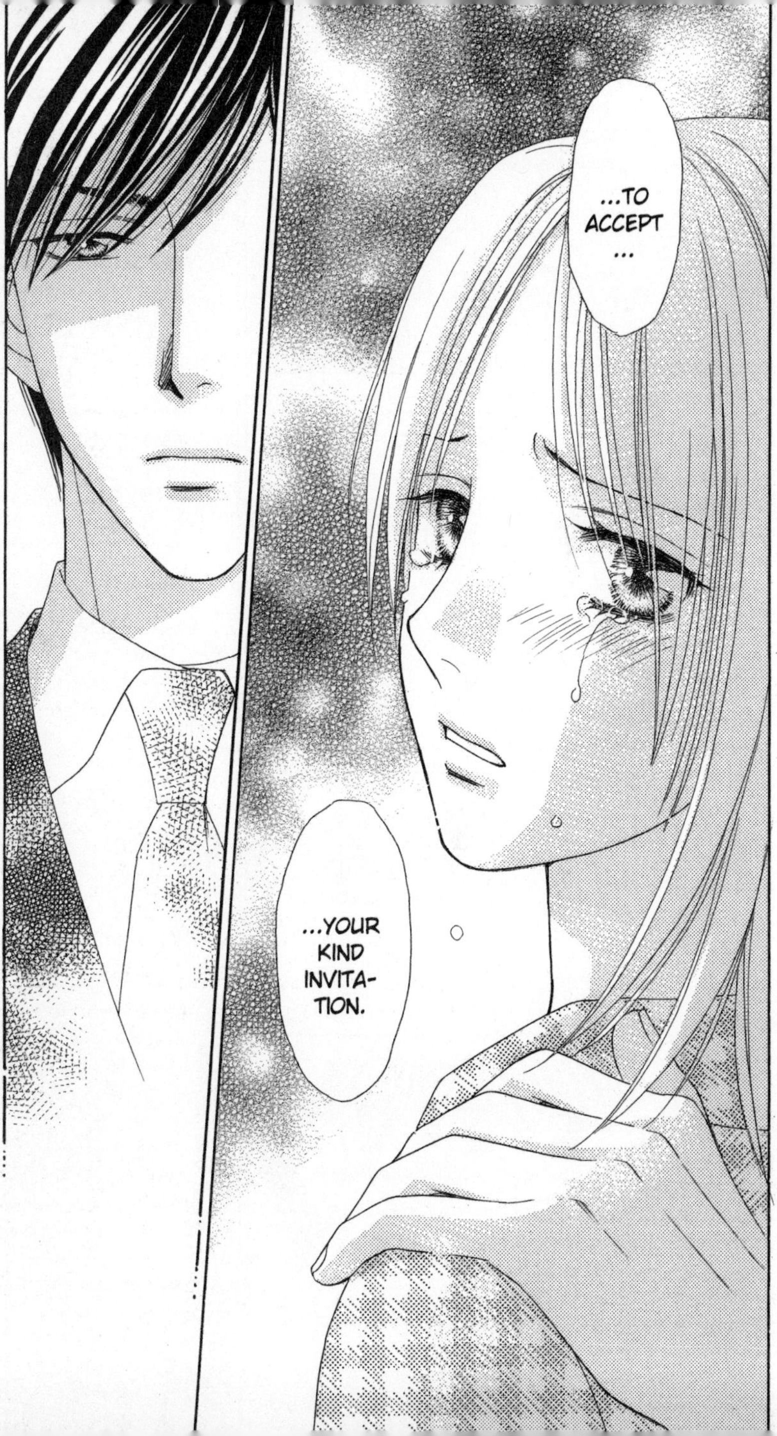
...TO ACCEPT ...
...YOUR KIND INVITATION.

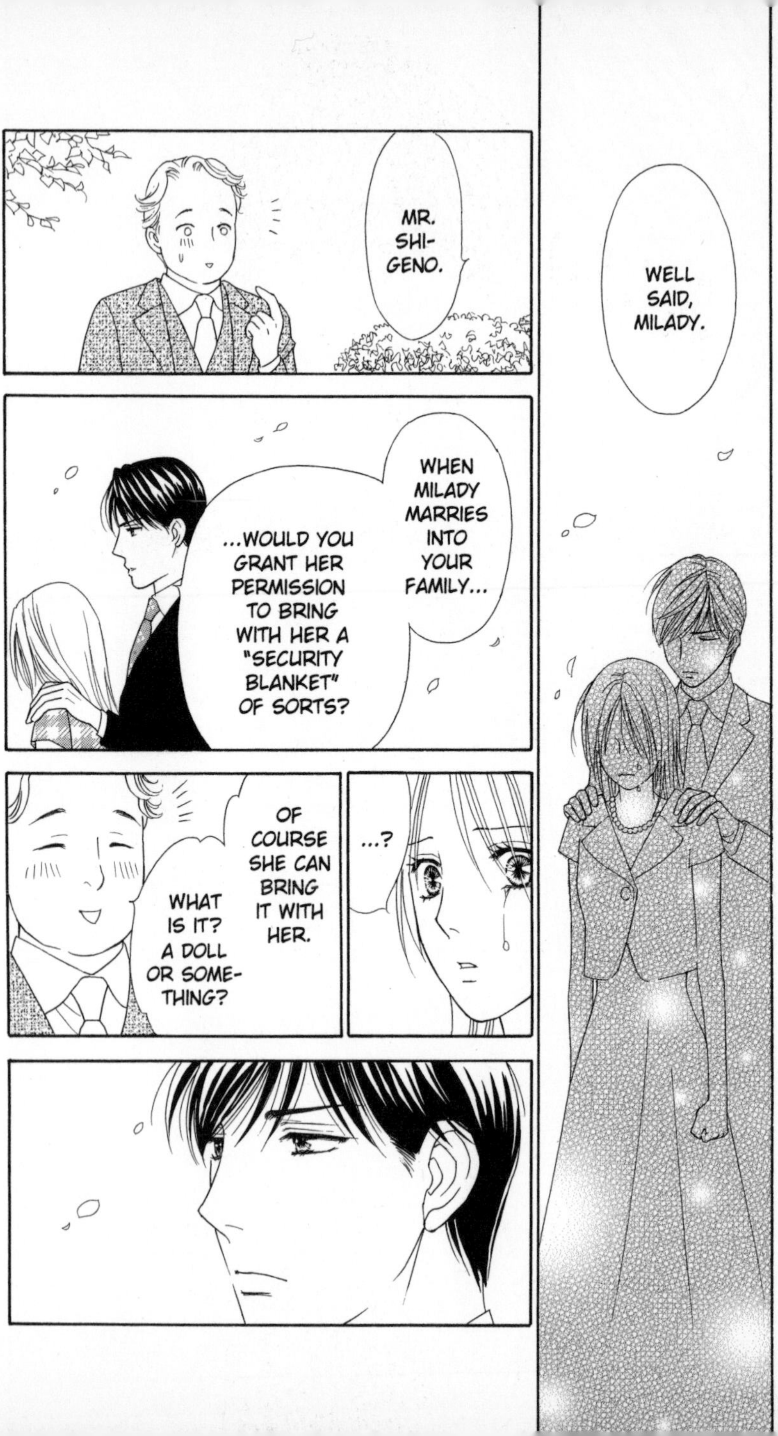
WELL SAID, MILADY.
MR. SHIGENO.
WHEN MILADY MARRIES INTO YOUR FAMILY...
...WOULD YOU GRANT HER PERMISSION TO BRING WITH HER A "SECURITY BLANKET" OF SORTS?
...?
OF COURSE SHE CAN BRING IT WITH HER.
WHAT IS IT? A DOLL OR SOME-THING?

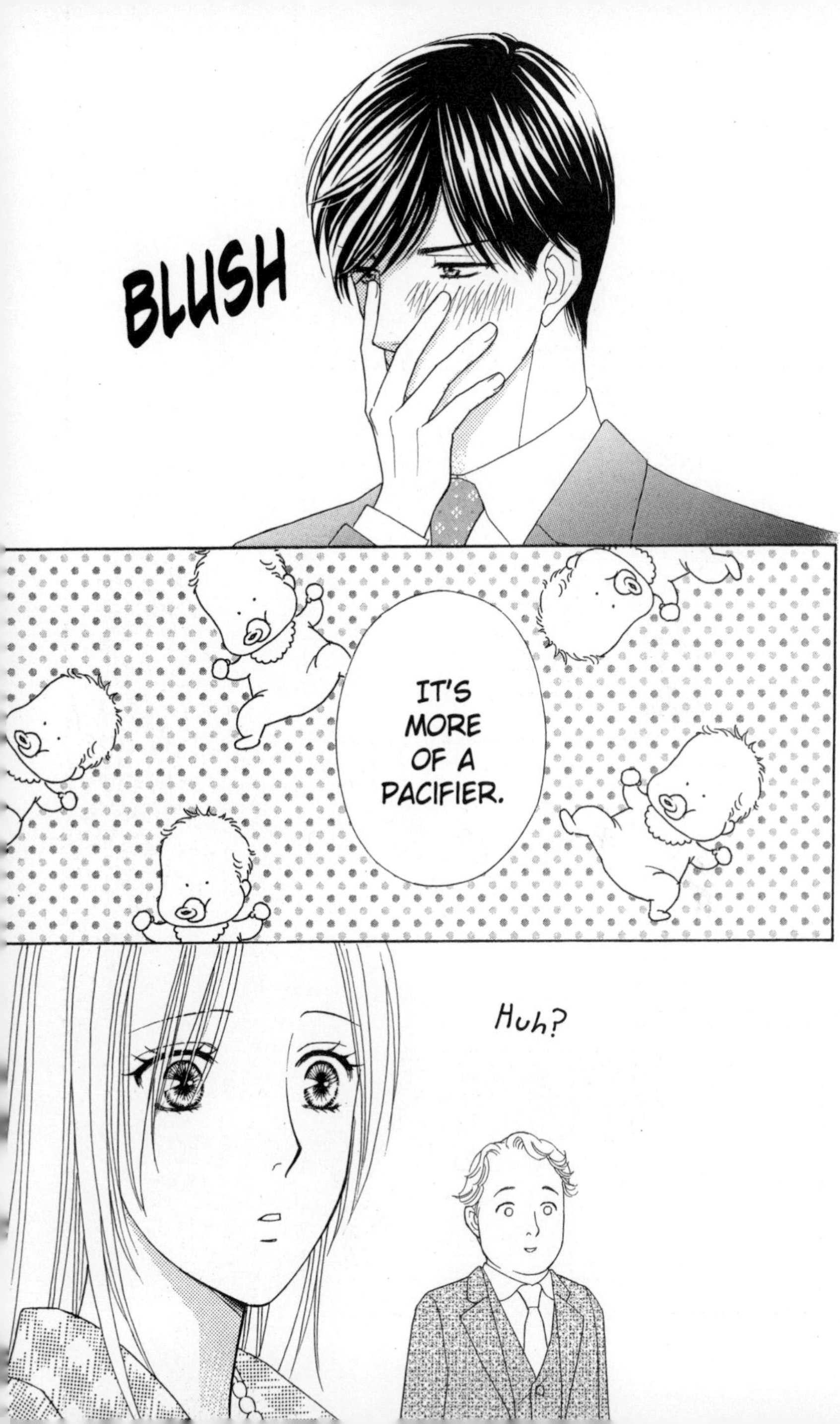
BLUSH
IT'S MORE OF A PACIFIER.
Huh?

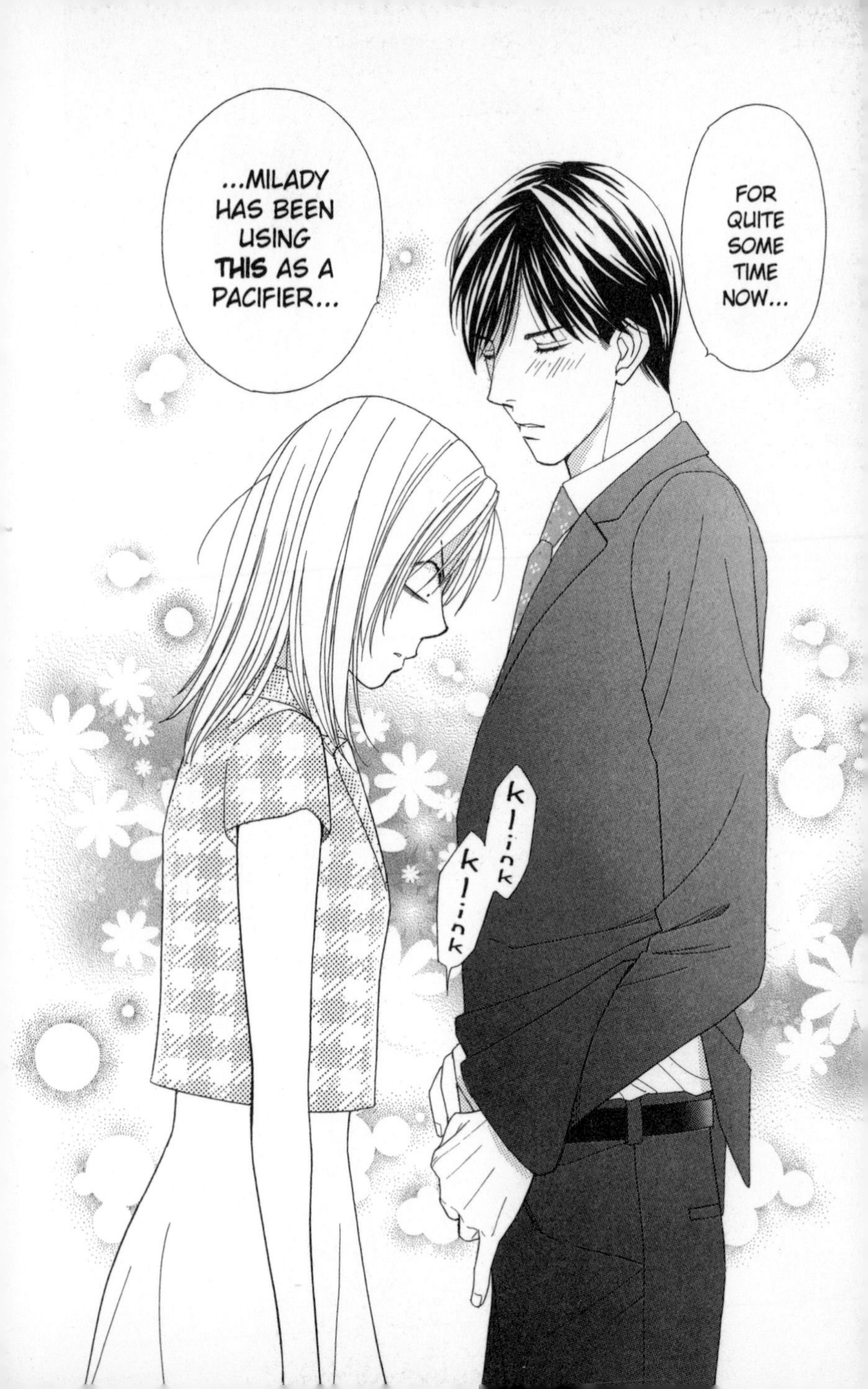
FOR QUITE SOME TIME NOW...
...MILADY HAS BEEN USING THIS AS A PACIFIER...
klink
klink

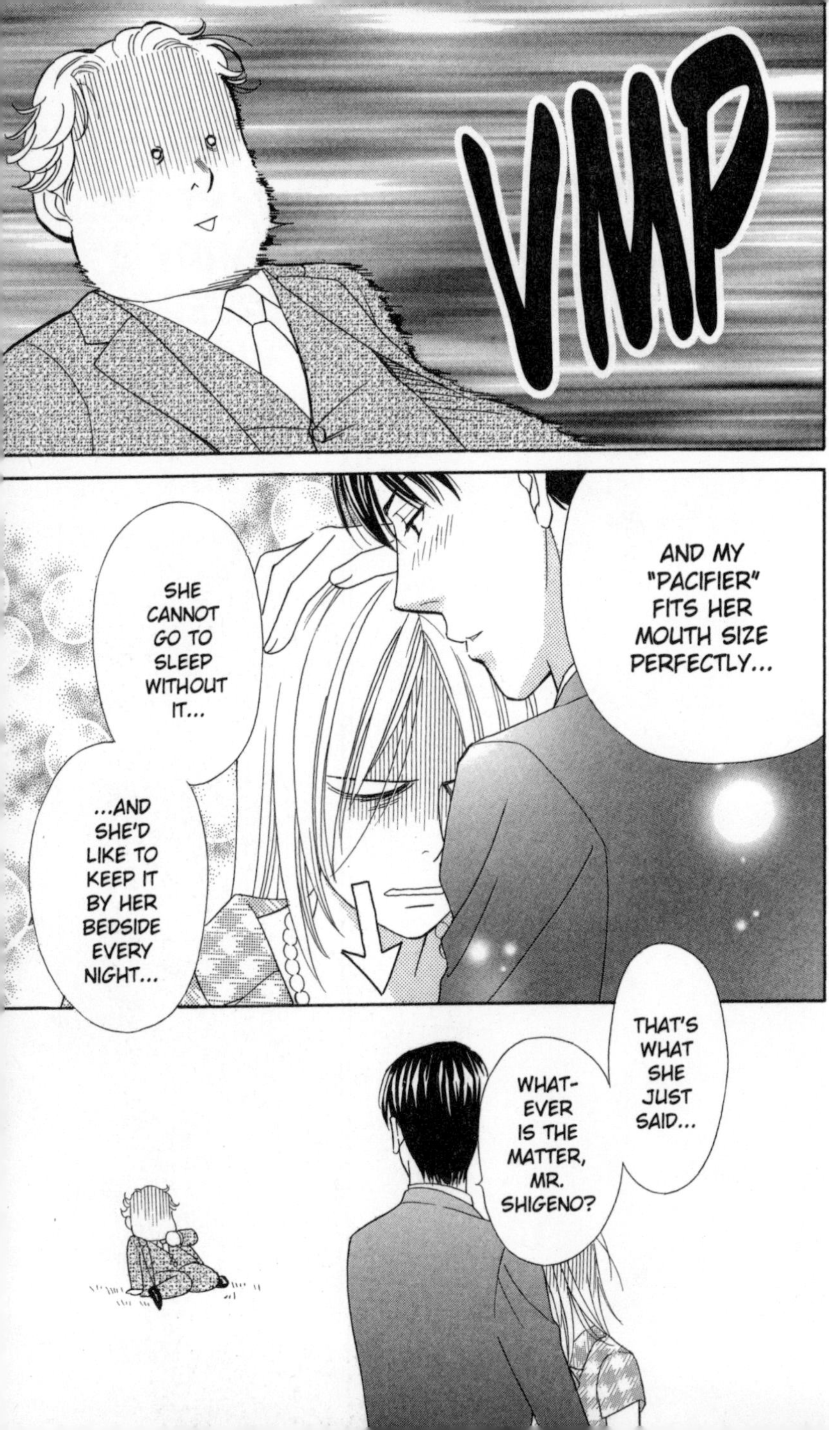
VMP
AND MY "PACIFIER" FITS HER MOUTH SIZE PERFECTLY...
SHE CANNOT GO TO SLEEP WITHOUT IT...
...AND SHE'D LIKE TO KEEP IT BY HER BEDSIDE EVERY NIGHT...
THAT'S WHAT SHE JUST SAID...
WHAT-EVER IS THE MATTER, MR. SHIGENO?

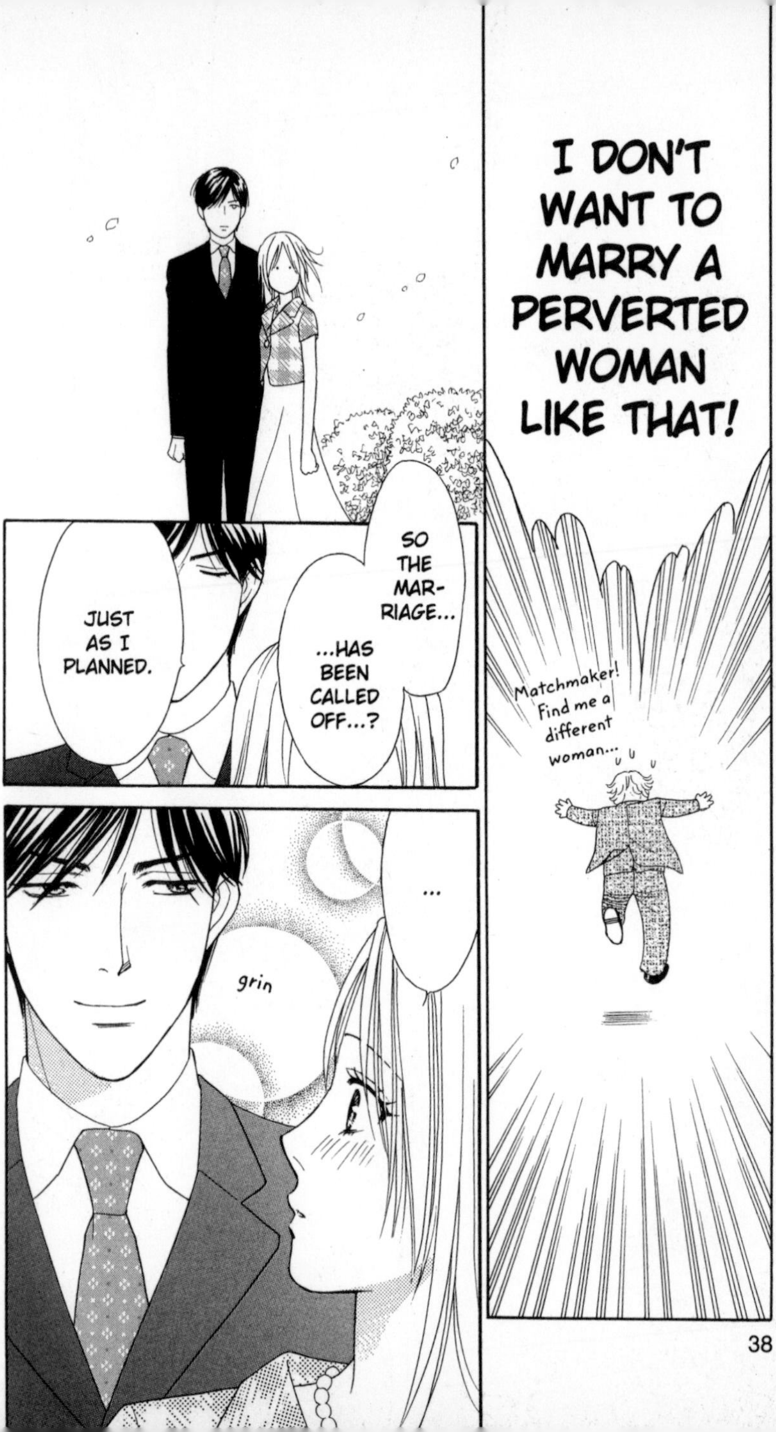
I DON'T WANT TO MARRY A PERVERTED WOMAN LIKE THAT!
Matchmaker! Find me a different woman...
SO THE MAR-RIAGE...
...HAS BEEN CALLED OFF...?
JUST AS I PLANNED.
...
grin

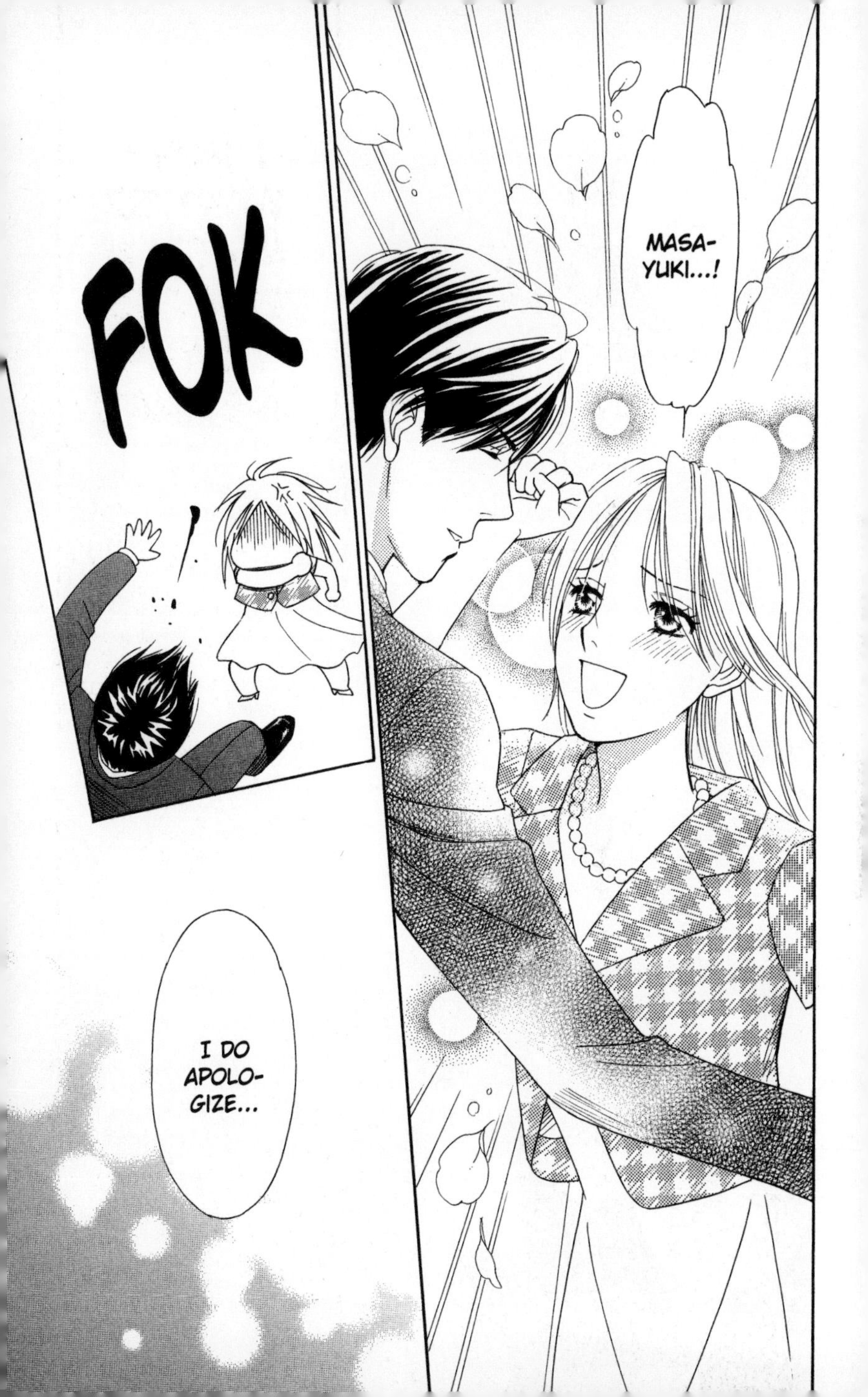
MASA-YUKI...!
FOK
I DO APOLO-GIZE...

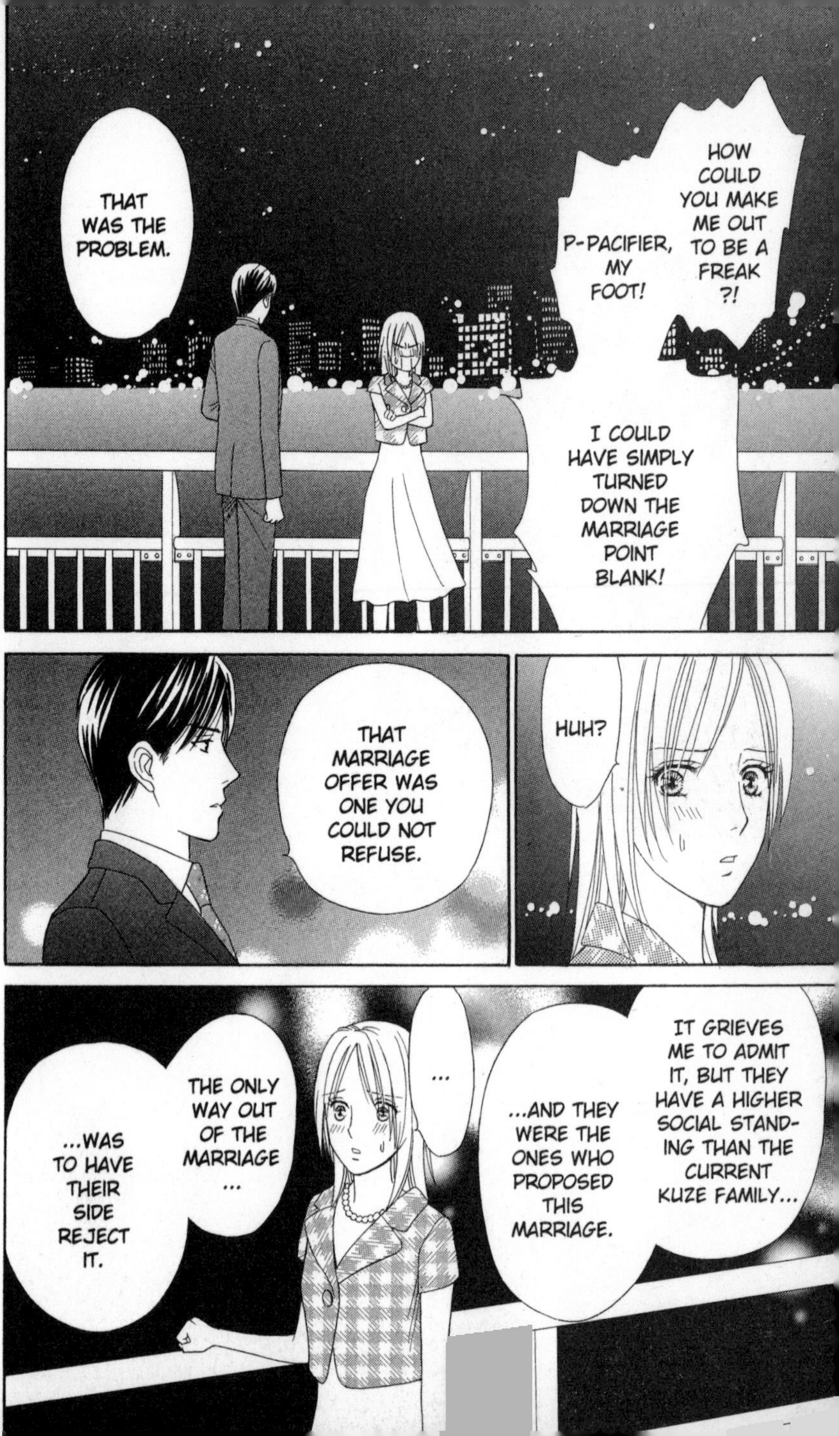
HOW COULD YOU MAKE ME OUT TO BE A FREAK ?!
P-PACIFIER, MY FOOT!
I COULD HAVE SIMPLY TURNED DOWN THE MARRIAGE POINT BLANK!
THAT WAS THE PROBLEM.
HUH?
THAT MARRIAGE OFFER WAS ONE YOU COULD NOT REFUSE.
IT GRIEVES ME TO ADMIT IT, BUT THEY HAVE A HIGHER SOCIAL STAND-ING THAN THE CURRENT KUZE FAMILY...
...AND THEY WERE THE ONES WHO PROPOSED THIS MARRIAGE.
...
THE ONLY WAY OUT OF THE MARRIAGE ...
...WAS TO HAVE THEIR SIDE REJECT IT.

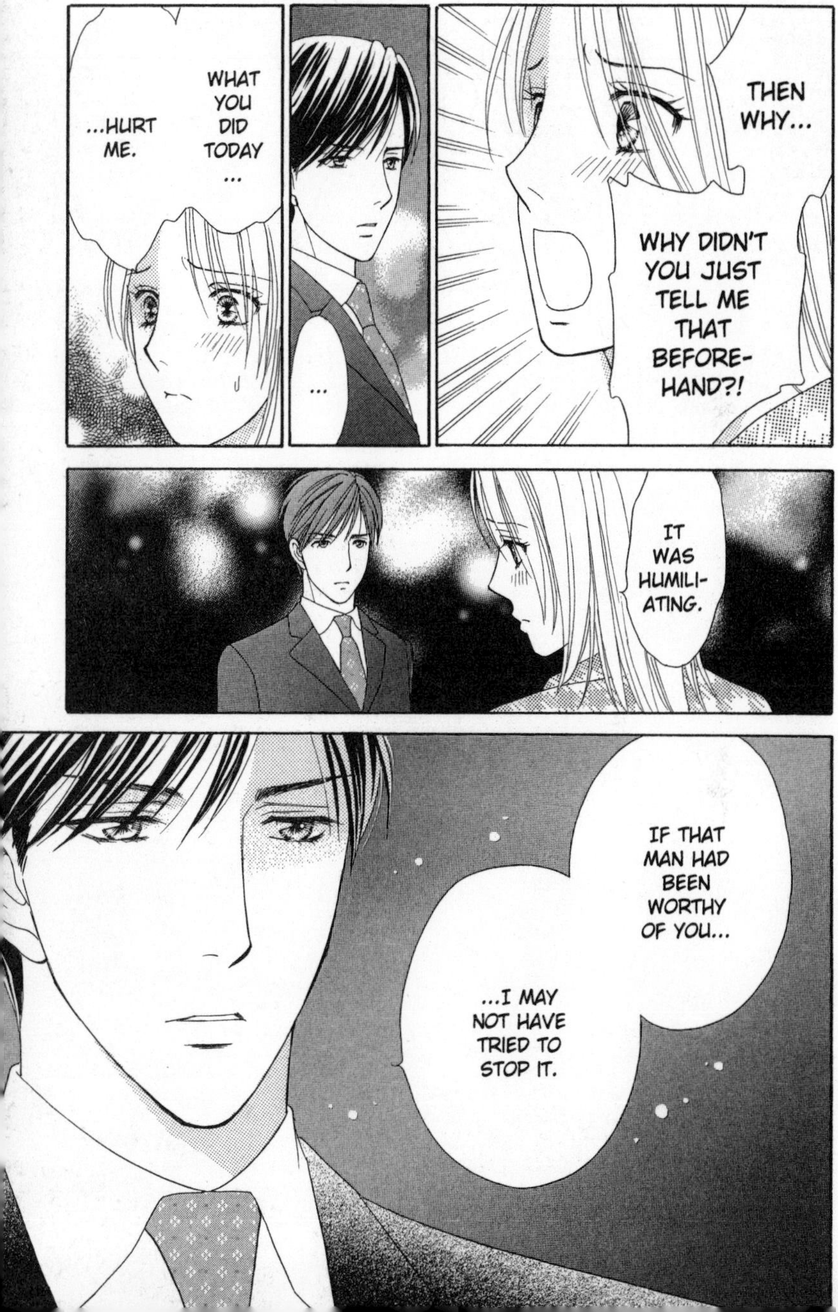
THEN WHY...
WHY DIDN'T YOU JUST TELL ME THAT BEFORE-HAND?!
...
WHAT YOU DID TODAY...
...HURT ME.
IT WAS HUMILI-ATING.
IF THAT MAN HAD BEEN WORTHY OF YOU...
...I MAY NOT HAVE TRIED TO STOP IT.

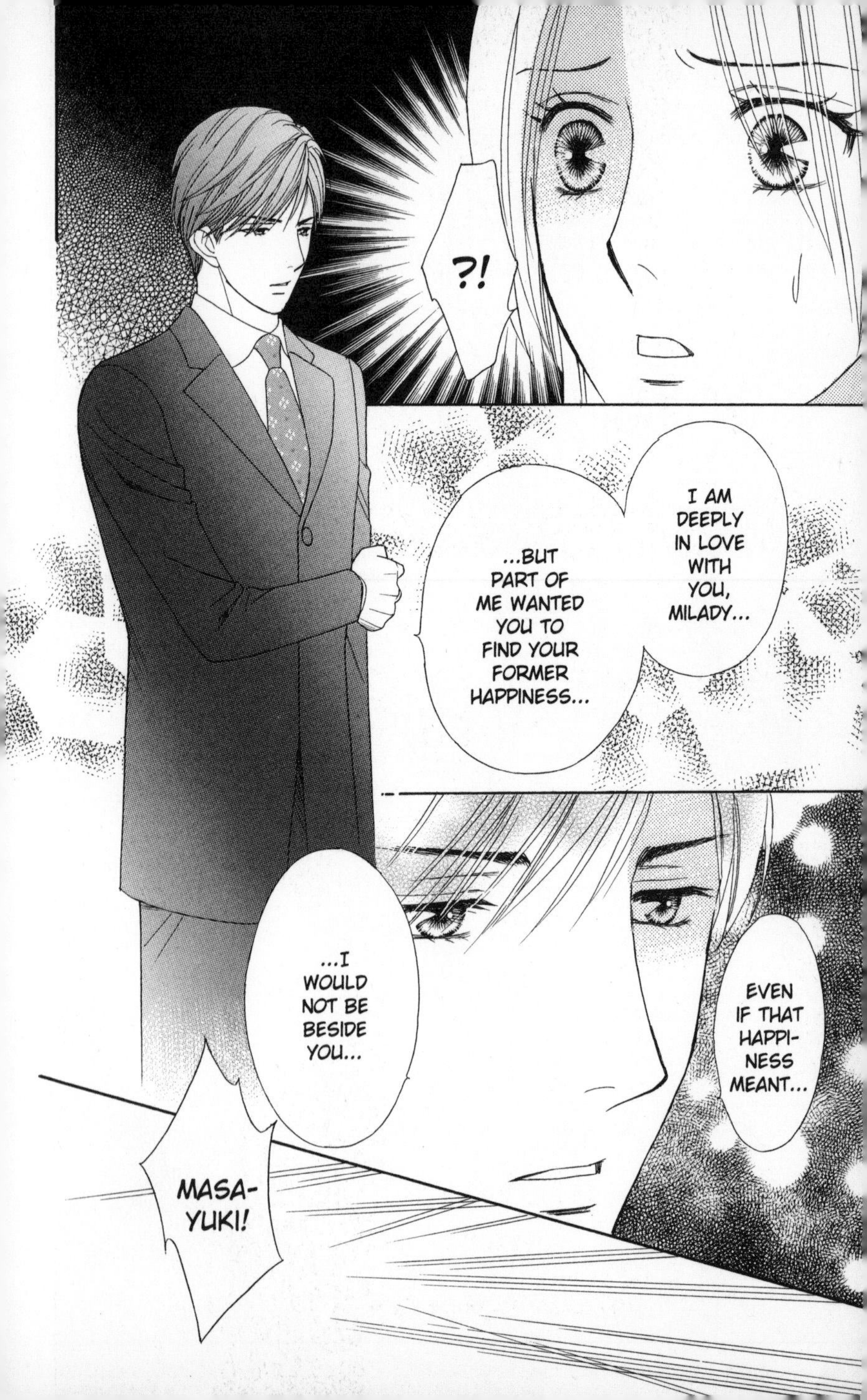
?!
I AM DEEPLY IN LOVE WITH YOU, MILADY...
...BUT PART OF ME WANTED YOU TO FIND YOUR FORMER HAPPINESS...
EVEN IF THAT HAPPI-NESS MEANT...
...I WOULD NOT BE BESIDE YOU...
MASA-YUKI!

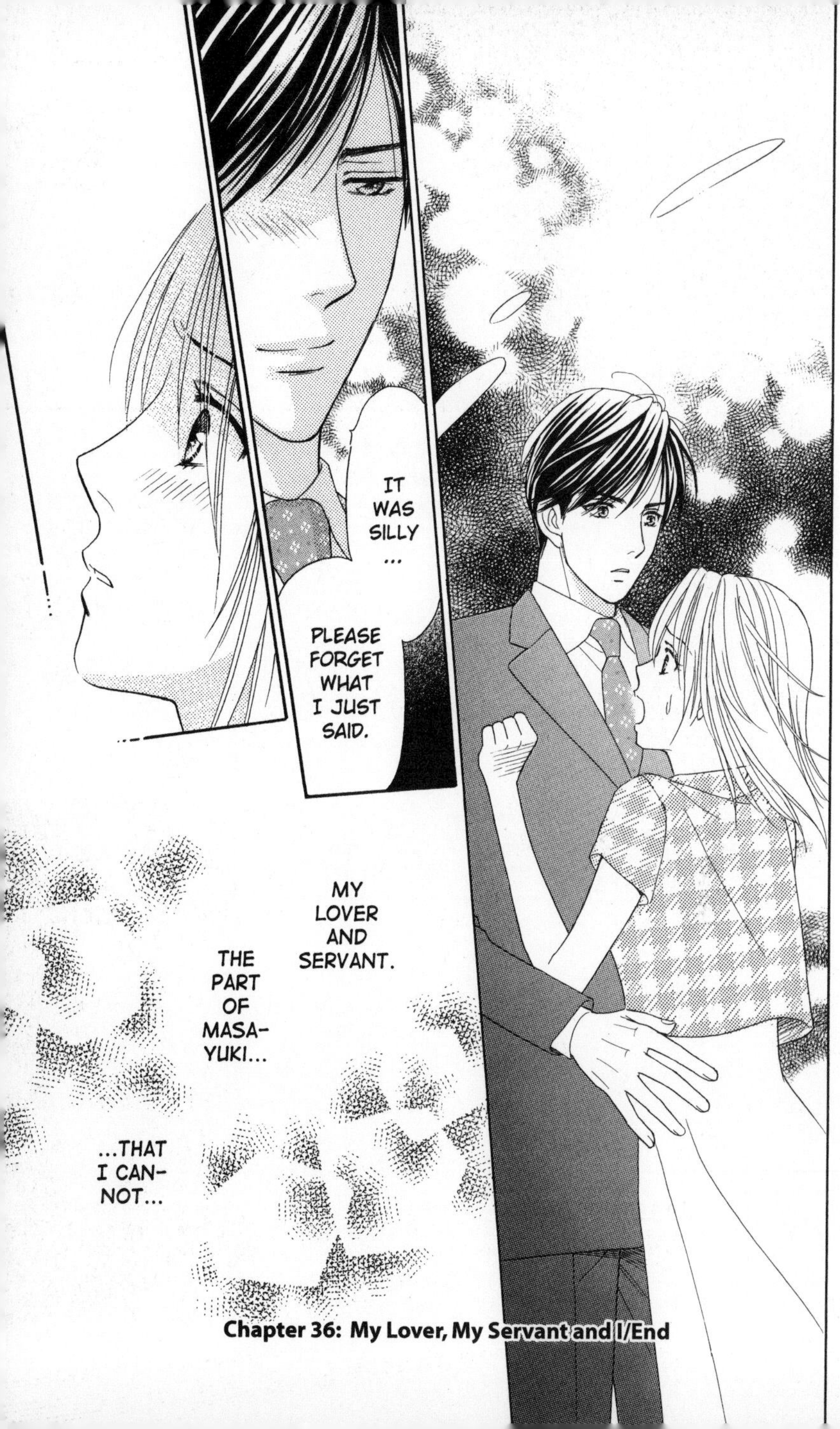
IT WAS SILLY...
PLEASE FORGET WHAT I JUST SAID.
MY LOVER AND SERVANT.
THE PART OF MASA-YUKI...
...THAT I CAN-NOT...

Chapter 36: My Lover, My Servant and I/End

FINAL VOLUME SPECIAL BUTTERFLIES, FLOWERS BACKSTAGE STORY

My second editor for *Butterflies, Flowers* kept coming up with taglines every month, such as...
"Masayuki Rising" and "Club Artesia"...
Or other kinds of taglines that sound like they are from Gundam (the original).
One month I even got "The Pursuit: Triple Masayuki!" Even though I am a Gundam otaku, I seriously wondered what my editor was asking me to draw, and I ended up getting an illness that rookie soldiers get...

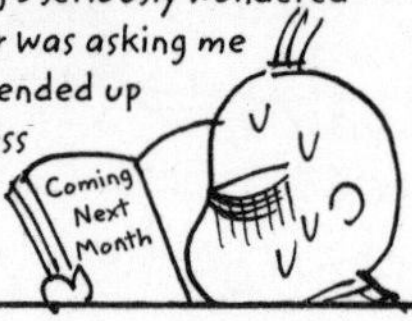
Coming Next Month

Ah, Gundam otaku are unbeliev-able...

Chapter 37
Vow and Wish

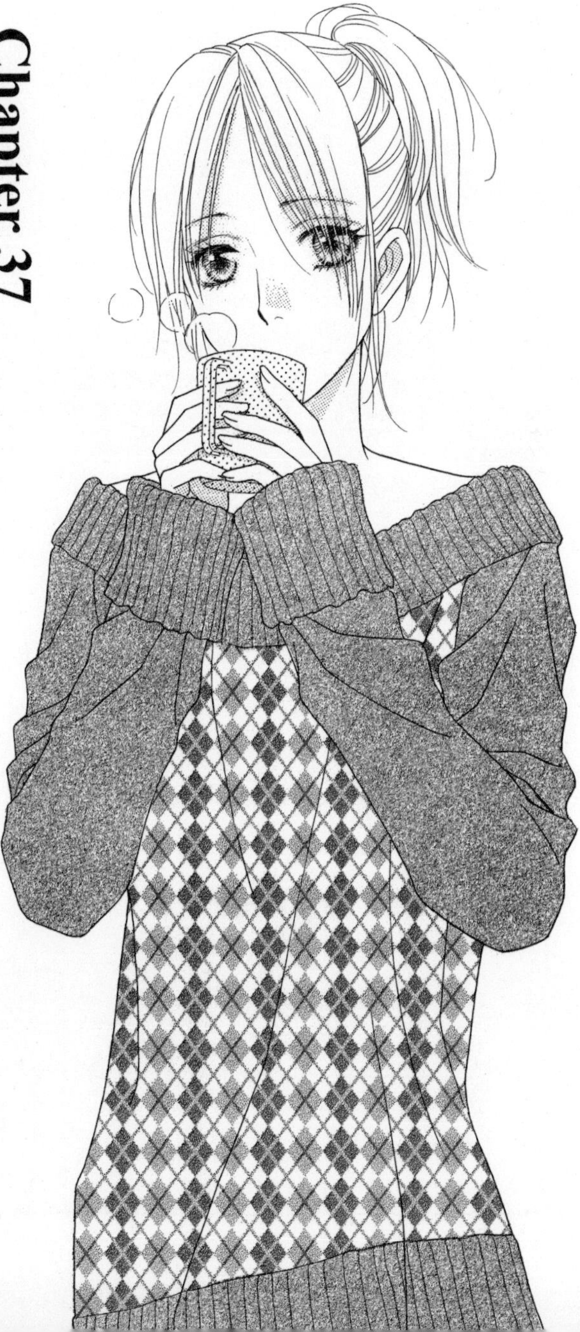

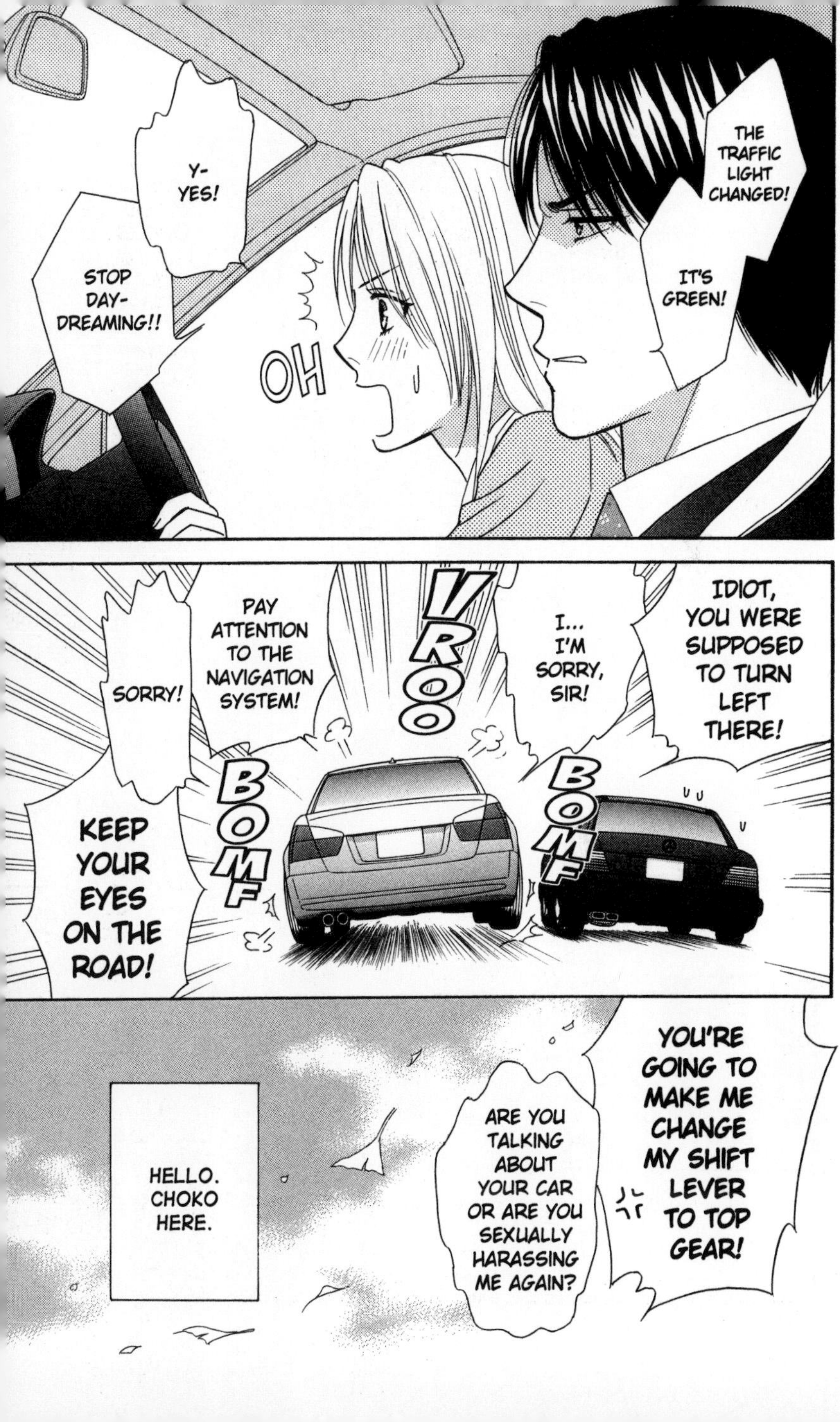
THE TRAFFIC LIGHT CHANGED!
IT'S GREEN!
OH
Y-YES!
STOP DAY-DREAMING!!
IDIOT, YOU WERE SUPPOSED TO TURN LEFT THERE!
I... I'M SORRY, SIR!
VROO
PAY ATTENTION TO THE NAVIGATION SYSTEM!
SORRY!
BOMF
BOMF
KEEP YOUR EYES ON THE ROAD!
YOU'RE GOING TO MAKE ME CHANGE MY SHIFT LEVER TO TOP GEAR!
ARE YOU TALKING ABOUT YOUR CAR OR ARE YOU SEXUALLY HARASSING ME AGAIN?
HELLO. CHOKO HERE.

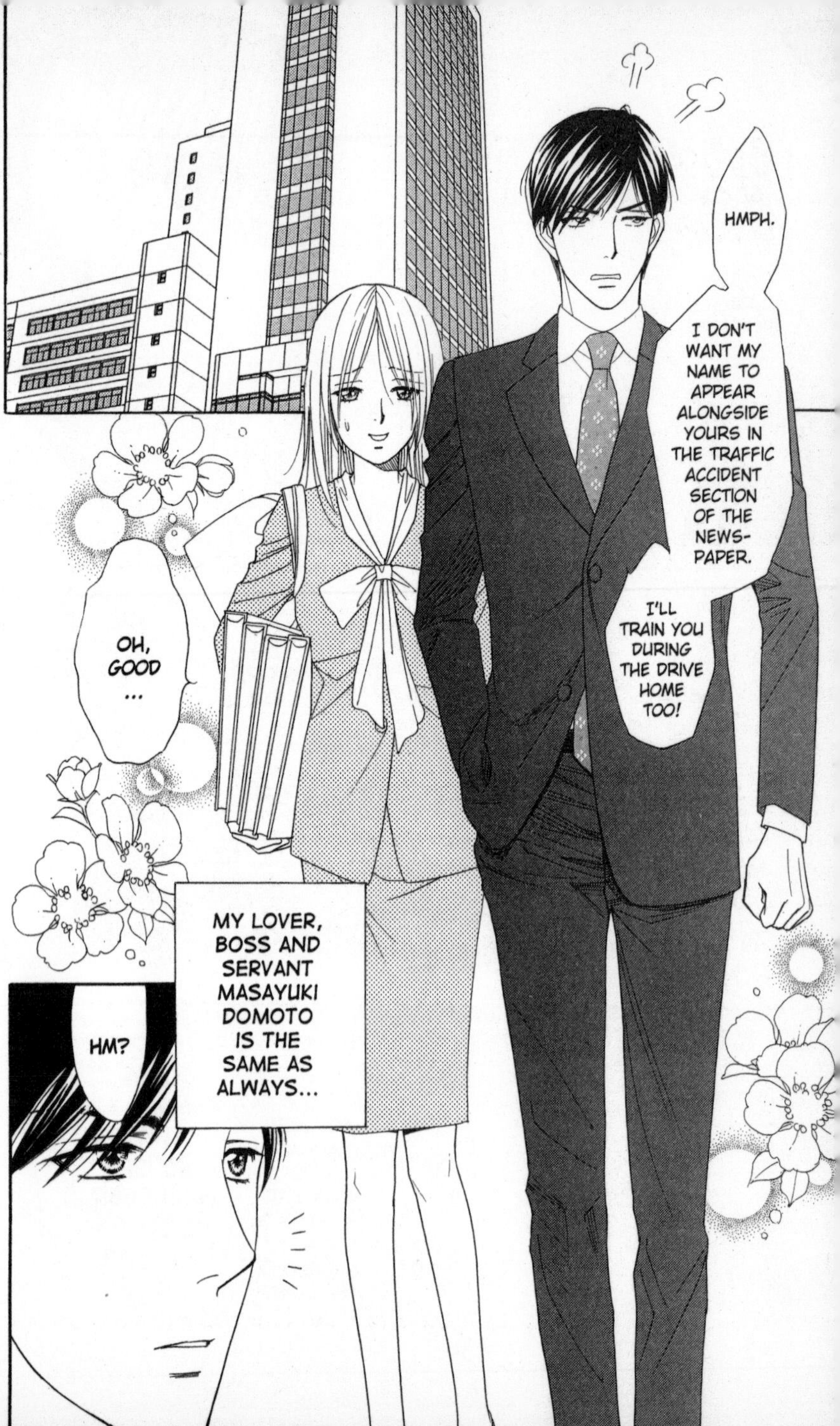
HMPH.
I DON'T WANT MY NAME TO APPEAR ALONGSIDE YOURS IN THE TRAFFIC ACCIDENT SECTION OF THE NEWS-PAPER.
I'LL TRAIN YOU DURING THE DRIVE HOME TOO!
OH, GOOD ...
MY LOVER, BOSS AND SERVANT MASAYUKI DOMOTO IS THE SAME AS ALWAYS...
HM?

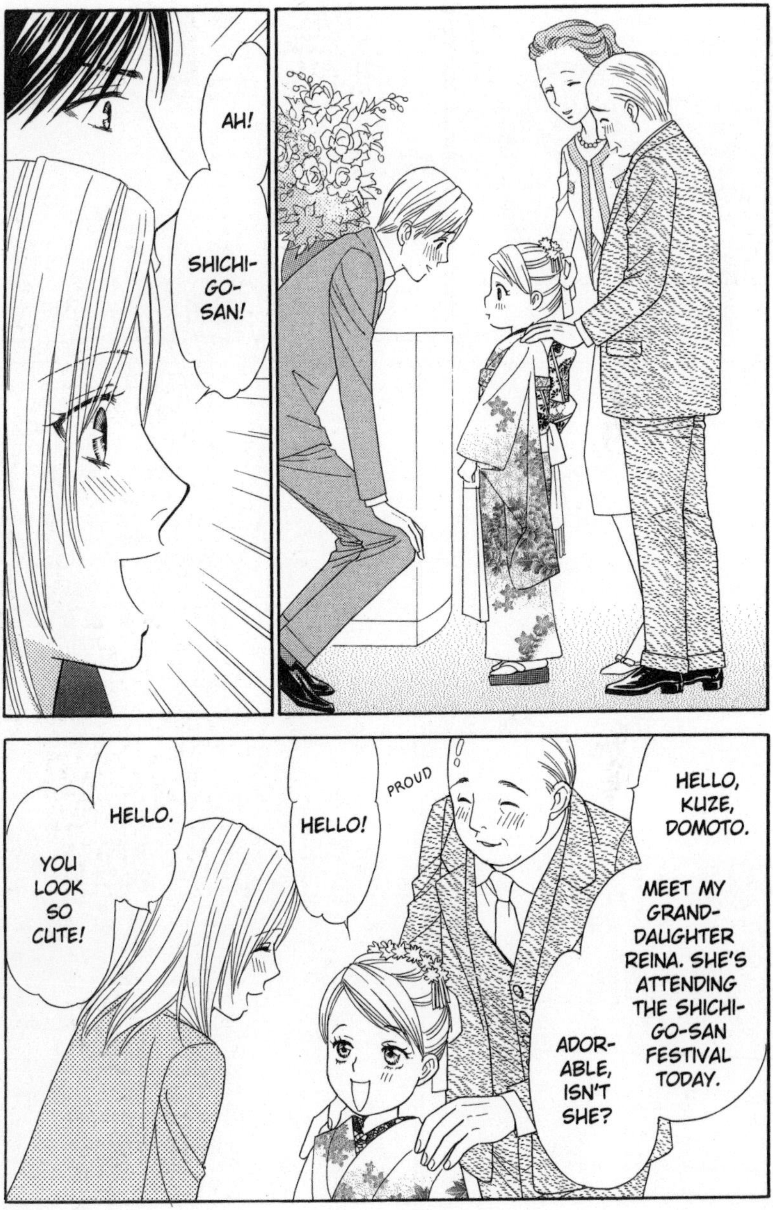
AH!
SHICHI-GO-SAN!
HELLO, KUZE, DOMOTO.
MEET MY GRAND-DAUGHTER REINA. SHE'S ATTENDING THE SHICHI-GO-SAN FESTIVAL TODAY.
ADOR-ABLE, ISN'T SHE?
PROUD
HELLO!
HELLO.
YOU LOOK SO CUTE!

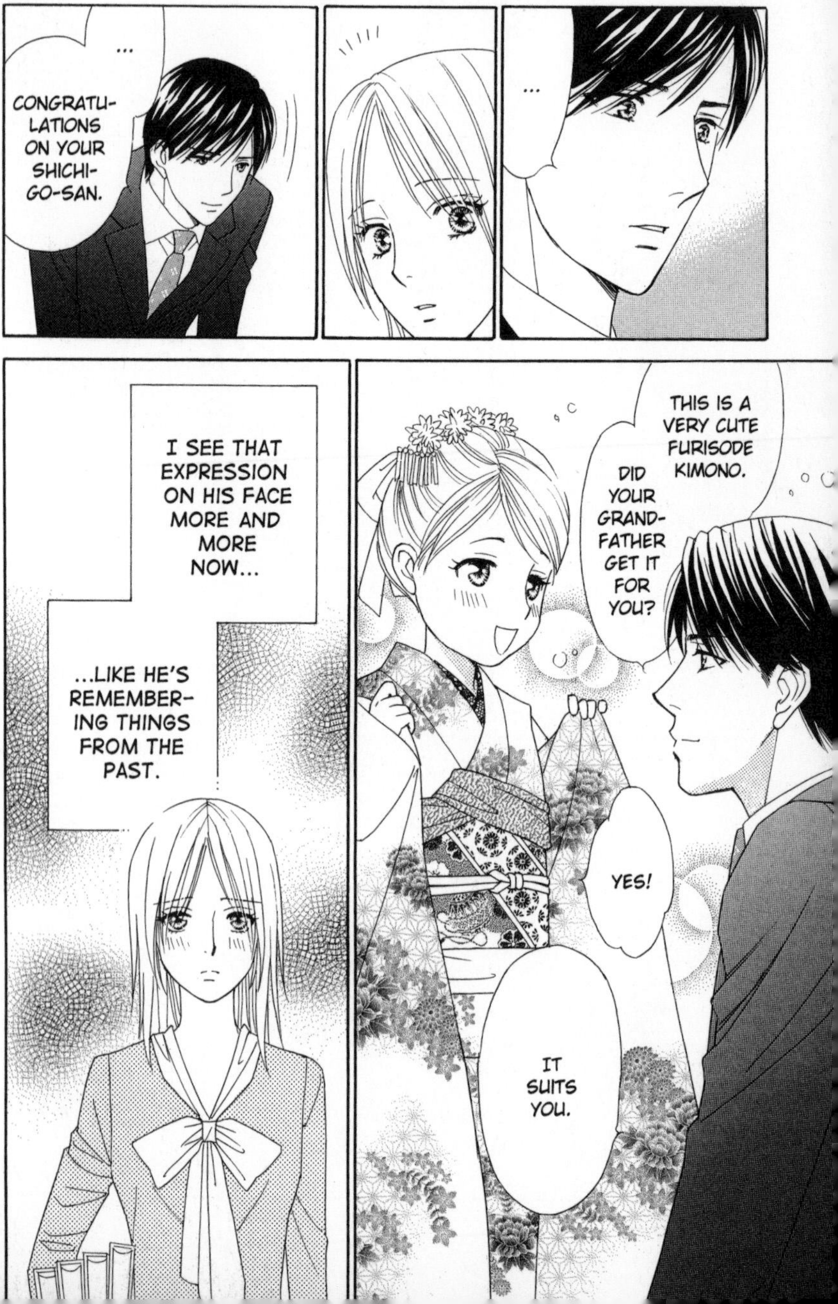
...
...
CONGRATULATIONS ON YOUR SHICHI-GO-SAN.
THIS IS A VERY CUTE FURISODE KIMONO.
DID YOUR GRANDFATHER GET IT FOR YOU?
YES!
IT SUITS YOU.
I SEE THAT EXPRESSION ON HIS FACE MORE AND MORE NOW...
...LIKE HE'S REMEMBERING THINGS FROM THE PAST.

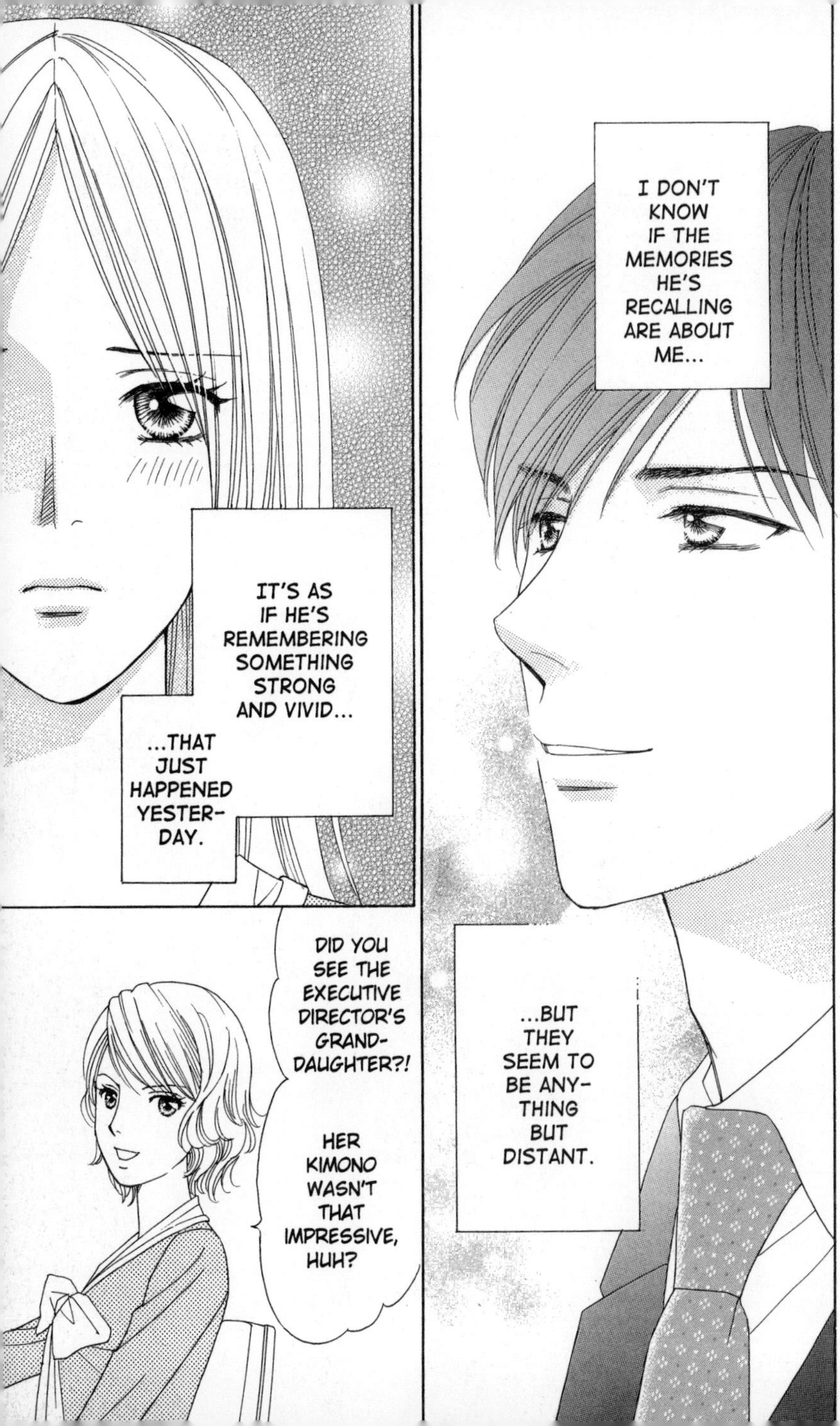
I DON'T KNOW IF THE MEMORIES HE'S RECALLING ARE ABOUT ME...
...BUT THEY SEEM TO BE ANY-THING BUT DISTANT.
IT'S AS IF HE'S REMEMBERING SOMETHING STRONG AND VIVID...
...THAT JUST HAPPENED YESTER-DAY.
DID YOU SEE THE EXECUTIVE DIRECTOR'S GRAND-DAUGHTER?!
HER KIMONO WASN'T THAT IMPRESSIVE, HUH?

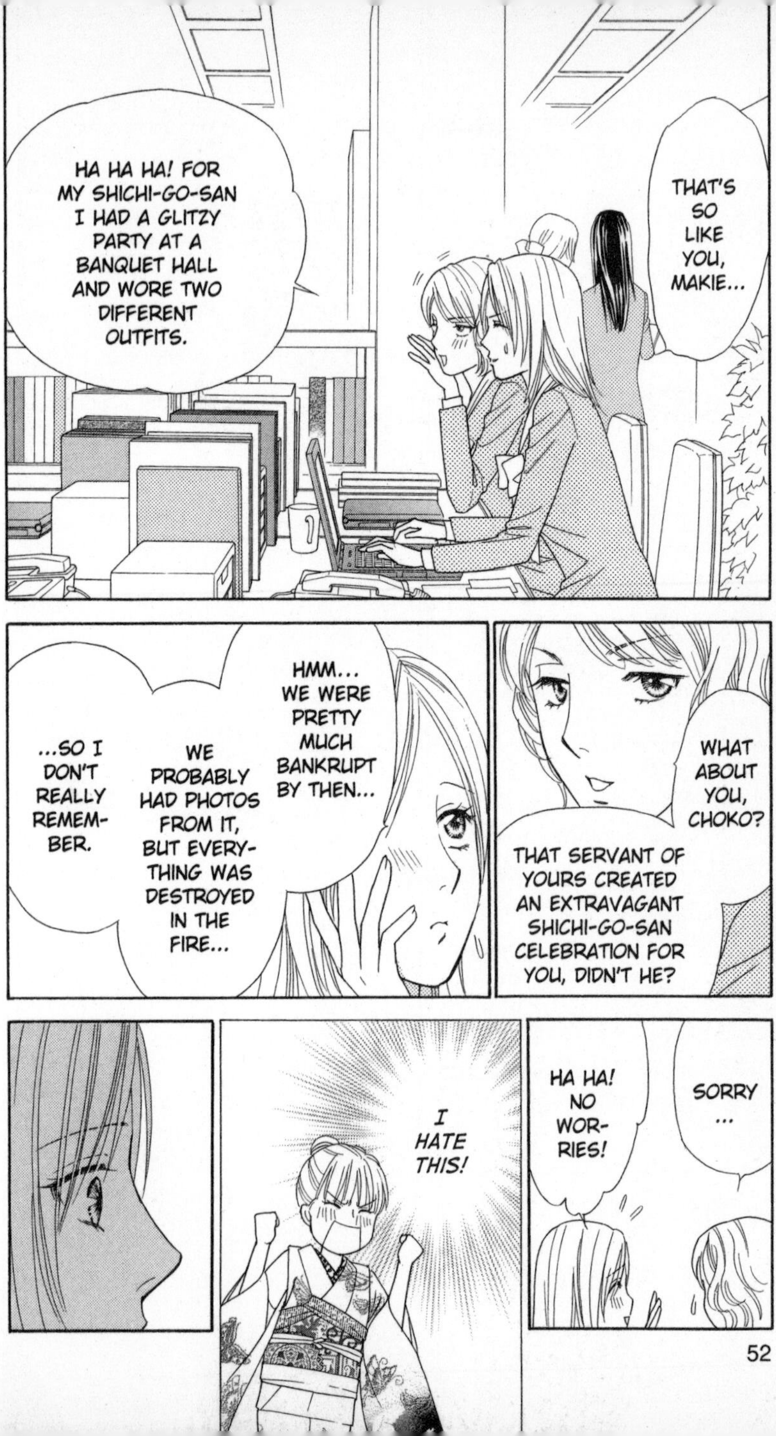
THAT'S SO LIKE YOU, MAKIE...
HA HA HA! FOR MY SHICHI-GO-SAN I HAD A GLITZY PARTY AT A BANQUET HALL AND WORE TWO DIFFERENT OUTFITS.
WHAT ABOUT YOU, CHOKO?
THAT SERVANT OF YOURS CREATED AN EXTRAVAGANT SHICHI-GO-SAN CELEBRATION FOR YOU, DIDN'T HE?
HMM... WE WERE PRETTY MUCH BANKRUPT BY THEN...
WE PROBABLY HAD PHOTOS FROM IT, BUT EVERYTHING WAS DESTROYED IN THE FIRE...
...SO I DON'T REALLY REMEMBER.
SORRY ...
HA HA! NO WORRIES!
I HATE THIS!

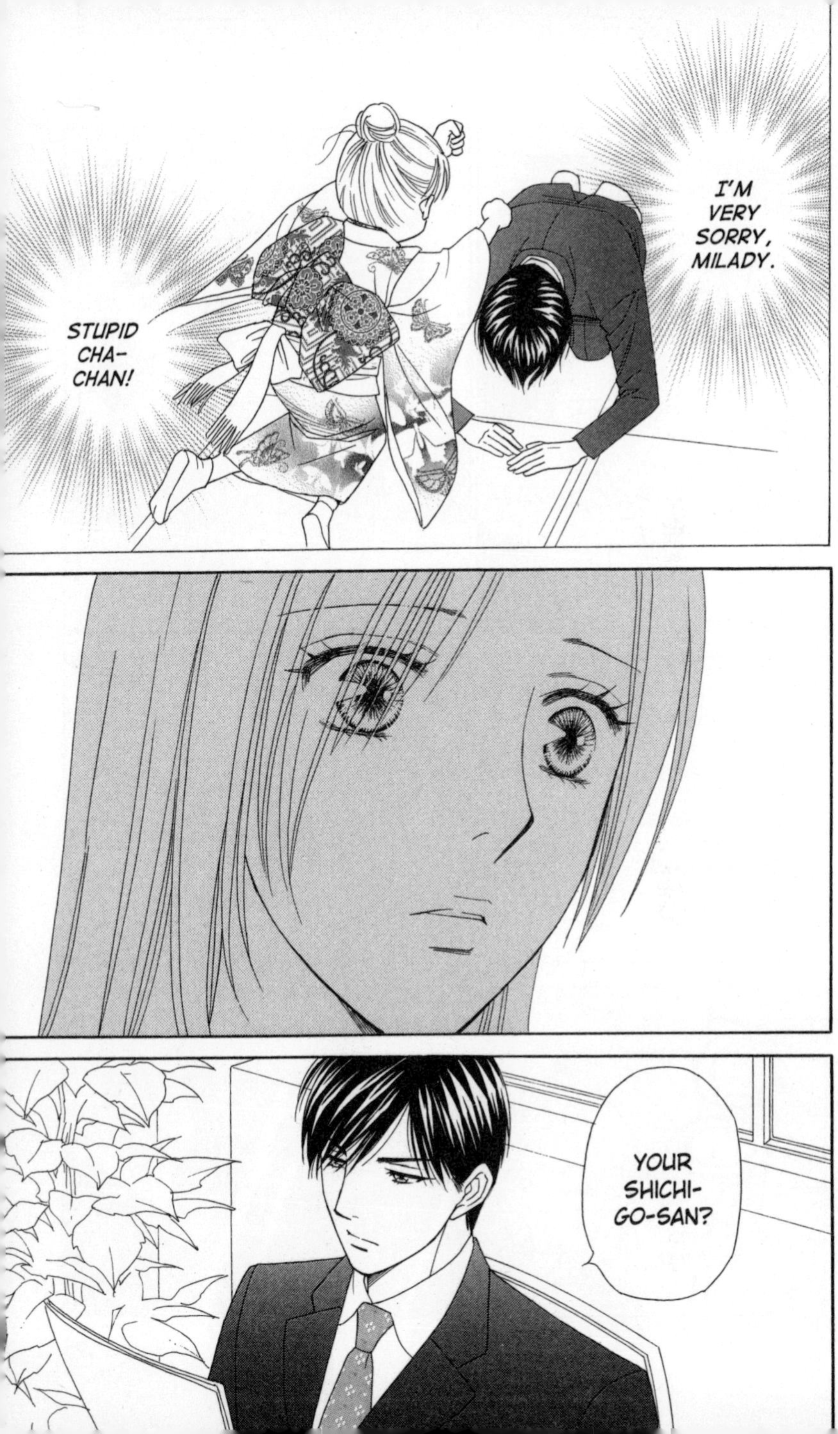
I'M VERY SORRY, MILADY.
STUPID CHA-CHAN!
YOUR SHICHI-GO-SAN?

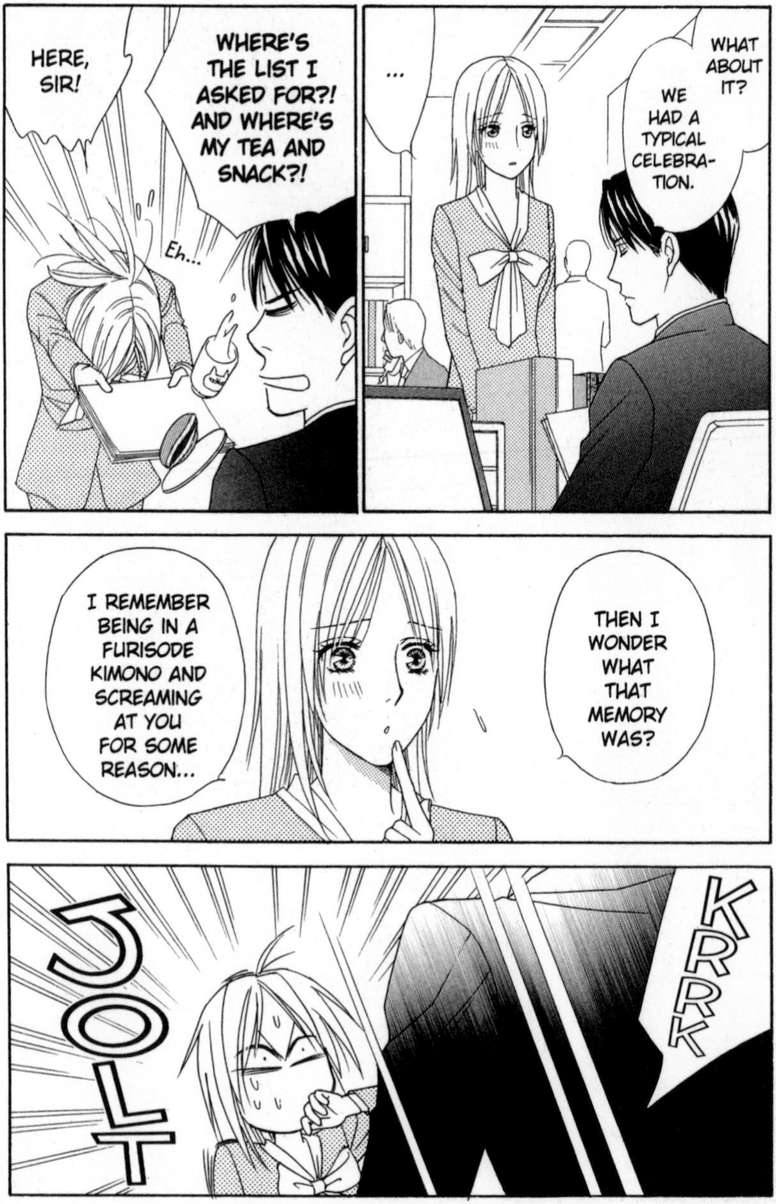
WHAT ABOUT IT?
WE HAD A TYPICAL CELEBRATION.
...
WHERE'S THE LIST I ASKED FOR?! AND WHERE'S MY TEA AND SNACK?!
HERE, SIR!
Eh...
THEN I WONDER WHAT THAT MEMORY WAS?
I REMEMBER BEING IN A FURISODE KIMONO AND SCREAMING AT YOU FOR SOME REASON...
KRRK
JOLT

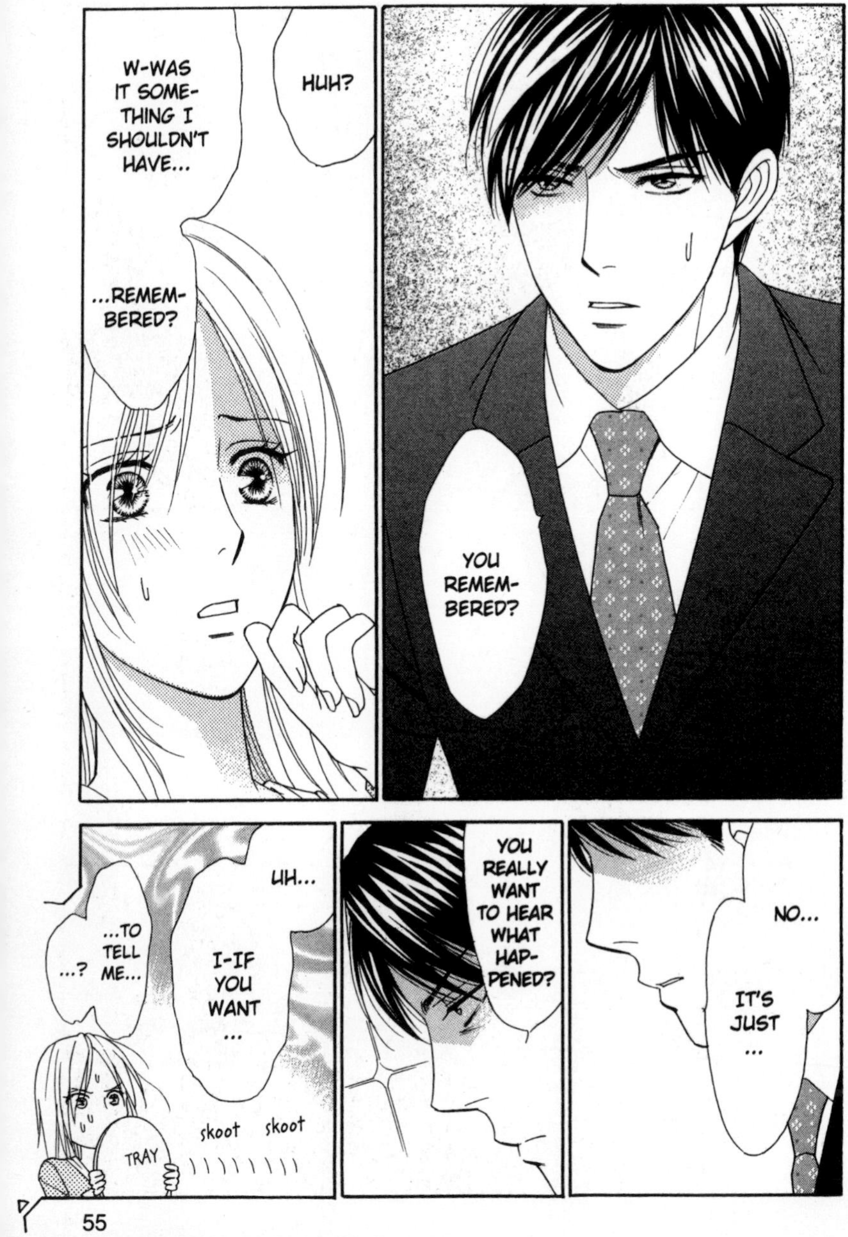
YOU REMEMBERED?
HUH?
W-WAS IT SOMETHING I SHOULDN'T HAVE...
...REMEMBERED?
NO...
IT'S JUST ...
YOU REALLY WANT TO HEAR WHAT HAPPENED?
UH...
I-IF YOU WANT ...
...TO TELL ME...
...?
skoot skoot
TRAY

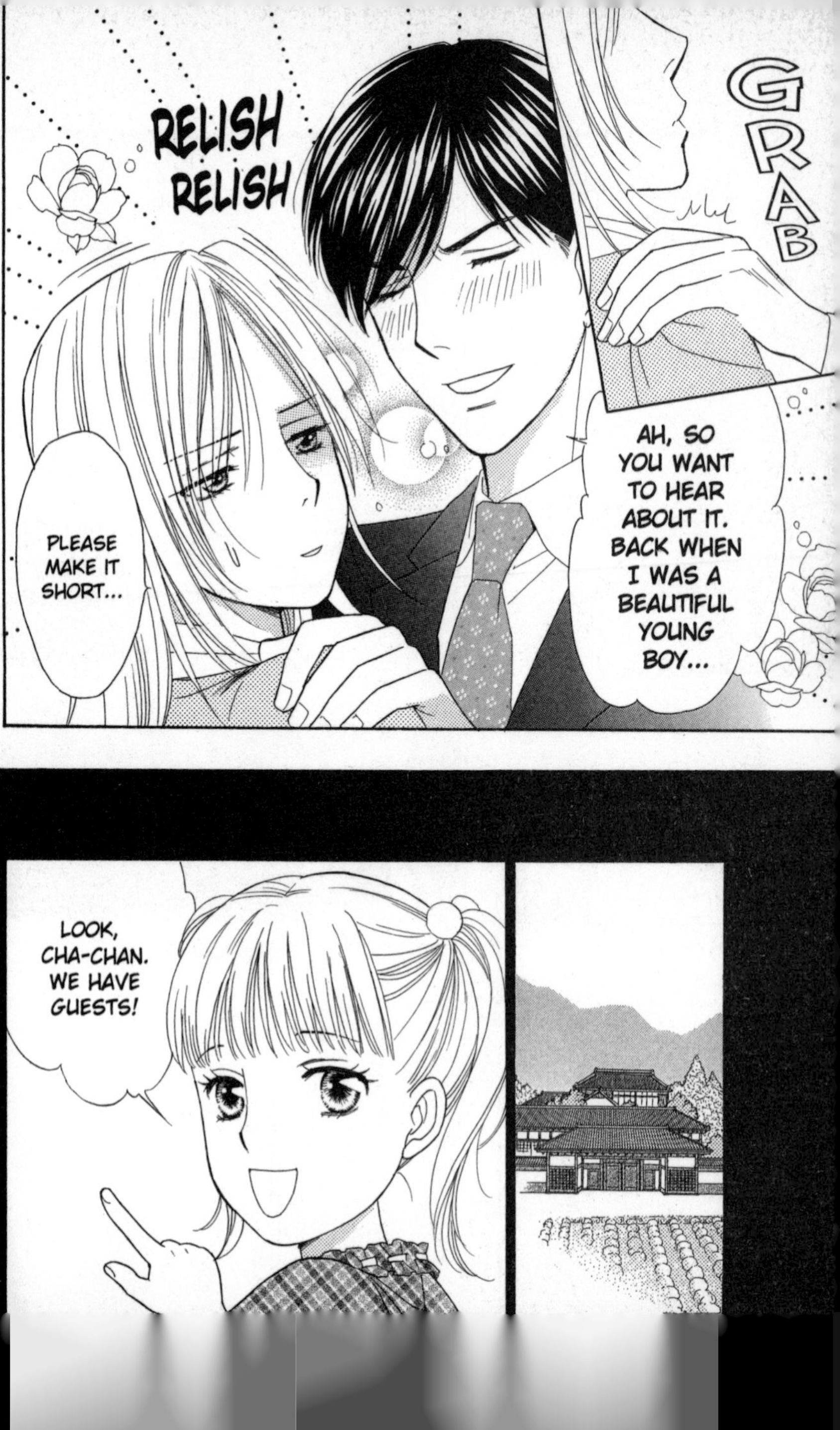
GRAB
RELISH RELISH
AH, SO YOU WANT TO HEAR ABOUT IT. BACK WHEN I WAS A BEAUTIFUL YOUNG BOY...
PLEASE MAKE IT SHORT...
LOOK, CHA-CHAN. WE HAVE GUESTS!

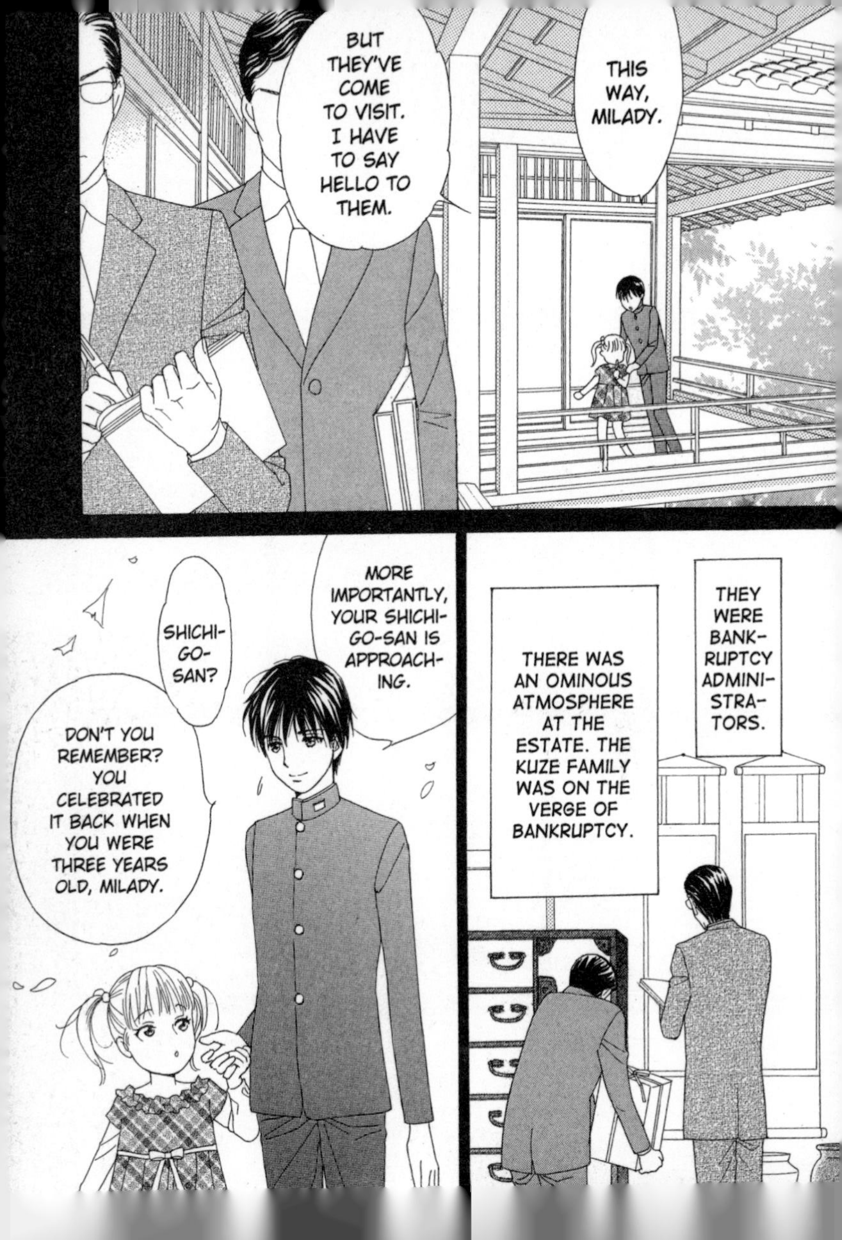
THIS WAY, MILADY.
BUT THEY'VE COME TO VISIT. I HAVE TO SAY HELLO TO THEM.
THEY WERE BANKRUPTCY ADMINISTRATORS.
THERE WAS AN OMINOUS ATMOSPHERE AT THE ESTATE. THE KUZE FAMILY WAS ON THE VERGE OF BANKRUPTCY.
MORE IMPORTANTLY, YOUR SHICHI-GO-SAN IS APPROACHING.
SHICHI-GO-SAN?
DON'T YOU REMEMBER? YOU CELEBRATED IT BACK WHEN YOU WERE THREE YEARS OLD, MILADY.

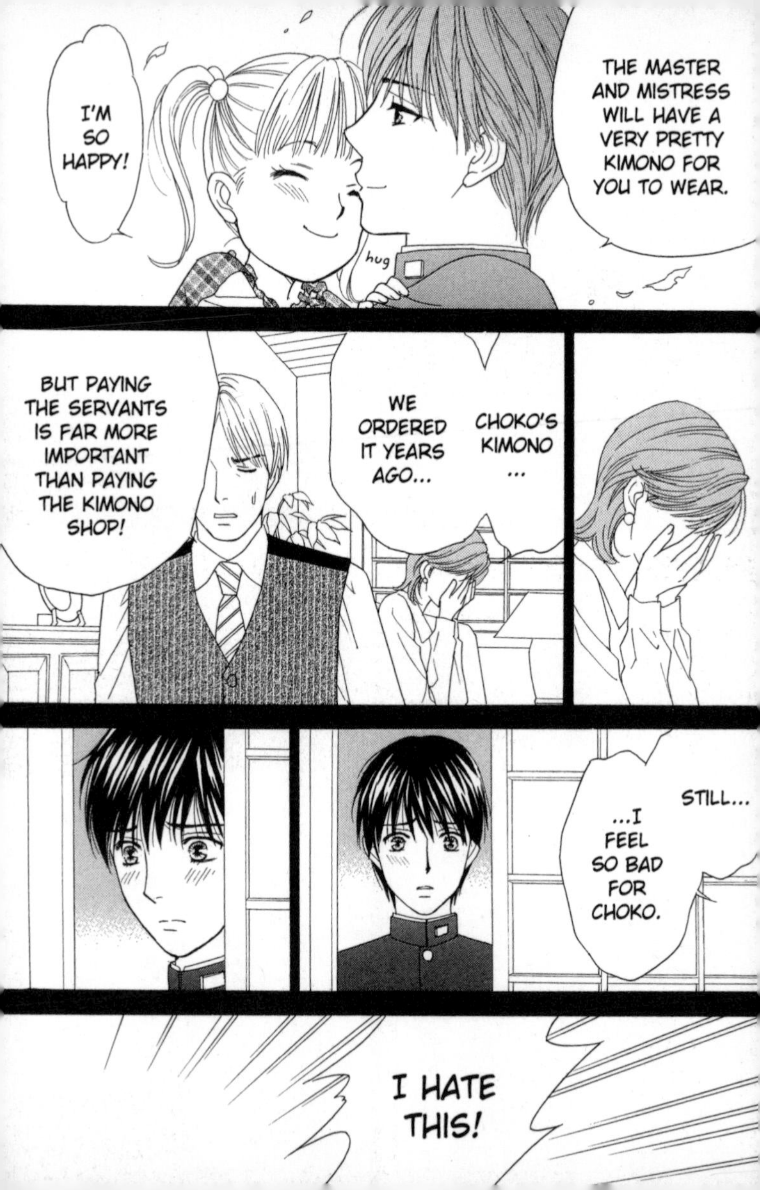
THE MASTER AND MISTRESS WILL HAVE A VERY PRETTY KIMONO FOR YOU TO WEAR.
I'M SO HAPPY!
hug
CHOKO'S KIMONO...
WE ORDERED IT YEARS AGO...
BUT PAYING THE SERVANTS IS FAR MORE IMPORTANT THAN PAYING THE KIMONO SHOP!
STILL...
...I FEEL SO BAD FOR CHOKO.
I HATE THIS!

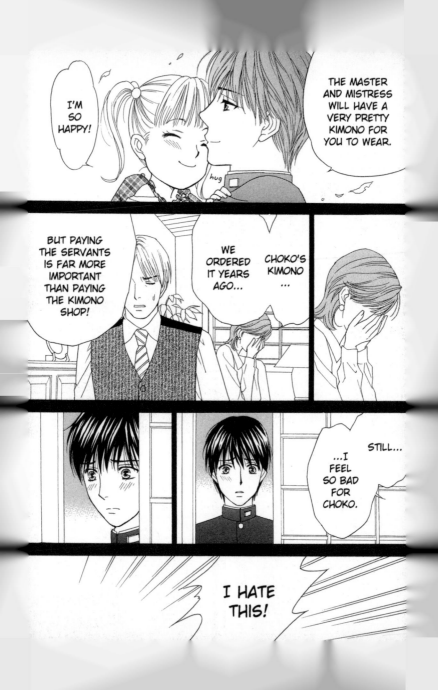

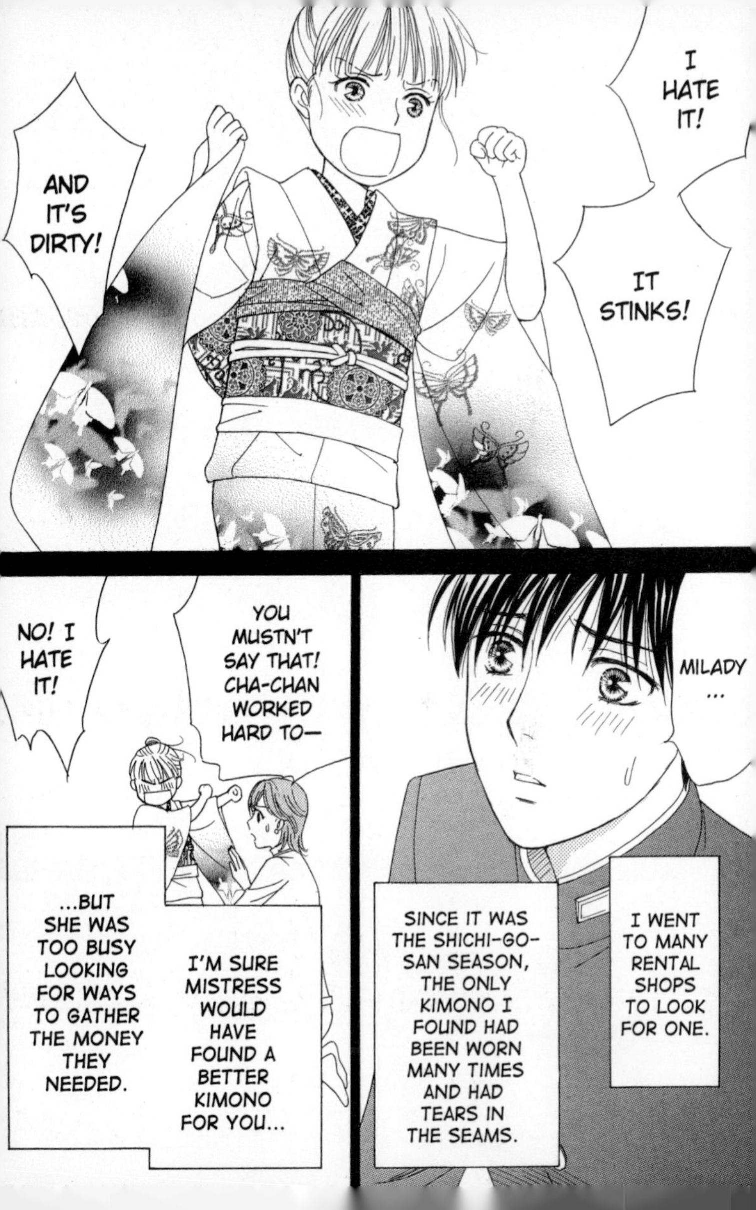
I HATE IT!
IT STINKS!
AND IT'S DIRTY!
MILADY...
I WENT TO MANY RENTAL SHOPS TO LOOK FOR ONE.
SINCE IT WAS THE SHICHI-GO-SAN SEASON, THE ONLY KIMONO I FOUND HAD BEEN WORN MANY TIMES AND HAD TEARS IN THE SEAMS.
YOU MUSTN'T SAY THAT! CHA-CHAN WORKED HARD TO—
NO! I HATE IT!
I'M SURE MISTRESS WOULD HAVE FOUND A BETTER KIMONO FOR YOU...
...BUT SHE WAS TOO BUSY LOOKING FOR WAYS TO GATHER THE MONEY THEY NEEDED.

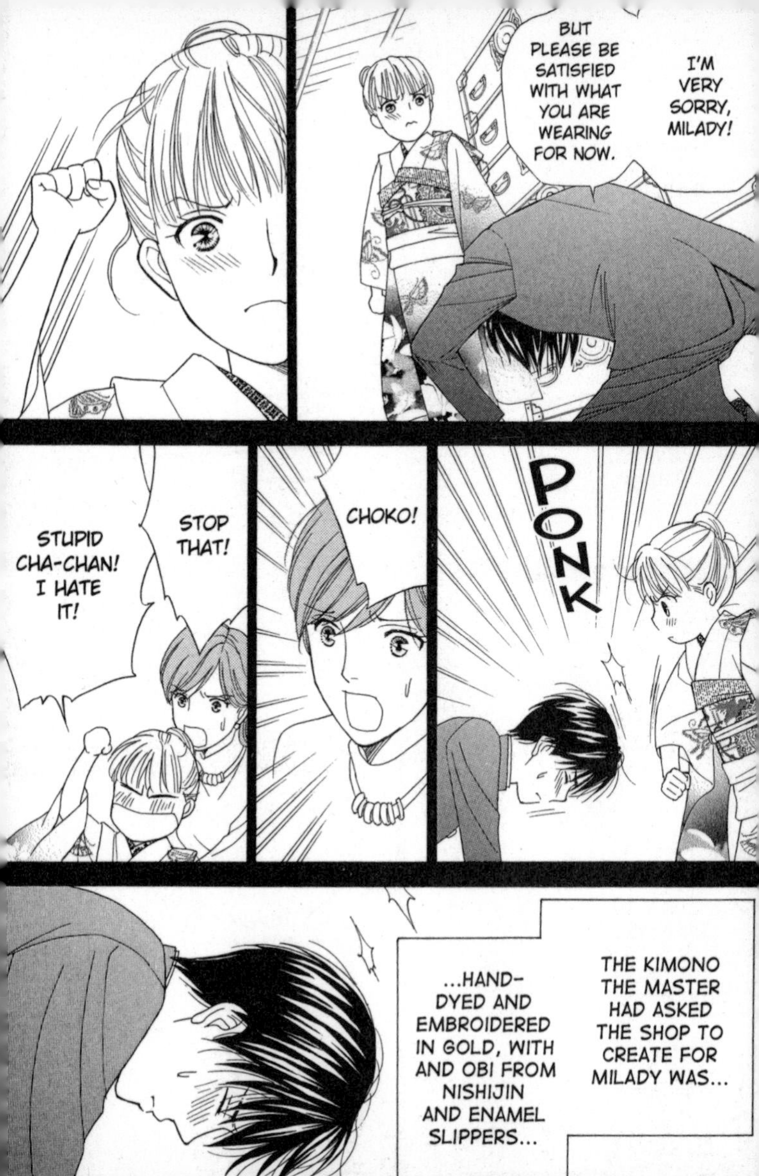
I'M VERY SORRY, MILADY!
BUT PLEASE BE SATISFIED WITH WHAT YOU ARE WEARING FOR NOW.
PONK
CHOKO!
STOP THAT!
STUPID CHA-CHAN! I HATE IT!
THE KIMONO THE MASTER HAD ASKED THE SHOP TO CREATE FOR MILADY WAS...
...HAND-DYED AND EMBROIDERED IN GOLD, WITH AND OBI FROM NISHIJIN AND ENAMEL SLIPPERS...

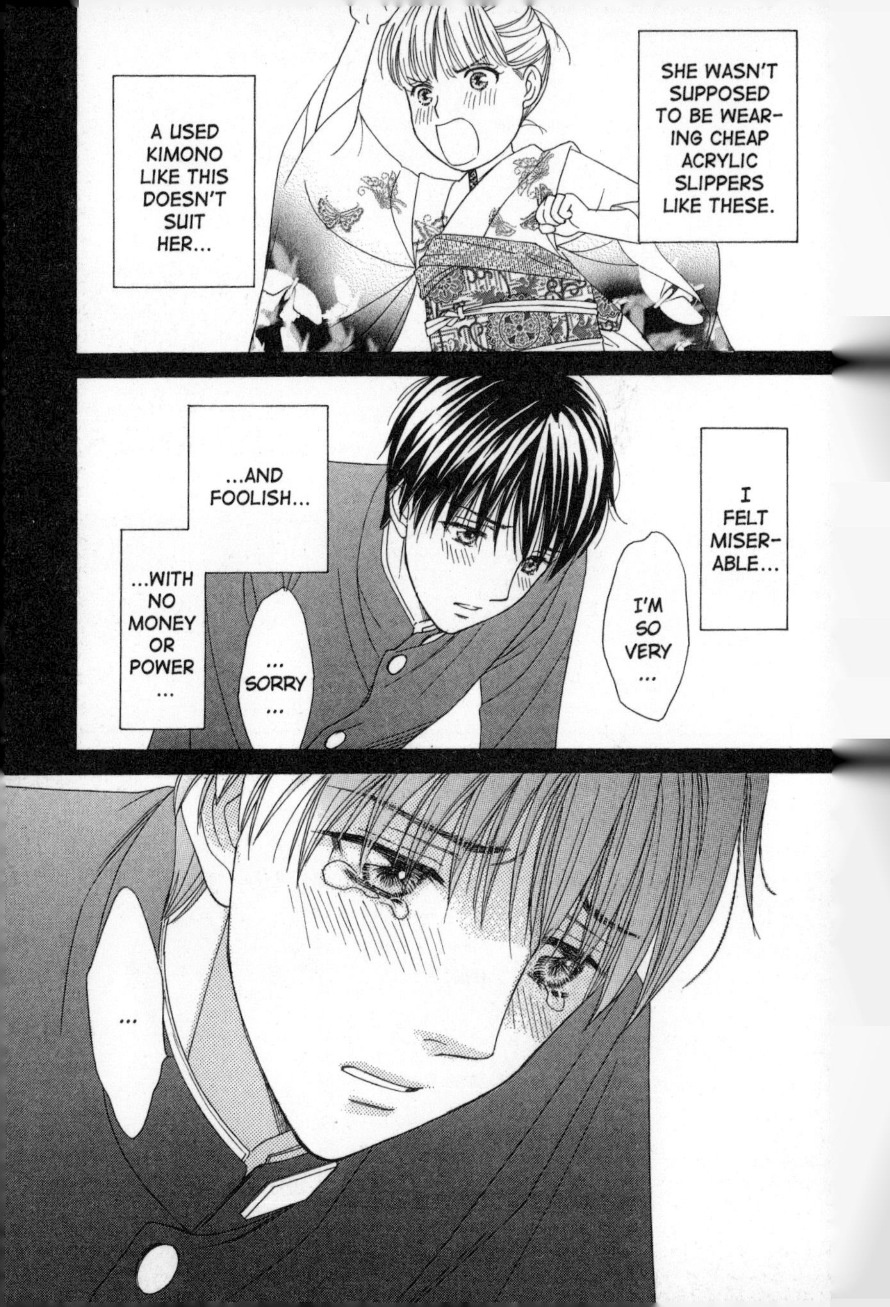
SHE WASN'T SUPPOSED TO BE WEAR-ING CHEAP ACRYLIC SLIPPERS LIKE THESE.
A USED KIMONO LIKE THIS DOESN'T SUIT HER...
I FELT MISER-ABLE...
I'M SO VERY ...
...AND FOOLISH...
...WITH NO MONEY OR POWER ...
... SORRY ...
...

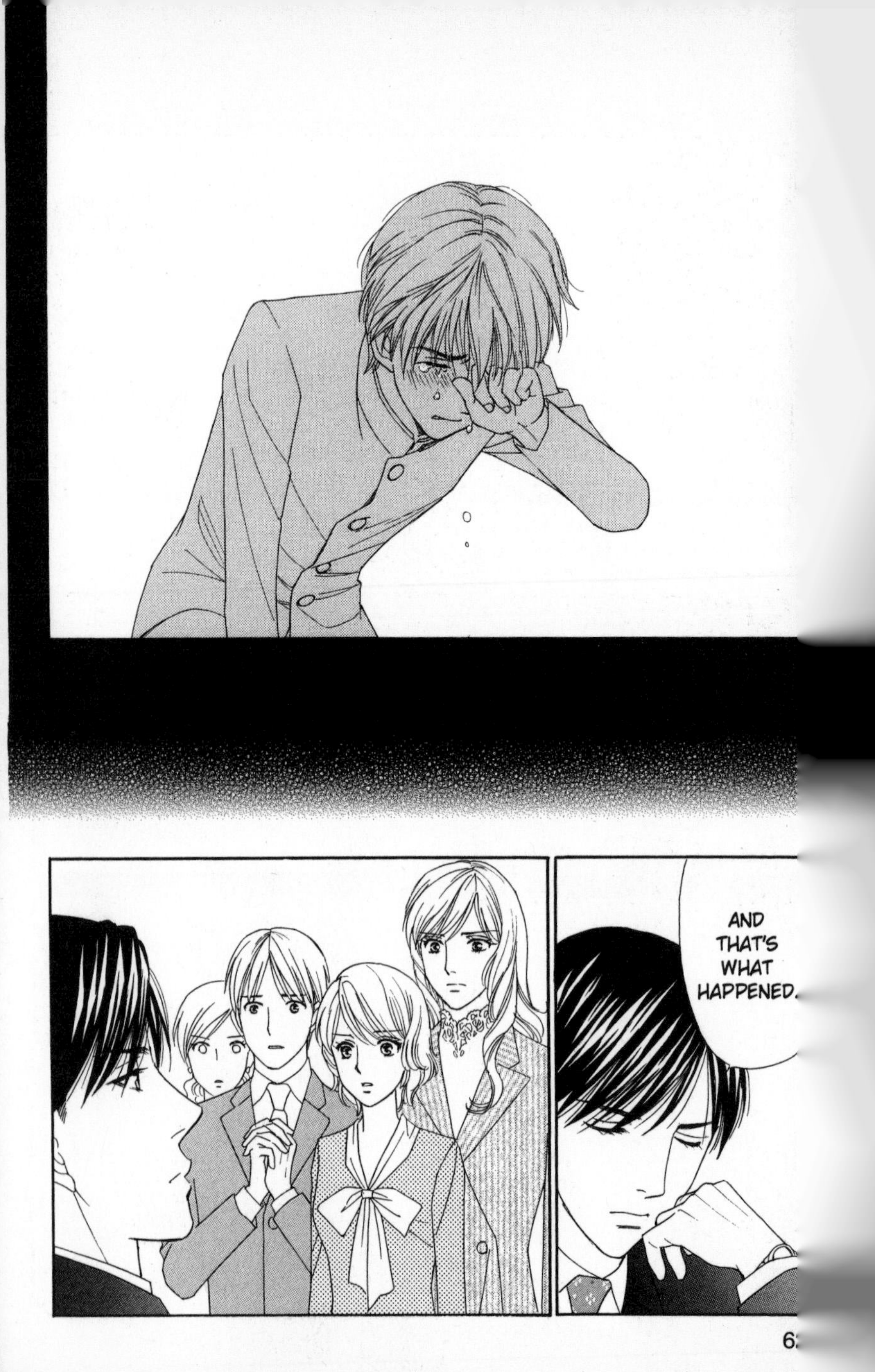
AND THAT'S WHAT HAPPENED.

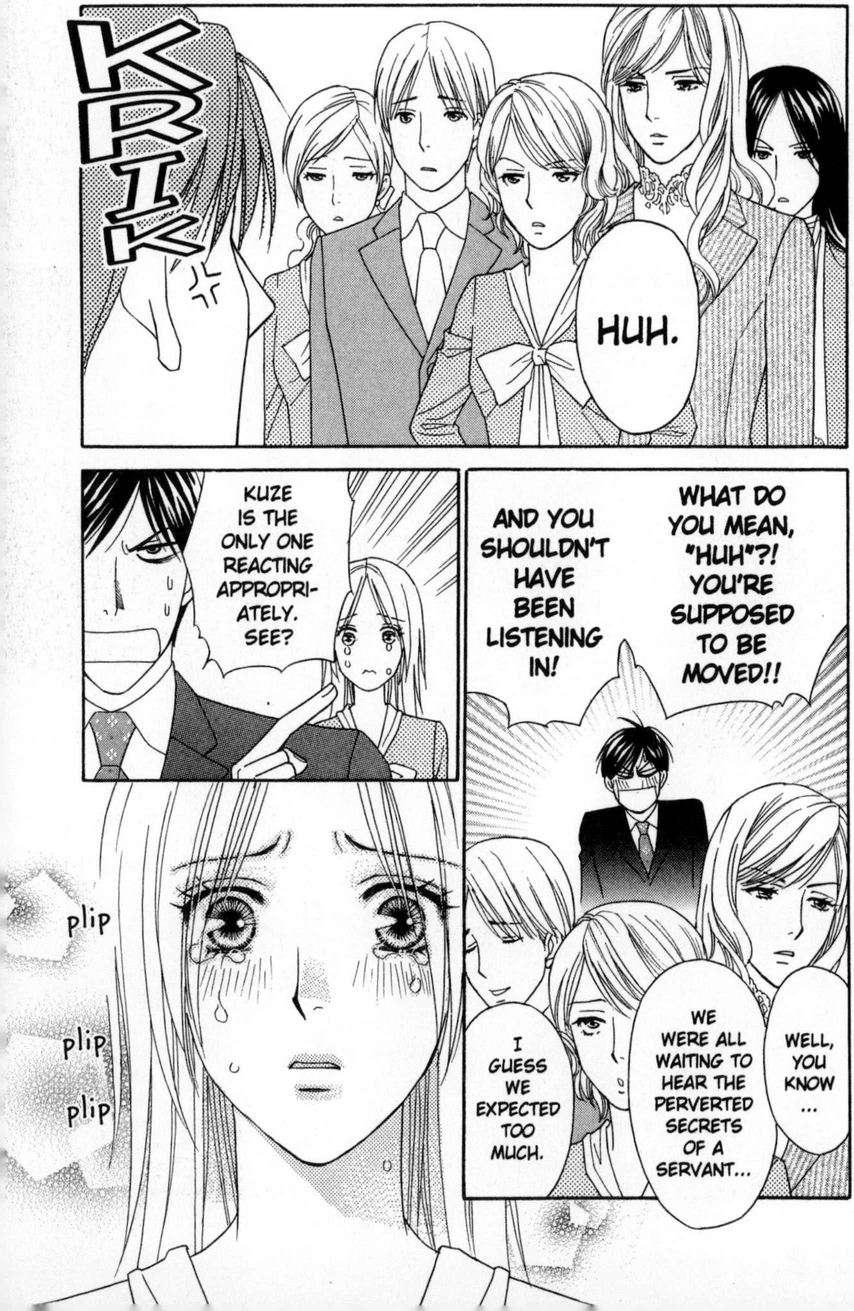
HUH.
KRIK
WHAT DO YOU MEAN, "HUH"?! YOU'RE SUPPOSED TO BE MOVED!!
AND YOU SHOULDN'T HAVE BEEN LISTENING IN!
WELL, YOU KNOW ...
WE WERE ALL WAITING TO HEAR THE PERVERTED SECRETS OF A SERVANT...
I GUESS WE EXPECTED TOO MUCH.
KUZE IS THE ONLY ONE REACTING APPROPRI-ATELY. SEE?
plip
plip
plip

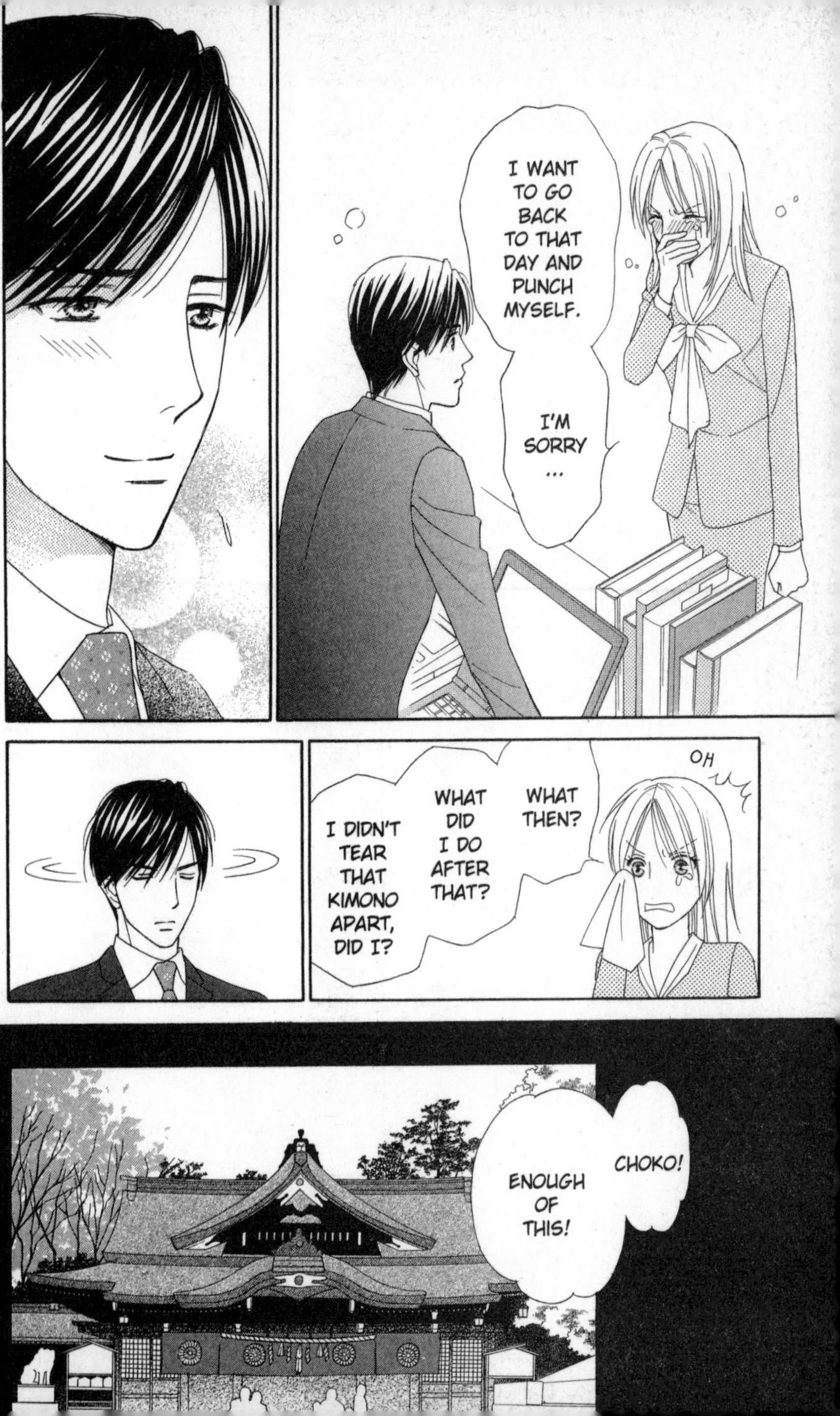
I WANT TO GO BACK TO THAT DAY AND PUNCH MYSELF.
I'M SORRY ...
OH
WHAT THEN?
WHAT DID I DO AFTER THAT?
I DIDN'T TEAR THAT KIMONO APART, DID I?
CHOKO!
ENOUGH OF THIS!

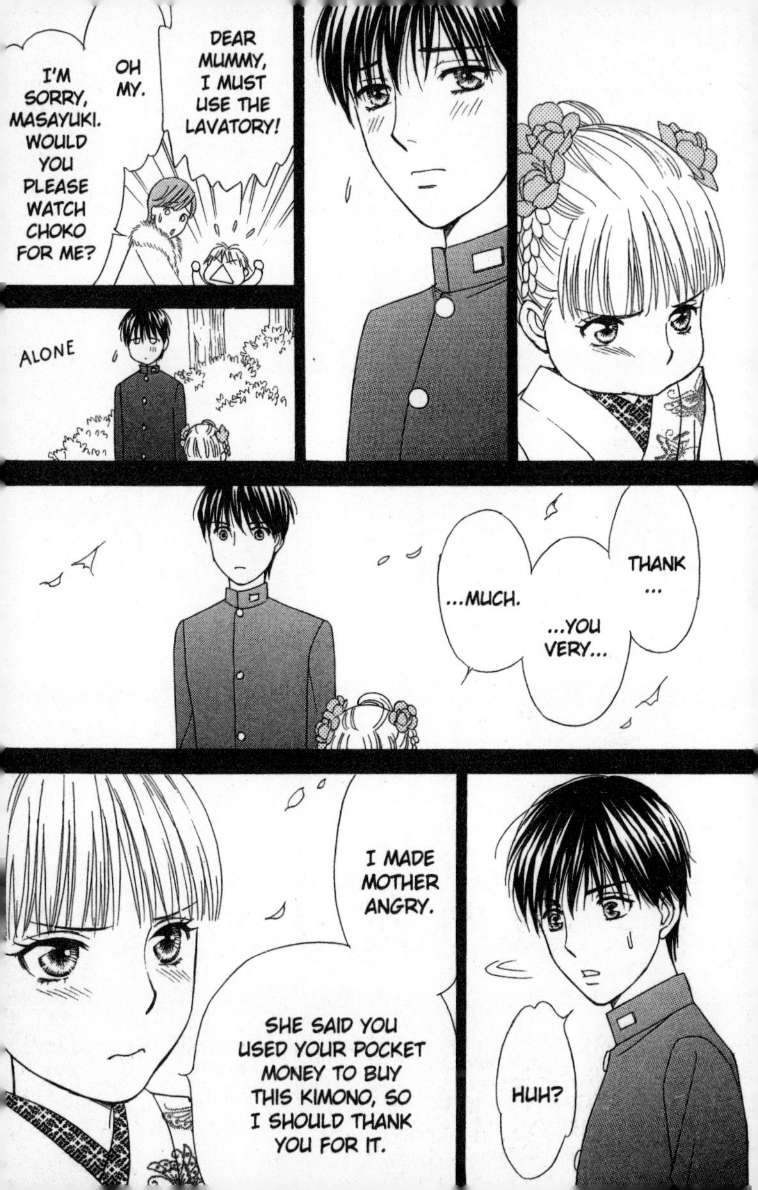
DEAR MUMMY, I MUST USE THE LAVATORY!
OH MY.
I'M SORRY, MASAYUKI. WOULD YOU PLEASE WATCH CHOKO FOR ME?
ALONE
THANK...
...YOU VERY...
...MUCH.
HUH?
I MADE MOTHER ANGRY.
SHE SAID YOU USED YOUR POCKET MONEY TO BUY THIS KIMONO, SO I SHOULD THANK YOU FOR IT.

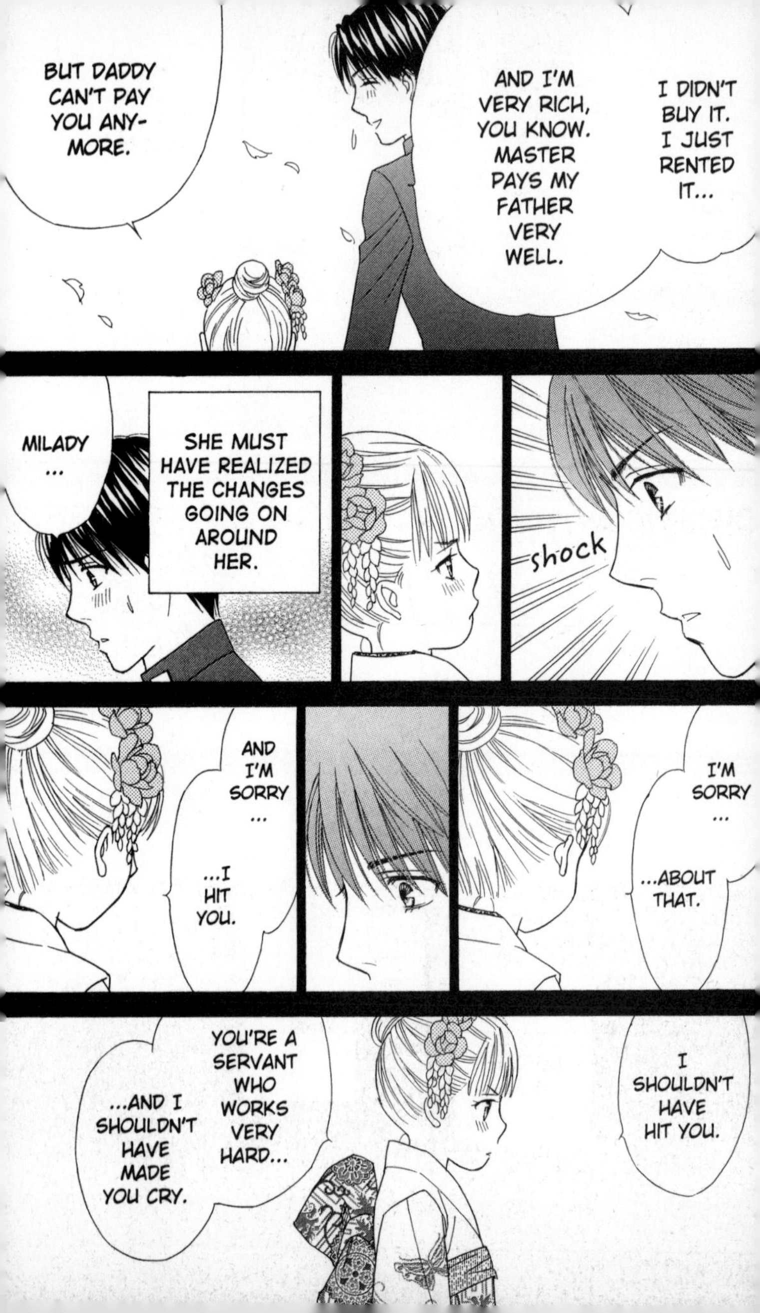
I DIDN'T BUY IT. I JUST RENTED IT...
AND I'M VERY RICH, YOU KNOW. MASTER PAYS MY FATHER VERY WELL.
BUT DADDY CAN'T PAY YOU ANY-MORE.
shock
SHE MUST HAVE REALIZED THE CHANGES GOING ON AROUND HER.
MILADY...
I'M SORRY...
...ABOUT THAT.
AND I'M SORRY...
...I HIT YOU.
I SHOULDN'T HAVE HIT YOU.
YOU'RE A SERVANT WHO WORKS VERY HARD...
...AND I SHOULDN'T HAVE MADE YOU CRY.

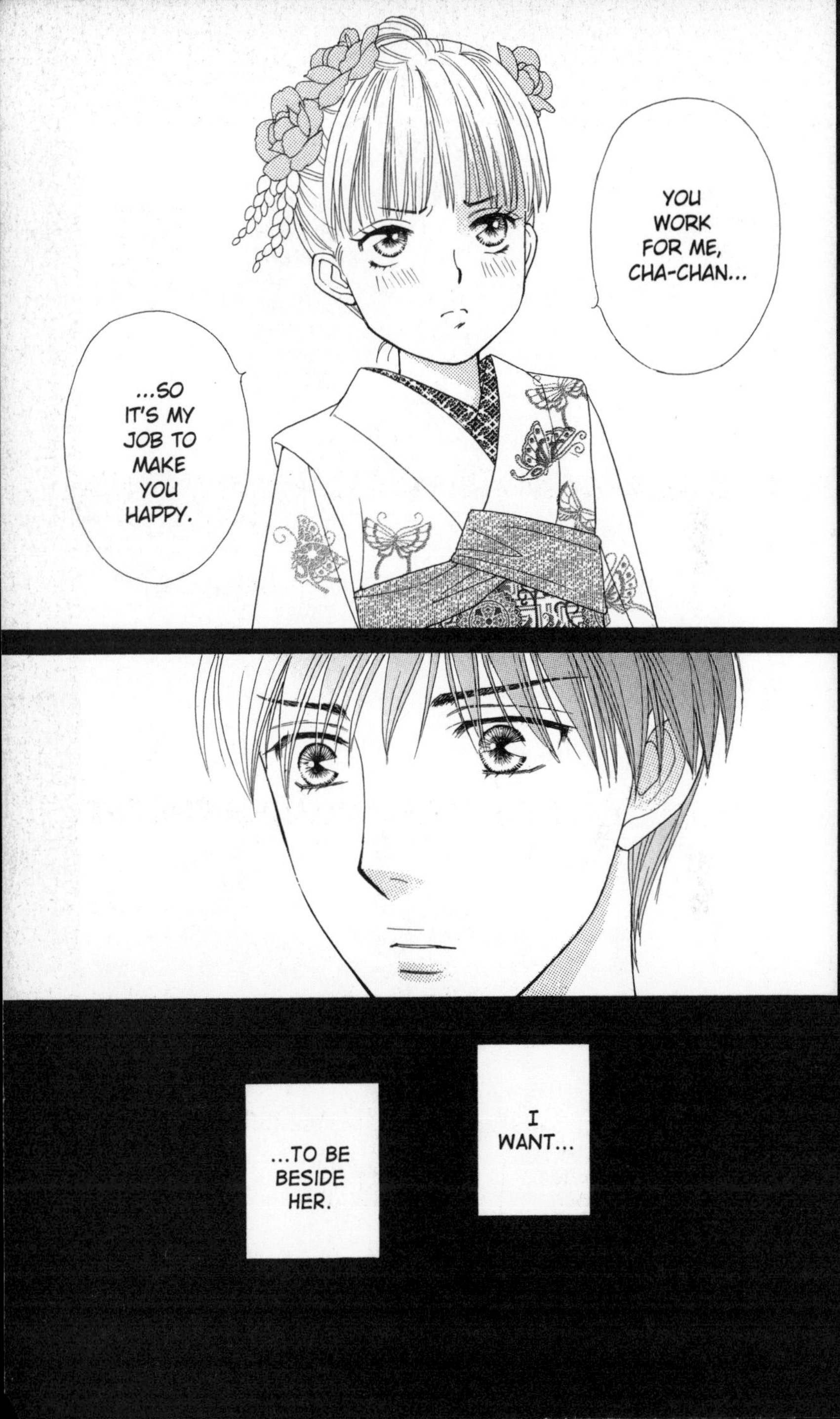
YOU WORK FOR ME, CHA-CHAN...
...SO IT'S MY JOB TO MAKE YOU HAPPY.
I WANT...
...TO BE BESIDE HER.

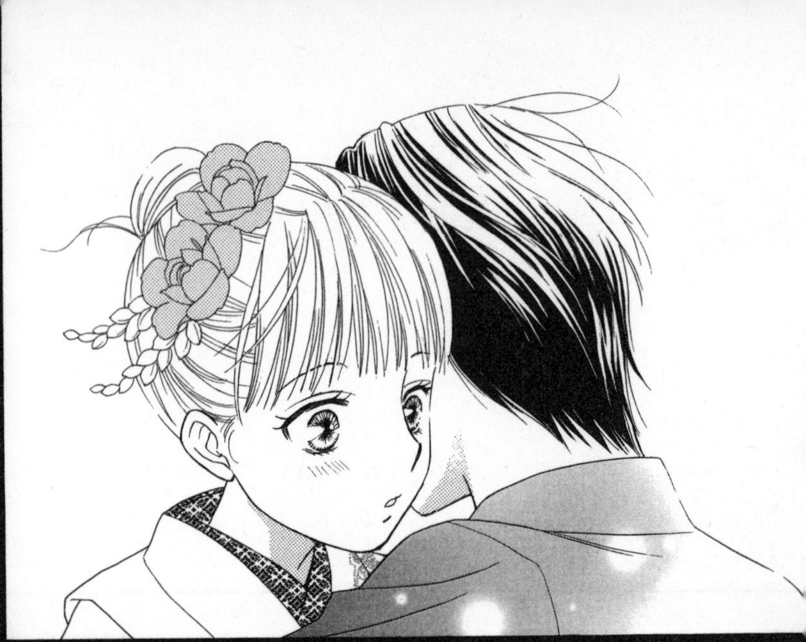

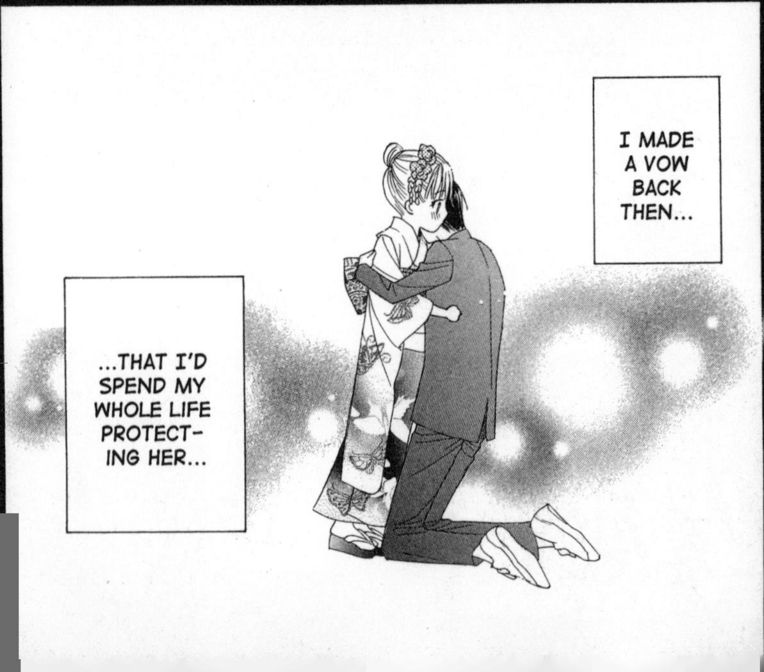
I MADE A VOW BACK THEN...
...THAT I'D SPEND MY WHOLE LIFE PROTECT-ING HER...

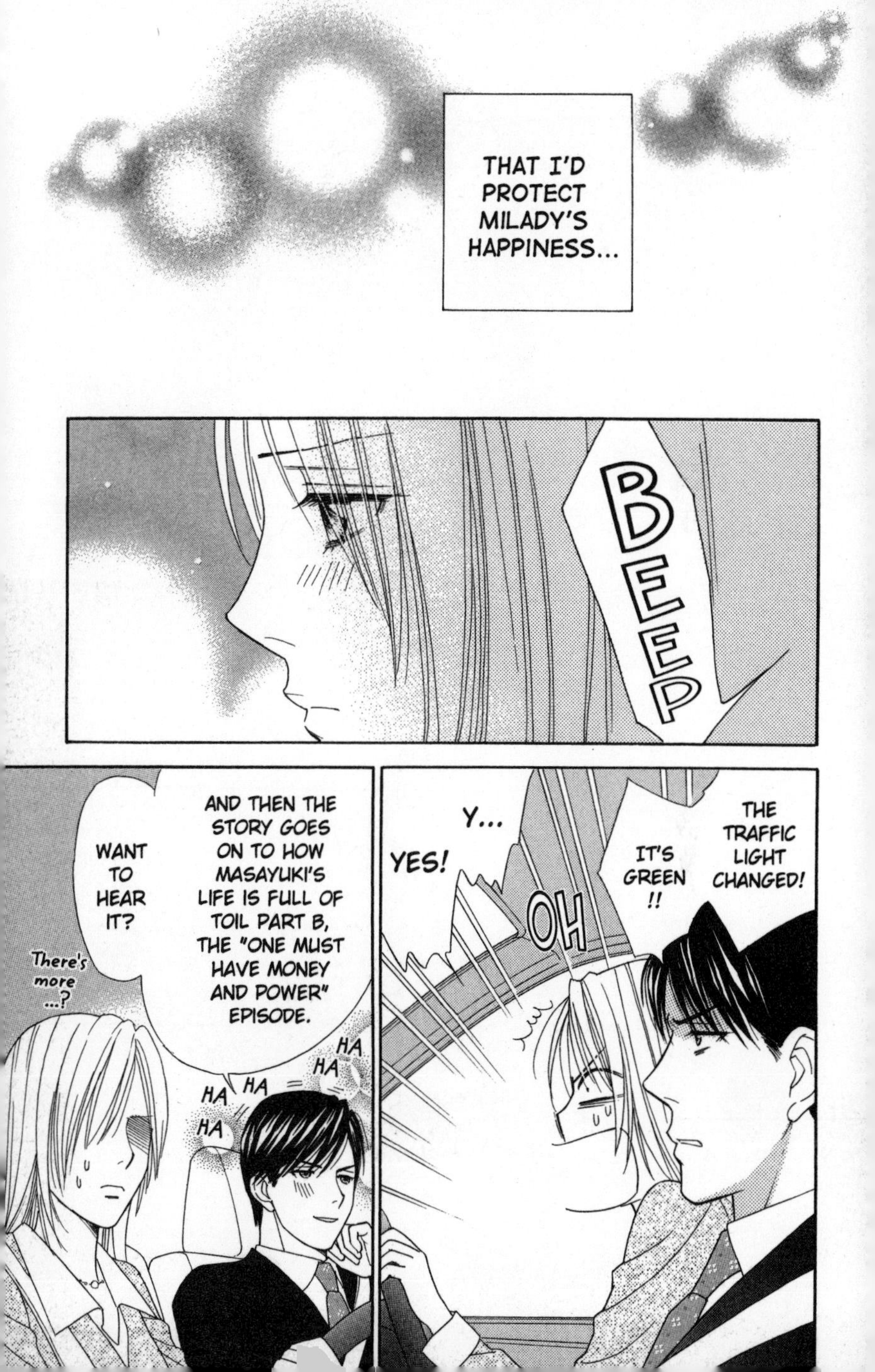
THAT I'D PROTECT MILADY'S HAPPINESS...
BEEP
THE TRAFFIC LIGHT CHANGED!
IT'S GREEN !!
Y... YES!
OH
AND THEN THE STORY GOES ON TO HOW MASAYUKI'S LIFE IS FULL OF TOIL PART B, THE "ONE MUST HAVE MONEY AND POWER" EPISODE.
WANT TO HEAR IT?
HA HA HA HA HA
There's more ...?

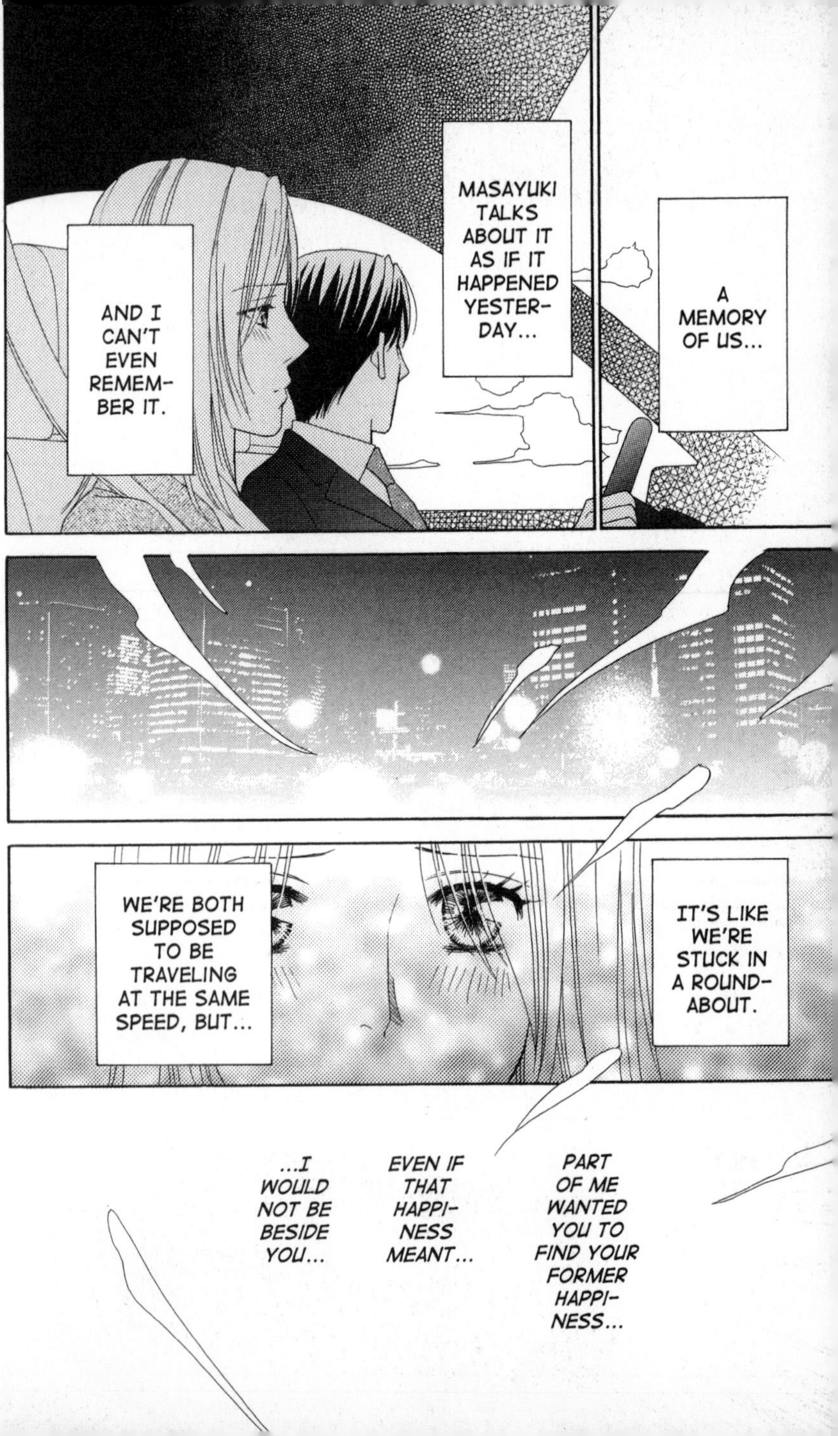
A MEMORY OF US...
MASAYUKI TALKS ABOUT IT AS IF IT HAPPENED YESTER-DAY...
AND I CAN'T EVEN REMEM-BER IT.
IT'S LIKE WE'RE STUCK IN A ROUND-ABOUT.
WE'RE BOTH SUPPOSED TO BE TRAVELING AT THE SAME SPEED, BUT...
PART OF ME WANTED YOU TO FIND YOUR FORMER HAPPI-NESS...
EVEN IF THAT HAPPI-NESS MEANT...
...I WOULD NOT BE BESIDE YOU...

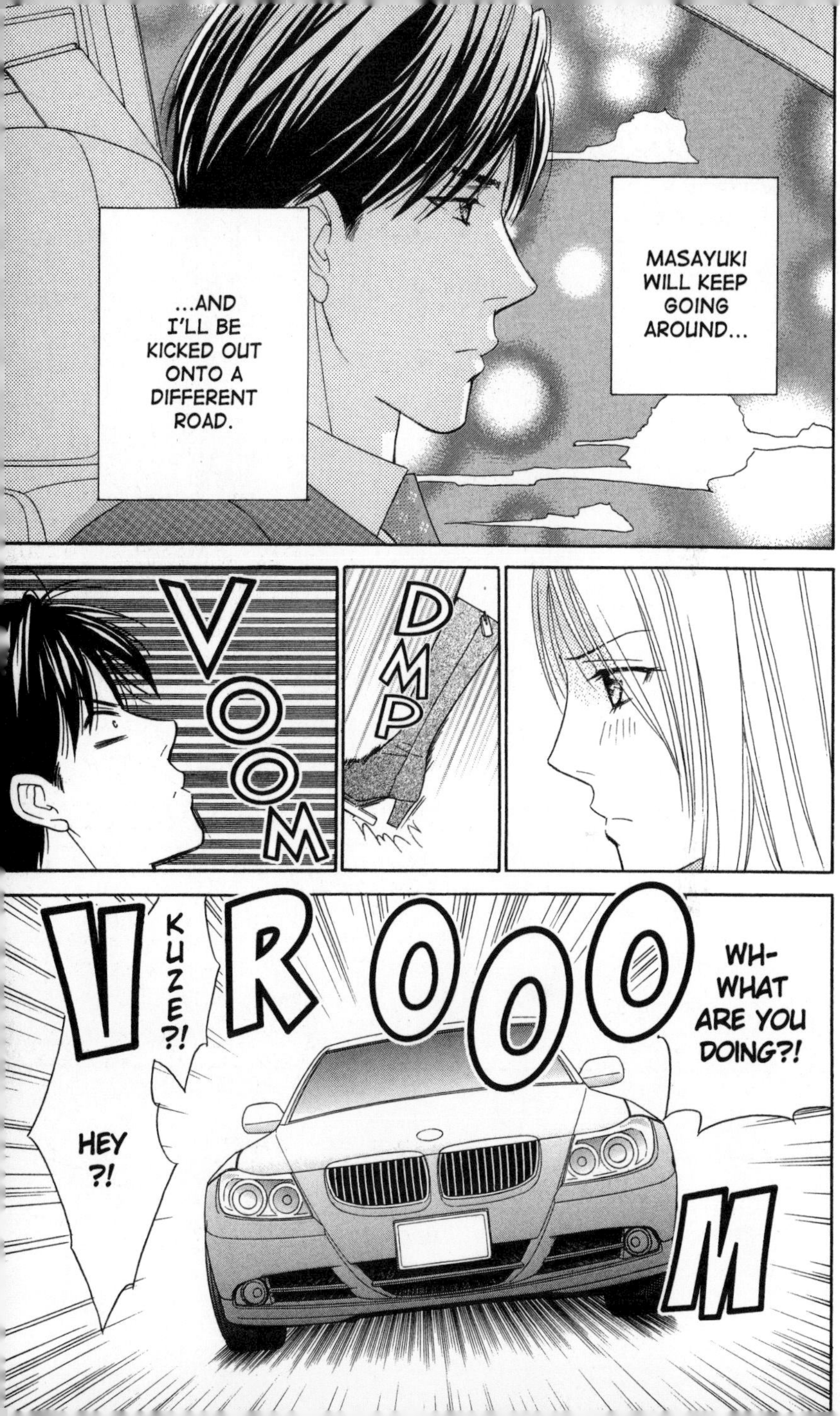
MASAYUKI WILL KEEP GOING AROUND...
...AND I'LL BE KICKED OUT ONTO A DIFFERENT ROAD.
DMP
VOOM
WH-WHAT ARE YOU DOING?!
VROOOM
KUZE?!
HEY?!

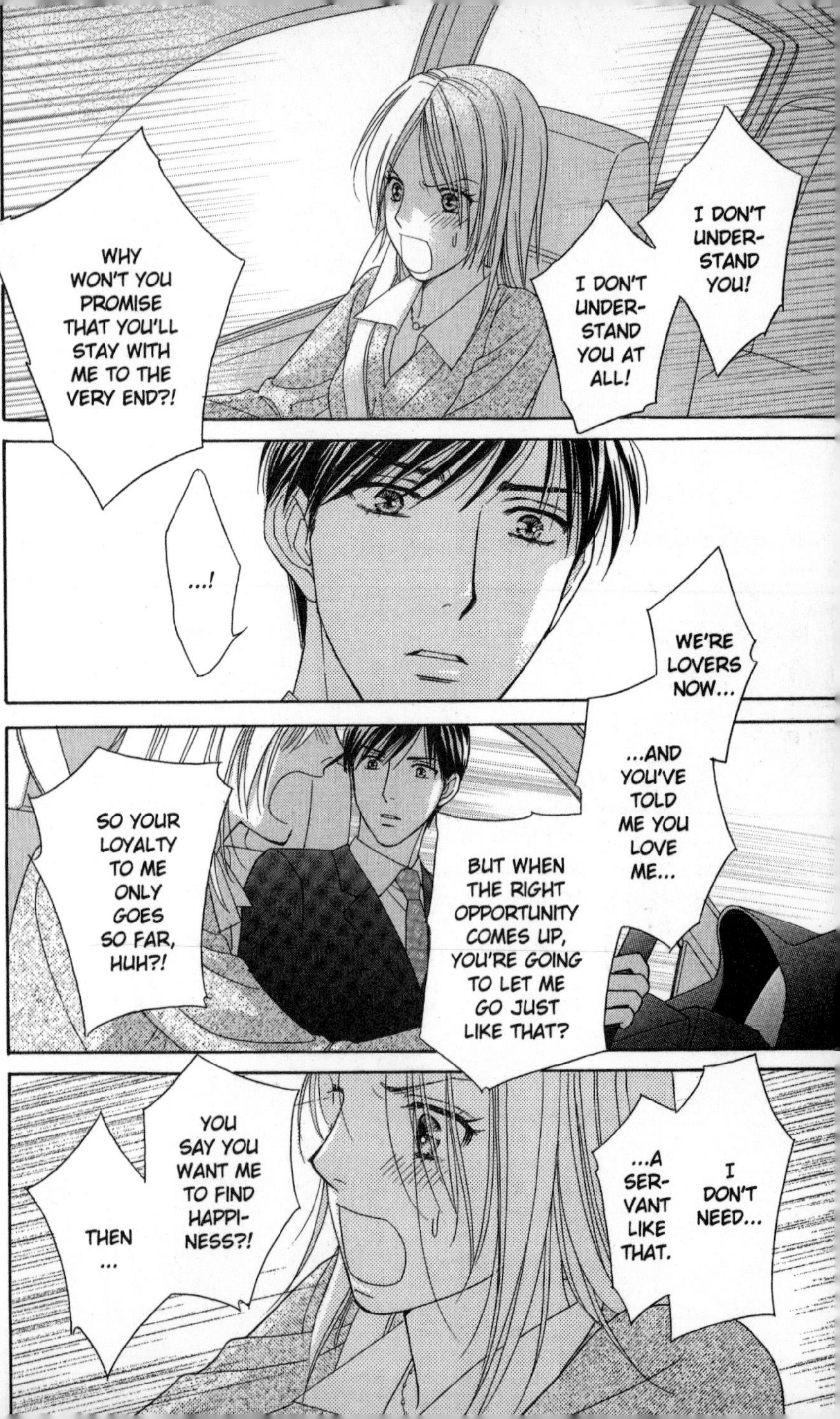
I DON'T UNDER-STAND YOU!
I DON'T UNDER-STAND YOU AT ALL!
WHY WON'T YOU PROMISE THAT YOU'LL STAY WITH ME TO THE VERY END?!
...!
WE'RE LOVERS NOW...
...AND YOU'VE TOLD ME YOU LOVE ME...
BUT WHEN THE RIGHT OPPORTUNITY COMES UP, YOU'RE GOING TO LET ME GO JUST LIKE THAT?
SO YOUR LOYALTY TO ME ONLY GOES SO FAR, HUH?!
I DON'T NEED...
...A SER-VANT LIKE THAT.
YOU SAY YOU WANT ME TO FIND HAPPI-NESS?!
THEN ...

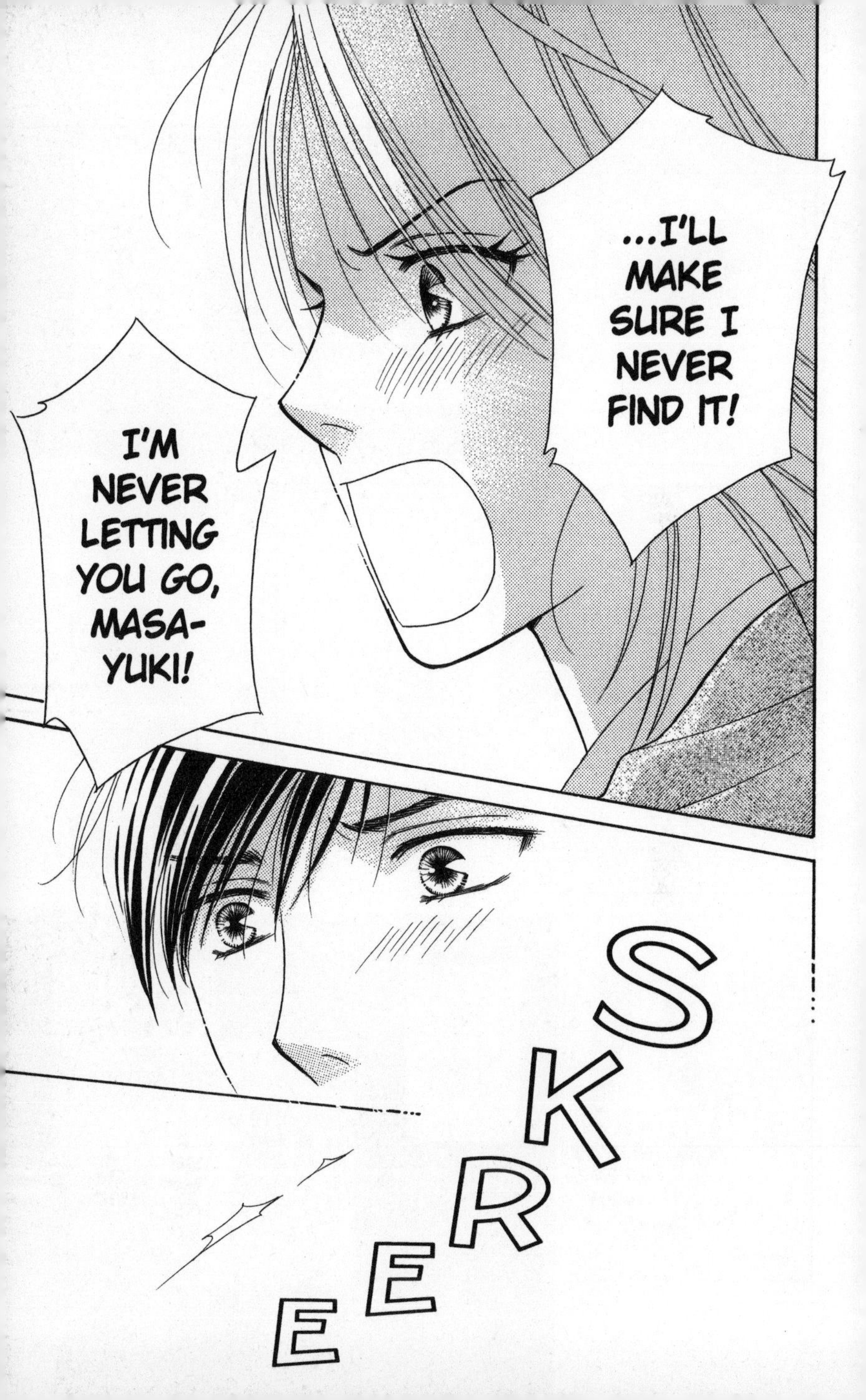
...I'LL MAKE SURE I NEVER FIND IT!
I'M NEVER LETTING YOU GO, MASA-YUKI!
SKREEE

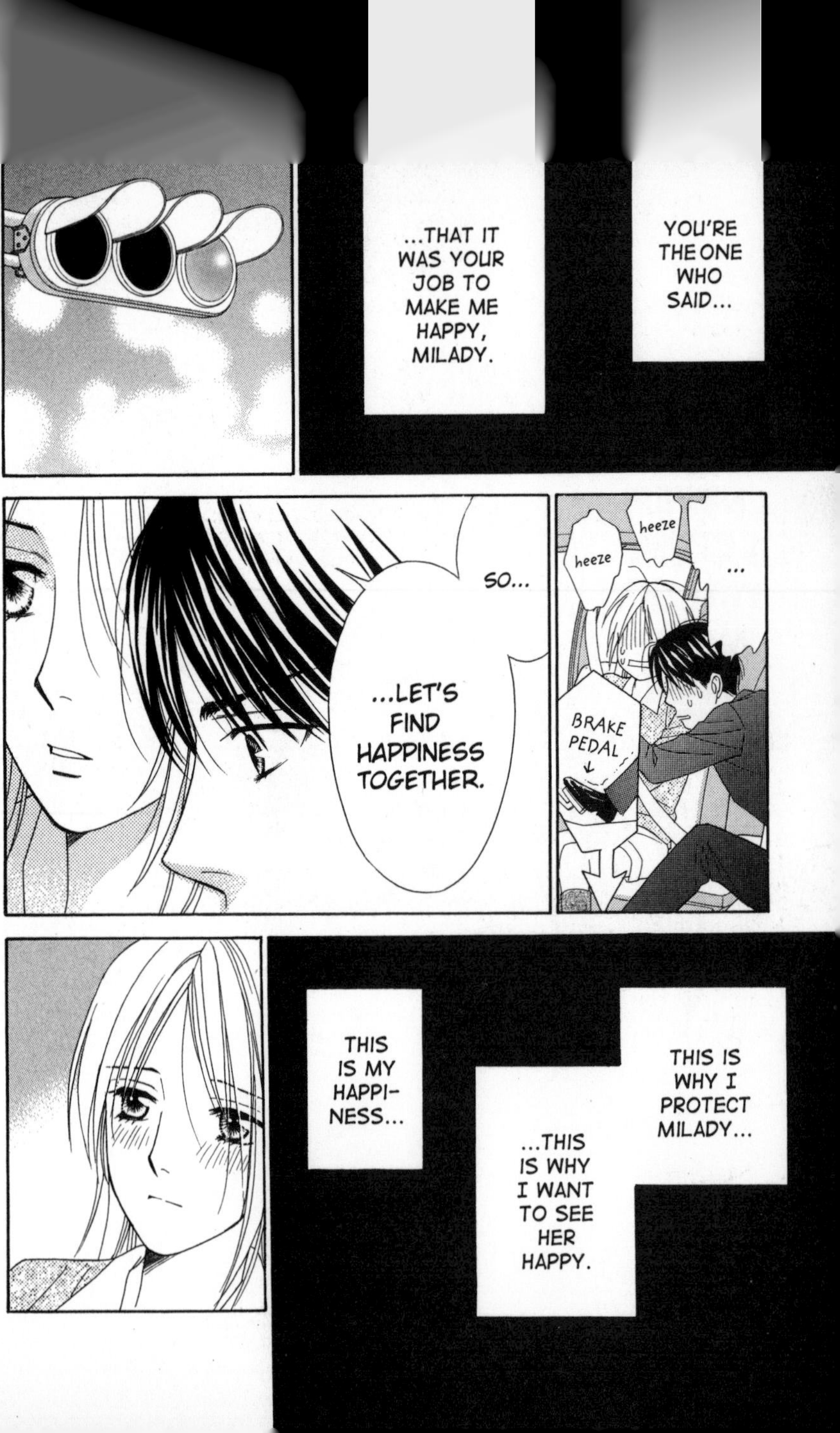
YOU'RE THE ONE WHO SAID...
...THAT IT WAS YOUR JOB TO MAKE ME HAPPY, MILADY.
heeze
heeze
...
BRAKE PEDAL
SO...
...LET'S FIND HAPPINESS TOGETHER.
THIS IS WHY I PROTECT MILADY...
...THIS IS WHY I WANT TO SEE HER HAPPY.
THIS IS MY HAPPI-NESS...

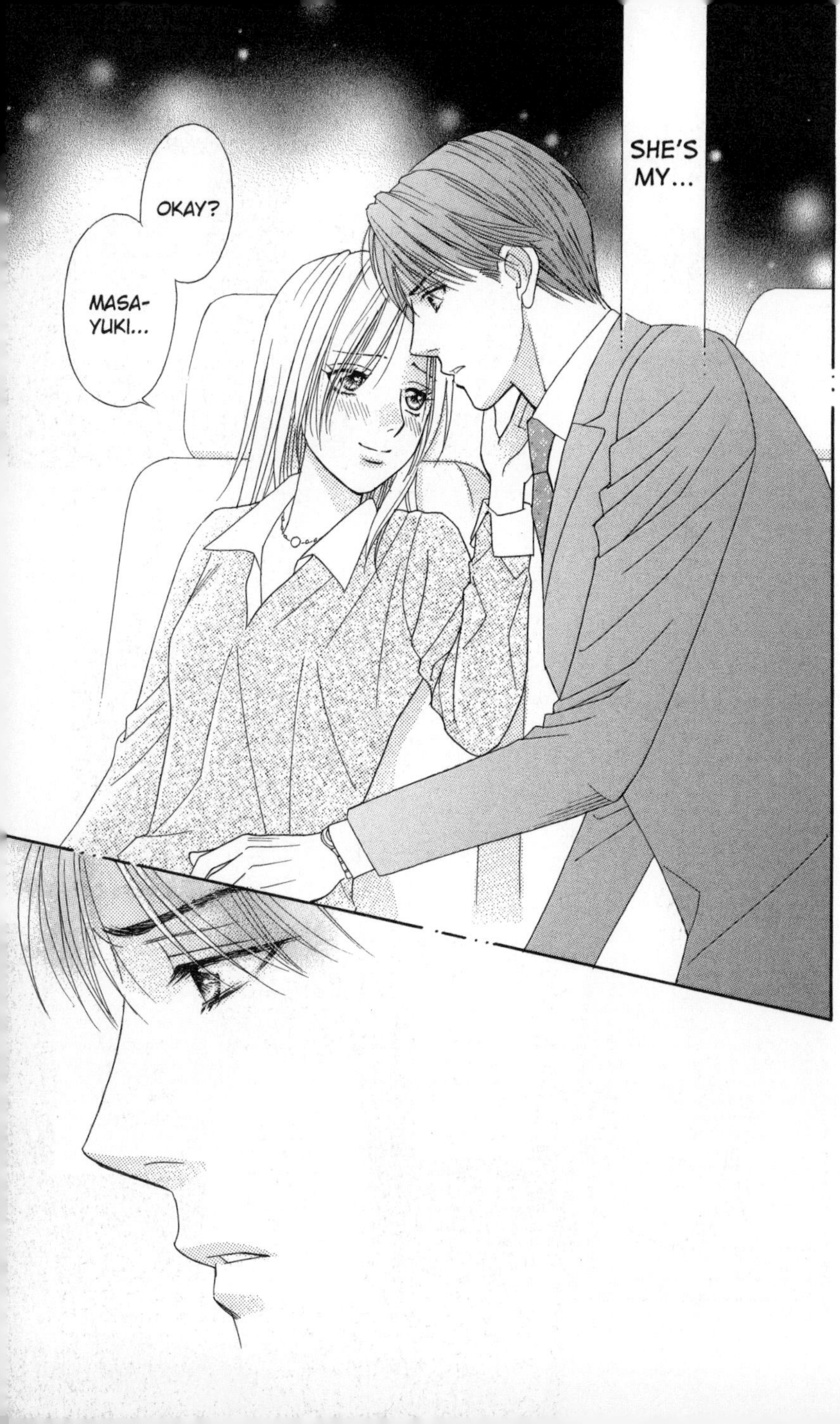
SHE'S MY...
OKAY?
MASA-YUKI...

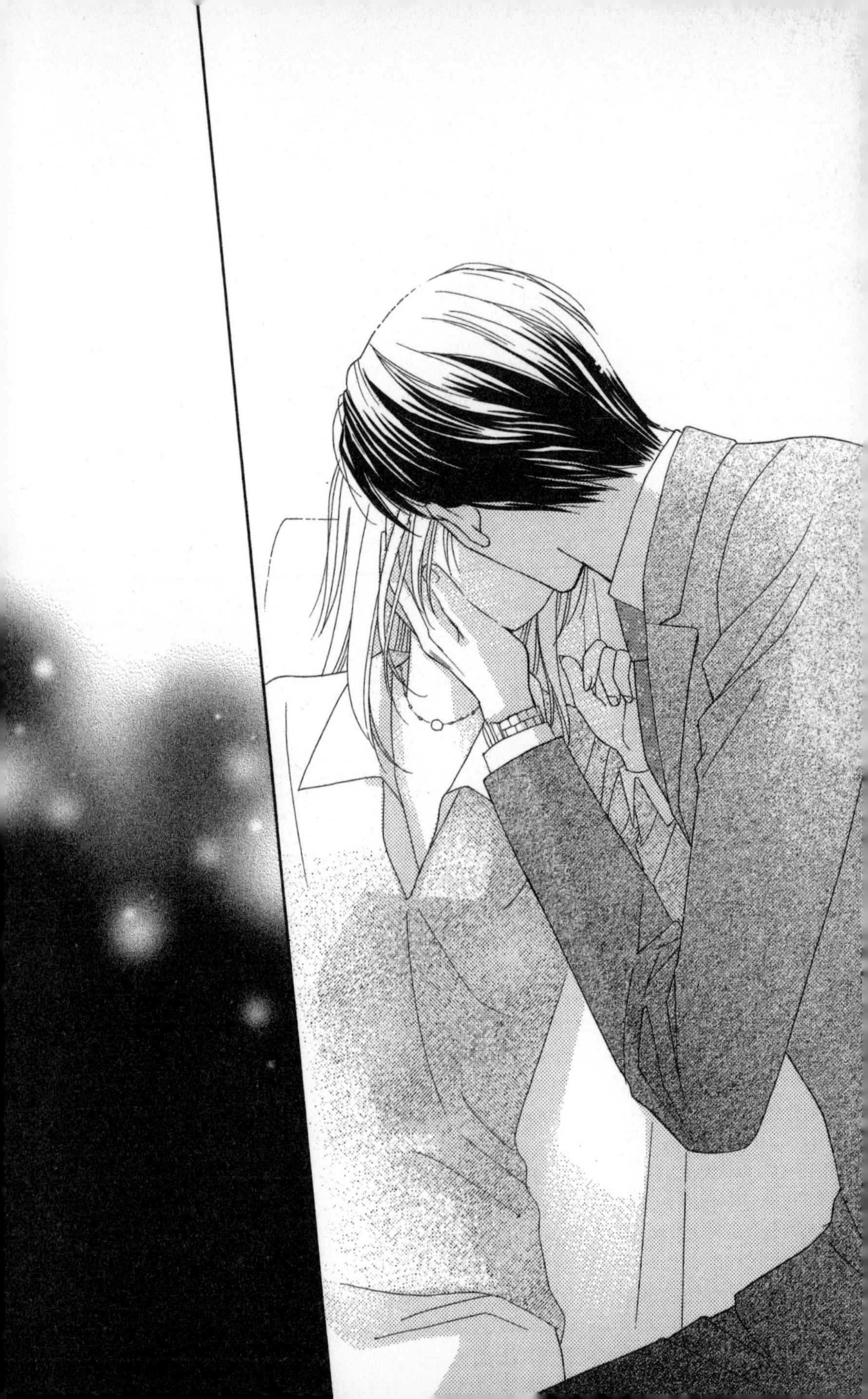

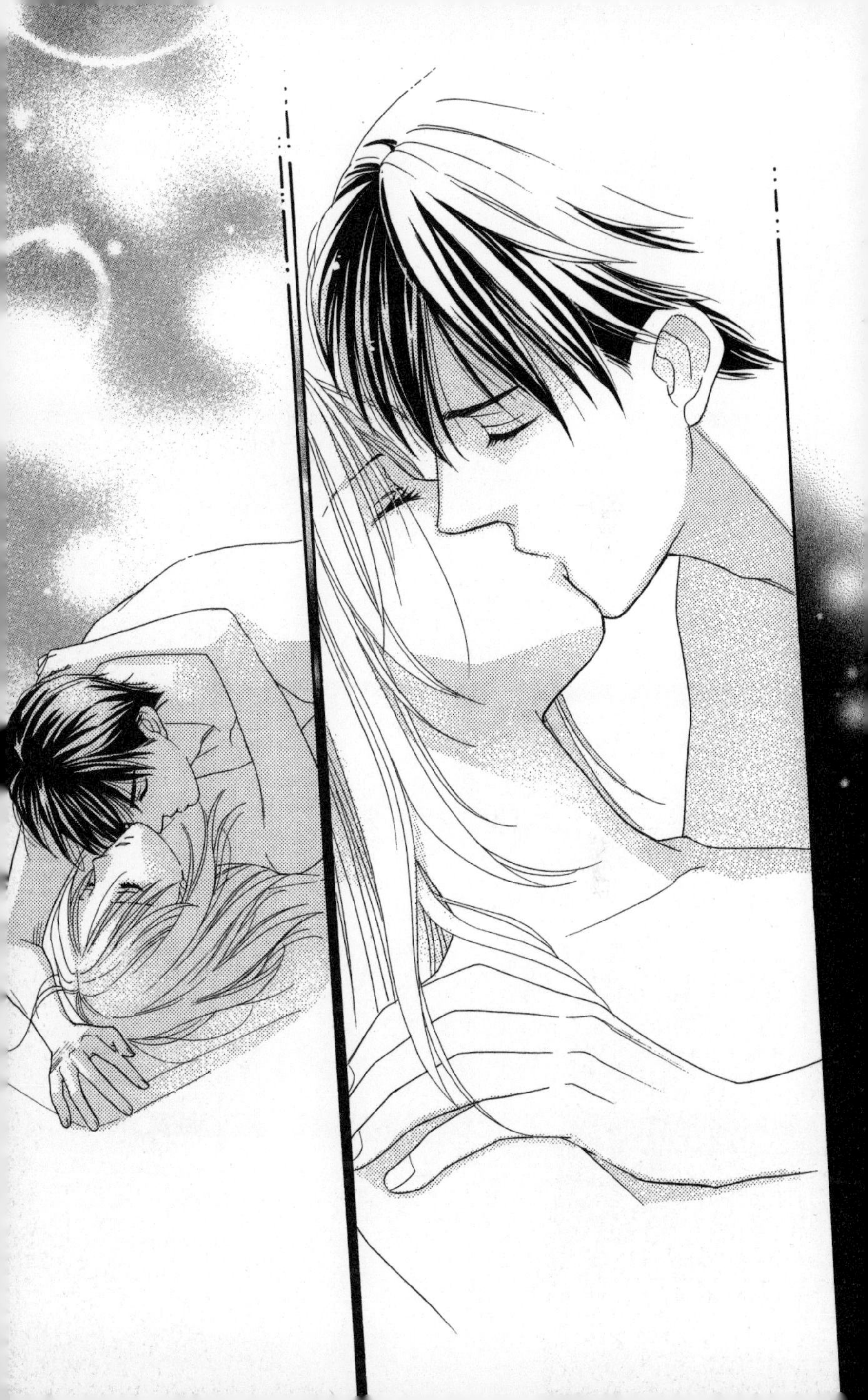

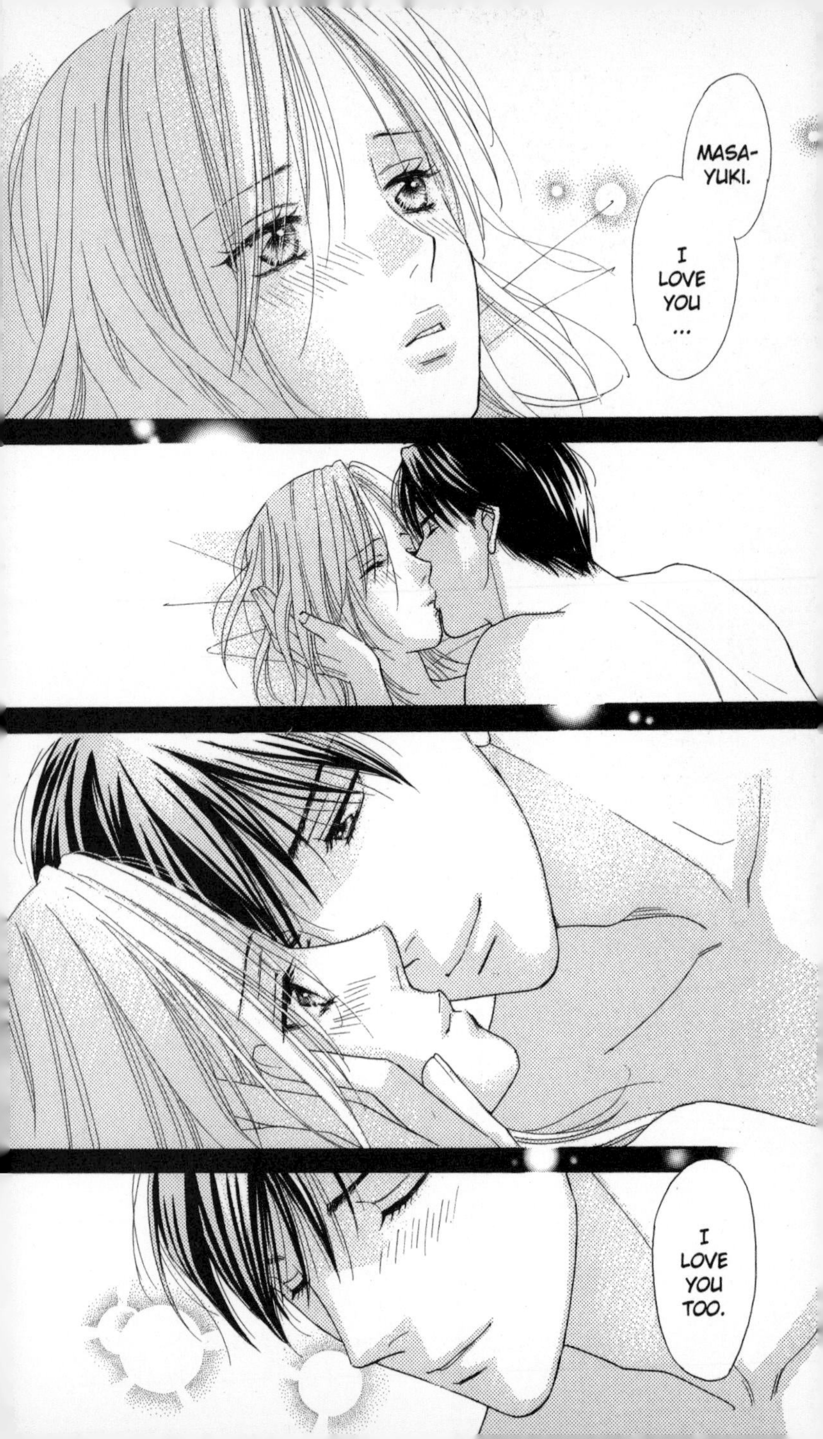
MASA-YUKI.
I LOVE YOU ...
I LOVE YOU TOO.

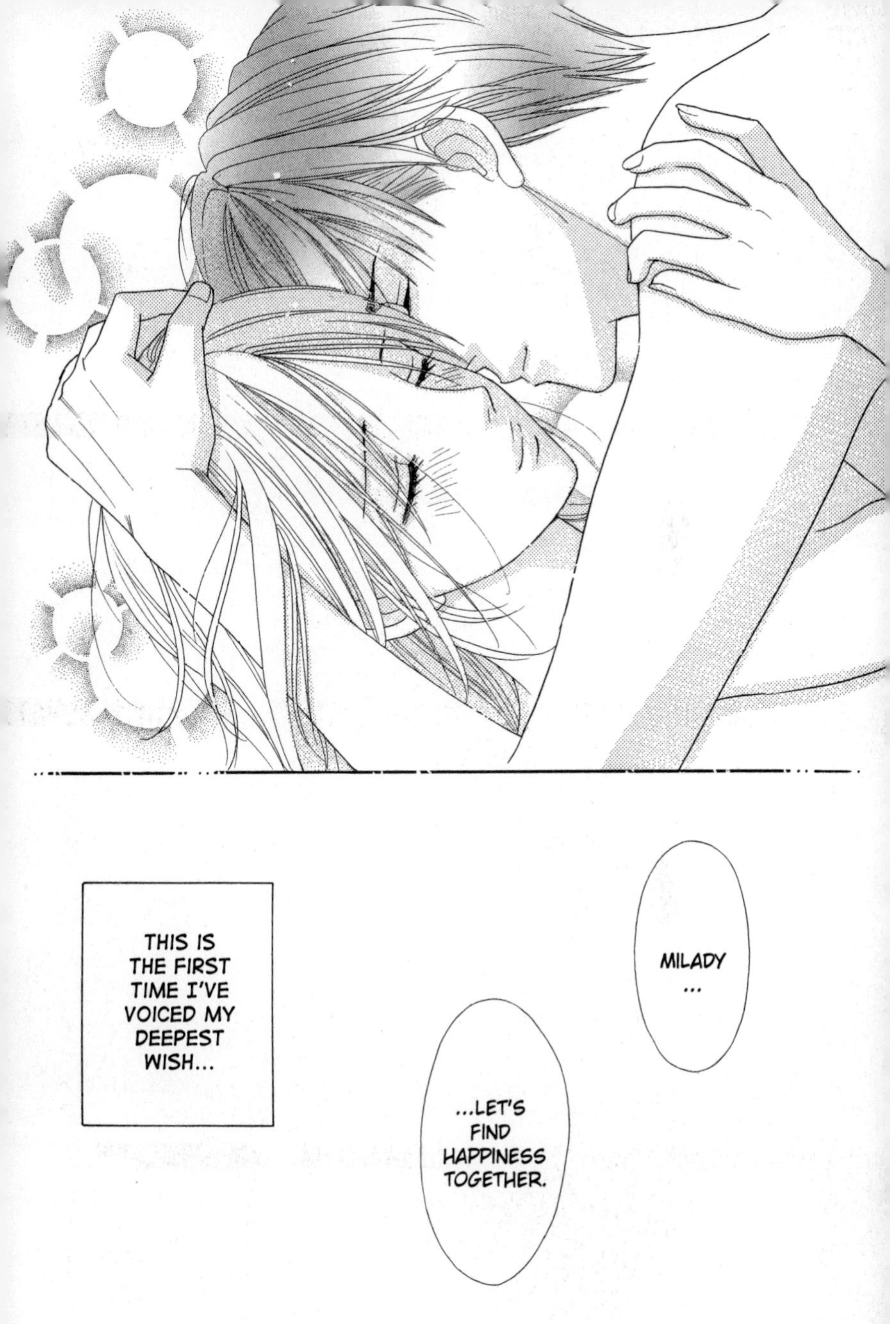
MILADY ...
...LET'S FIND HAPPINESS TOGETHER.
THIS IS THE FIRST TIME I'VE VOICED MY DEEPEST WISH...

Chapter 37: Vow and Wish/End

FINAL VOLUME SPECIAL WOW STORY

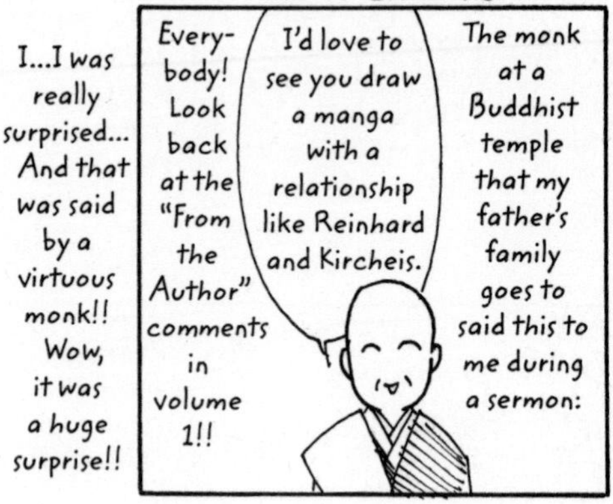
The monk at a Buddhist temple that my father's family goes to said this to me during a sermon:
I'd love to see you draw a manga with a relationship like Reinhard and Kircheis.
Everybody! Look back at the "From the Author" comments in volume 1!!
I...I was really surprised... And that was said by a virtuous monk!! Wow, it was a huge surprise!!

Chapter 38
An Important Place

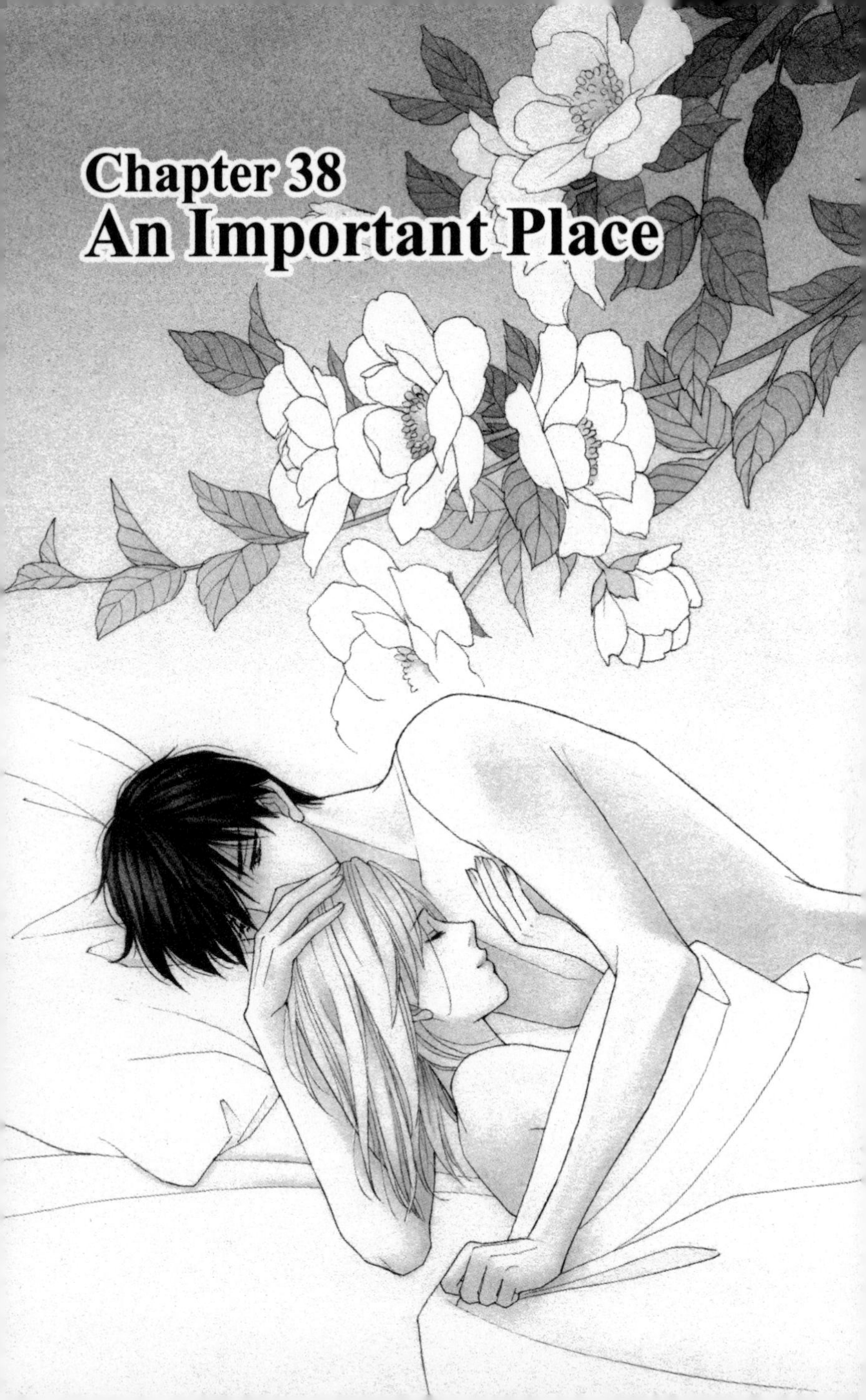

FINAL VOLUME
HMM, IS THAT SO... STORY

After all, it's a country
that claims to be the
center of the world,
that screams and
shouts about many
things, so I really don't
care who becomes
the leader...

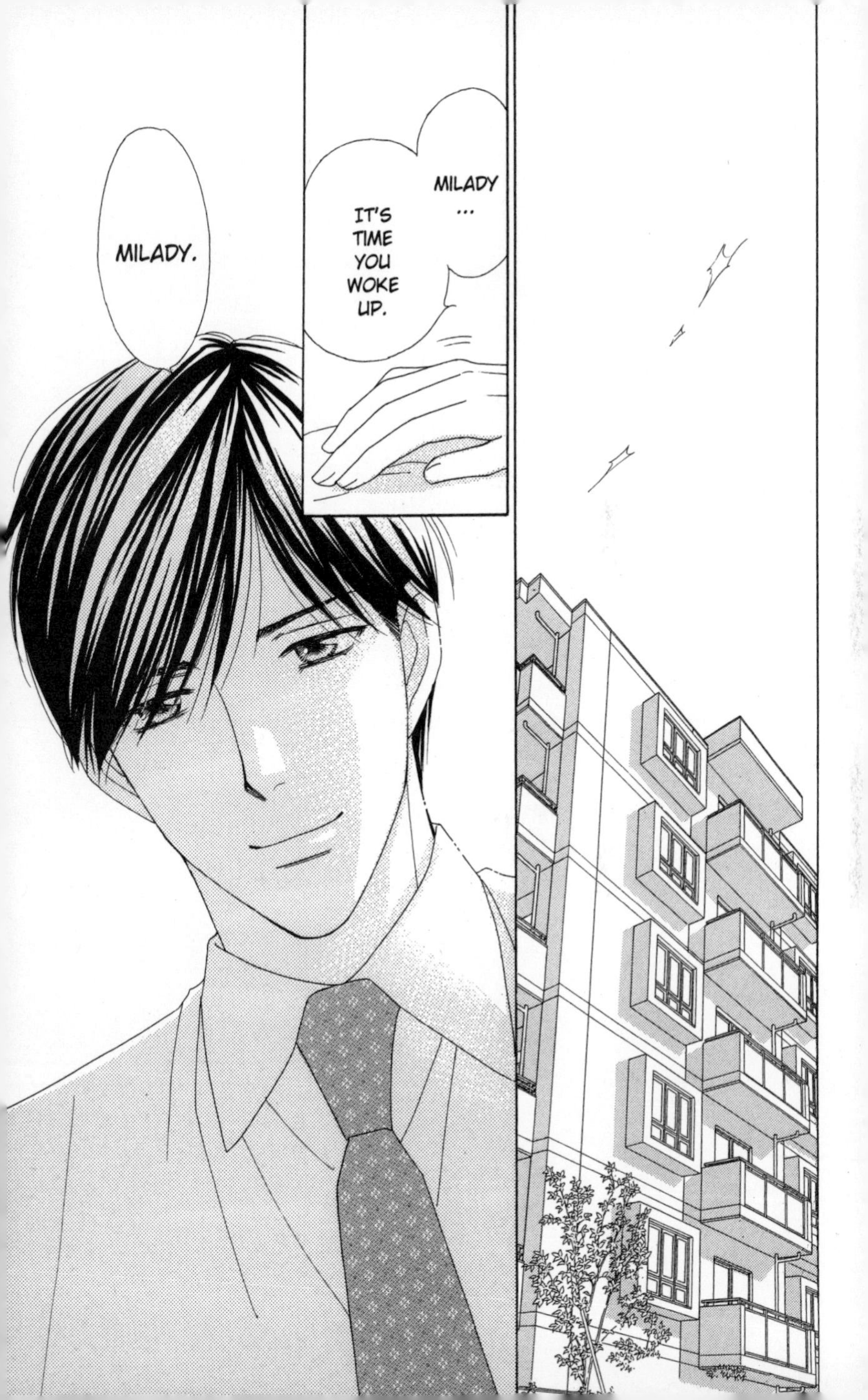
MILADY ...
IT'S TIME YOU WOKE UP.
MILADY.

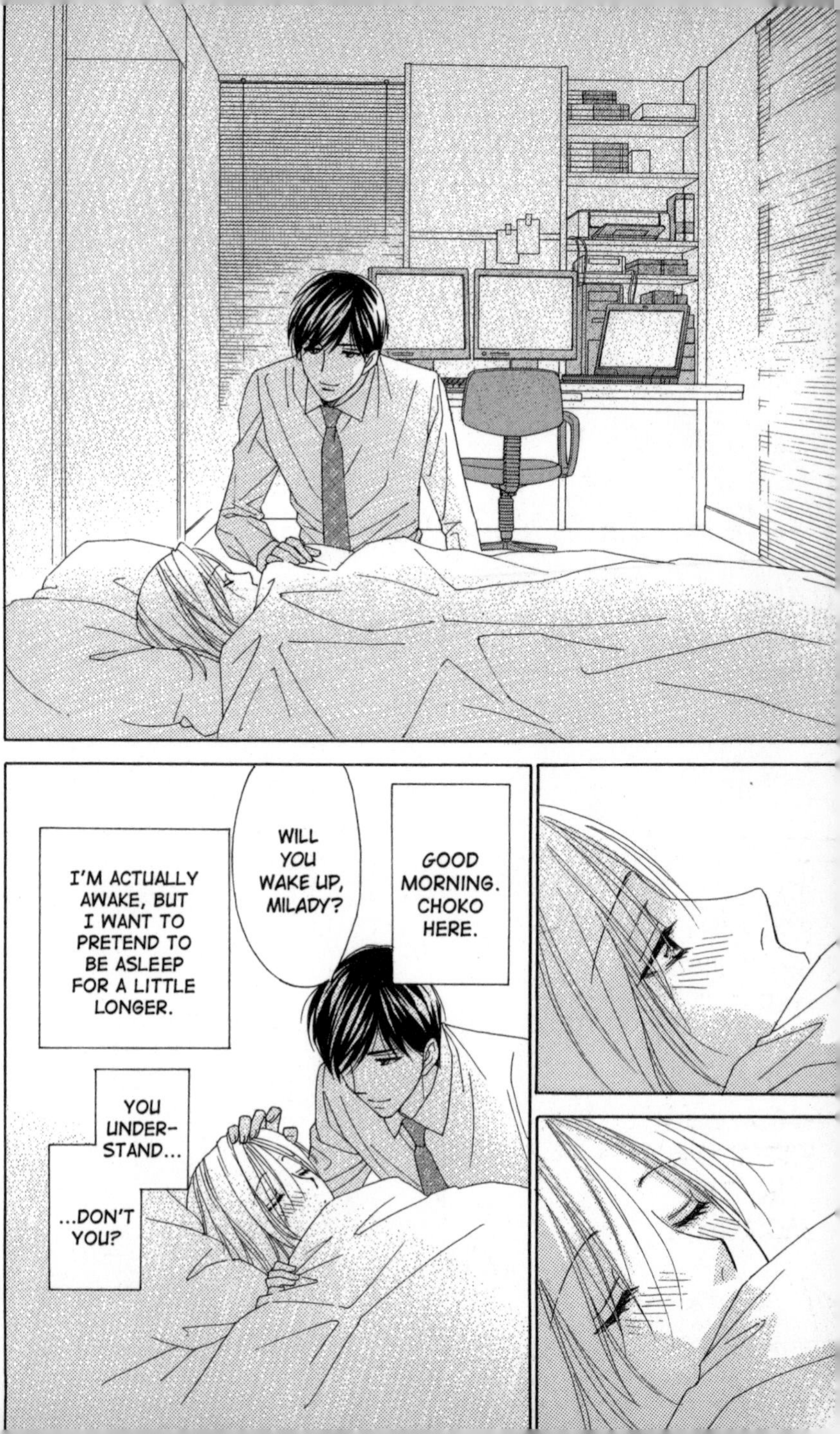
GOOD MORNING. CHOKO HERE.
WILL YOU WAKE UP, MILADY?
I'M ACTUALLY AWAKE, BUT I WANT TO PRETEND TO BE ASLEEP FOR A LITTLE LONGER.
YOU UNDER-STAND...
...DON'T YOU?

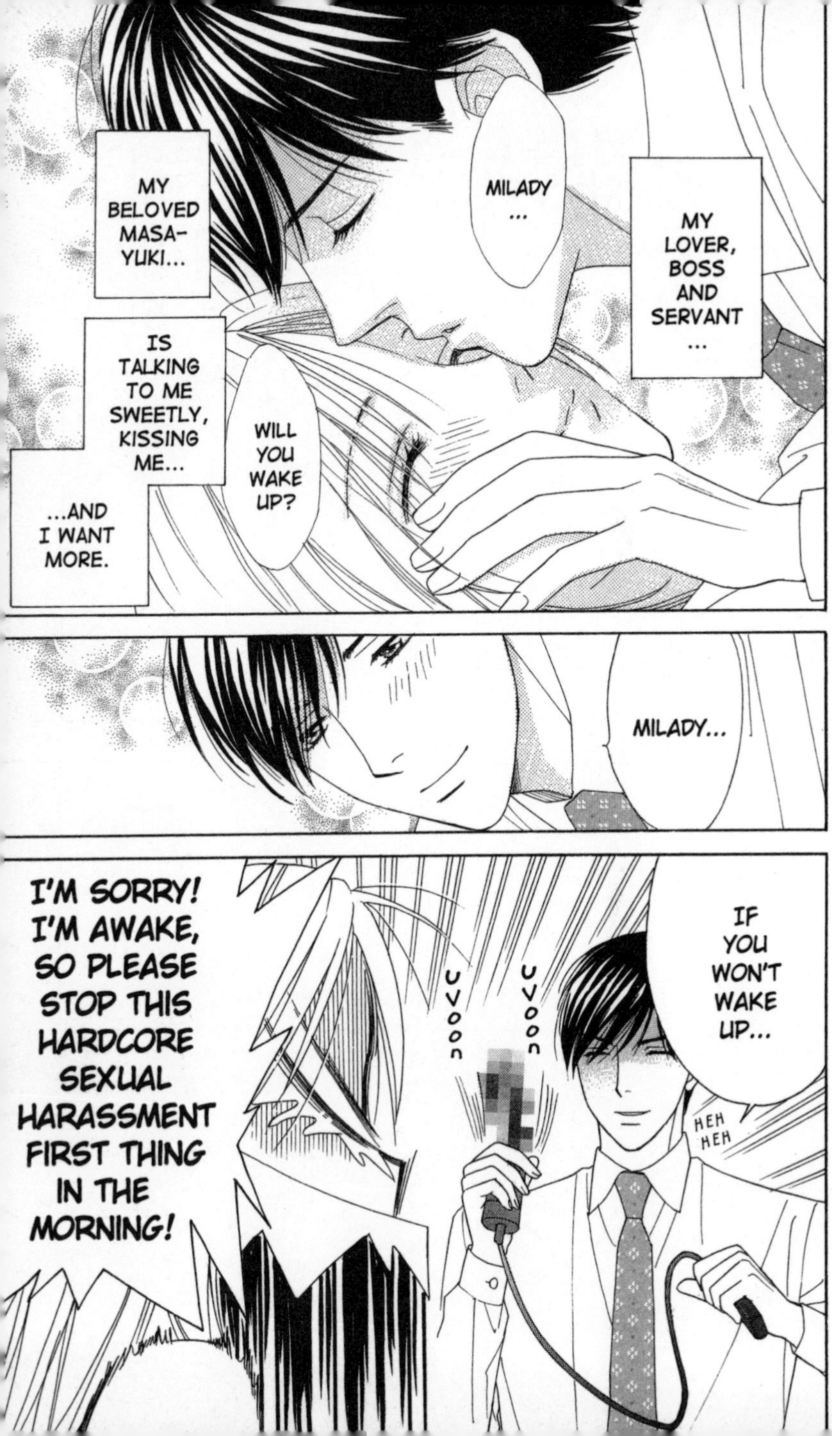
MY LOVER, BOSS AND SERVANT...
MILADY...
MY BELOVED MASA-YUKI...
IS TALKING TO ME SWEETLY, KISSING ME...
WILL YOU WAKE UP?
...AND I WANT MORE.
MILADY...
IF YOU WON'T WAKE UP...
HEH HEH
UVOON
UVOON
I'M SORRY! I'M AWAKE, SO PLEASE STOP THIS HARDCORE SEXUAL HARASSMENT FIRST THING IN THE MORNING!

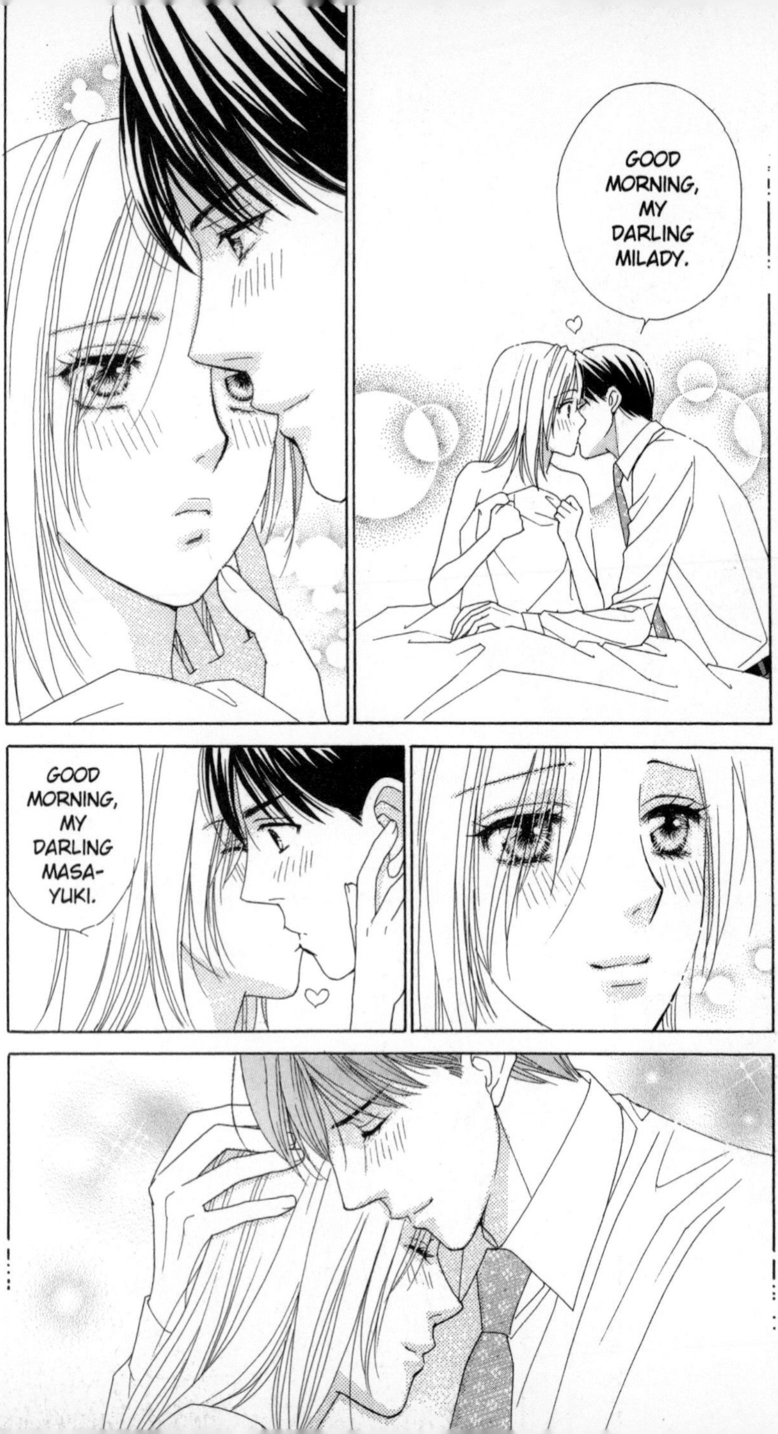
GOOD MORNING, MY DARLING MILADY.
GOOD MORNING, MY DARLING MASA-YUKI.

A MOMENT AGO YOU WERE TRYING TO GET ME UP.

...

I'M SORRY ...

BUT ...

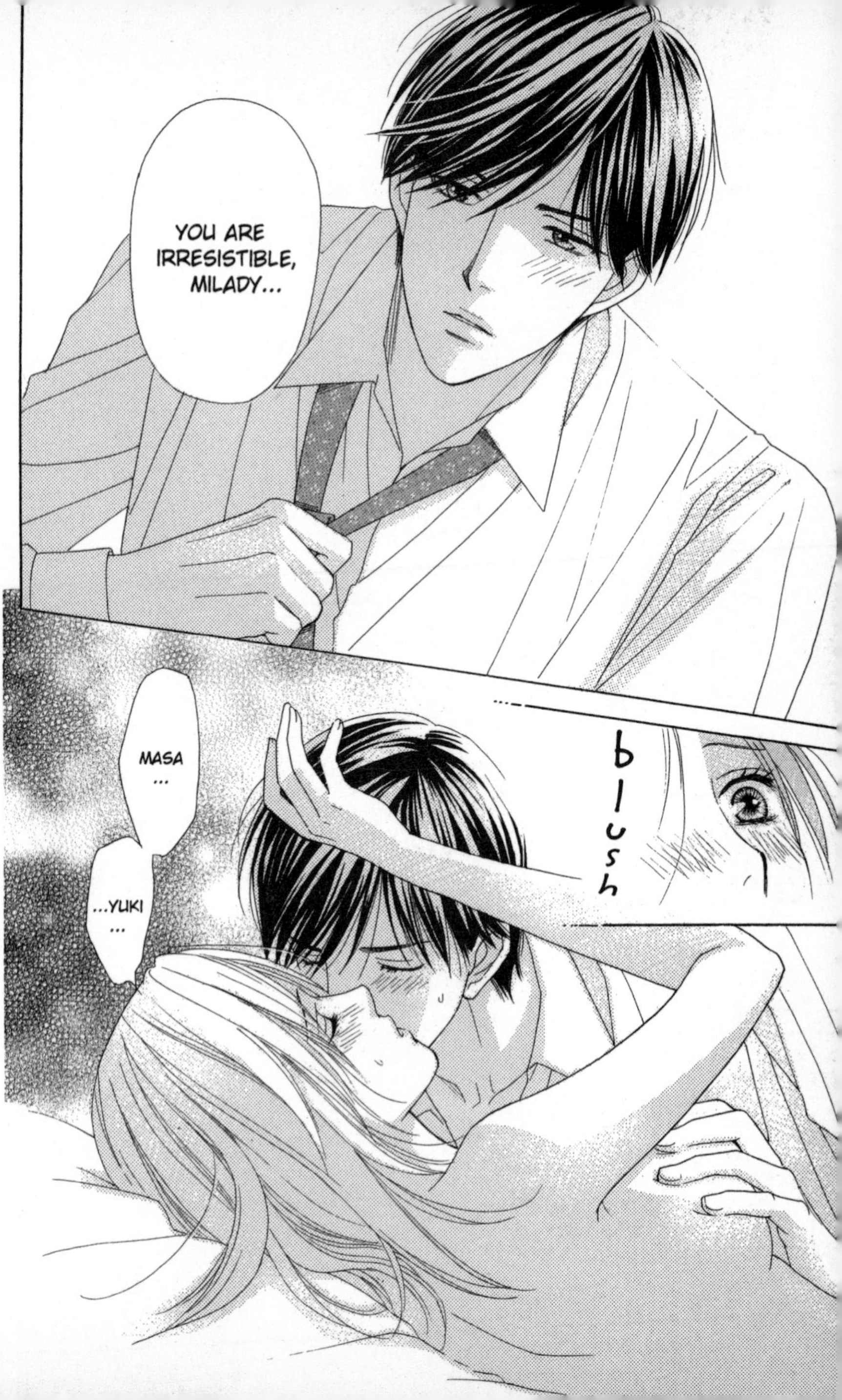
YOU ARE IRRESISTIBLE, MILADY...
blush
MASA ...
...YUKI ...

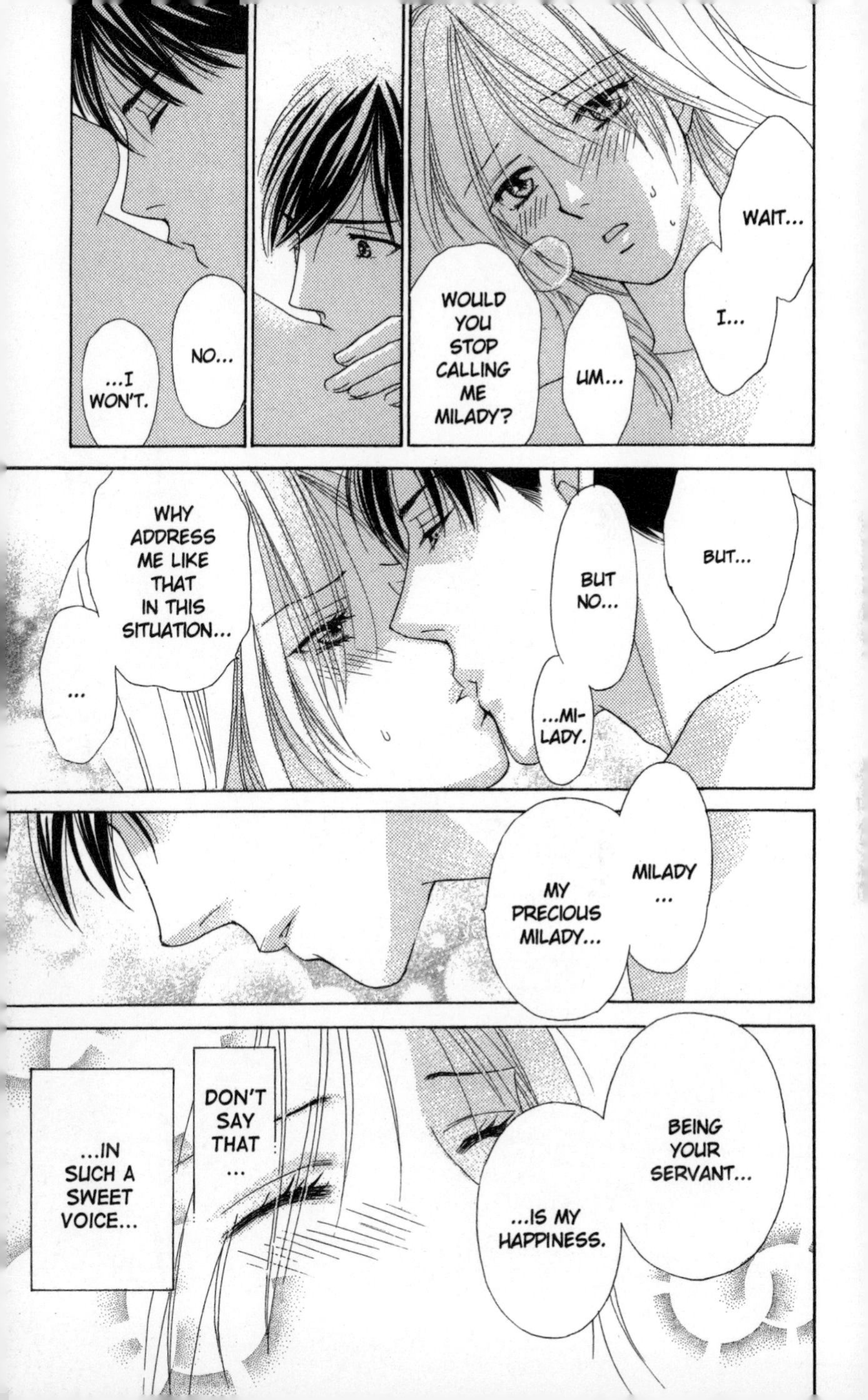
WAIT...
I...
UM...
WOULD YOU STOP CALLING ME MILADY?
NO...
...I WON'T.
BUT...
BUT NO...
...MI-LADY.
WHY ADDRESS ME LIKE THAT IN THIS SITUATION...
...
MILADY ...
MY PRECIOUS MILADY...
BEING YOUR SERVANT...
...IS MY HAPPINESS.
DON'T SAY THAT ...
...IN SUCH A SWEET VOICE...

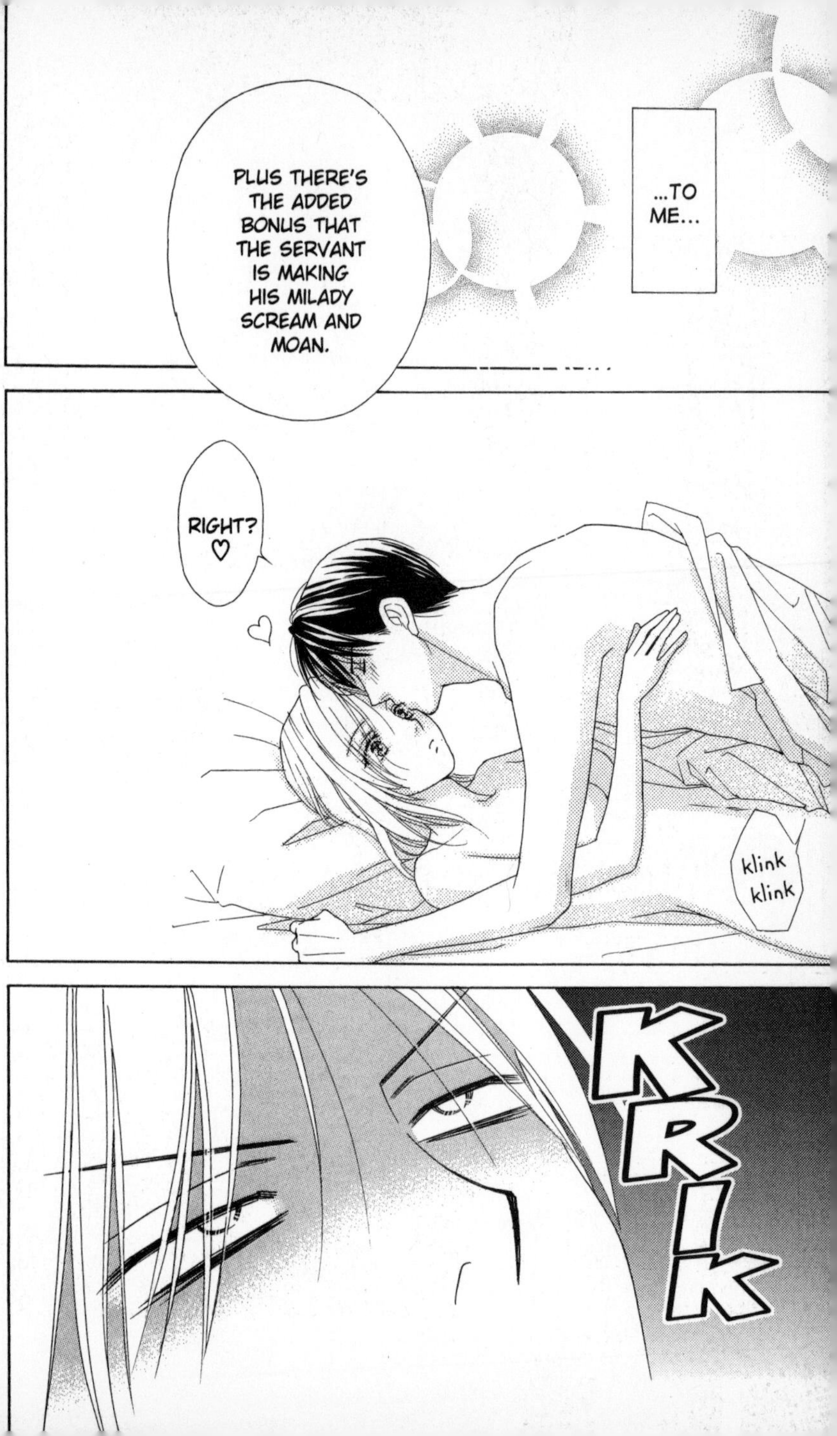
...TO ME...
PLUS THERE'S THE ADDED BONUS THAT THE SERVANT IS MAKING HIS MILADY SCREAM AND MOAN.
RIGHT? ♡
klink klink
KRIK

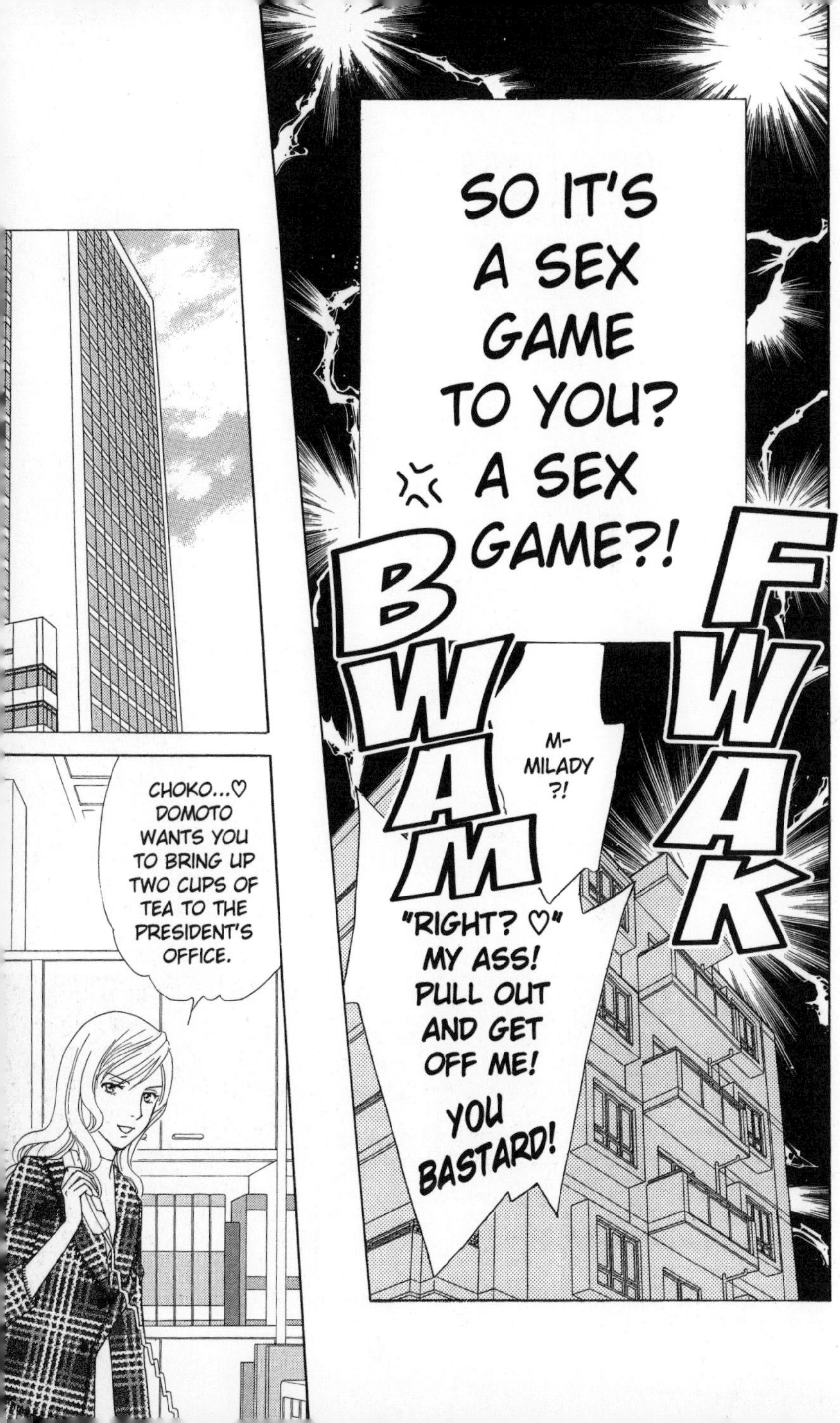
SO IT'S A SEX GAME TO YOU? A SEX GAME?!
FWAK
BWAM
M-MILADY?!
"RIGHT? ♡" MY ASS! PULL OUT AND GET OFF ME!
YOU BASTARD!
CHOKO...♡ DOMOTO WANTS YOU TO BRING UP TWO CUPS OF TEA TO THE PRESIDENT'S OFFICE.

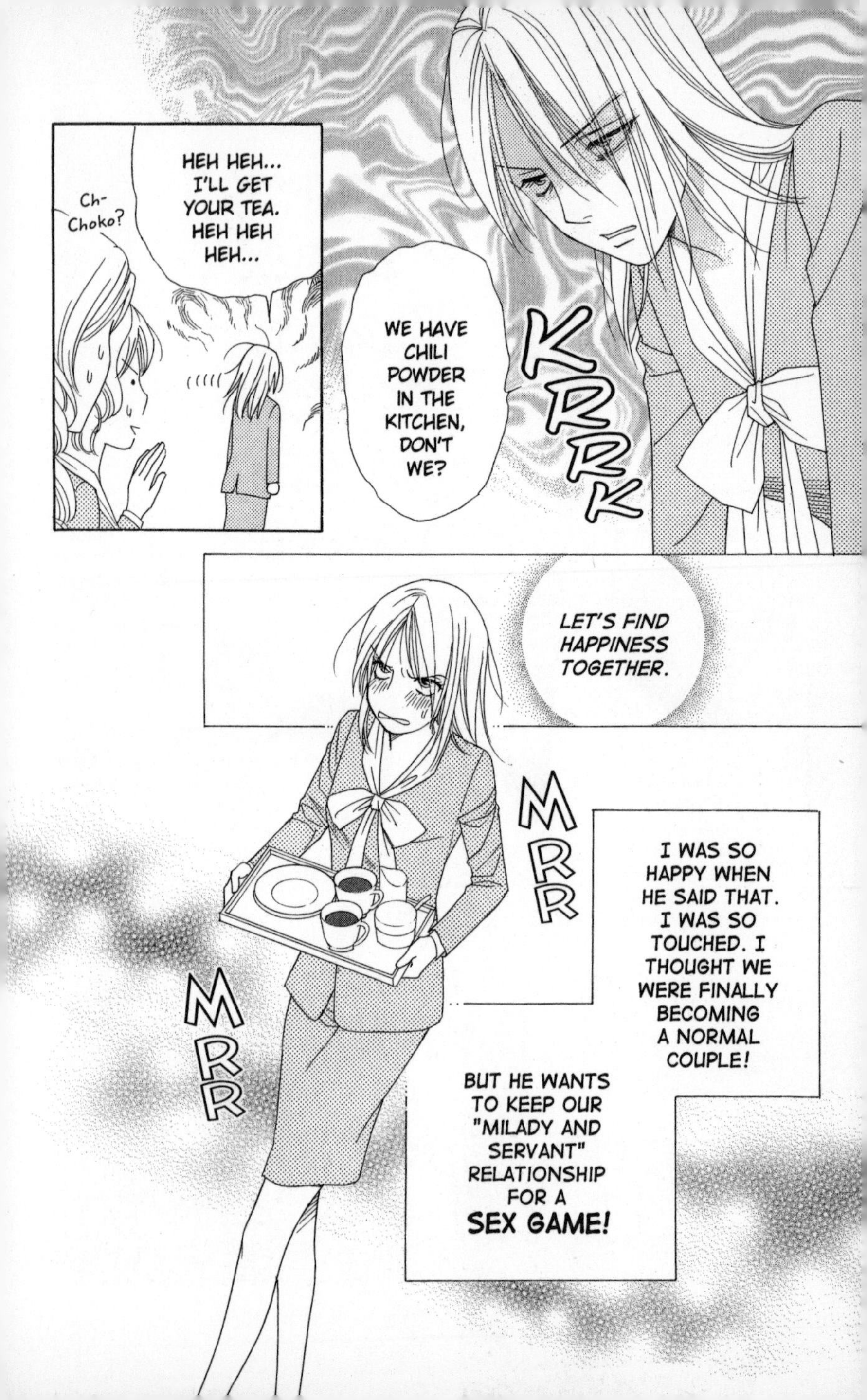
KRRK
WE HAVE CHILI POWDER IN THE KITCHEN, DON'T WE?
HEH HEH... I'LL GET YOUR TEA. HEH HEH HEH...
Ch-Choko?
LET'S FIND HAPPINESS TOGETHER.
I WAS SO HAPPY WHEN HE SAID THAT. I WAS SO TOUCHED. I THOUGHT WE WERE FINALLY BECOMING A NORMAL COUPLE!
MRR
MRR
BUT HE WANTS TO KEEP OUR "MILADY AND SERVANT" RELATIONSHIP FOR A **SEX GAME!**

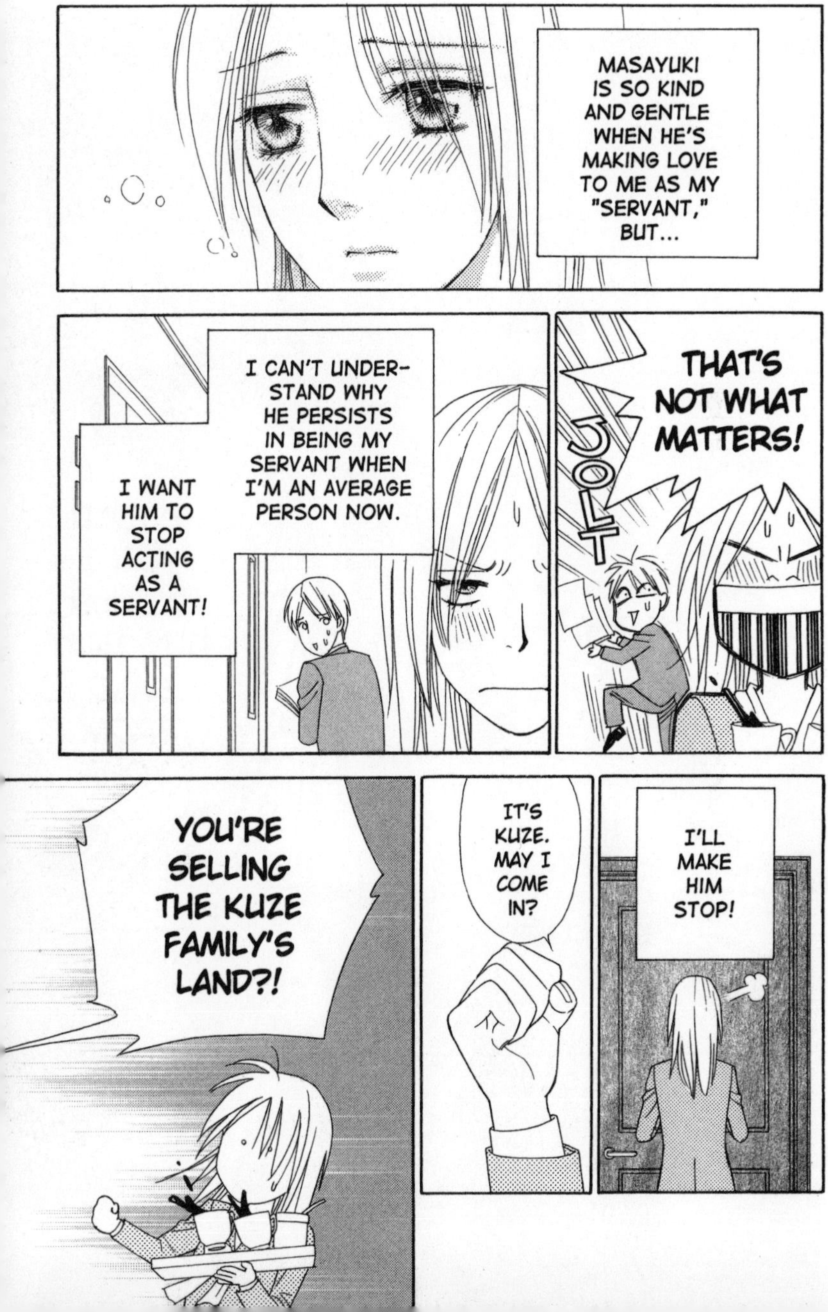
MASAYUKI IS SO KIND AND GENTLE WHEN HE'S MAKING LOVE TO ME AS MY "SERVANT," BUT...
THAT'S NOT WHAT MATTERS!
JOLT
I CAN'T UNDER-STAND WHY HE PERSISTS IN BEING MY SERVANT WHEN I'M AN AVERAGE PERSON NOW.
I WANT HIM TO STOP ACTING AS A SERVANT!
I'LL MAKE HIM STOP!
IT'S KUZE. MAY I COME IN?
YOU'RE SELLING THE KUZE FAMILY'S LAND?!

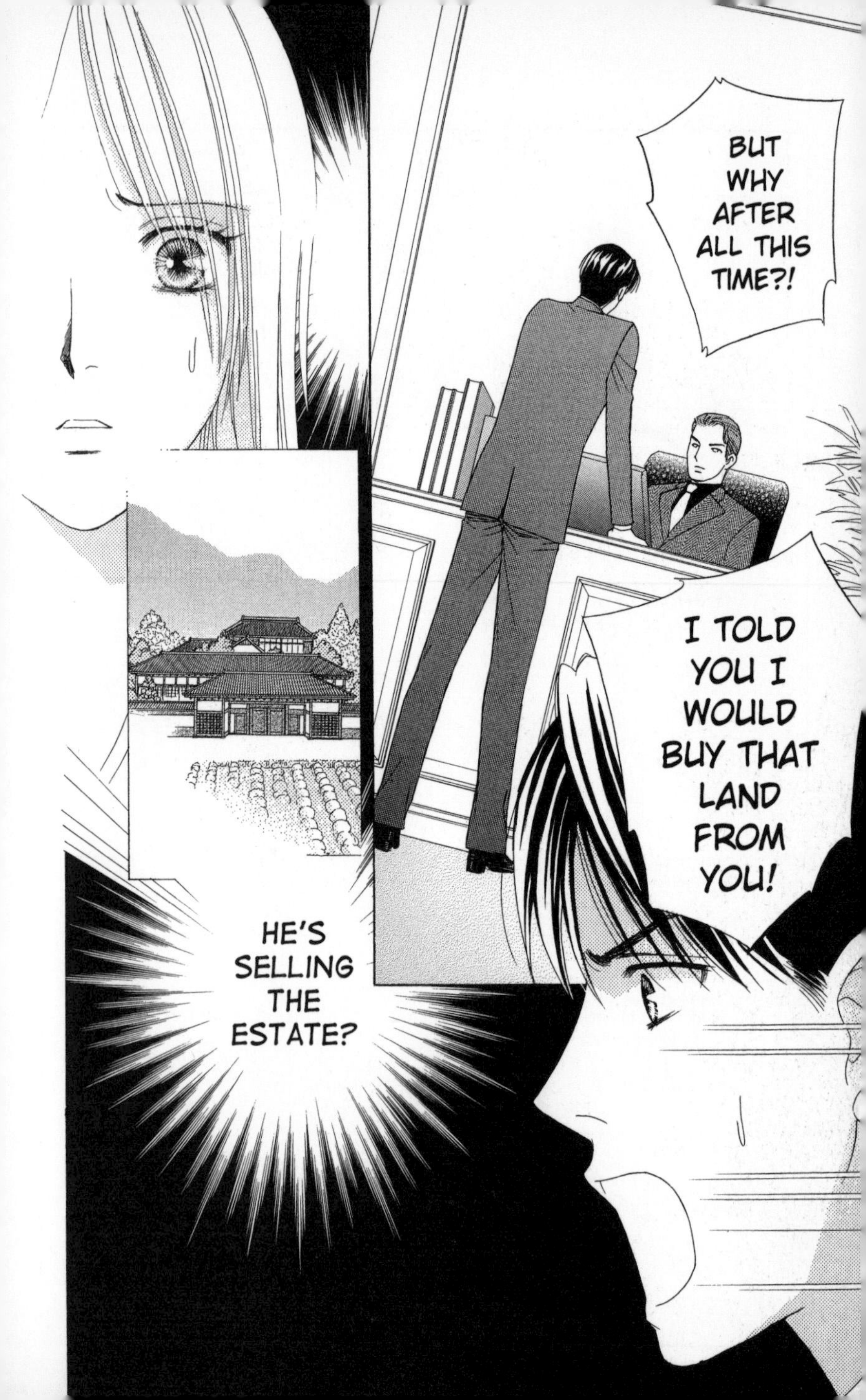
BUT WHY AFTER ALL THIS TIME?!
I TOLD YOU I WOULD BUY THAT LAND FROM YOU!
HE'S SELLING THE ESTATE?

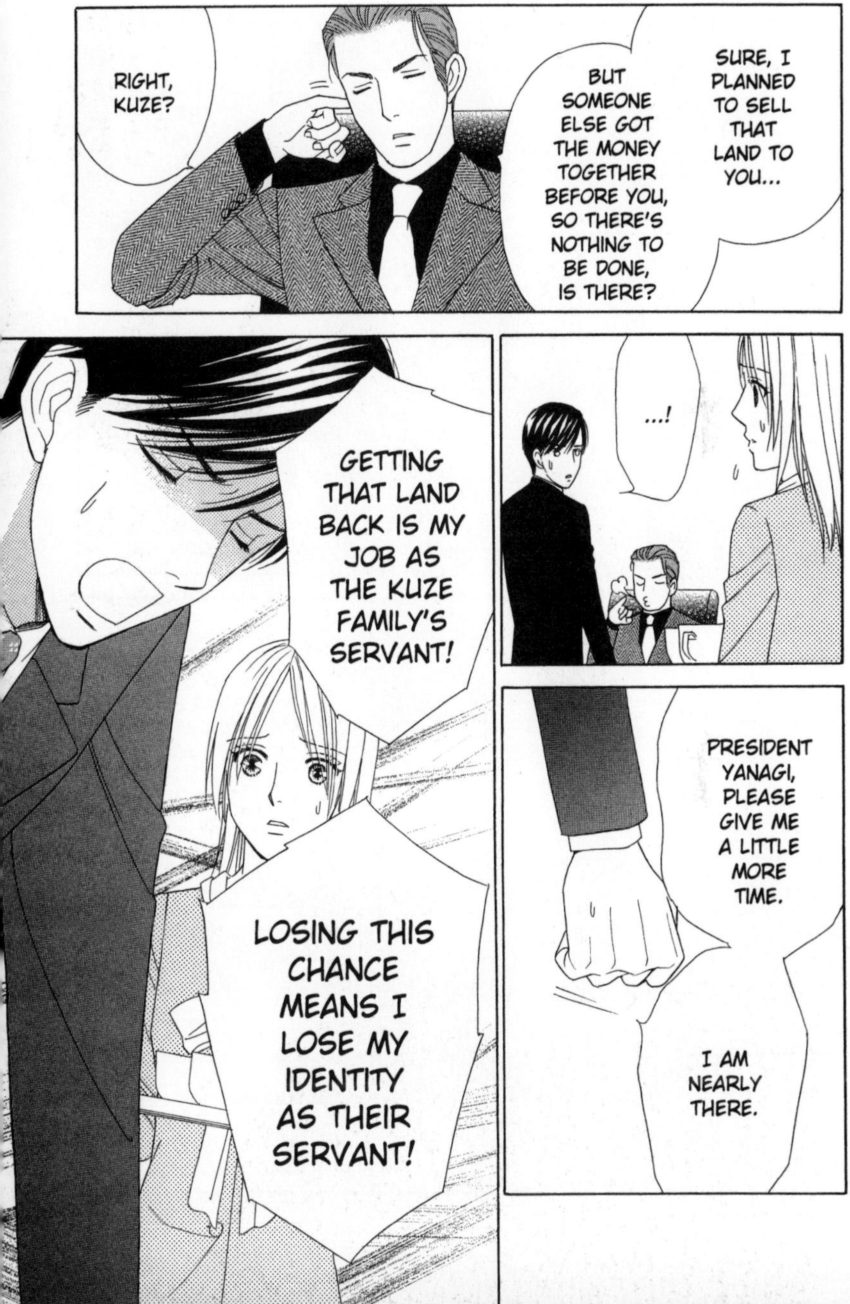
SURE, I PLANNED TO SELL THAT LAND TO YOU...
BUT SOMEONE ELSE GOT THE MONEY TOGETHER BEFORE YOU, SO THERE'S NOTHING TO BE DONE, IS THERE?
RIGHT, KUZE?
...!
PRESIDENT YANAGI, PLEASE GIVE ME A LITTLE MORE TIME.
I AM NEARLY THERE.
GETTING THAT LAND BACK IS MY JOB AS THE KUZE FAMILY'S SERVANT!
LOSING THIS CHANCE MEANS I LOSE MY IDENTITY AS THEIR SERVANT!

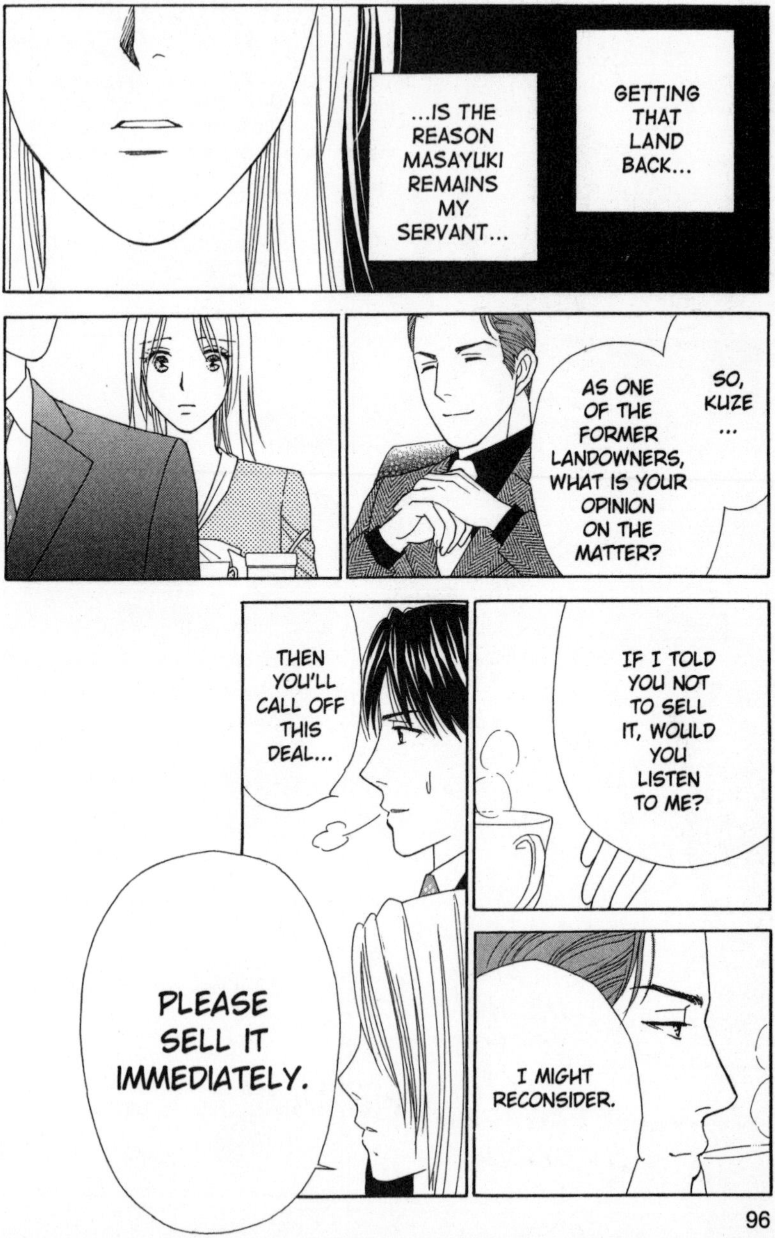
GETTING THAT LAND BACK...
...IS THE REASON MASAYUKI REMAINS MY SERVANT...
SO, KUZE...
AS ONE OF THE FORMER LANDOWNERS, WHAT IS YOUR OPINION ON THE MATTER?
IF I TOLD YOU NOT TO SELL IT, WOULD YOU LISTEN TO ME?
THEN YOU'LL CALL OFF THIS DEAL...
I MIGHT RECONSIDER.
PLEASE SELL IT IMMEDIATELY.

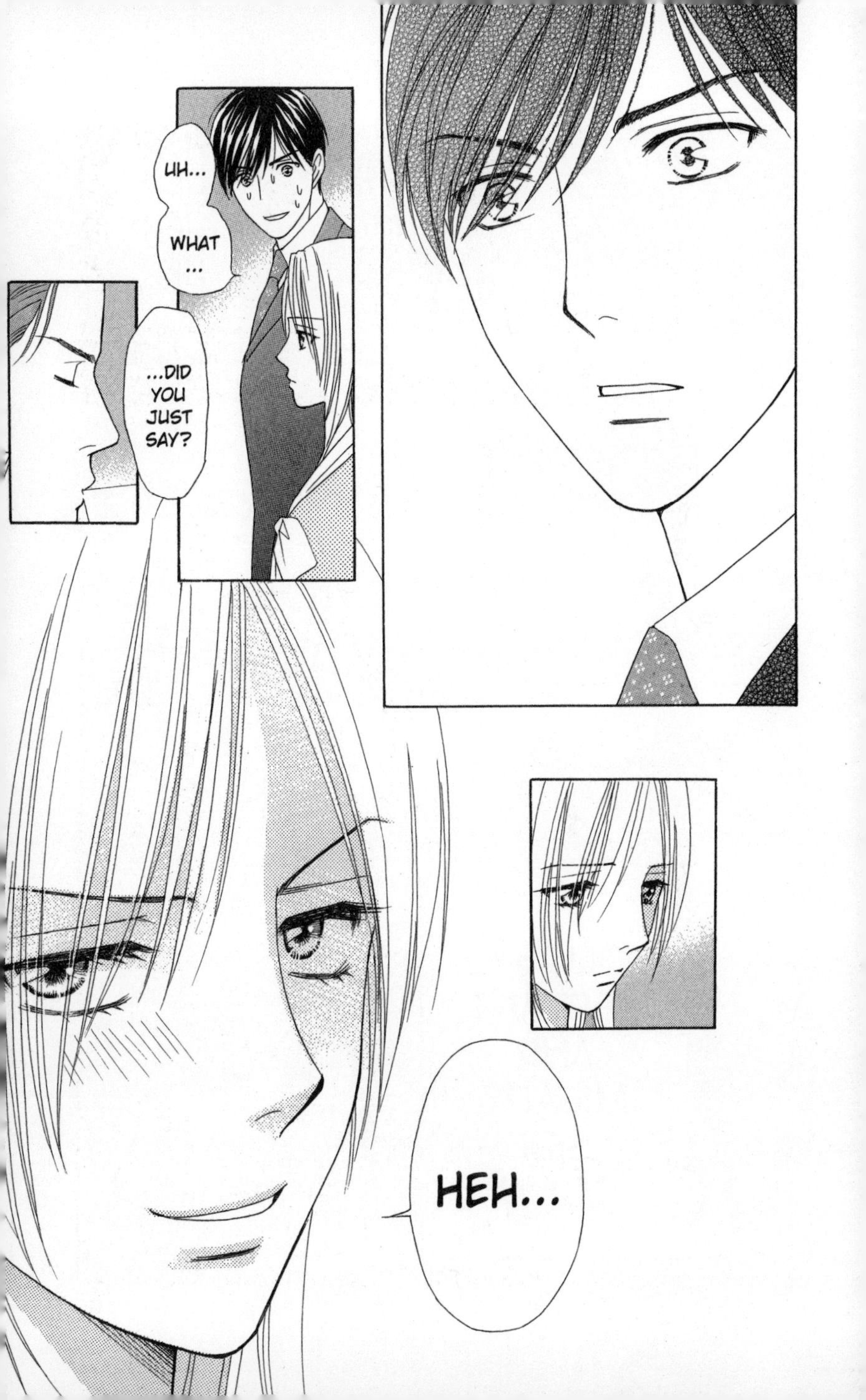
UH...
WHAT ...
...DID YOU JUST SAY?
HEH...

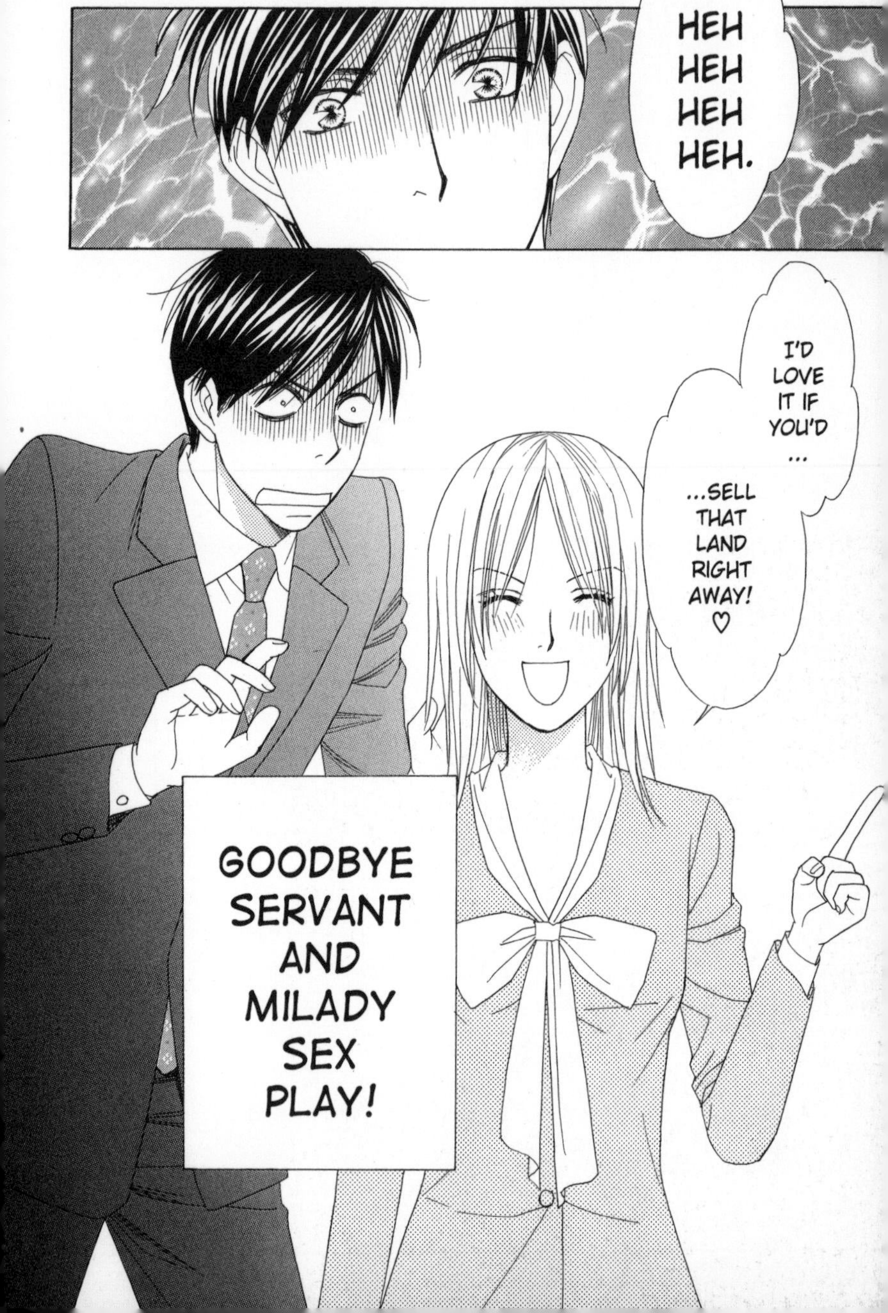
HEH HEH HEH HEH.
I'D LOVE IT IF YOU'D ...
...SELL THAT LAND RIGHT AWAY! ♡
GOODBYE SERVANT AND MILADY SEX PLAY!

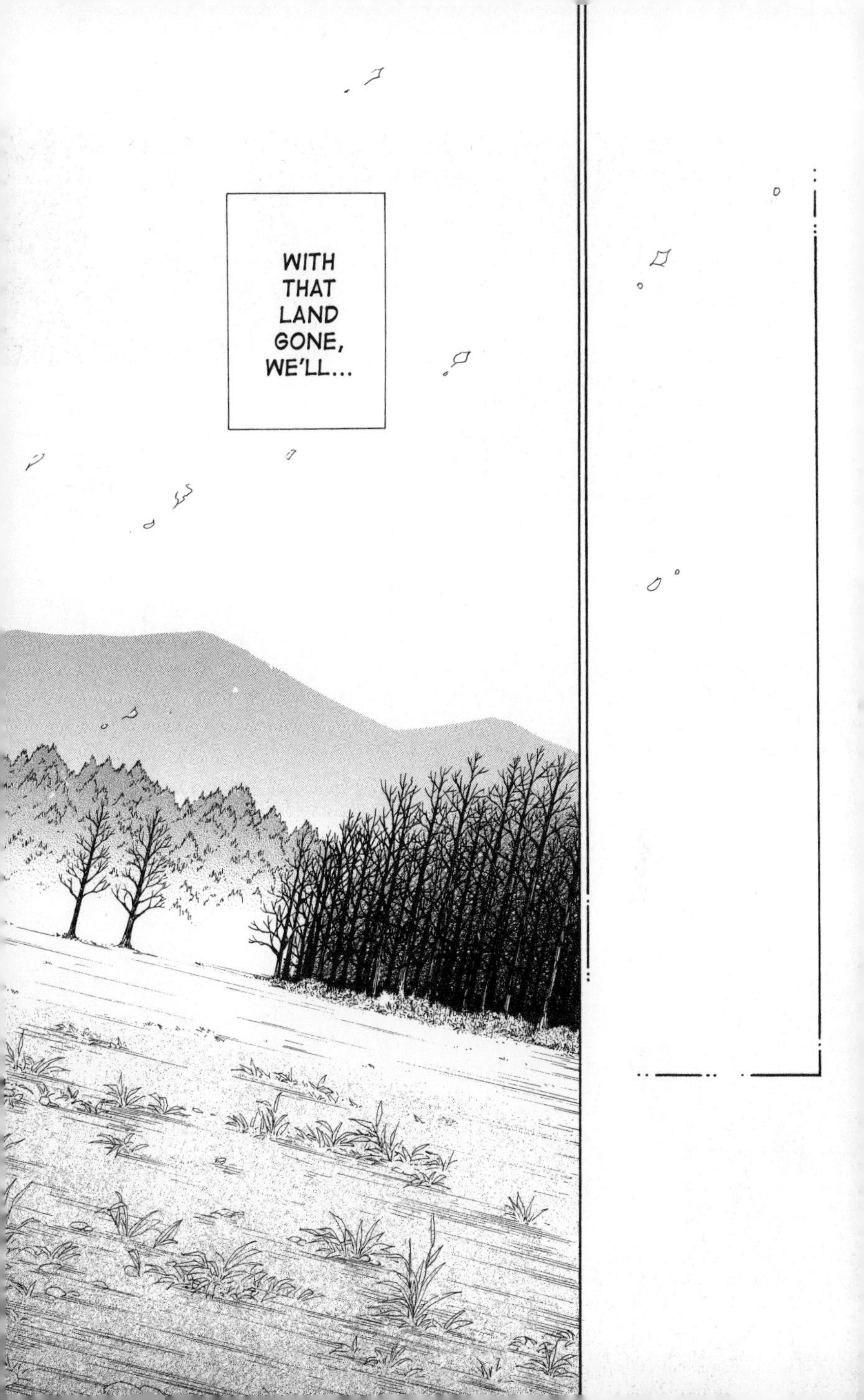
WITH THAT LAND GONE, WE'LL...

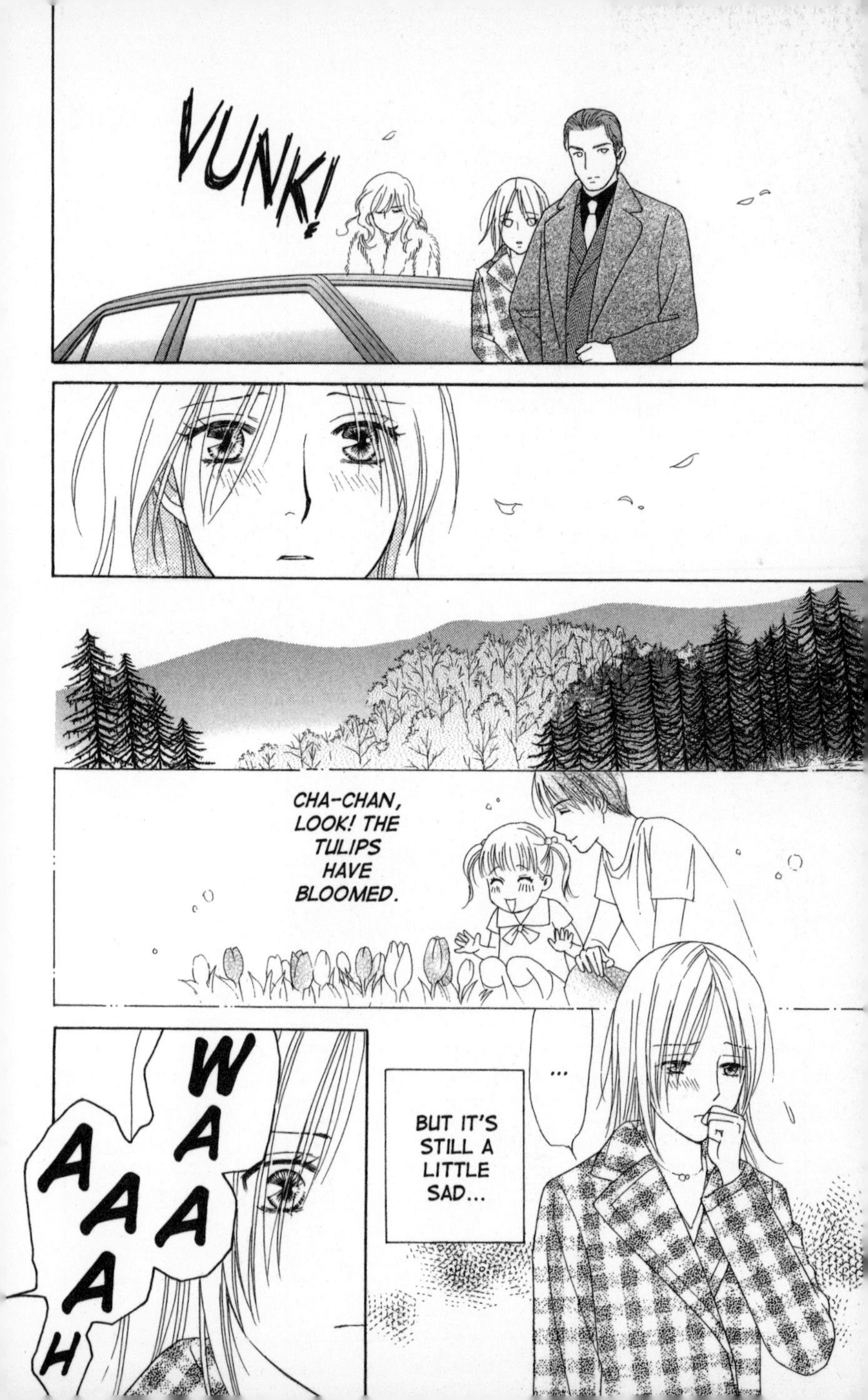
VUNK!
CHA-CHAN, LOOK! THE TULIPS HAVE BLOOMED.
...
BUT IT'S STILL A LITTLE SAD...
WAAAAAH

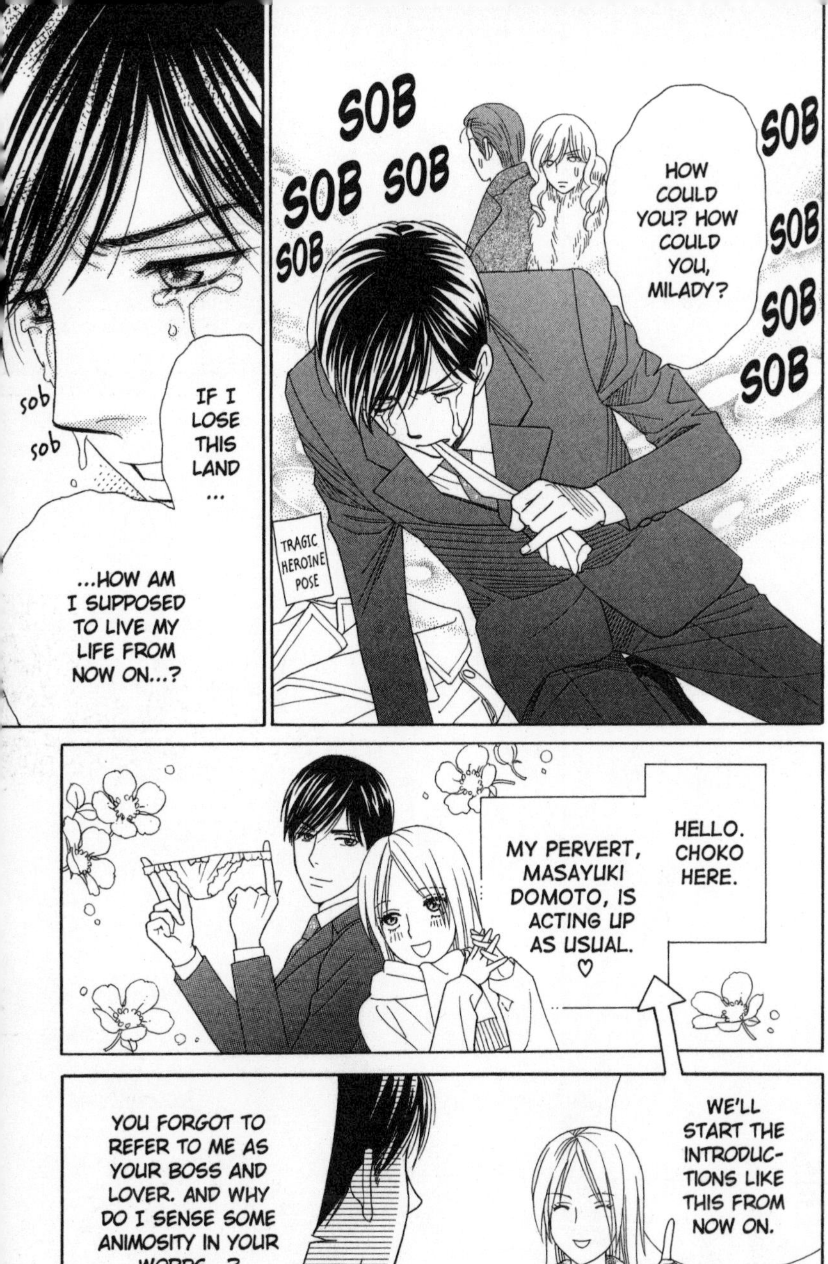
SOB SOB SOB SOB
HOW COULD YOU? HOW COULD YOU, MILADY?
SOB SOB SOB SOB
TRAGIC HEROINE POSE
IF I LOSE THIS LAND ...
sob sob
...HOW AM I SUPPOSED TO LIVE MY LIFE FROM NOW ON...?
HELLO. CHOKO HERE.
MY PERVERT, MASAYUKI DOMOTO, IS ACTING UP AS USUAL. ♡
WE'LL START THE INTRODUCTIONS LIKE THIS FROM NOW ON.
YOU FORGOT TO REFER TO ME AS YOUR BOSS AND LOVER. AND WHY DO I SENSE SOME ANIMOSITY IN YOUR WORDS...?

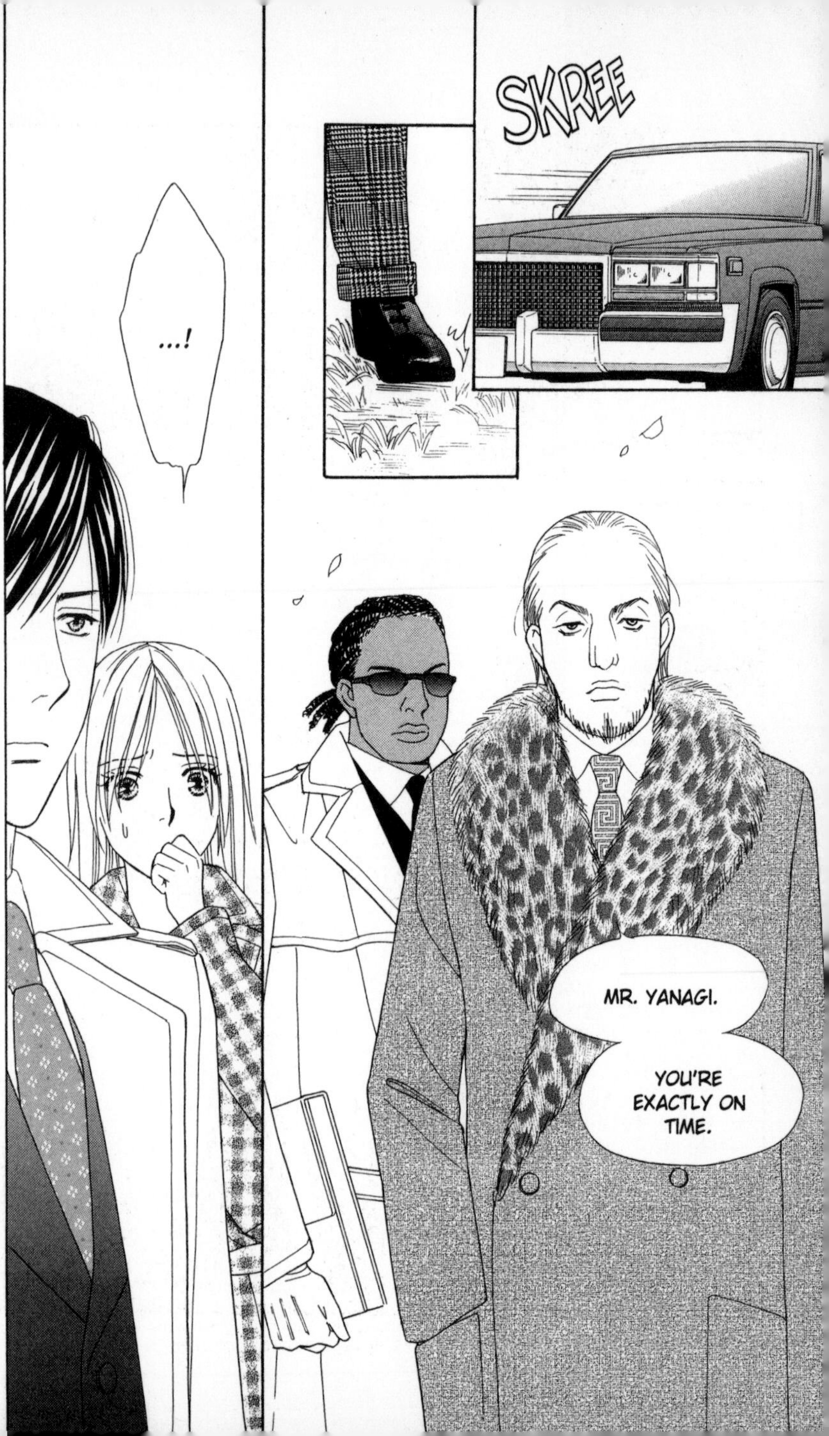
SKREE
MR. YANAGI.
YOU'RE EXACTLY ON TIME.
...!

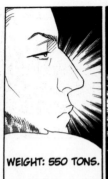

HEIGHT: 57 METERS.
WEIGHT: 550 TONS.
HA HA HA
Chodenji yo-yo...
Chodenji spin.
HO HO HO
...
HE'S MR. BARRYMORE, THE PRESIDENT OF AN INVESTMENT COMPANY AND THE BRANCH MANAGER OF THE '70S ANIME LOVERS ASSOCIATION IN NEW YORK.
COMBATTLER V...
AN AMERICAN IS GOING TO BUY THIS LAND?
...
...

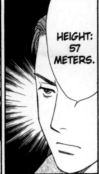

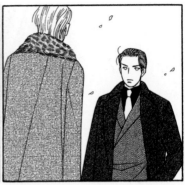

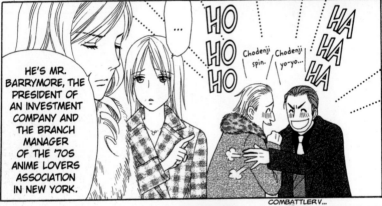

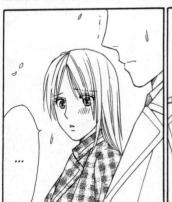

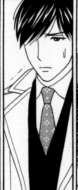

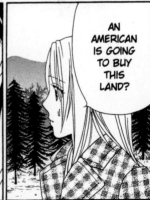

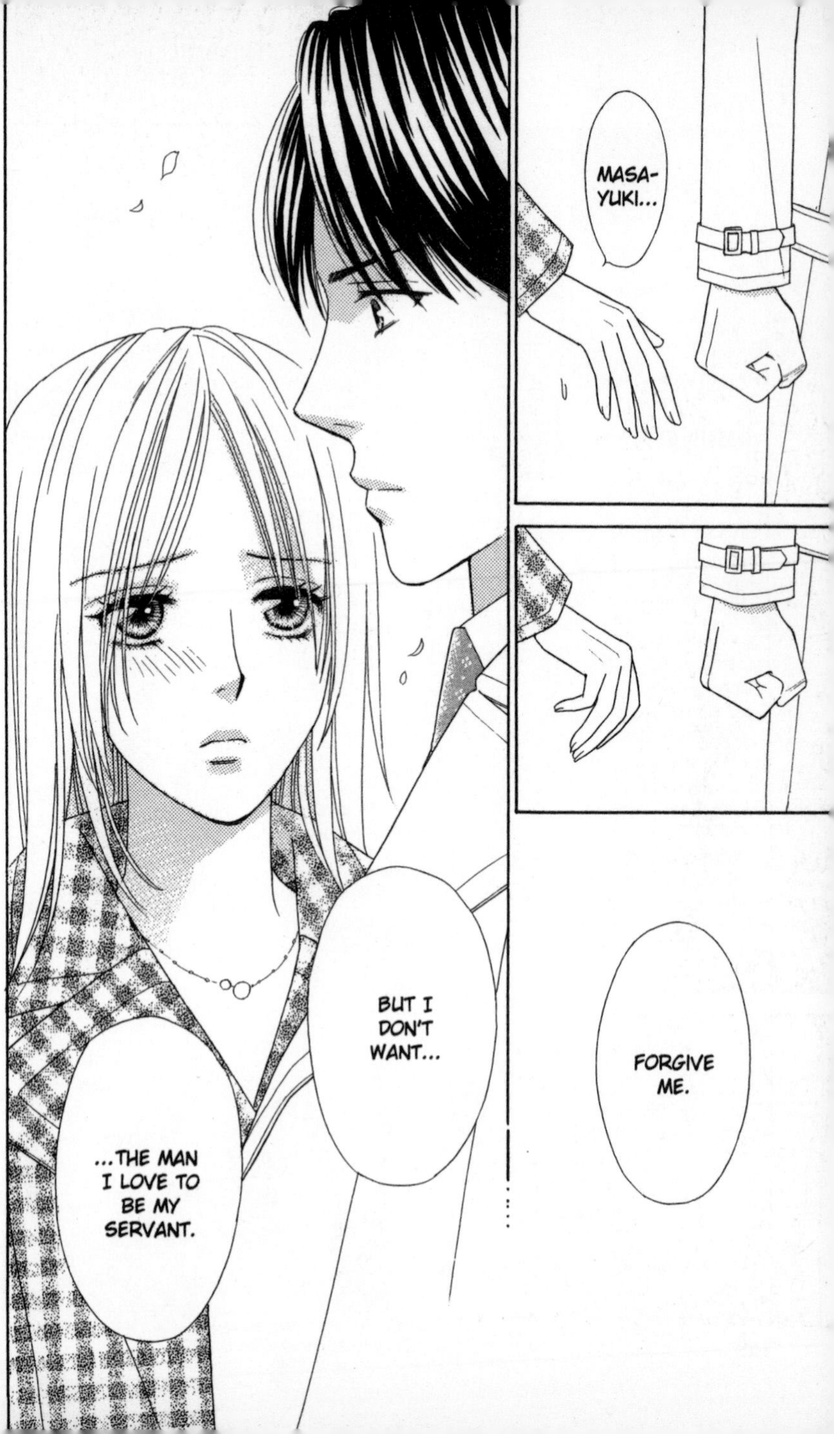
MASA-YUKI...
FORGIVE ME.
BUT I DON'T WANT...
...THE MAN I LOVE TO BE MY SERVANT.

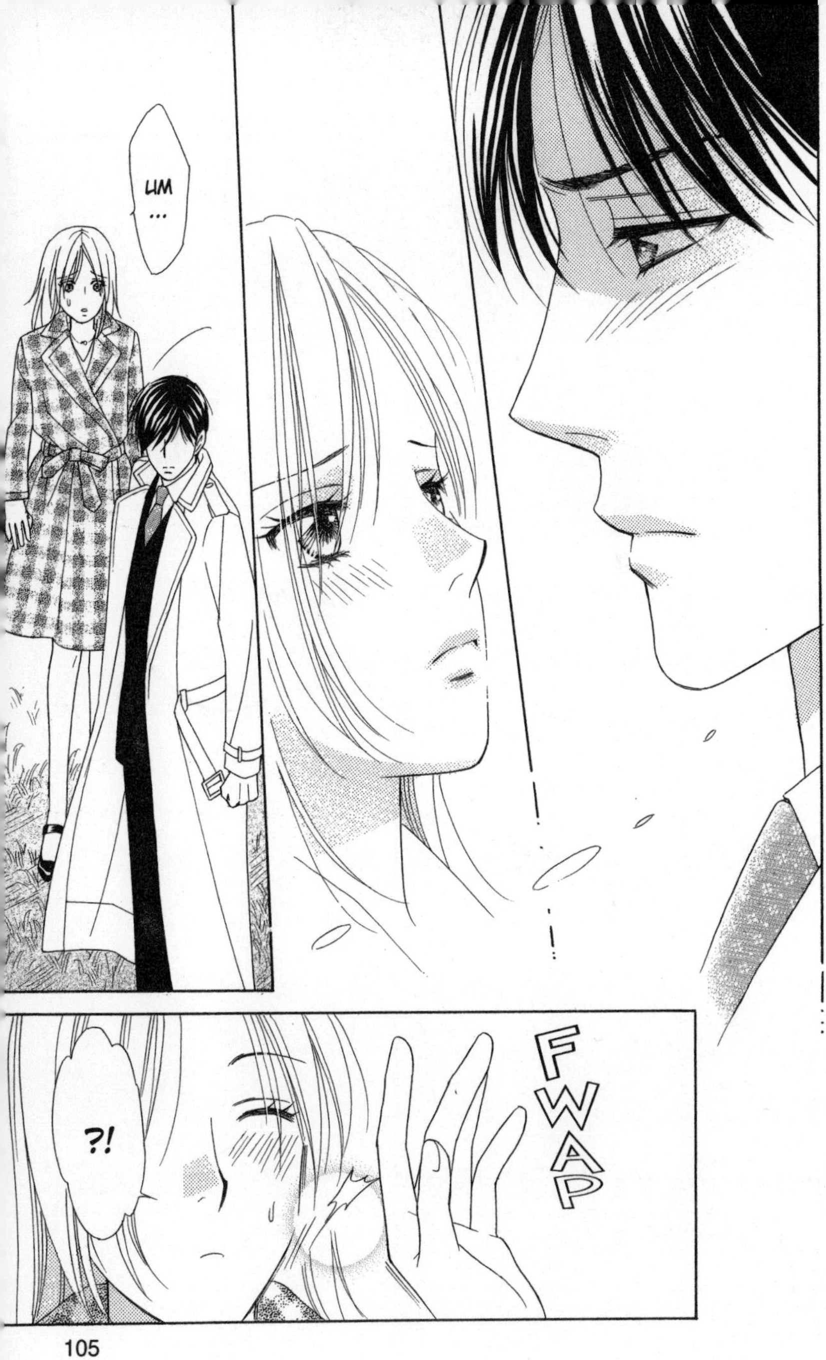
UM ...
?!
FWAP

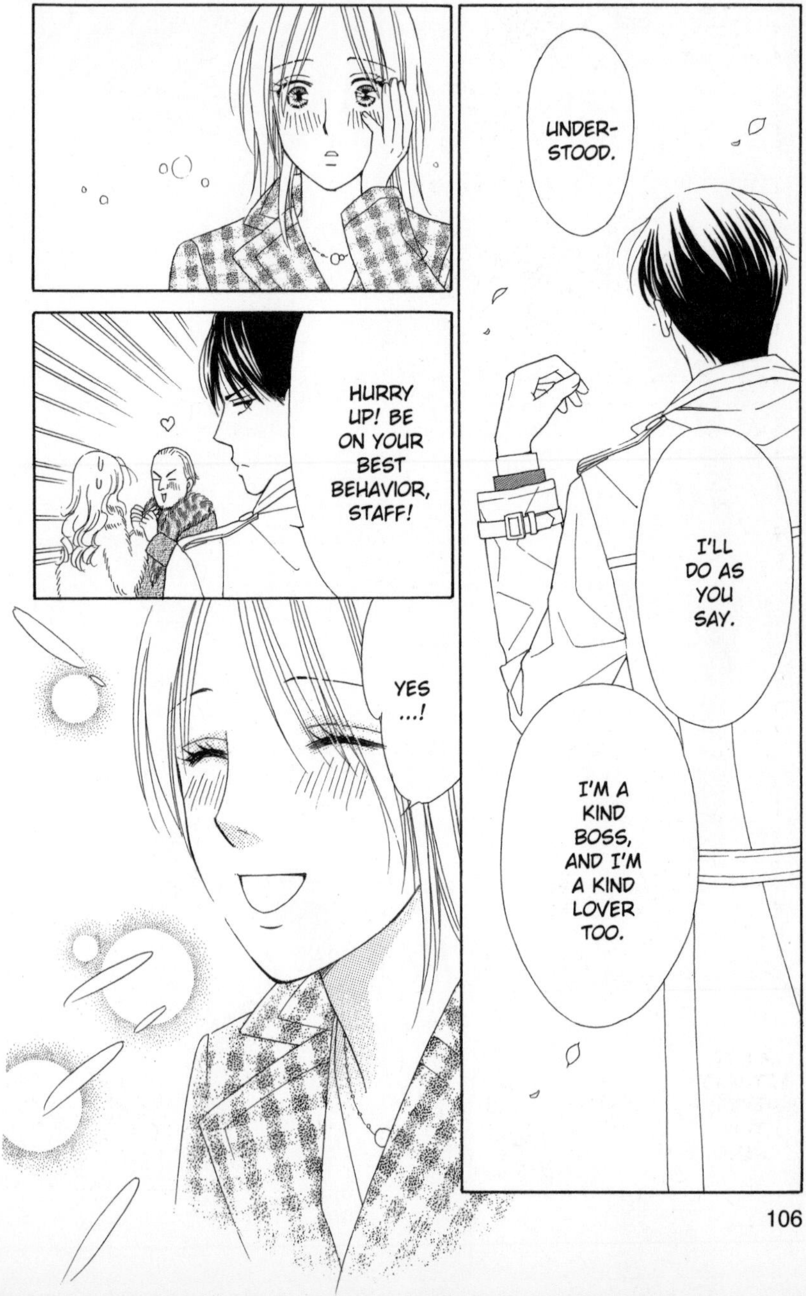
UNDER-STOOD.
I'LL DO AS YOU SAY.
I'M A KIND BOSS, AND I'M A KIND LOVER TOO.
HURRY UP! BE ON YOUR BEST BEHAVIOR, STAFF!
YES ...!

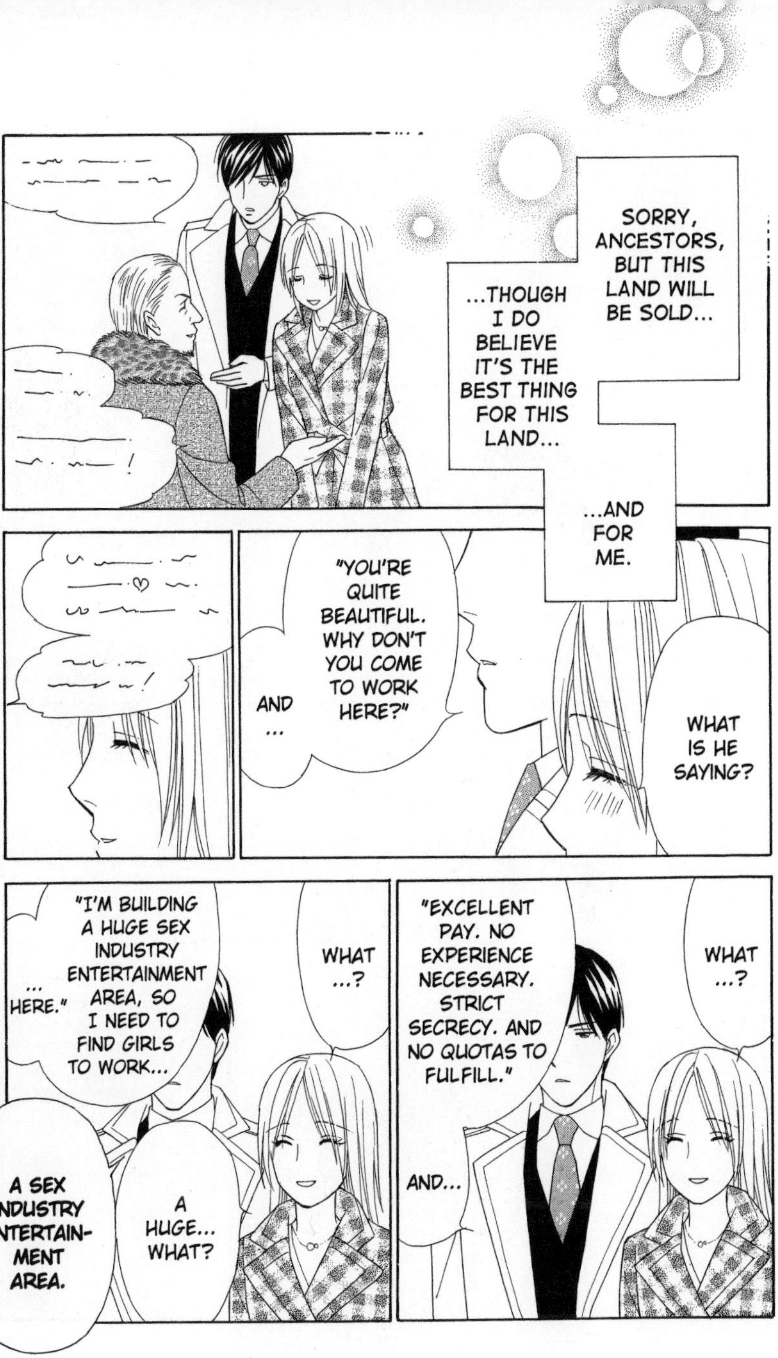
SORRY, ANCESTORS, BUT THIS LAND WILL BE SOLD...
...THOUGH I DO BELIEVE IT'S THE BEST THING FOR THIS LAND...
...AND FOR ME.
WHAT IS HE SAYING?
"YOU'RE QUITE BEAUTIFUL. WHY DON'T YOU COME TO WORK HERE?"
AND ...
WHAT ...?
"EXCELLENT PAY. NO EXPERIENCE NECESSARY. STRICT SECRECY. AND NO QUOTAS TO FULFILL."
AND...
WHAT ...?
"I'M BUILDING A HUGE SEX INDUSTRY ENTERTAINMENT AREA, SO I NEED TO FIND GIRLS TO WORK...
... HERE."
A HUGE... WHAT?
A SEX INDUSTRY ENTERTAIN-MENT AREA.

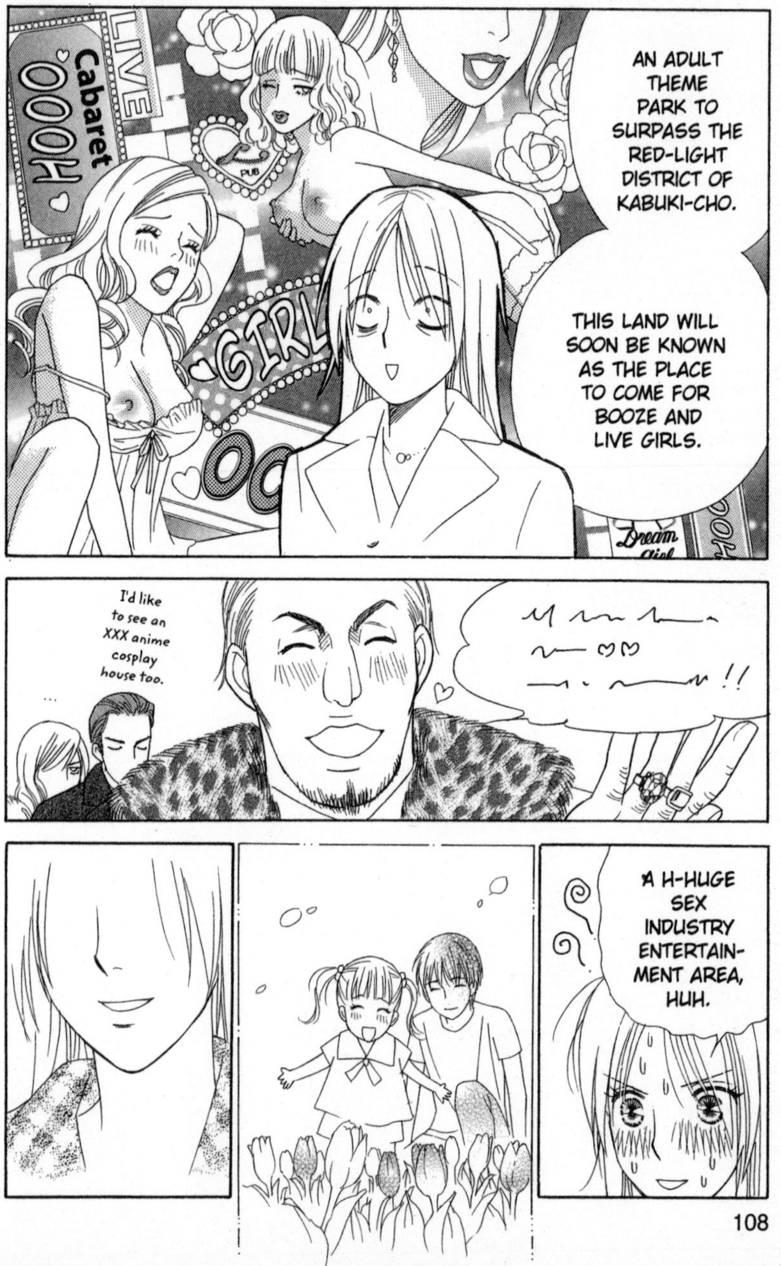
AN ADULT THEME PARK TO SURPASS THE RED-LIGHT DISTRICT OF KABUKI-CHO.
THIS LAND WILL SOON BE KNOWN AS THE PLACE TO COME FOR BOOZE AND LIVE GIRLS.
LIVE
Cabaret OOOH
PUB
GIRL
I'd like to see an XXX anime cosplay house too.
...
A H-HUGE SEX INDUSTRY ENTERTAIN-MENT AREA, HUH.

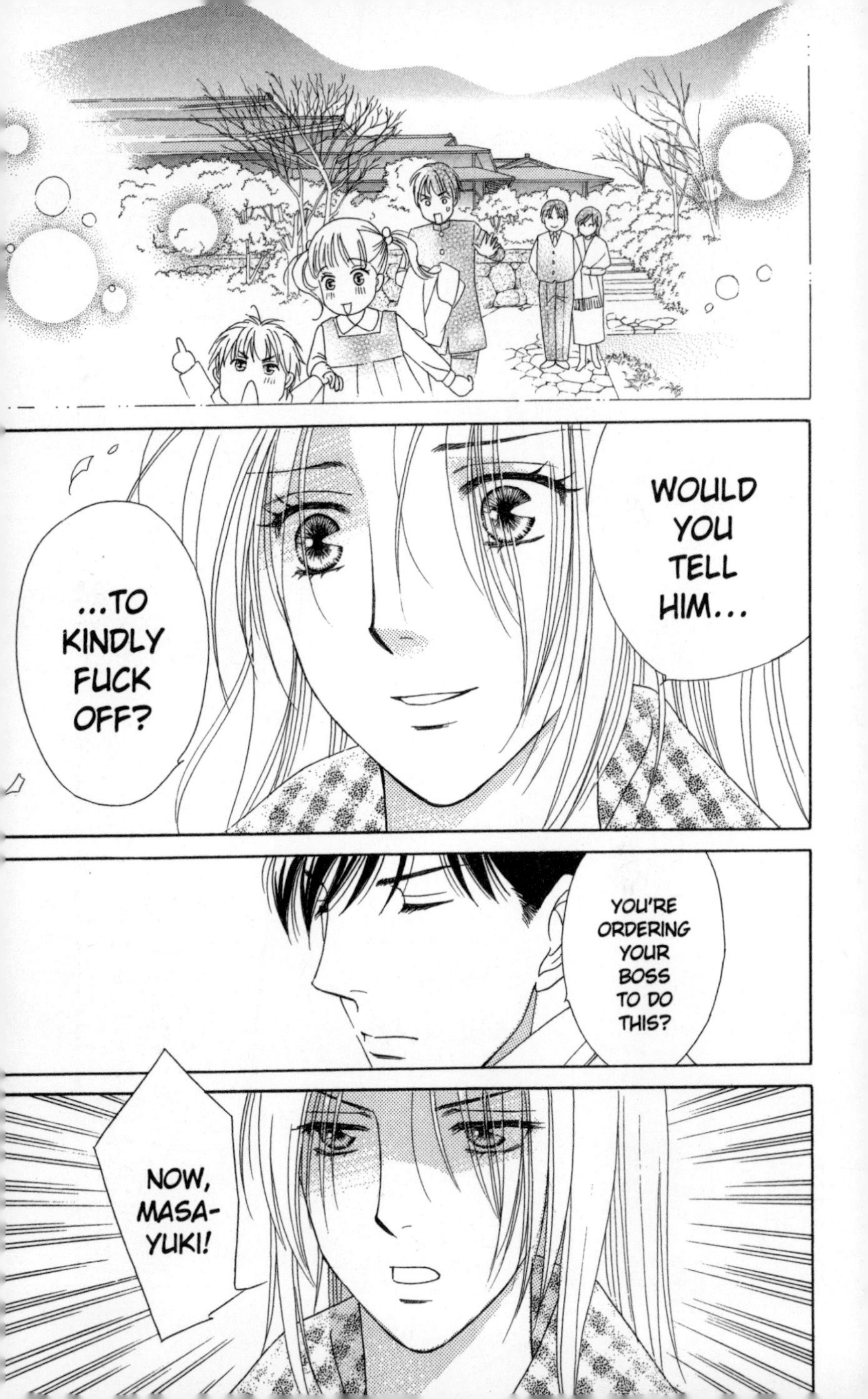
WOULD YOU TELL HIM...
...TO KINDLY FUCK OFF?
YOU'RE ORDERING YOUR BOSS TO DO THIS?
NOW, MASA-YUKI!

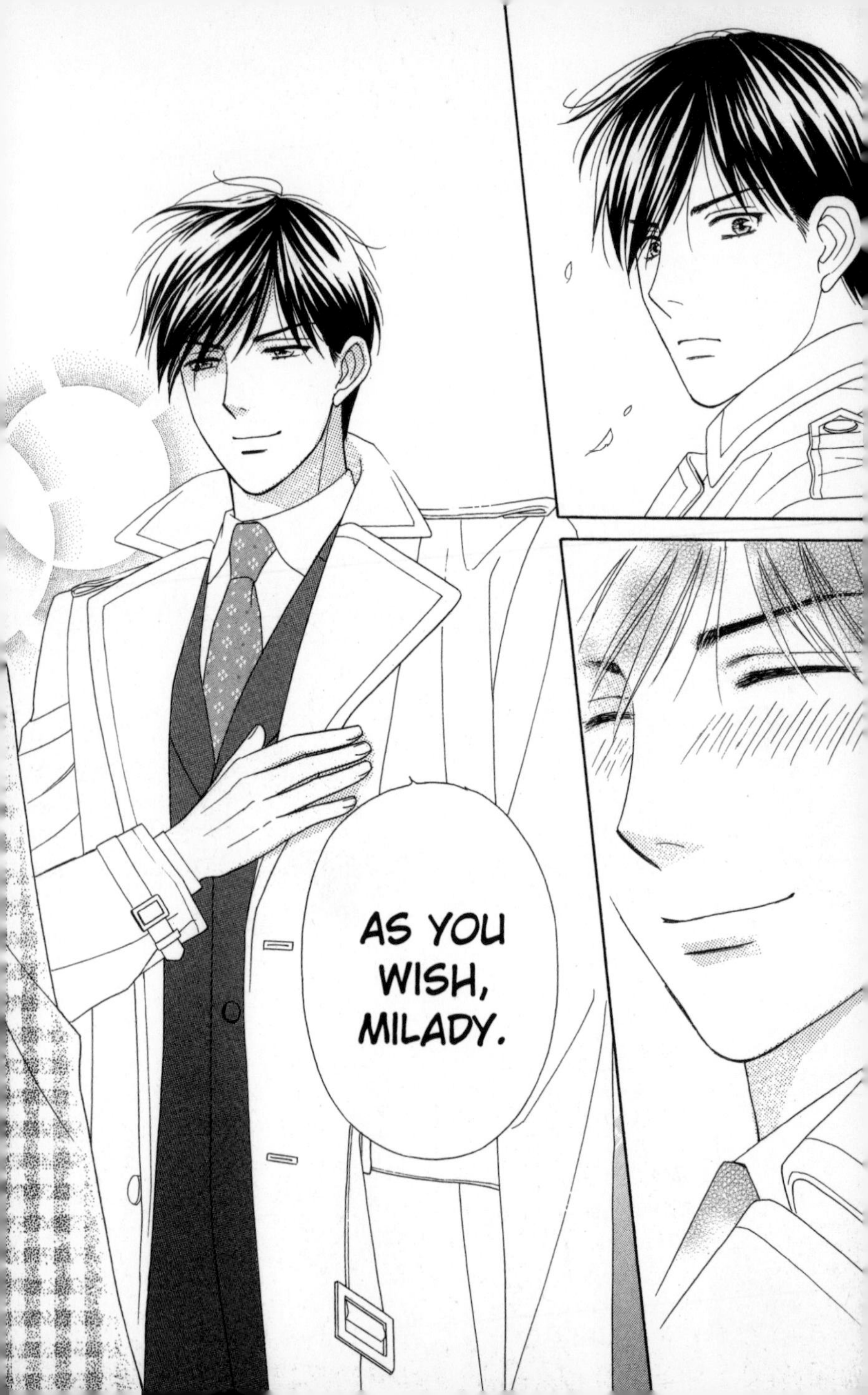
AS YOU WISH, MILADY.

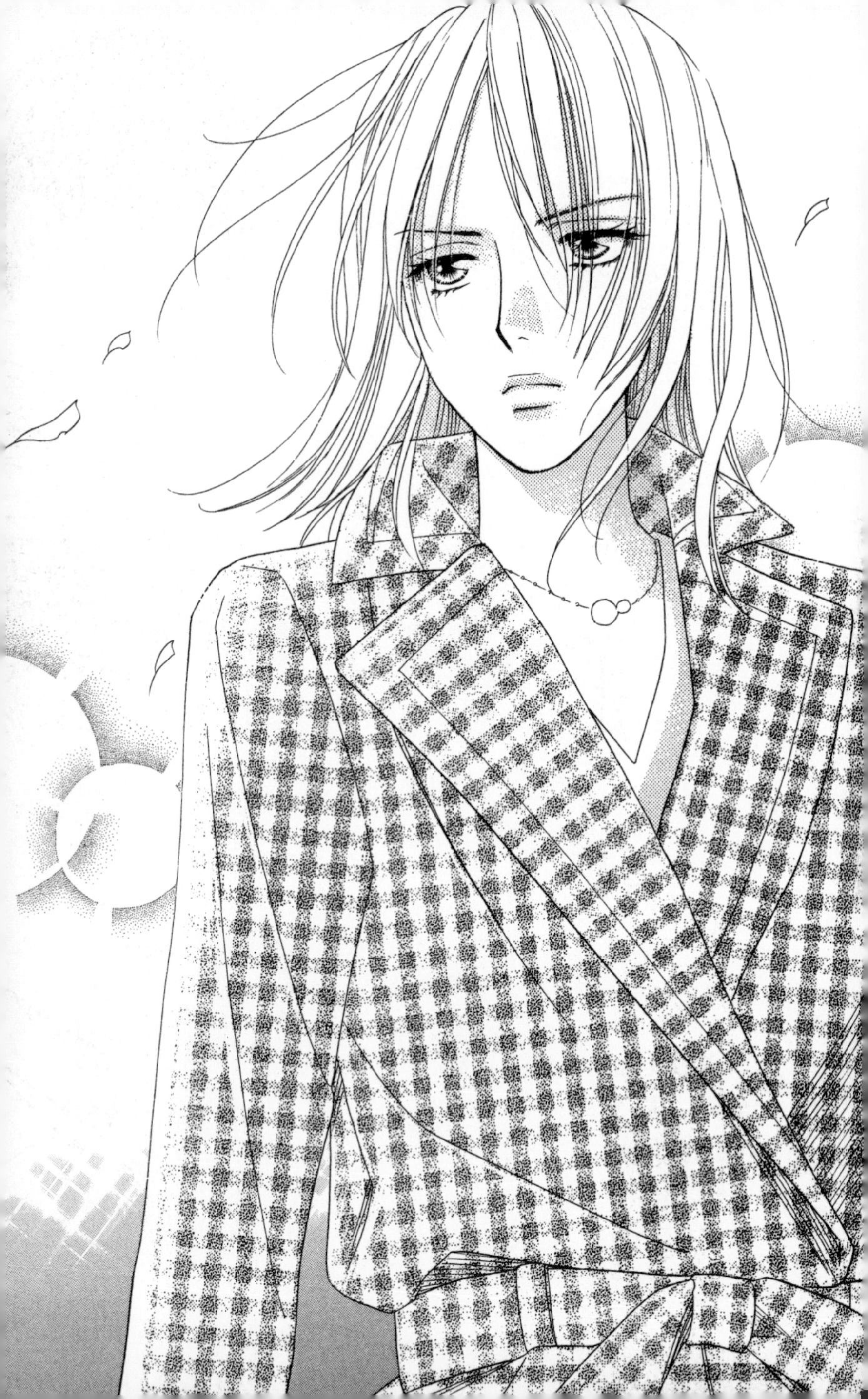

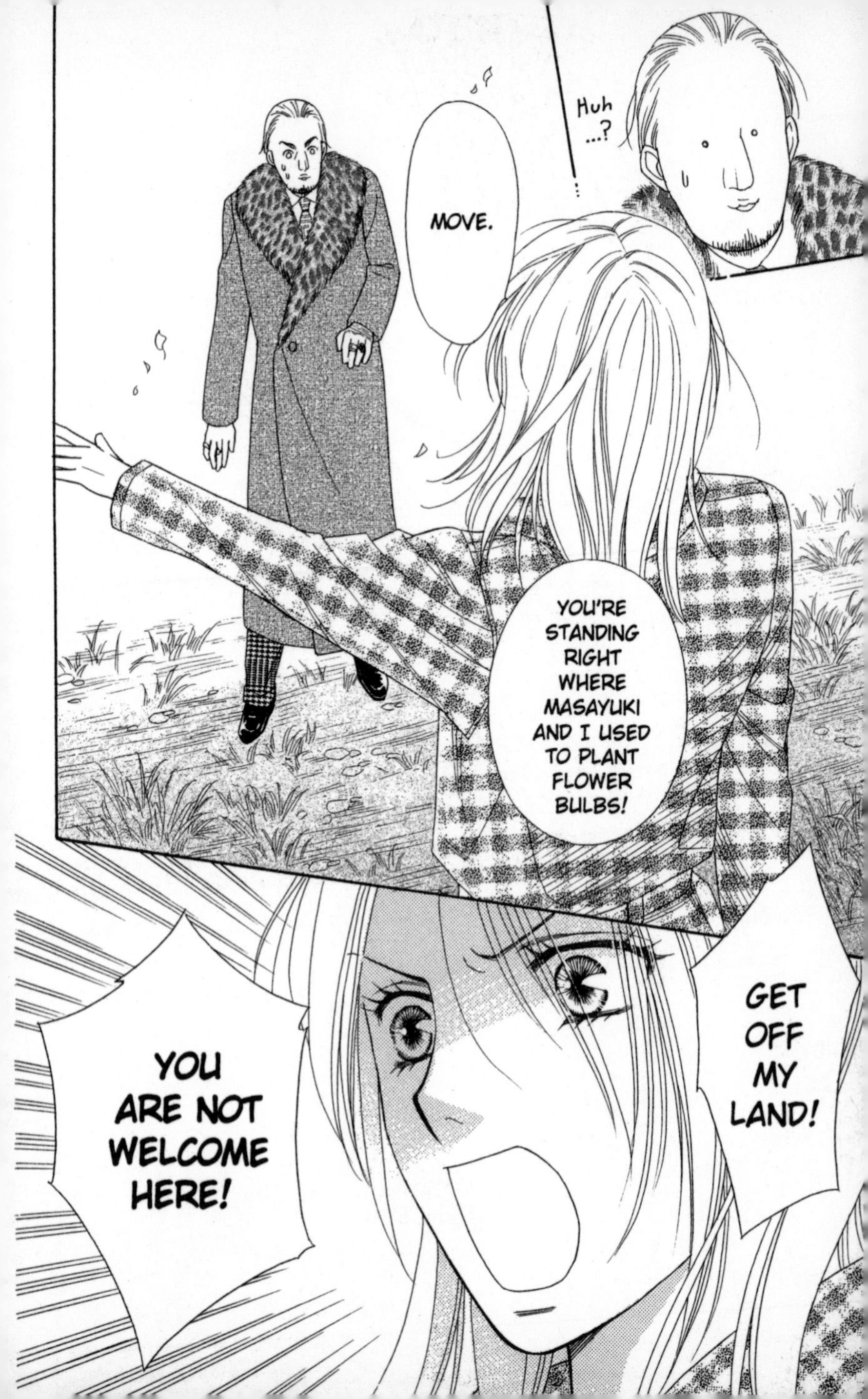
Huh ...?
MOVE.
YOU'RE STANDING RIGHT WHERE MASAYUKI AND I USED TO PLANT FLOWER BULBS!
GET OFF MY LAND!
YOU ARE NOT WELCOME HERE!

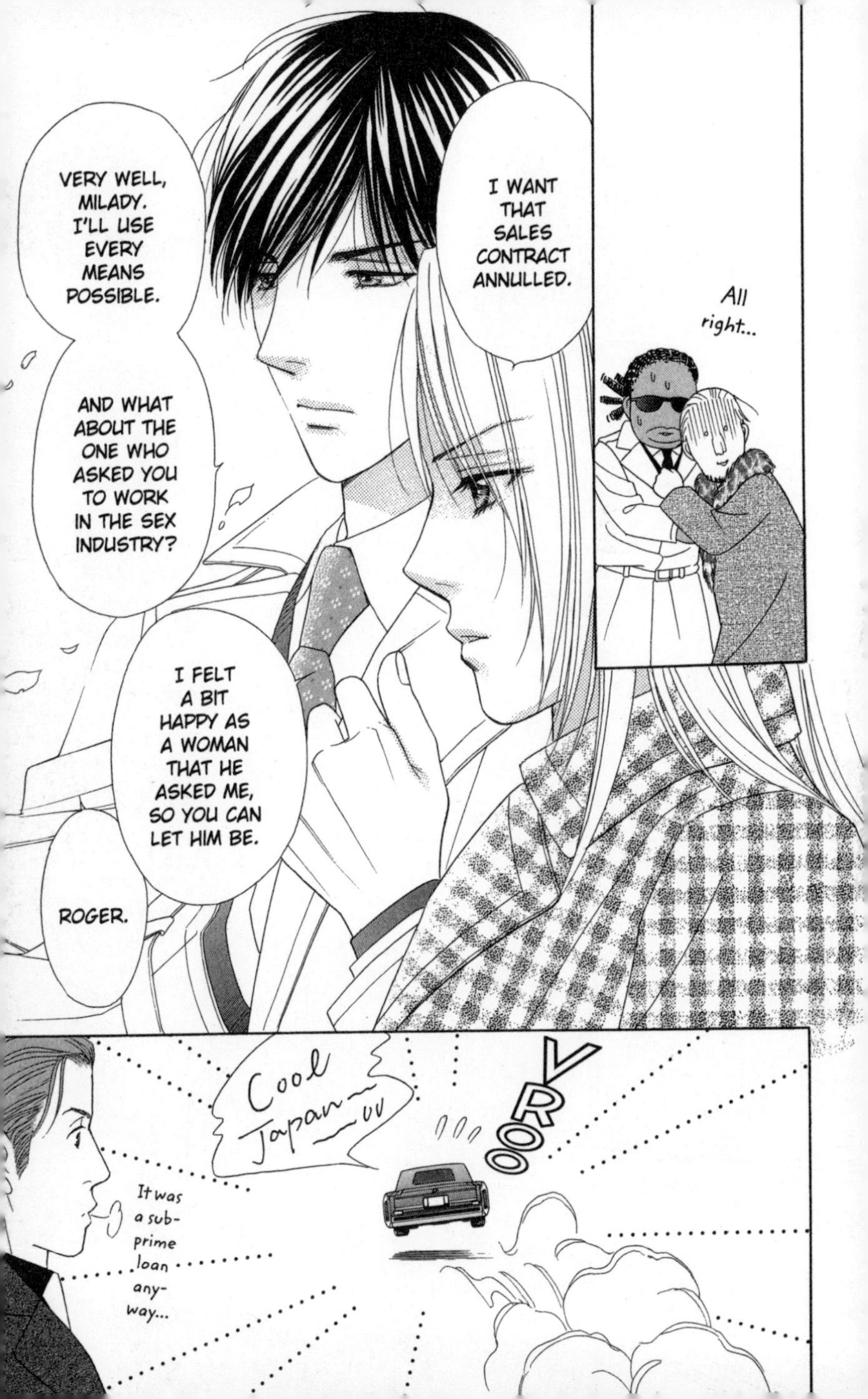
All right...
I WANT THAT SALES CONTRACT ANNULLED.
VERY WELL, MILADY. I'LL USE EVERY MEANS POSSIBLE.
AND WHAT ABOUT THE ONE WHO ASKED YOU TO WORK IN THE SEX INDUSTRY?
I FELT A BIT HAPPY AS A WOMAN THAT HE ASKED ME, SO YOU CAN LET HIM BE.
ROGER.
VROOO
Cool Japan~~
It was a sub-prime loan any-way...

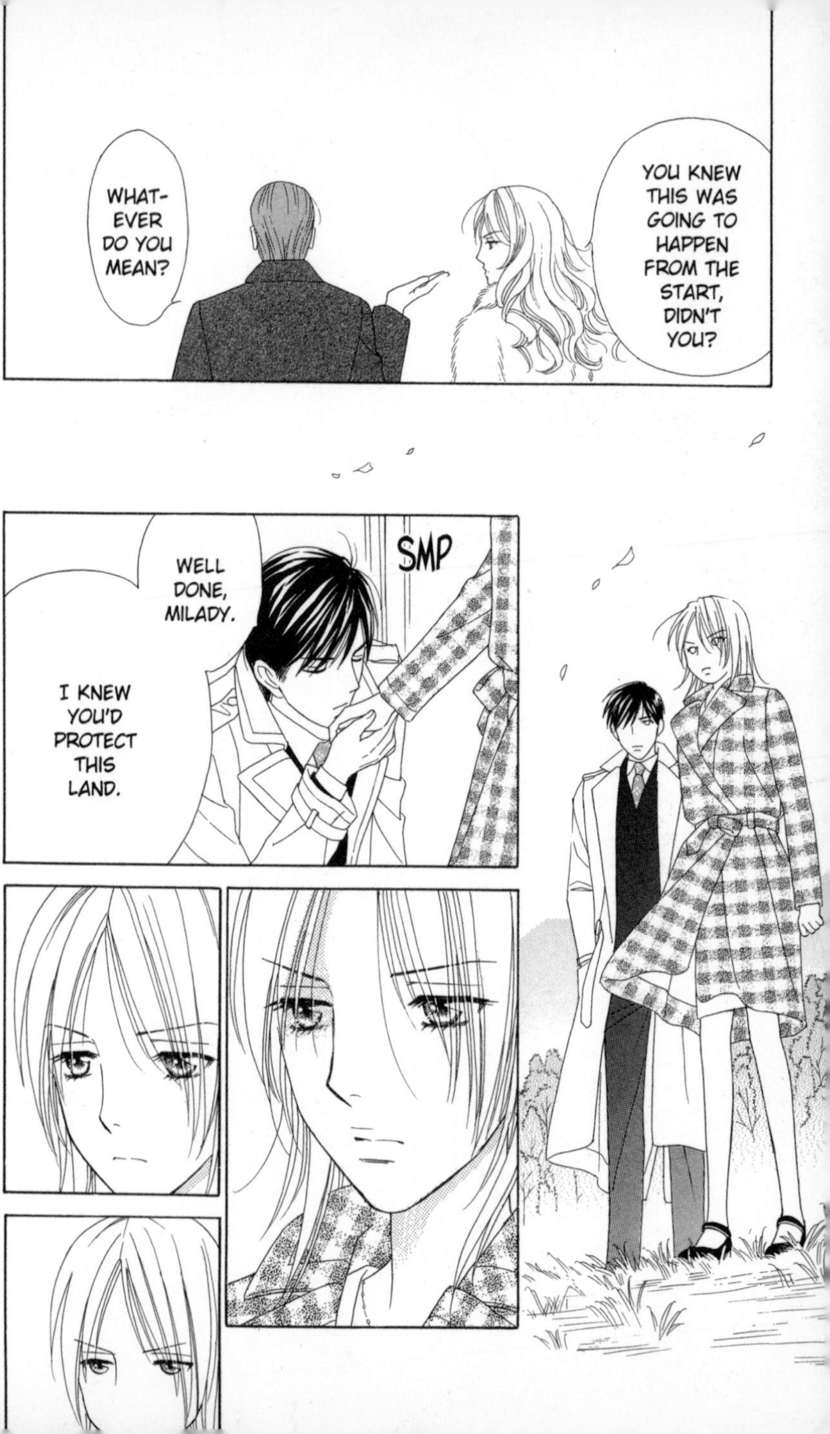
YOU KNEW THIS WAS GOING TO HAPPEN FROM THE START, DIDN'T YOU?
WHAT-EVER DO YOU MEAN?
SMP
WELL DONE, MILADY.
I KNEW YOU'D PROTECT THIS LAND.

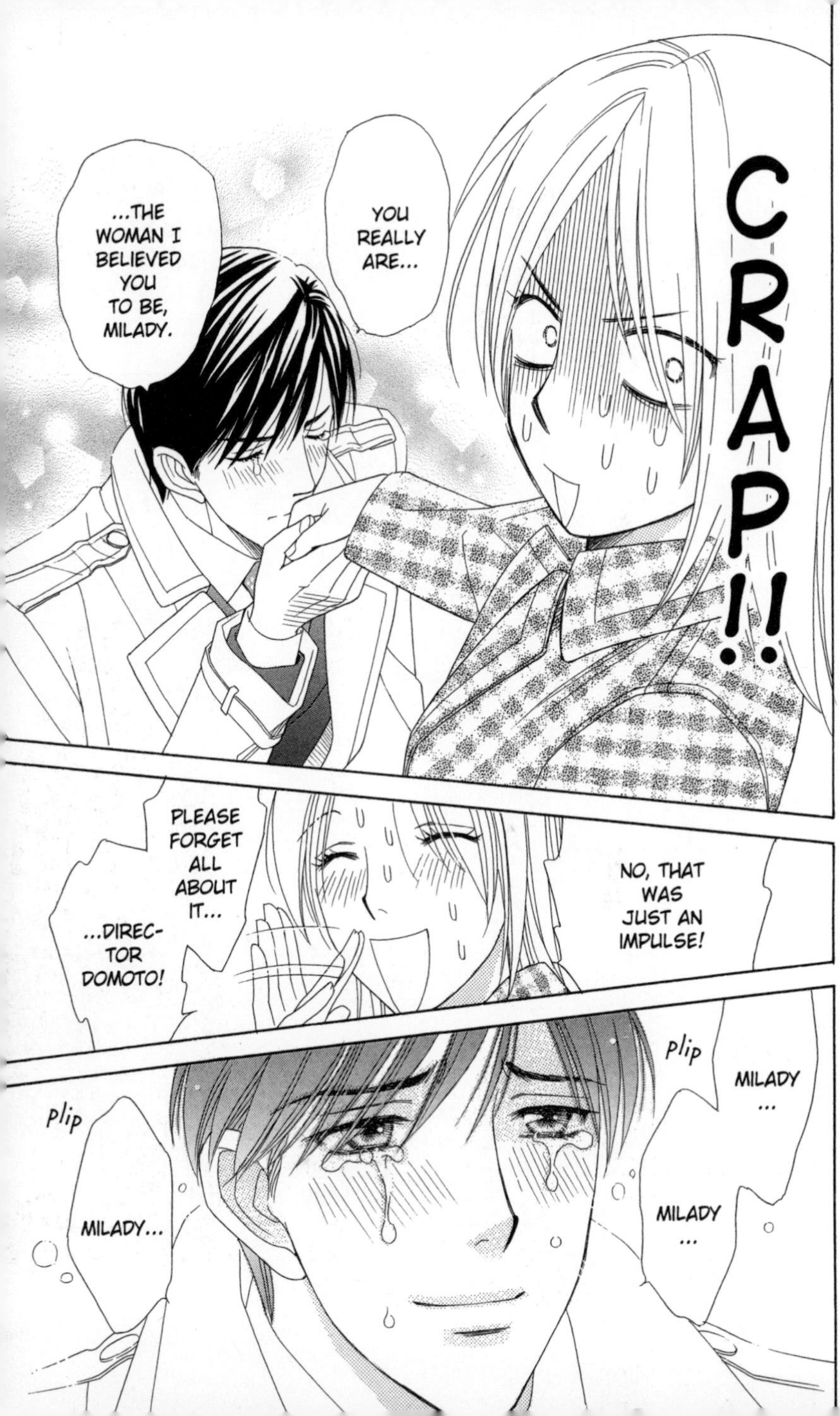
CRAP!!
YOU REALLY ARE...
...THE WOMAN I BELIEVED YOU TO BE, MILADY.
NO, THAT WAS JUST AN IMPULSE!
PLEASE FORGET ALL ABOUT IT...
...DIRECTOR DOMOTO!
plip
MILADY...
MILADY...
plip
MILADY...

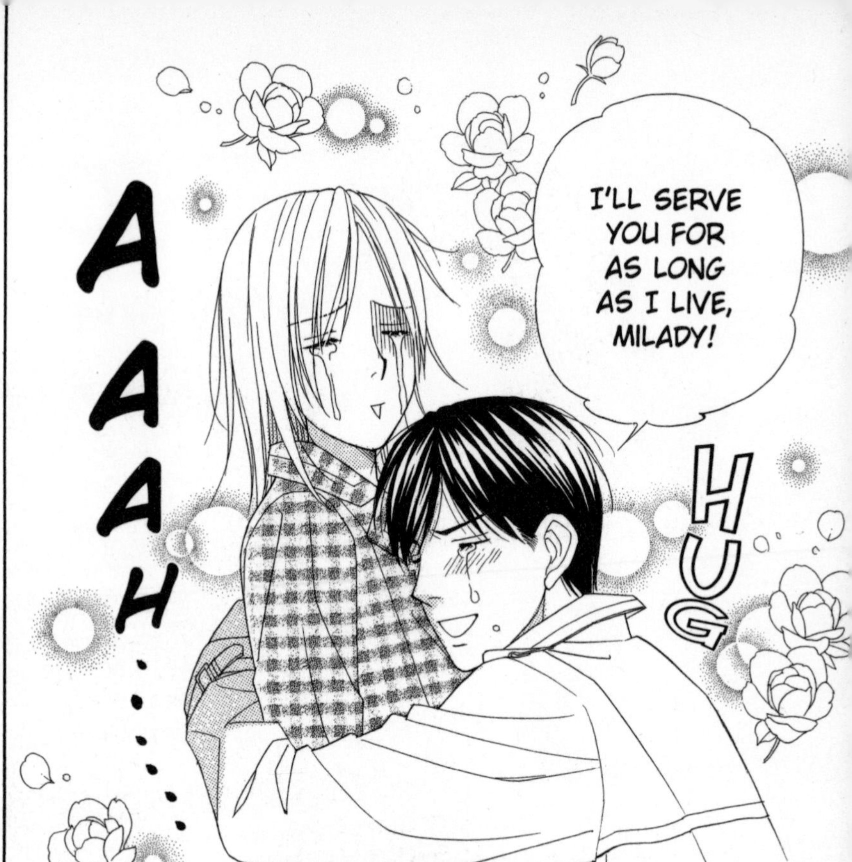
I'LL SERVE YOU FOR AS LONG AS I LIVE, MILADY!
HUG
AAAH.....

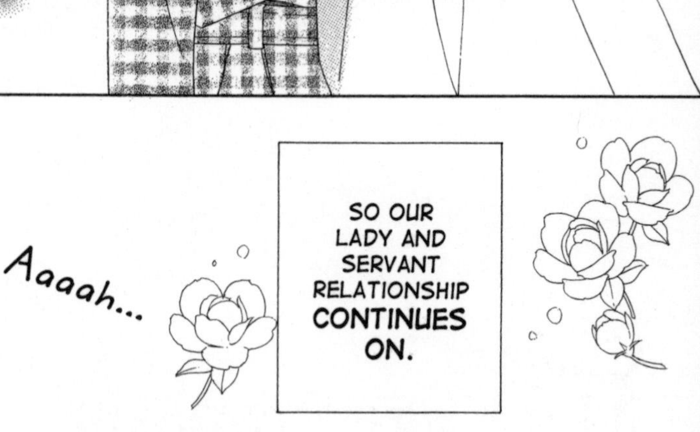
SO OUR LADY AND SERVANT RELATIONSHIP CONTINUES ON.
Aaaah...

Chapter 38: An Important Place/End

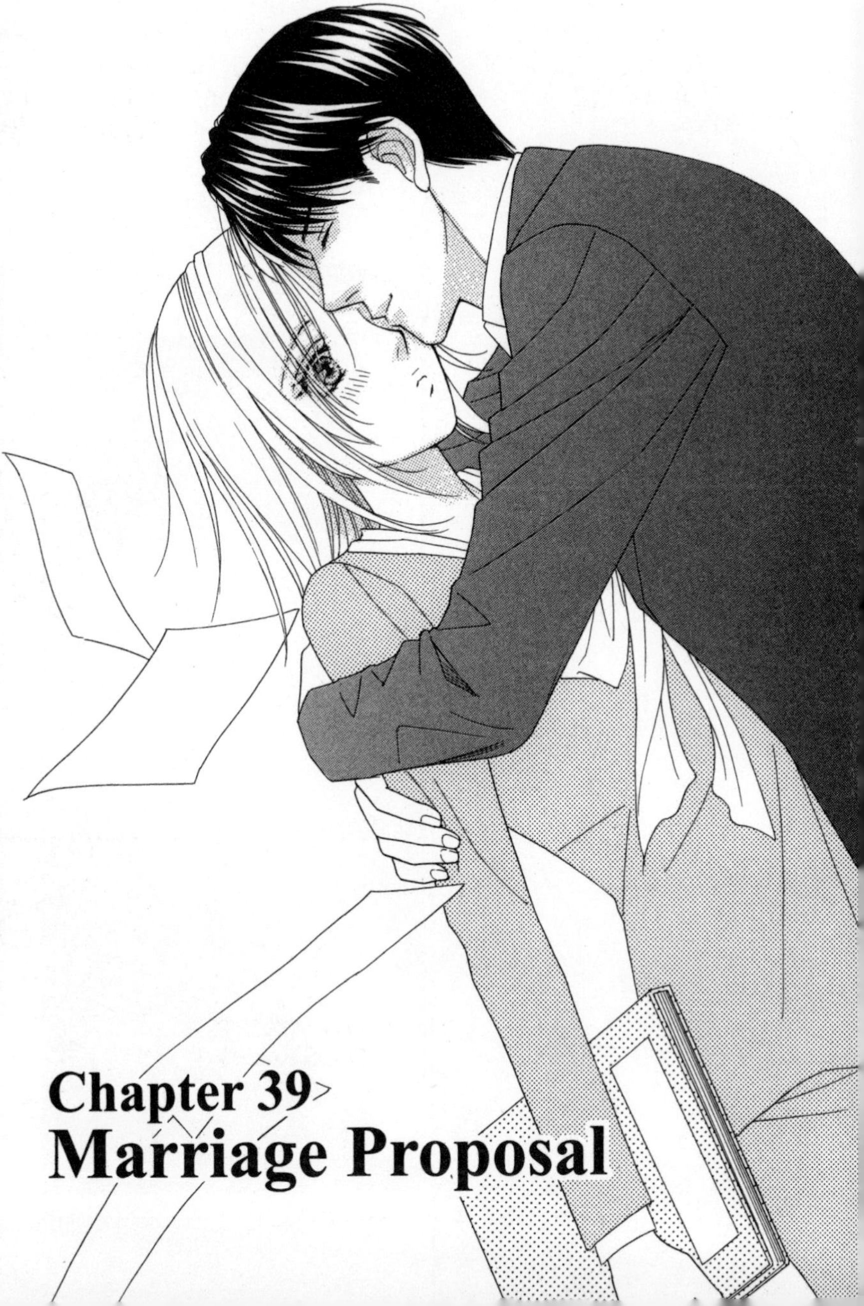

Chapter 39
Marriage Proposal

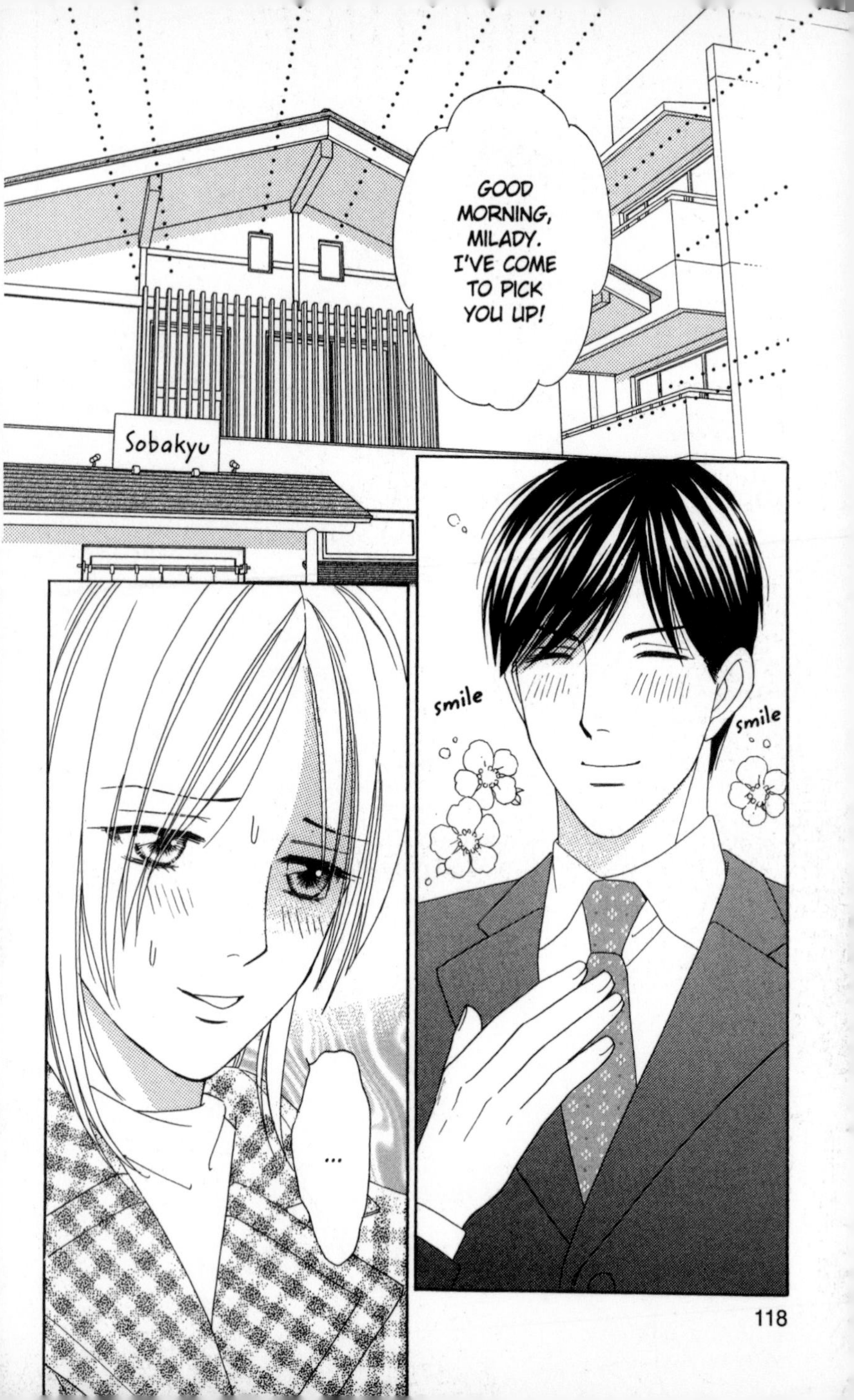
GOOD MORNING, MILADY. I'VE COME TO PICK YOU UP!
Sobakyu
smile
smile
...

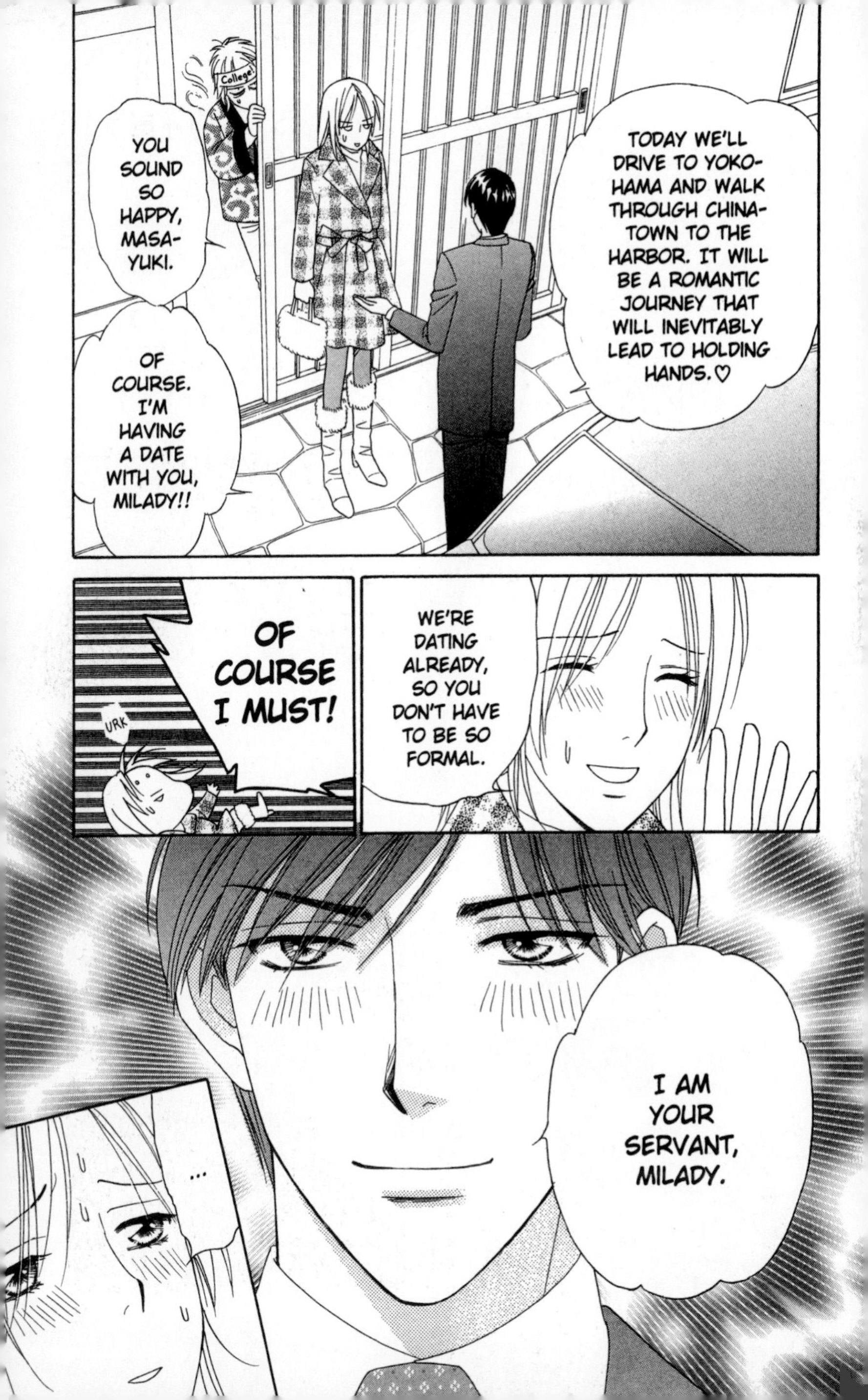
College!
TODAY WE'LL DRIVE TO YOKO-HAMA AND WALK THROUGH CHINA-TOWN TO THE HARBOR. IT WILL BE A ROMANTIC JOURNEY THAT WILL INEVITABLY LEAD TO HOLDING HANDS. ♡
YOU SOUND SO HAPPY, MASA-YUKI.
OF COURSE. I'M HAVING A DATE WITH YOU, MILADY!!
WE'RE DATING ALREADY, SO YOU DON'T HAVE TO BE SO FORMAL.
OF COURSE I MUST!
URK
I AM YOUR SERVANT, MILADY.
...

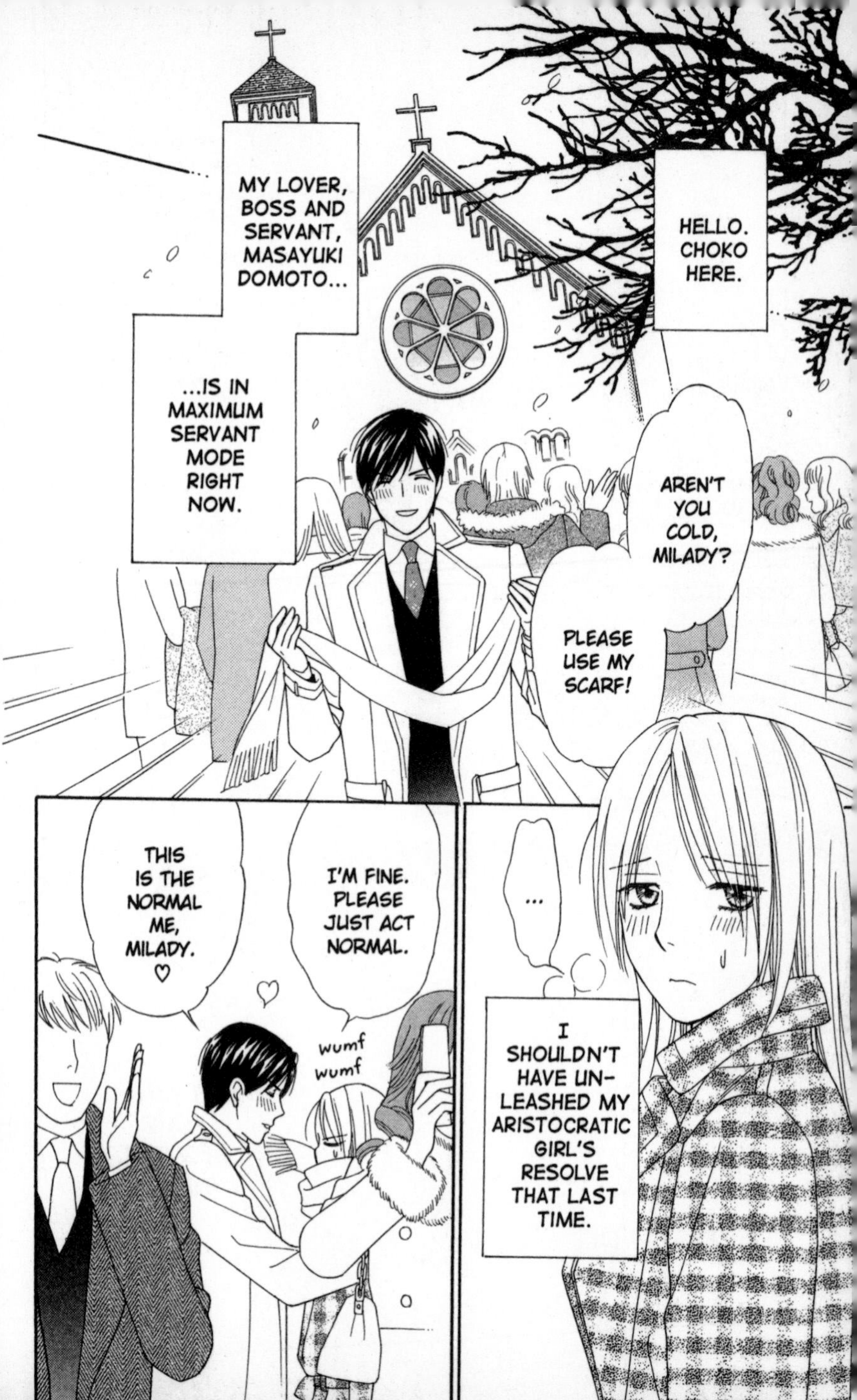
HELLO. CHOKO HERE.
MY LOVER, BOSS AND SERVANT, MASAYUKI DOMOTO...
...IS IN MAXIMUM SERVANT MODE RIGHT NOW.
AREN'T YOU COLD, MILADY?
PLEASE USE MY SCARF!
...
I SHOULDN'T HAVE UN-LEASHED MY ARISTOCRATIC GIRL'S RESOLVE THAT LAST TIME.
I'M FINE. PLEASE JUST ACT NORMAL.
THIS IS THE NORMAL ME, MILADY. ♡
wumf wumf

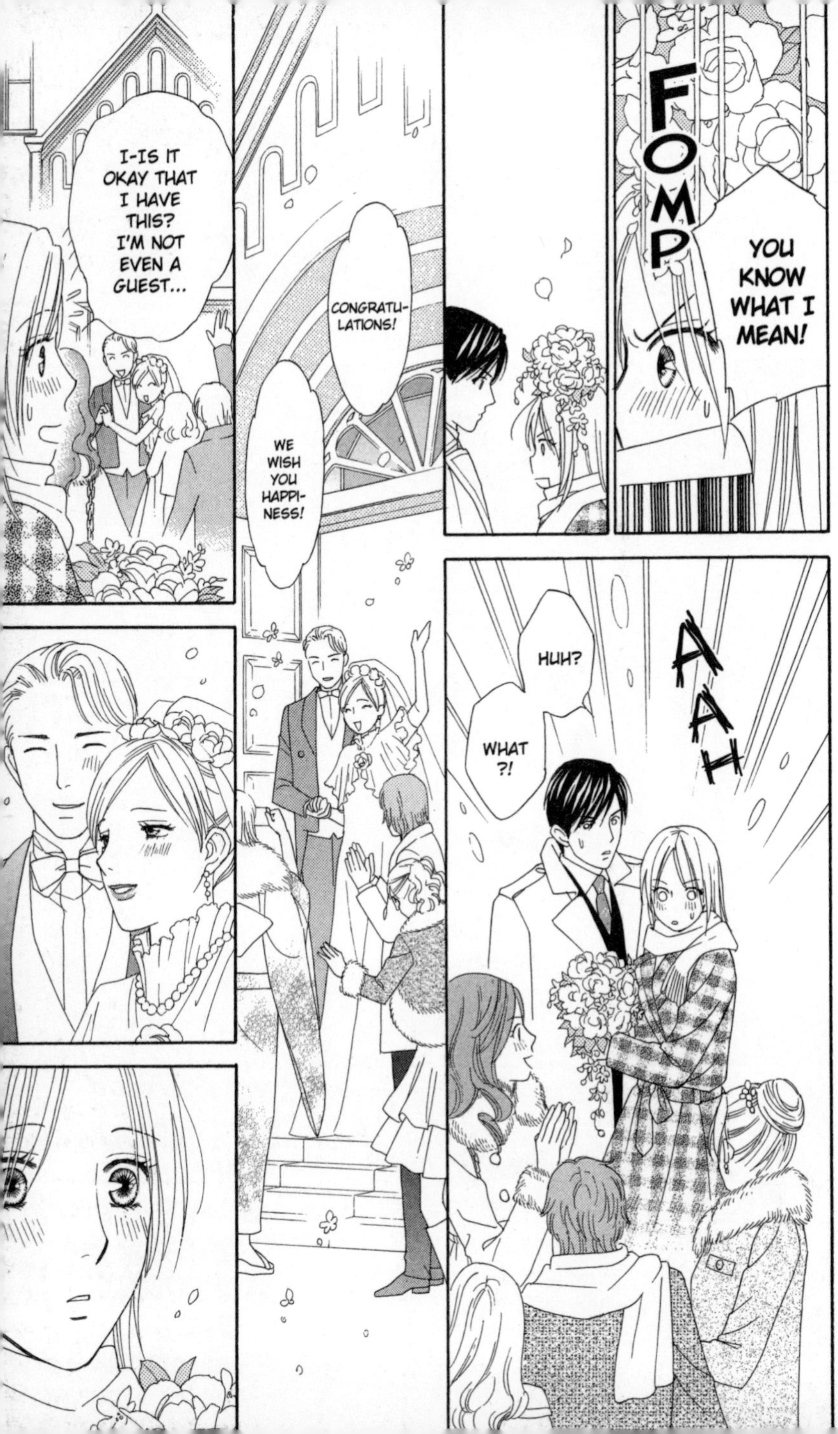
FOMP
YOU KNOW WHAT I MEAN!
HUH?
WHAT?!
AAAH
CONGRATULATIONS!
WE WISH YOU HAPPINESS!
I-IS IT OKAY THAT I HAVE THIS? I'M NOT EVEN A GUEST...

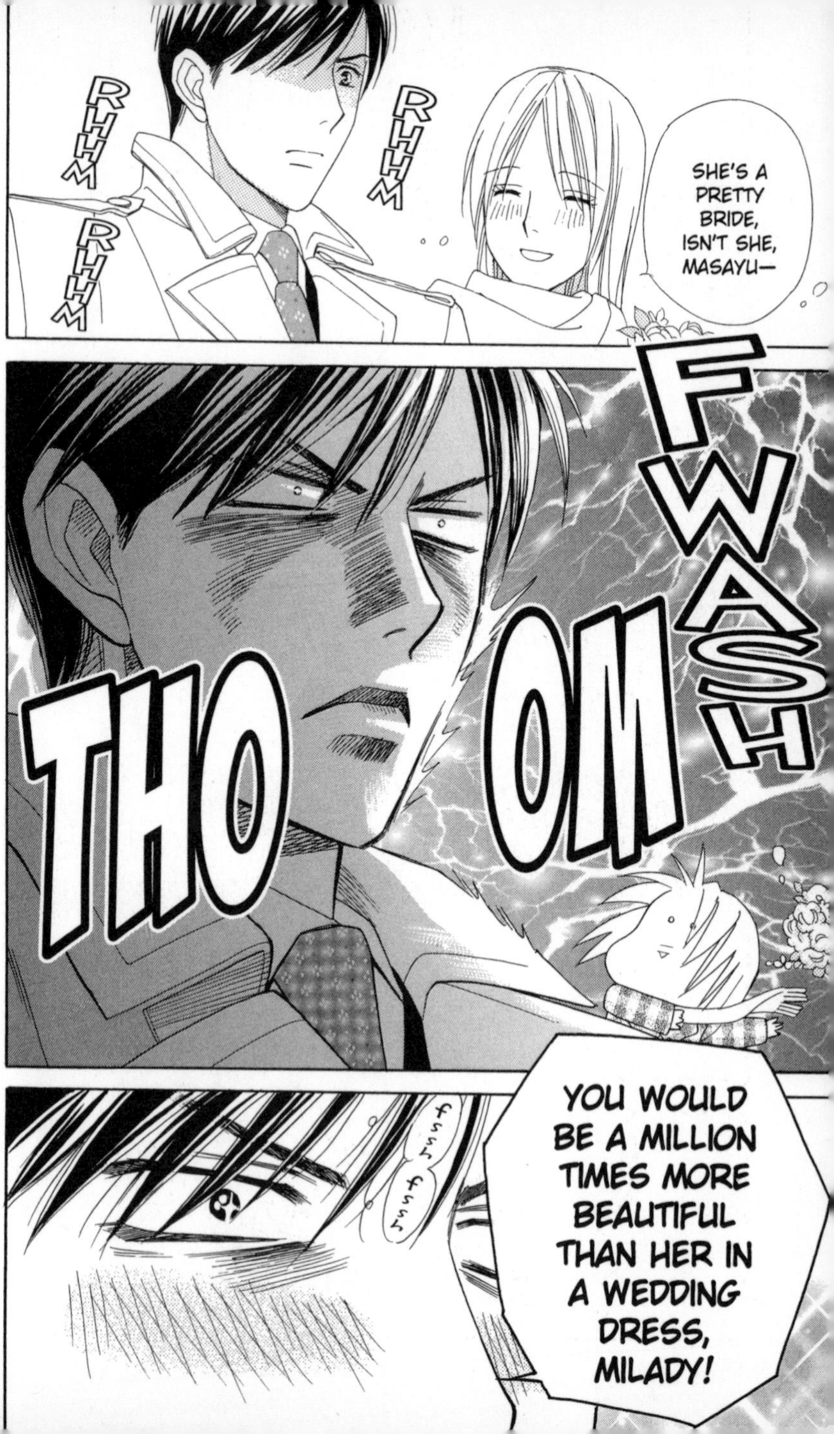
SHE'S A PRETTY BRIDE, ISN'T SHE, MASAYU—
RHHHM
RHHHM
RHHHM
FWASH
THOOM
YOU WOULD BE A MILLION TIMES MORE BEAUTIFUL THAN HER IN A WEDDING DRESS, MILADY!
fsss
fsss

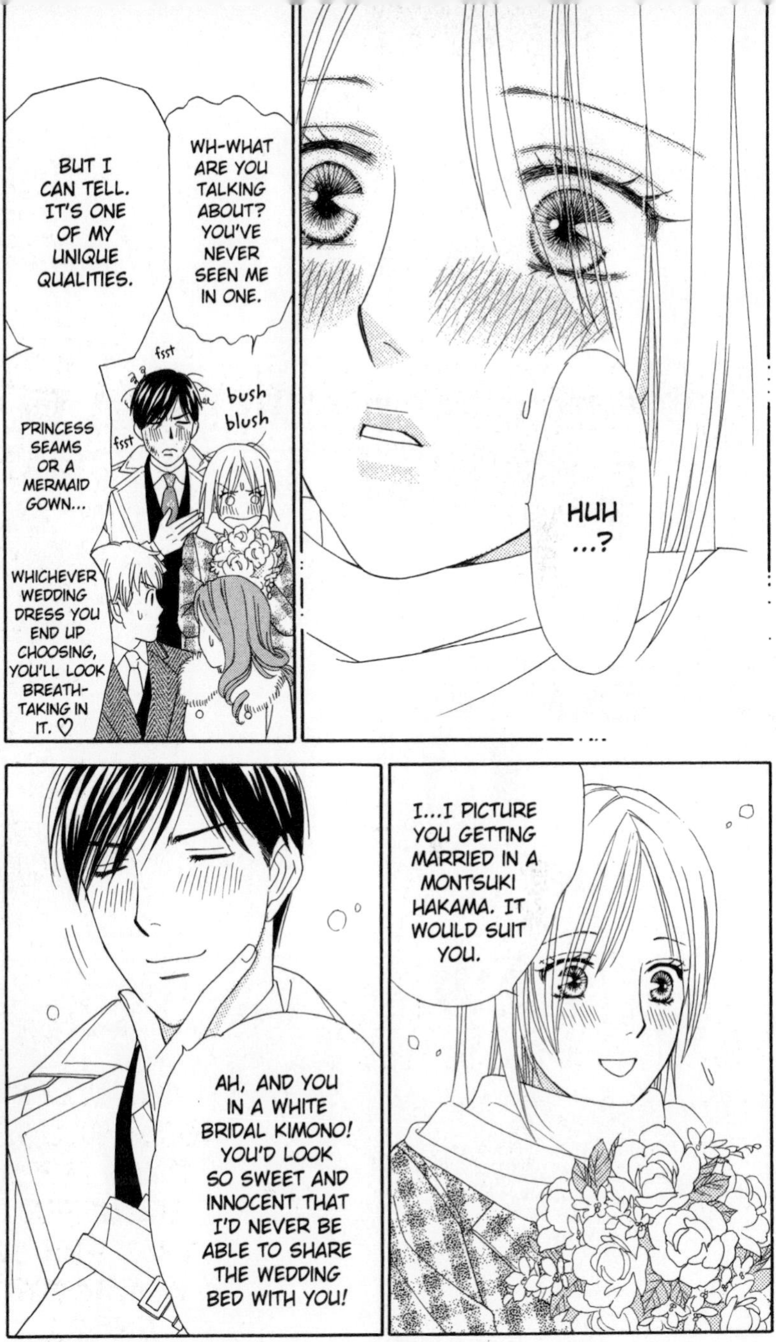
HUH ...?
WH-WHAT ARE YOU TALKING ABOUT? YOU'VE NEVER SEEN ME IN ONE.
BUT I CAN TELL. IT'S ONE OF MY UNIQUE QUALITIES.
fsst
bush blush
fsst
PRINCESS SEAMS OR A MERMAID GOWN...
WHICHEVER WEDDING DRESS YOU END UP CHOOSING, YOU'LL LOOK BREATH-TAKING IN IT. ♡
I...I PICTURE YOU GETTING MARRIED IN A MONTSUKI HAKAMA. IT WOULD SUIT YOU.
AH, AND YOU IN A WHITE BRIDAL KIMONO! YOU'D LOOK SO SWEET AND INNOCENT THAT I'D NEVER BE ABLE TO SHARE THE WEDDING BED WITH YOU!

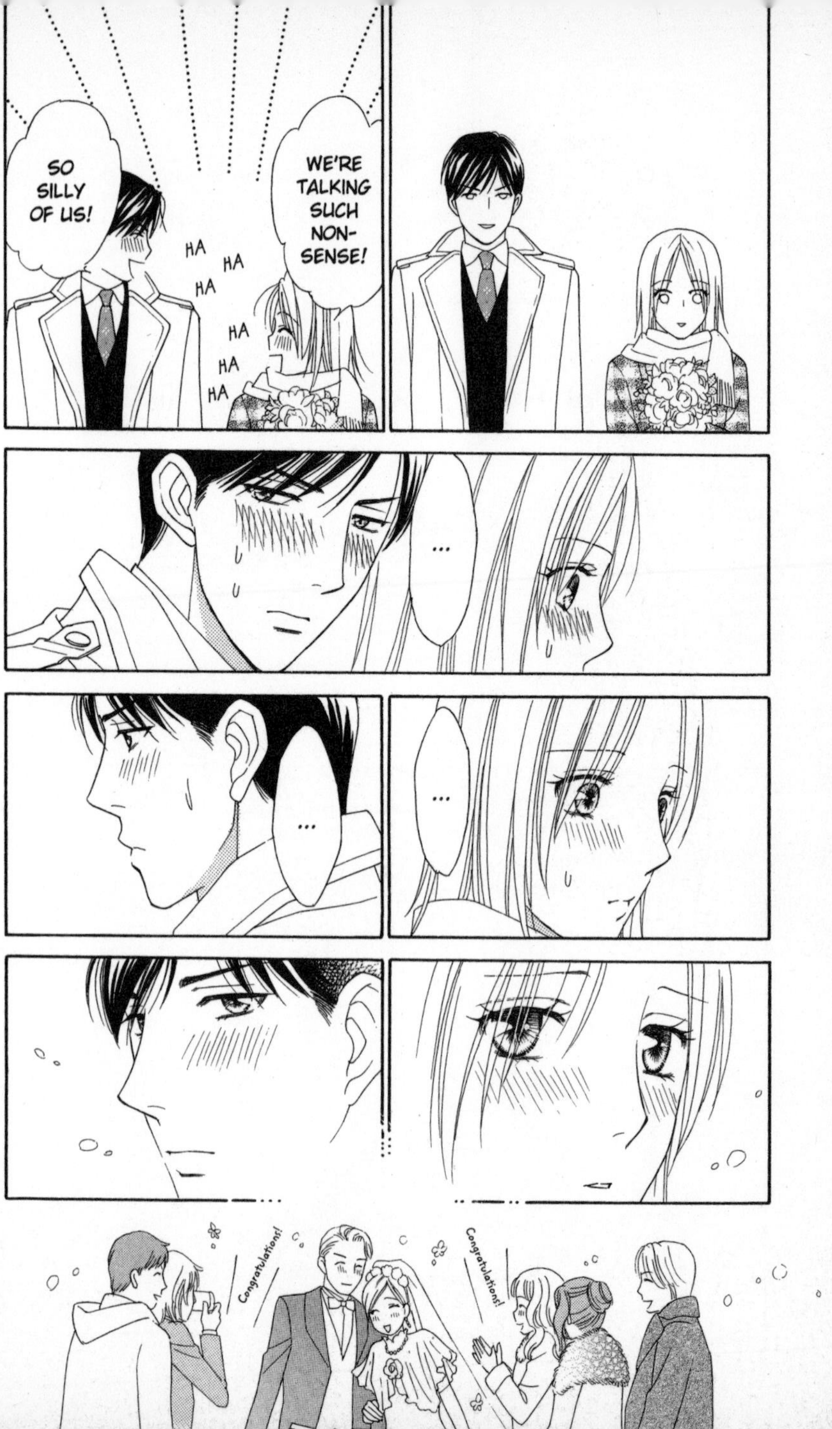
WE'RE TALKING SUCH NON-SENSE!
HA HA HA HA HA HA
SO SILLY OF US!
...
...
...
Congratulations!
Congratulations!

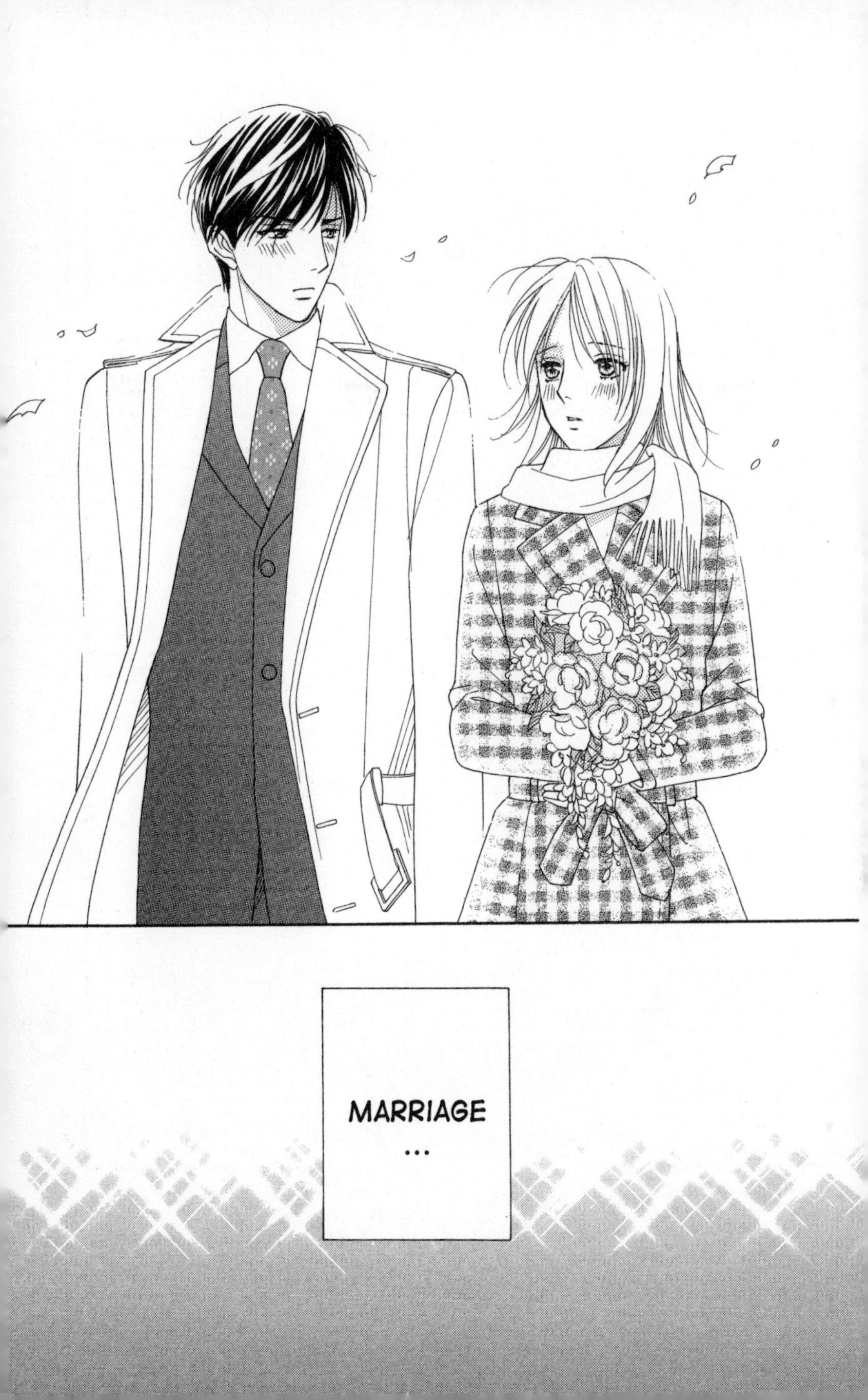
MARRIAGE
...

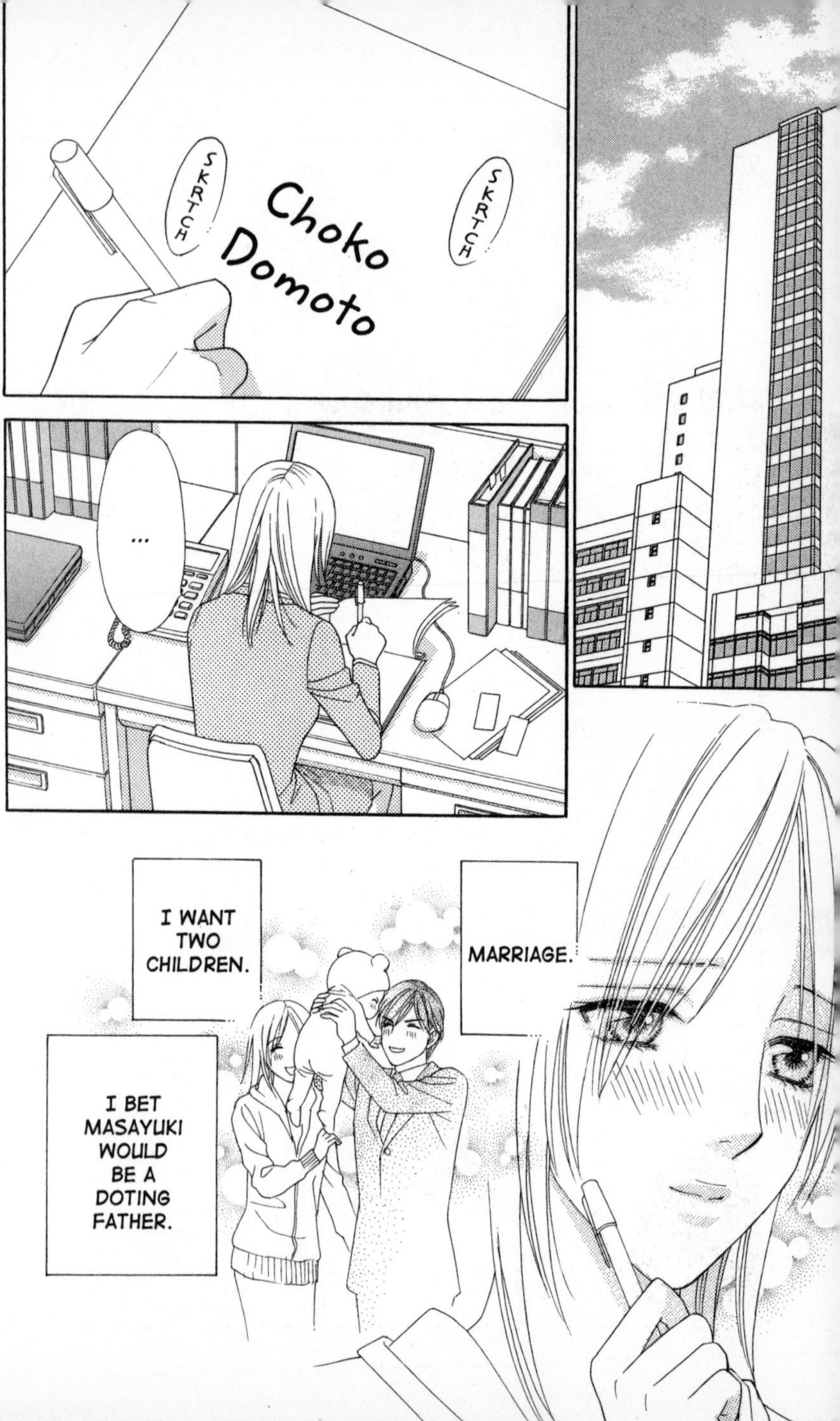
SKRTCH
Choko Domoto
SKRTCH
...
MARRIAGE.
I WANT TWO CHILDREN.
I BET MASAYUKI WOULD BE A DOTING FATHER.

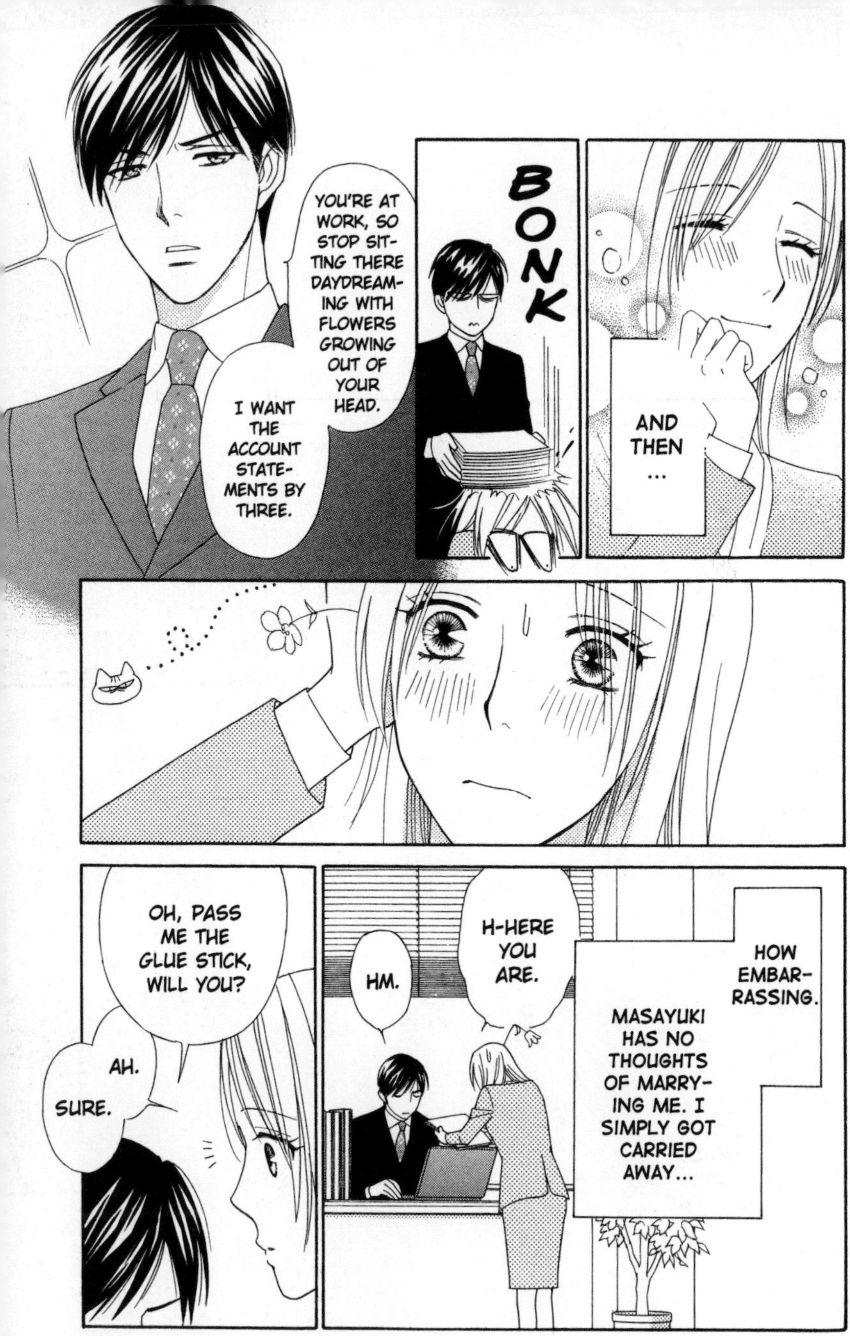
AND THEN ...
BONK
YOU'RE AT WORK, SO STOP SITTING THERE DAYDREAMING WITH FLOWERS GROWING OUT OF YOUR HEAD.
I WANT THE ACCOUNT STATEMENTS BY THREE.
HOW EMBARRASSING.
MASAYUKI HAS NO THOUGHTS OF MARRYING ME. I SIMPLY GOT CARRIED AWAY...
H-HERE YOU ARE.
HM.
OH, PASS ME THE GLUE STICK, WILL YOU?
AH. SURE.

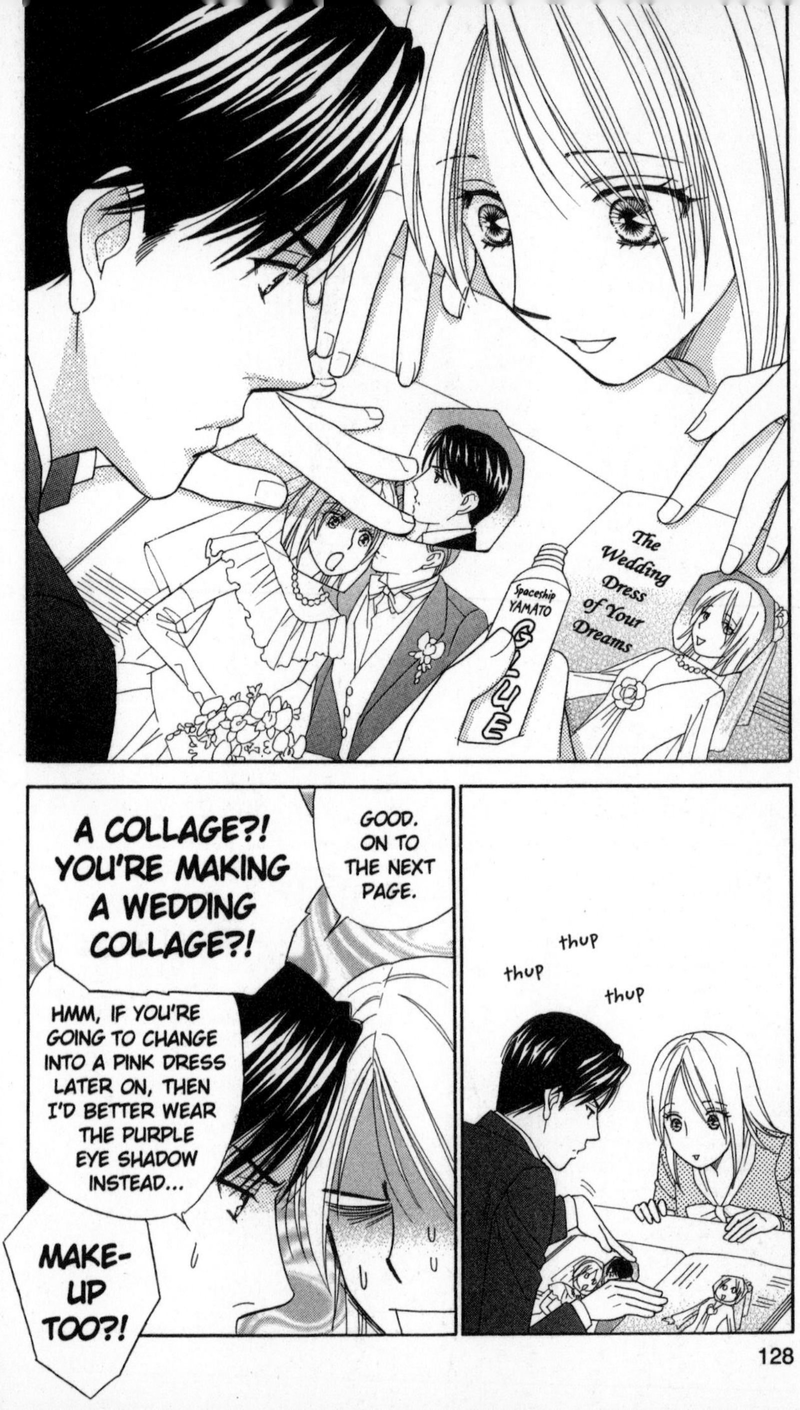
The Wedding Dress of Your Dreams
Spaceship YAMATO
GLUE
thup
thup
thup
GOOD. ON TO THE NEXT PAGE.
A COLLAGE?! YOU'RE MAKING A WEDDING COLLAGE?!
HMM, IF YOU'RE GOING TO CHANGE INTO A PINK DRESS LATER ON, THEN I'D BETTER WEAR THE PURPLE EYE SHADOW INSTEAD...
MAKE-UP TOO?!

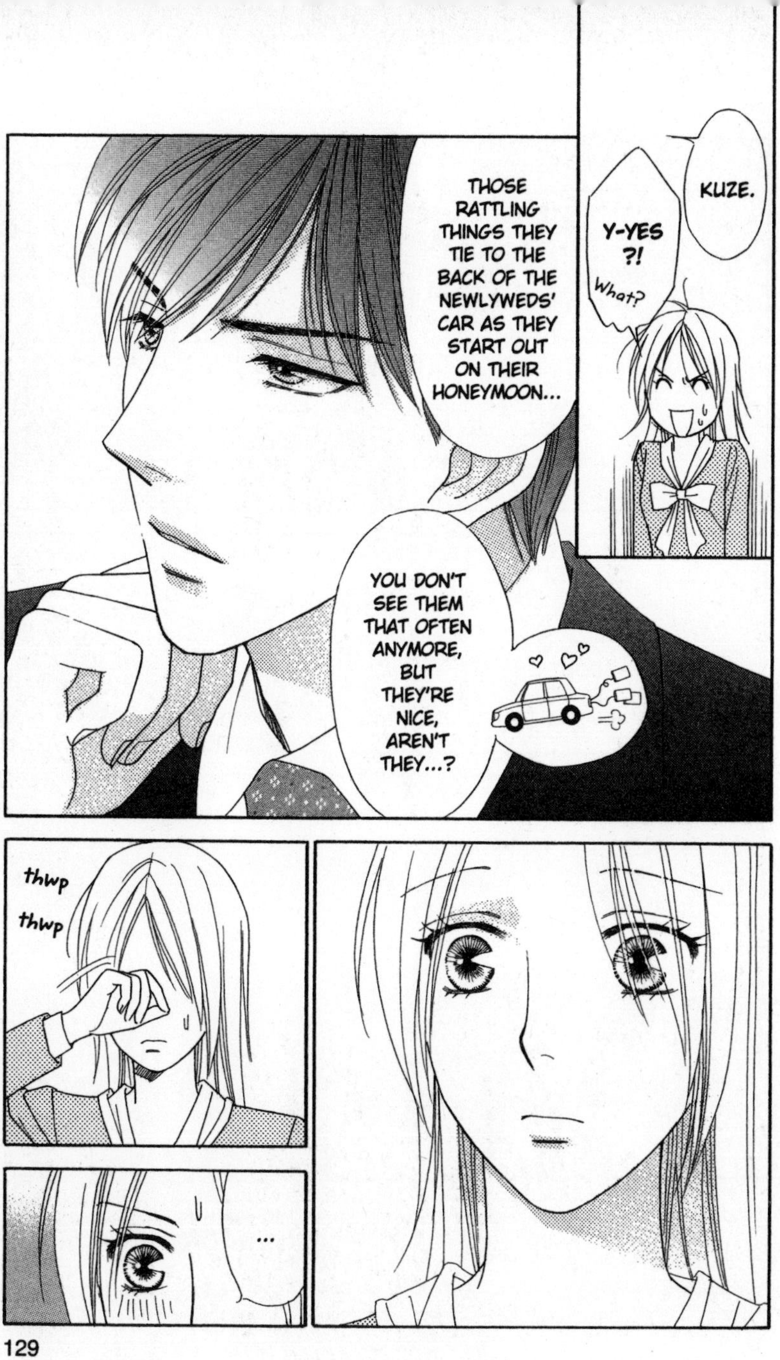
KUZE.
Y-YES ?!
What?
THOSE RATTLING THINGS THEY TIE TO THE BACK OF THE NEWLYWEDS' CAR AS THEY START OUT ON THEIR HONEYMOON...
YOU DON'T SEE THEM THAT OFTEN ANYMORE, BUT THEY'RE NICE, AREN'T THEY...?
thwp
thwp
...

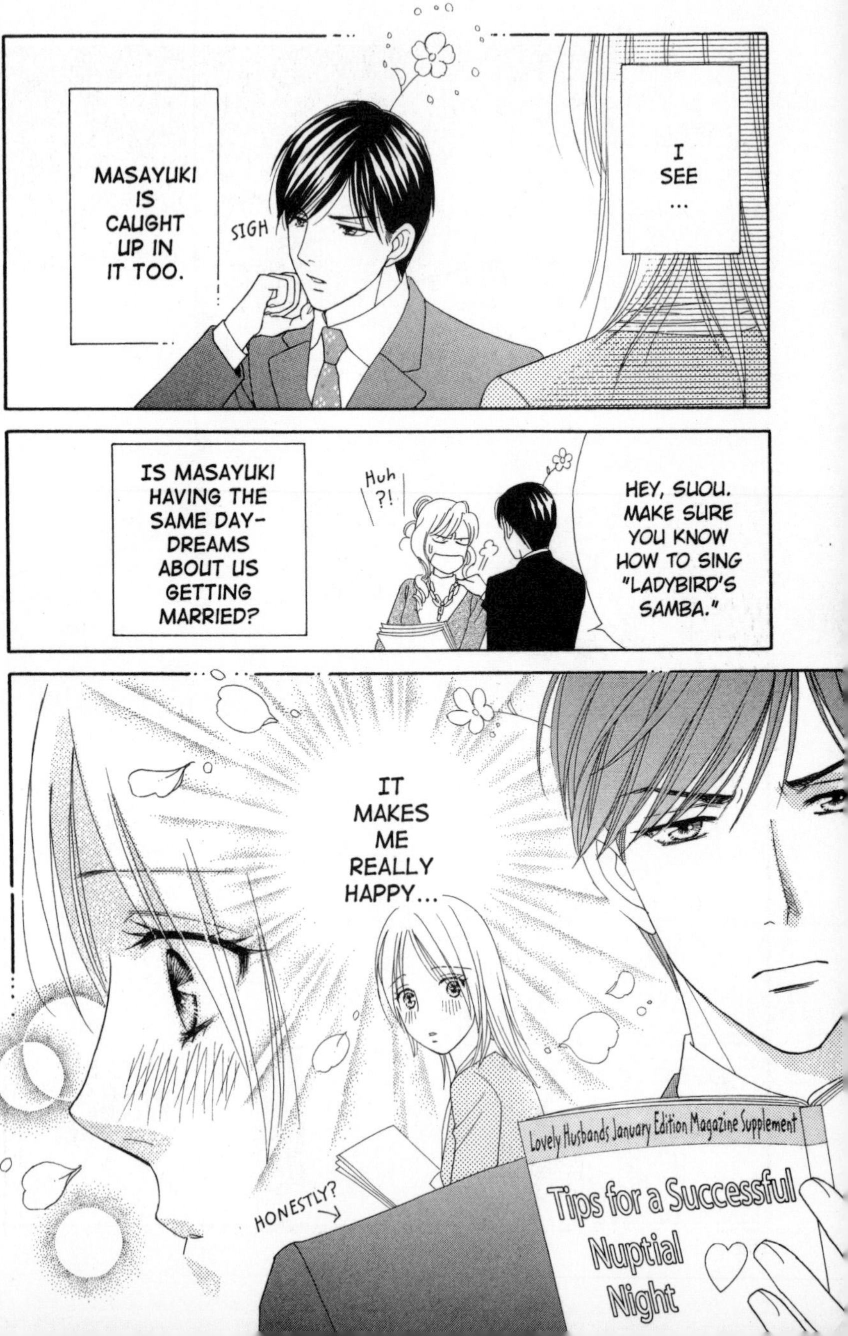
I SEE ...
SIGH
MASAYUKI IS CAUGHT UP IN IT TOO.
HEY, SUOU. MAKE SURE YOU KNOW HOW TO SING "LADYBIRD'S SAMBA."
Huh ?!
IS MASAYUKI HAVING THE SAME DAY-DREAMS ABOUT US GETTING MARRIED?
IT MAKES ME REALLY HAPPY...
Lovely Husbands January Edition Magazine Supplement
Tips for a Successful Nuptial Night
HONESTLY?

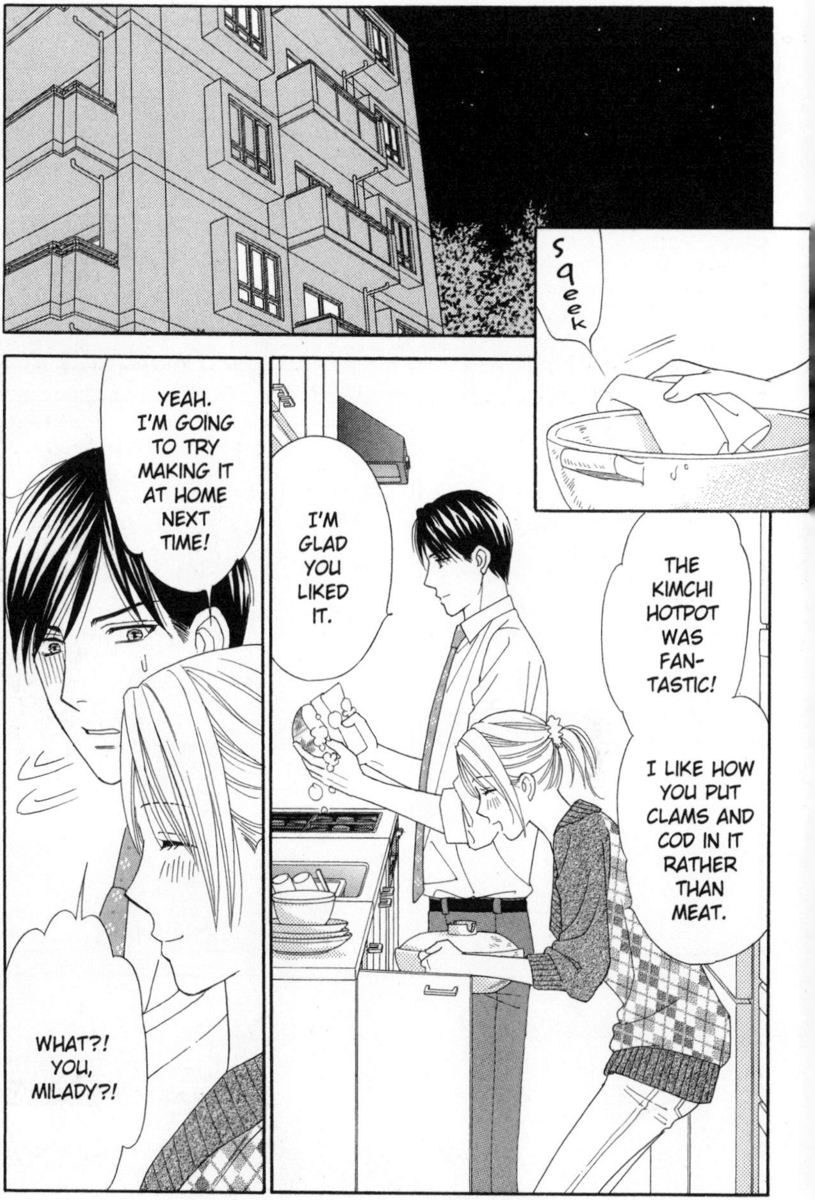
sqeek
THE KIMCHI HOTPOT WAS FAN-TASTIC!
I LIKE HOW YOU PUT CLAMS AND COD IN IT RATHER THAN MEAT.
I'M GLAD YOU LIKED IT.
YEAH. I'M GOING TO TRY MAKING IT AT HOME NEXT TIME!
WHAT?! YOU, MILADY?!

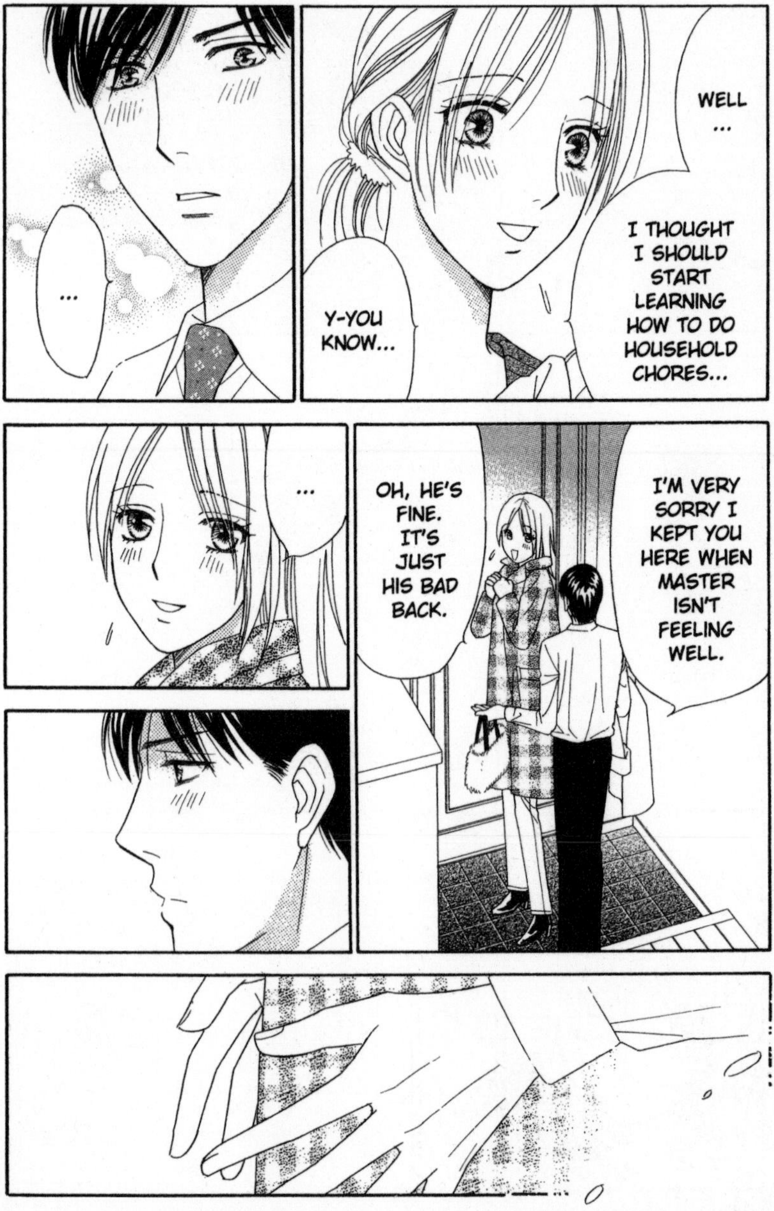
WELL ...
I THOUGHT I SHOULD START LEARNING HOW TO DO HOUSEHOLD CHORES...
Y-YOU KNOW...
...
I'M VERY SORRY I KEPT YOU HERE WHEN MASTER ISN'T FEELING WELL.
OH, HE'S FINE. IT'S JUST HIS BAD BACK.
...

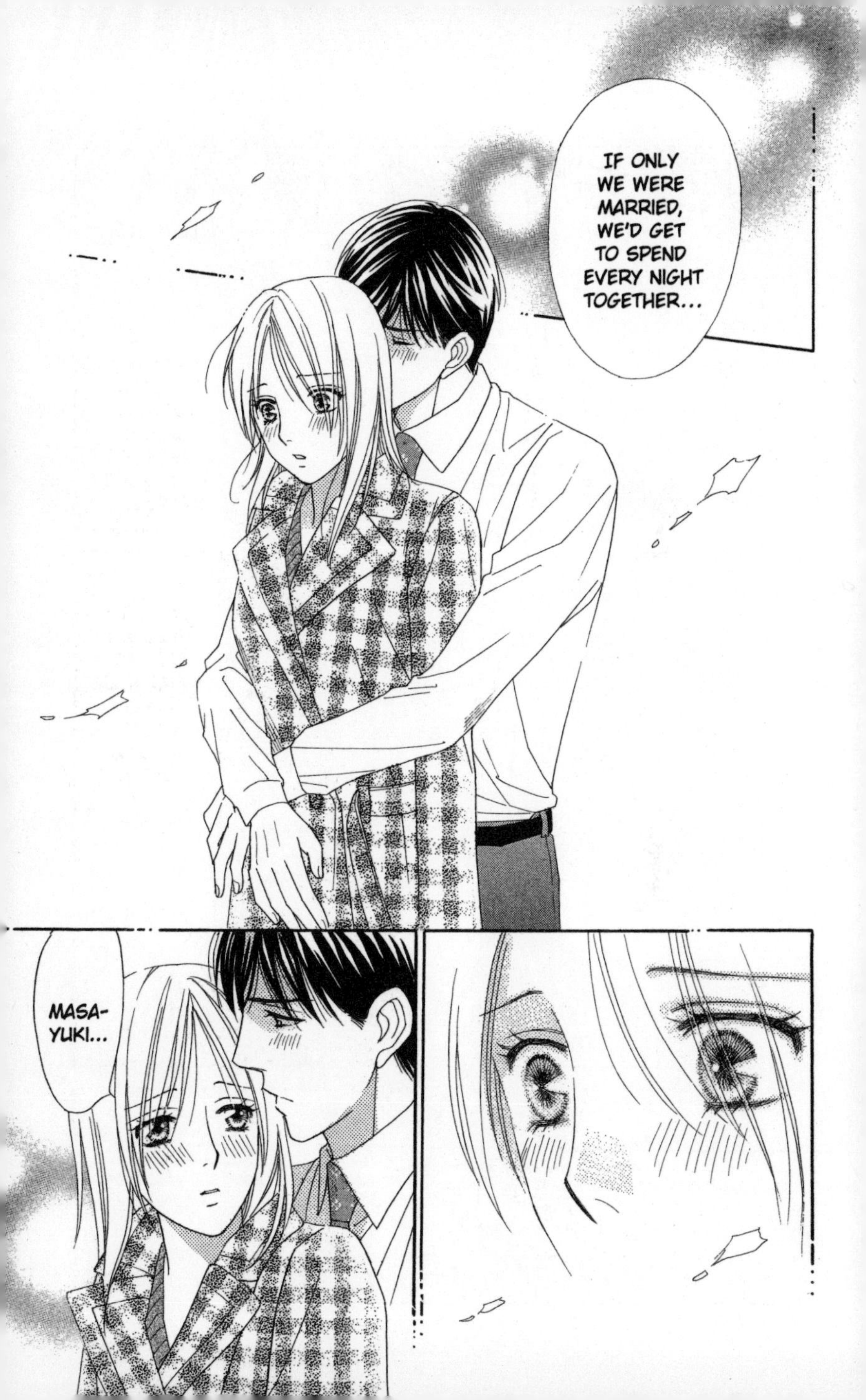
IF ONLY WE WERE MARRIED, WE'D GET TO SPEND EVERY NIGHT TOGETHER...
MASA-YUKI...

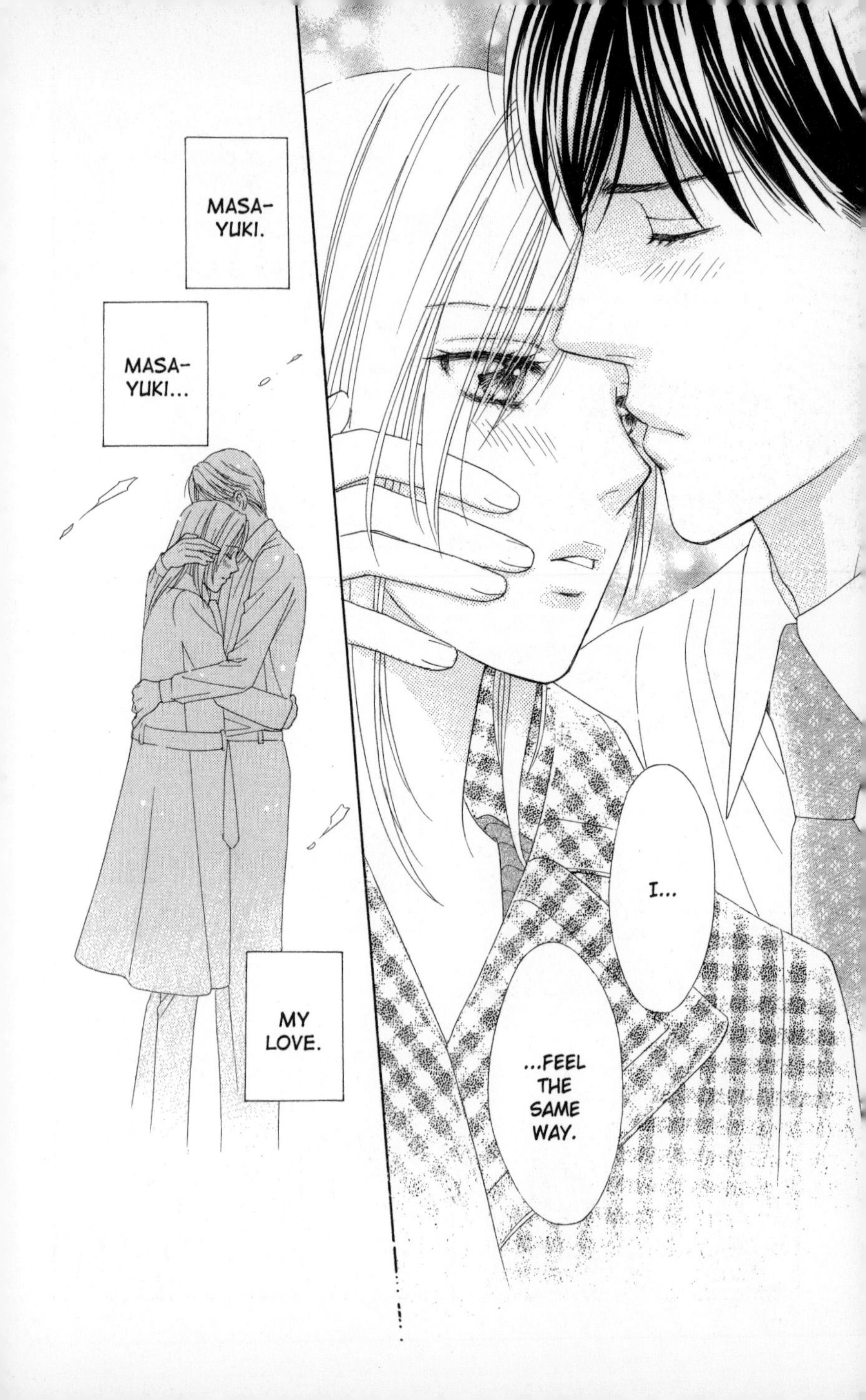
I...
...FEEL THE SAME WAY.
MASA-YUKI.
MASA-YUKI...
MY LOVE.

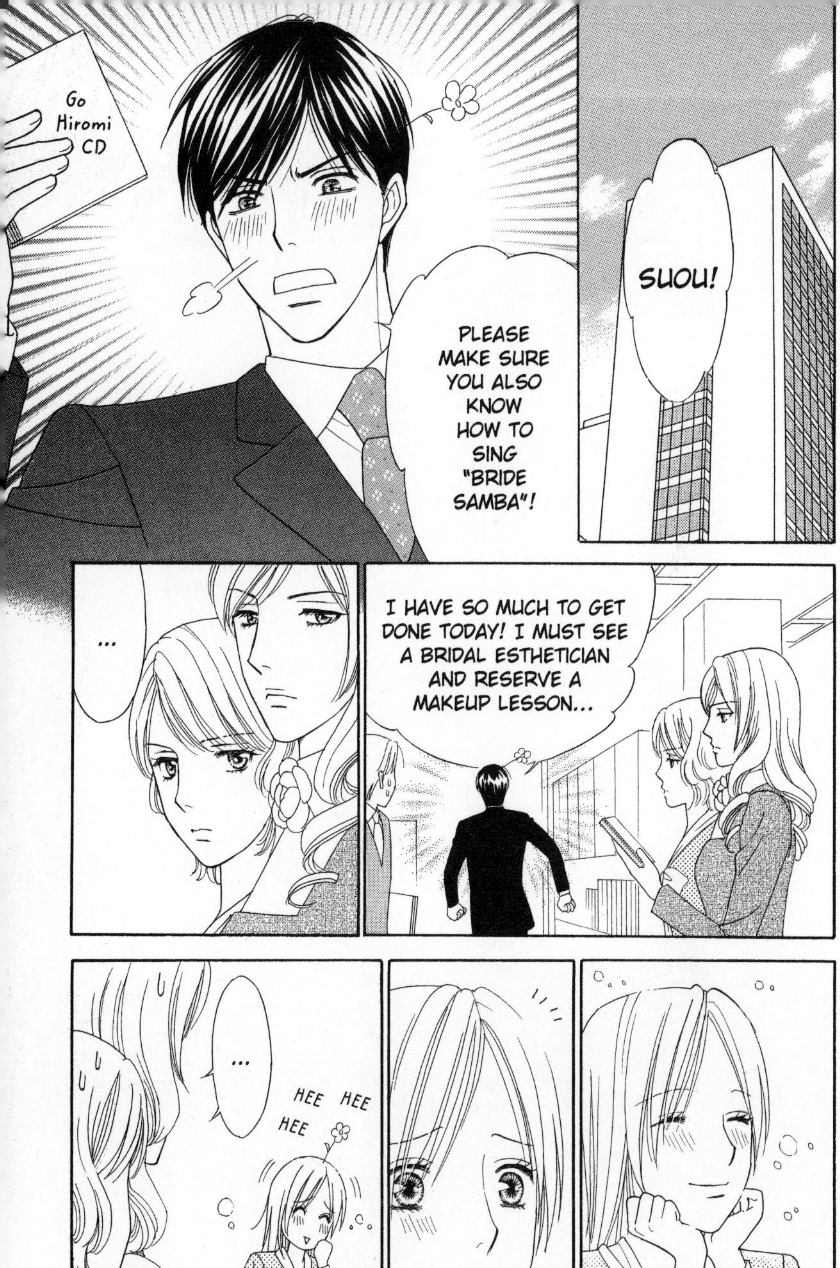
SUOU!
Go Hiromi CD
PLEASE MAKE SURE YOU ALSO KNOW HOW TO SING "BRIDE SAMBA"!
I HAVE SO MUCH TO GET DONE TODAY! I MUST SEE A BRIDAL ESTHETICIAN AND RESERVE A MAKEUP LESSON...
...
...
HEE HEE HEE

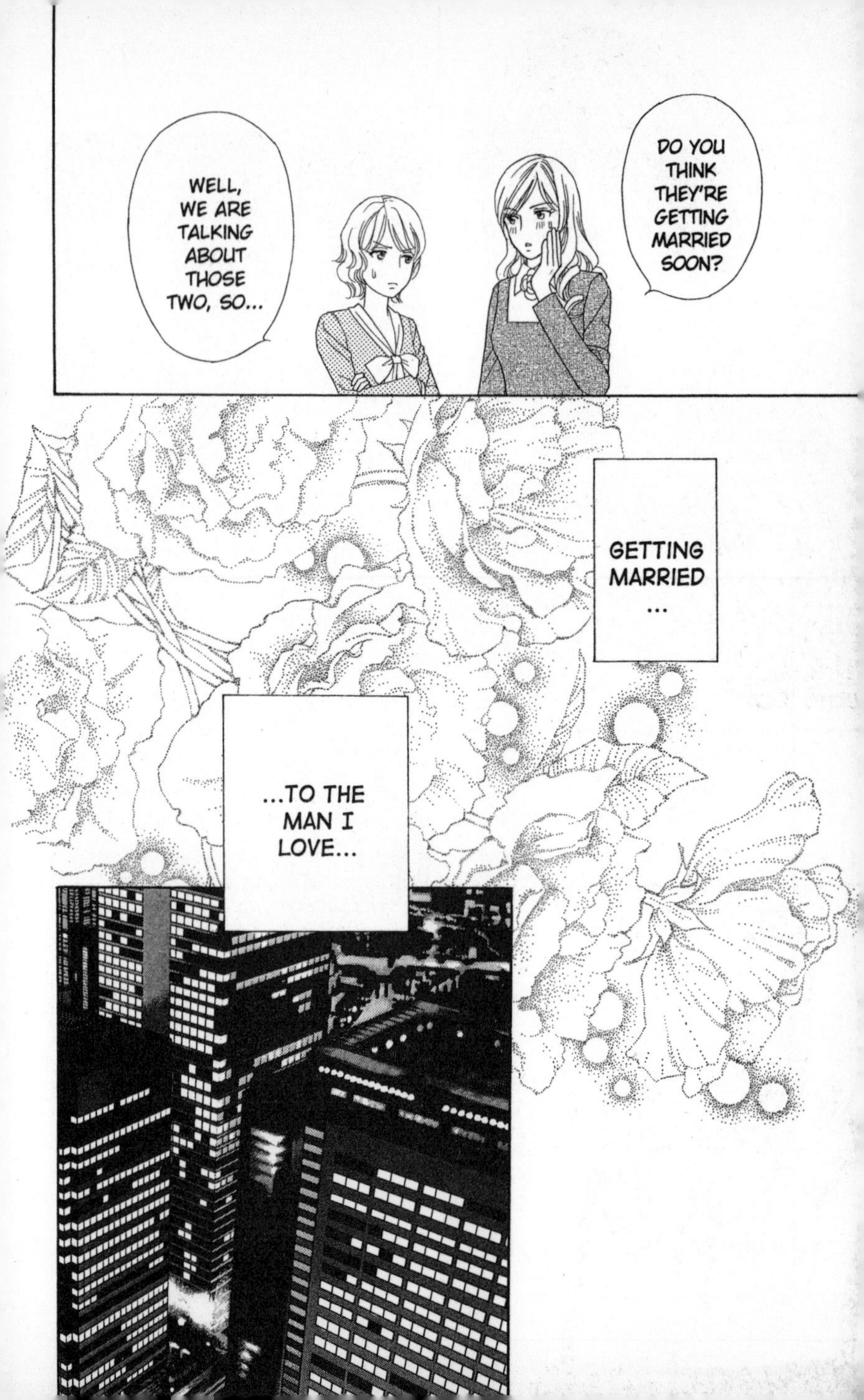
DO YOU THINK THEY'RE GETTING MARRIED SOON?
WELL, WE ARE TALKING ABOUT THOSE TWO, SO...
GETTING MARRIED ...
...TO THE MAN I LOVE...

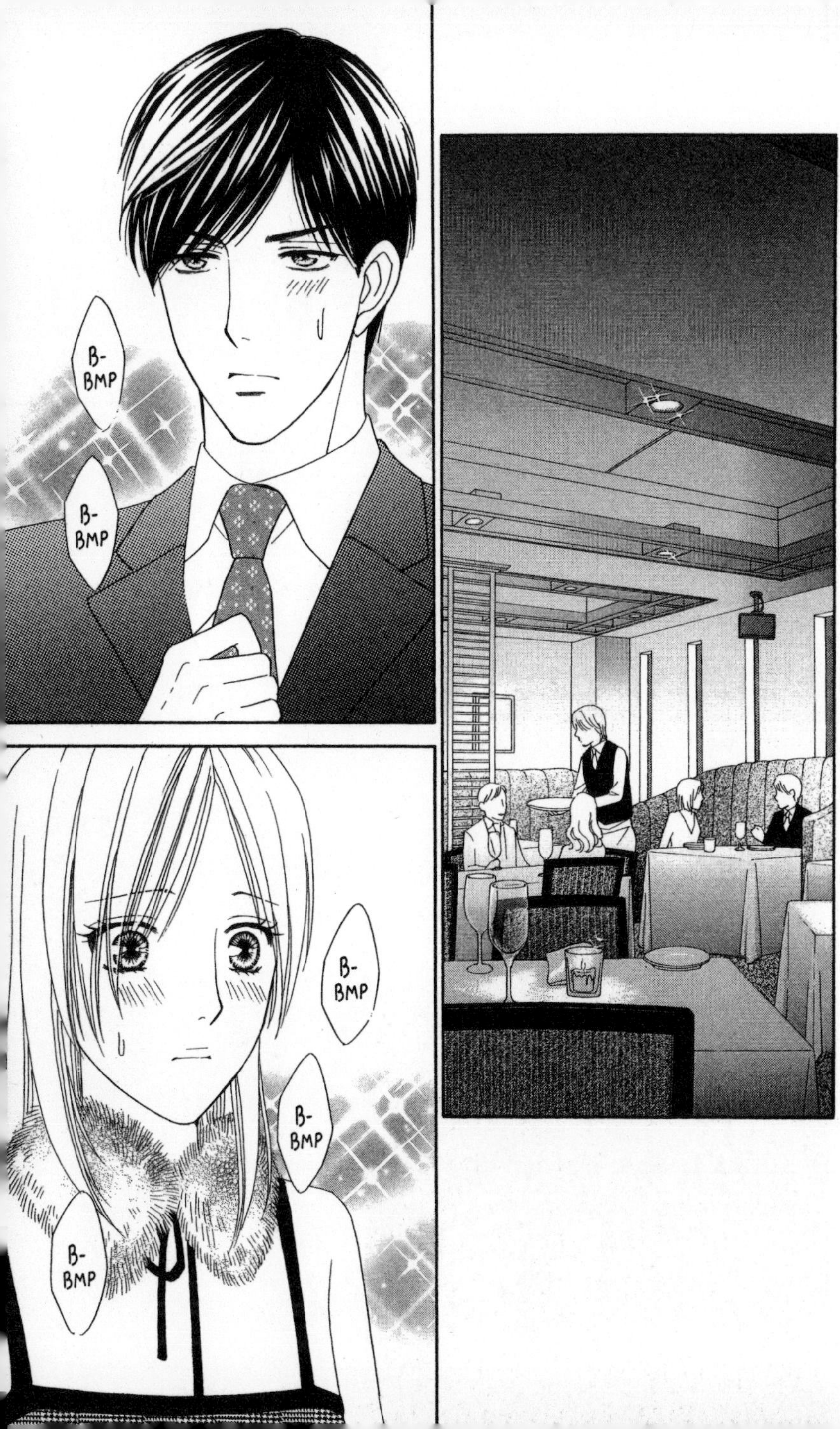
B-BMP
B-BMP
B-BMP
B-BMP
B-BMP

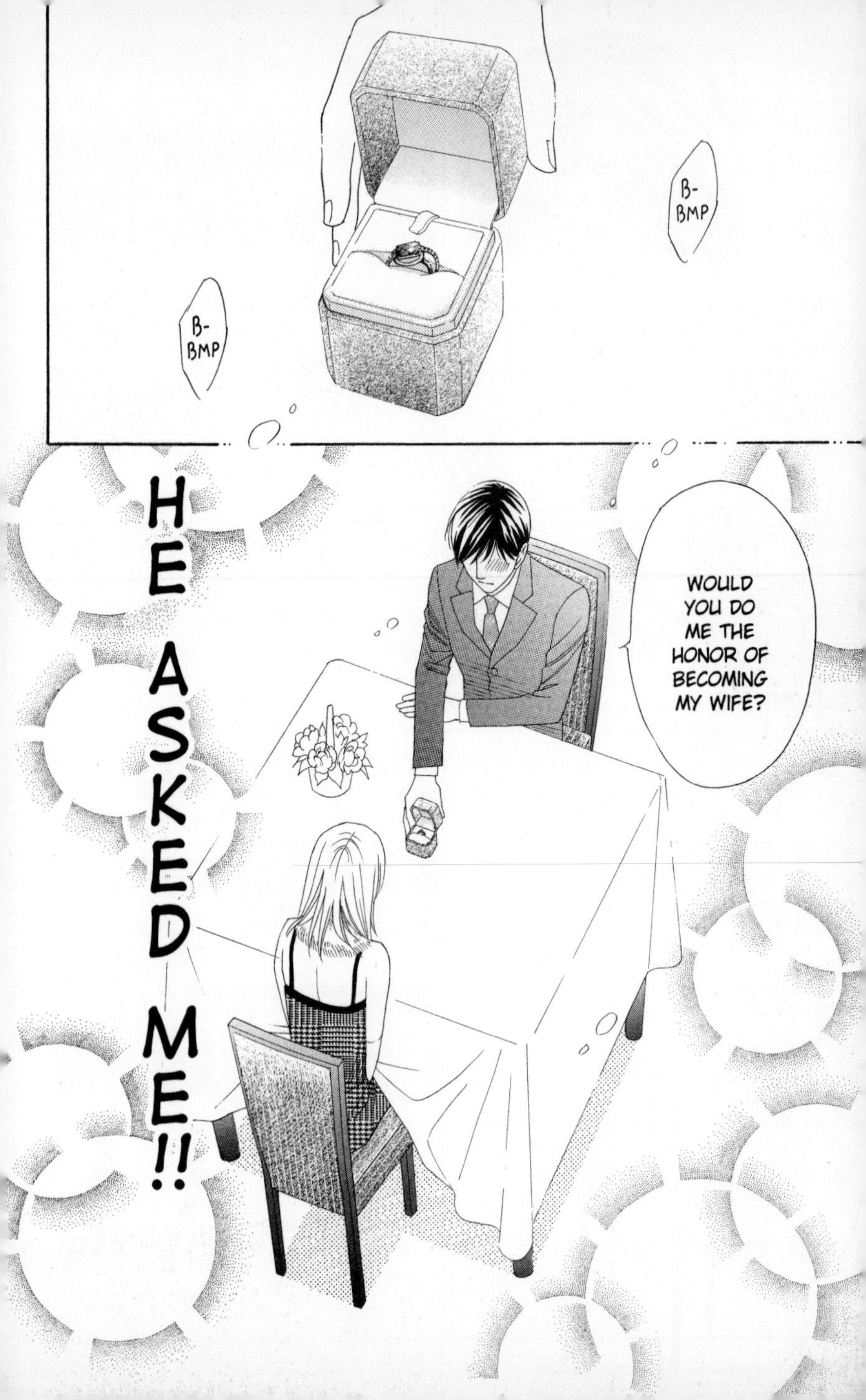
B-BMP
B-BMP
WOULD YOU DO ME THE HONOR OF BECOMING MY WIFE?
HE ASKED ME!!

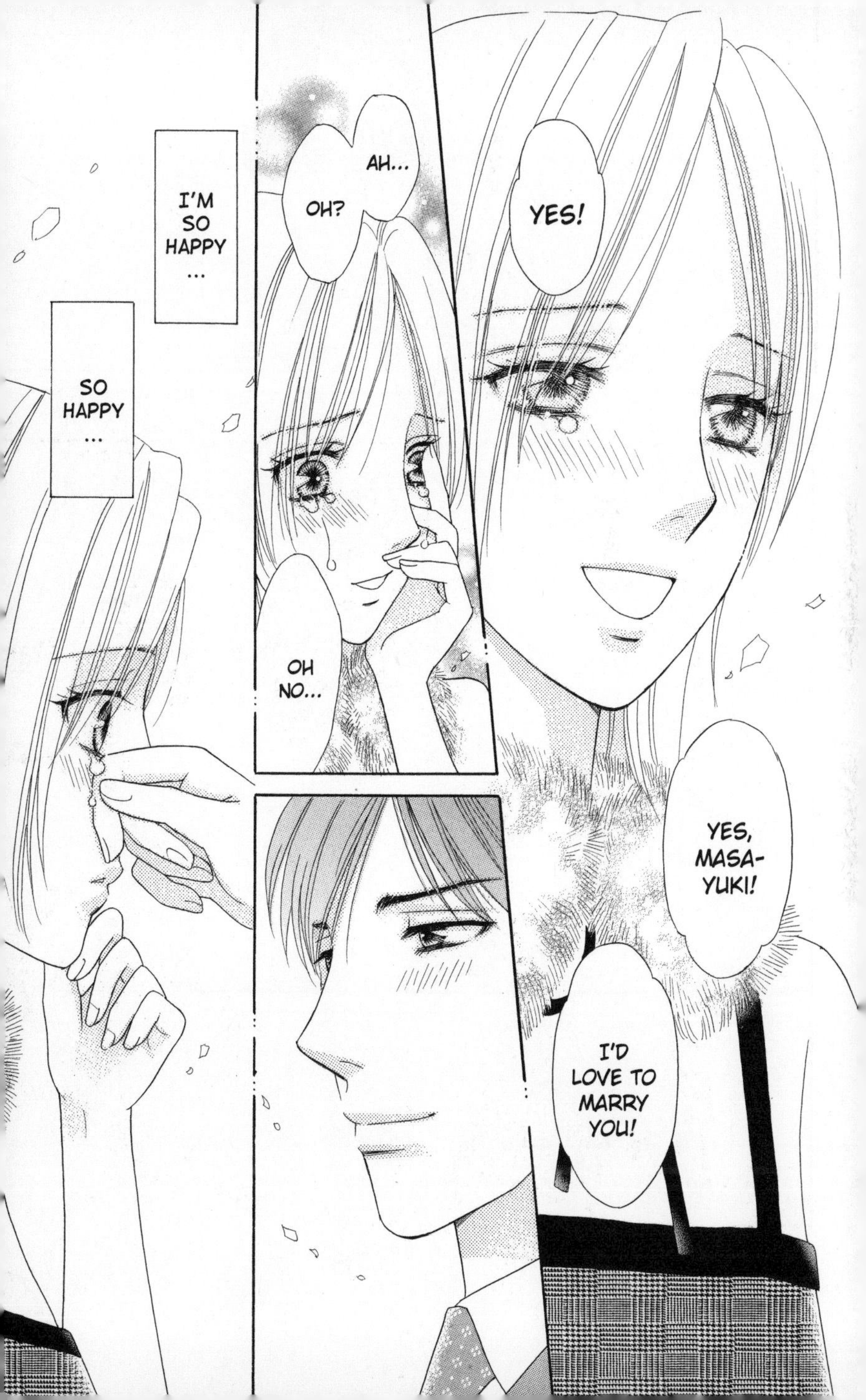
YES!
YES, MASAYUKI!
I'D LOVE TO MARRY YOU!
AH... OH?
OH NO...
I'M SO HAPPY...
SO HAPPY...

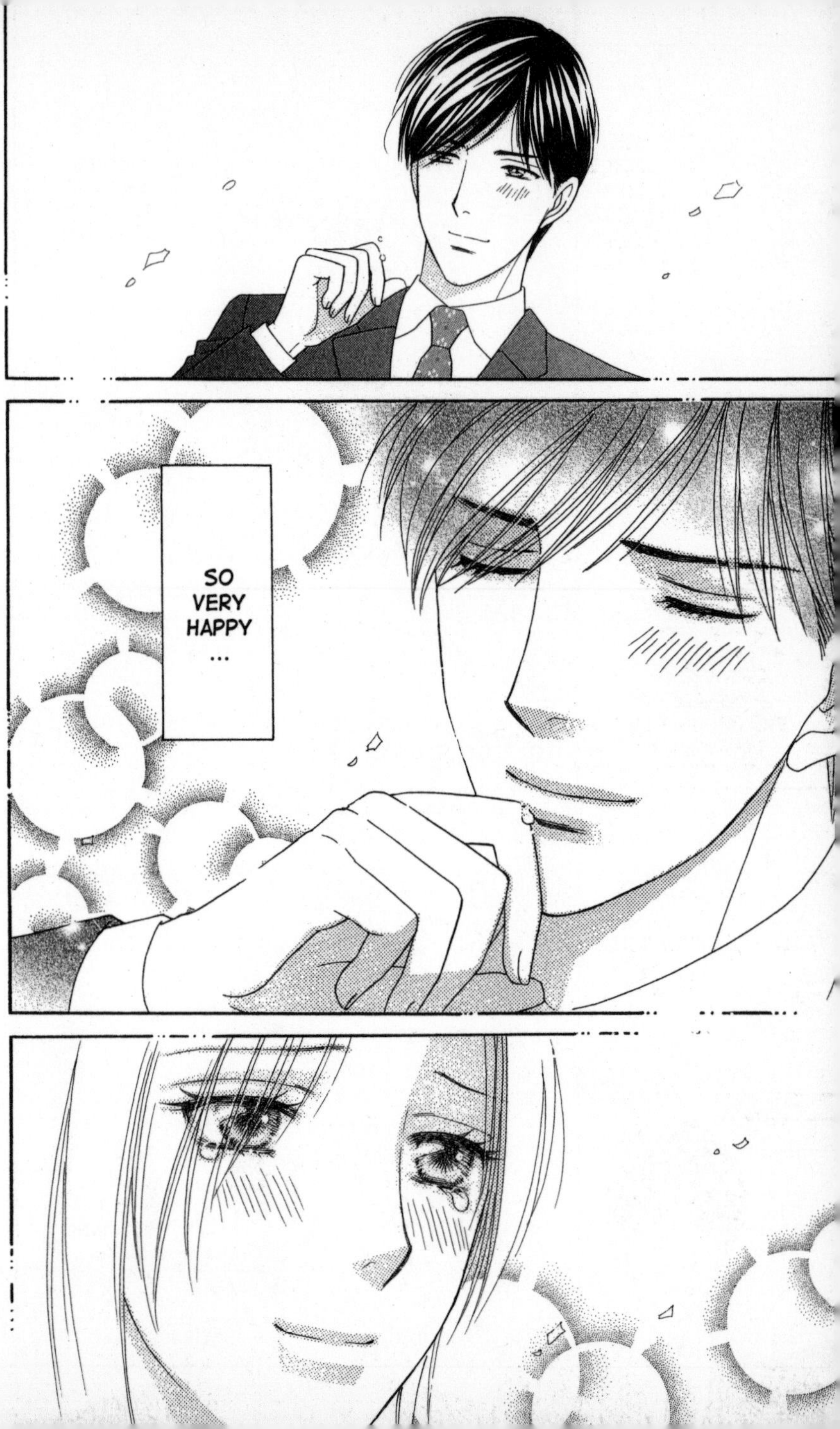
SO VERY HAPPY ...

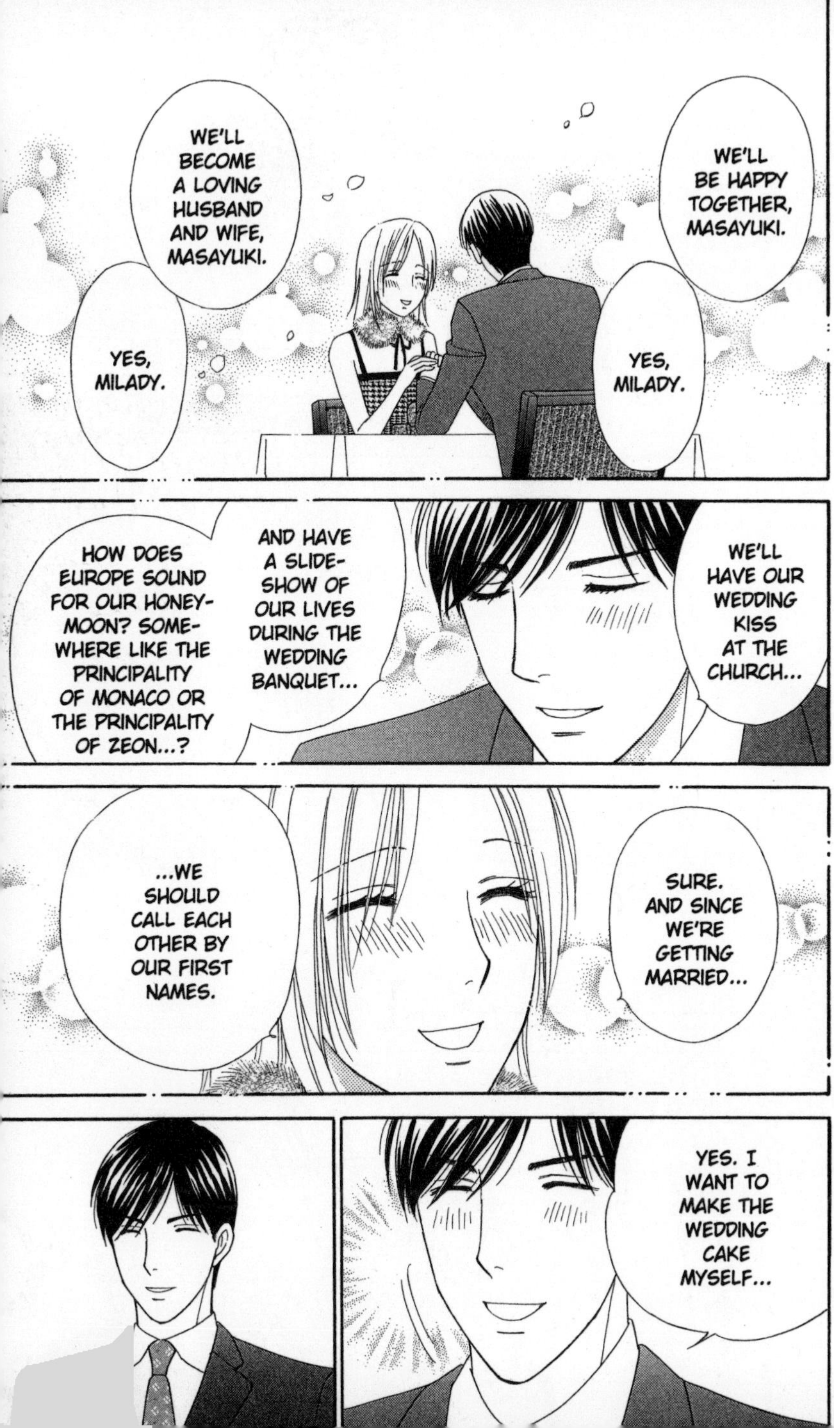
WE'LL BE HAPPY TOGETHER, MASAYUKI.
YES, MILADY.
WE'LL BECOME A LOVING HUSBAND AND WIFE, MASAYUKI.
YES, MILADY.
WE'LL HAVE OUR WEDDING KISS AT THE CHURCH...
AND HAVE A SLIDE-SHOW OF OUR LIVES DURING THE WEDDING BANQUET...
HOW DOES EUROPE SOUND FOR OUR HONEY-MOON? SOME-WHERE LIKE THE PRINCIPALITY OF MONACO OR THE PRINCIPALITY OF ZEON...?
SURE. AND SINCE WE'RE GETTING MARRIED...
...WE SHOULD CALL EACH OTHER BY OUR FIRST NAMES.
YES. I WANT TO MAKE THE WEDDING CAKE MYSELF...

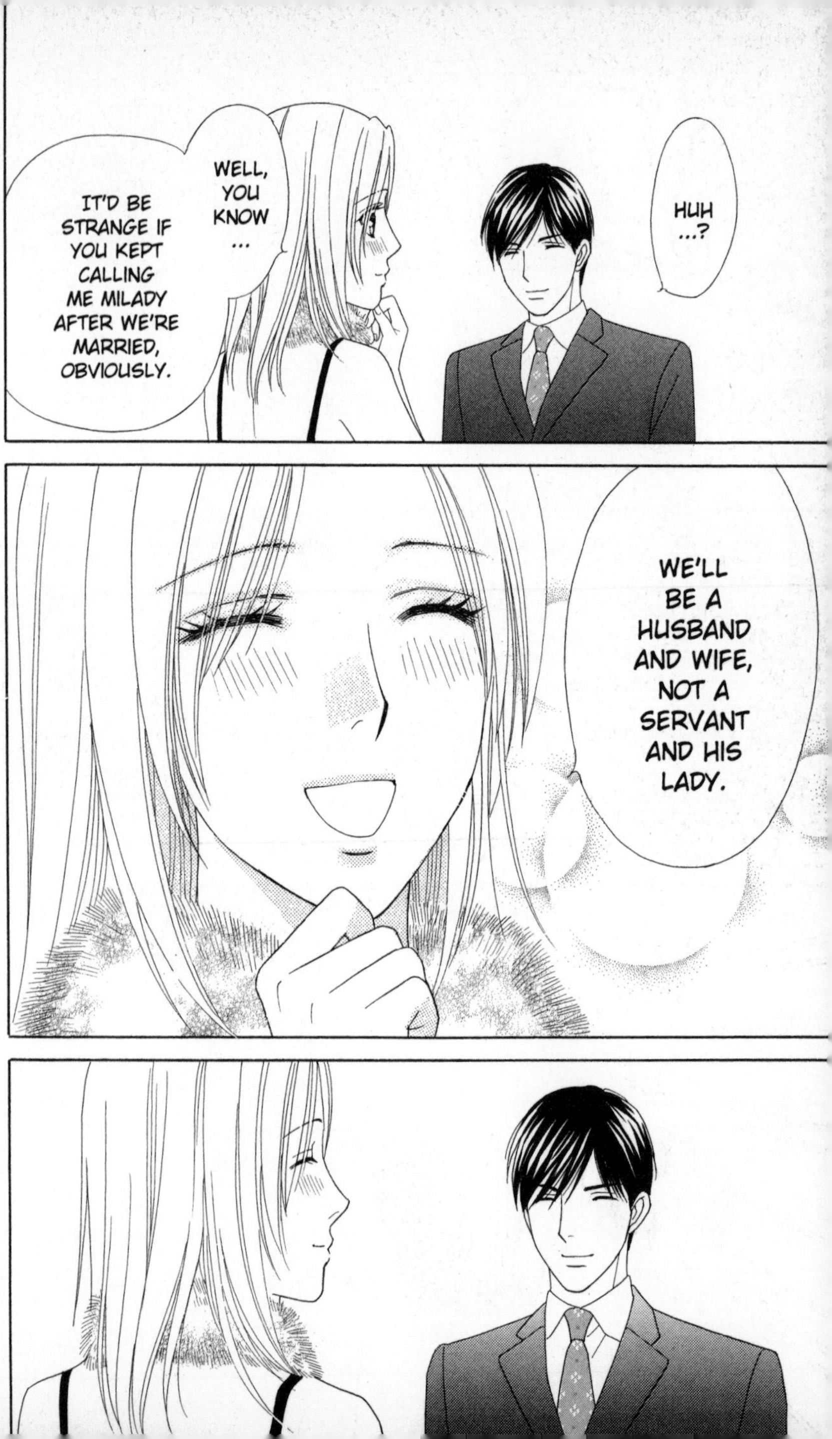
HUH ...?
WELL, YOU KNOW ...
IT'D BE STRANGE IF YOU KEPT CALLING ME MILADY AFTER WE'RE MARRIED, OBVIOUSLY.
WE'LL BE A HUSBAND AND WIFE, NOT A SERVANT AND HIS LADY.

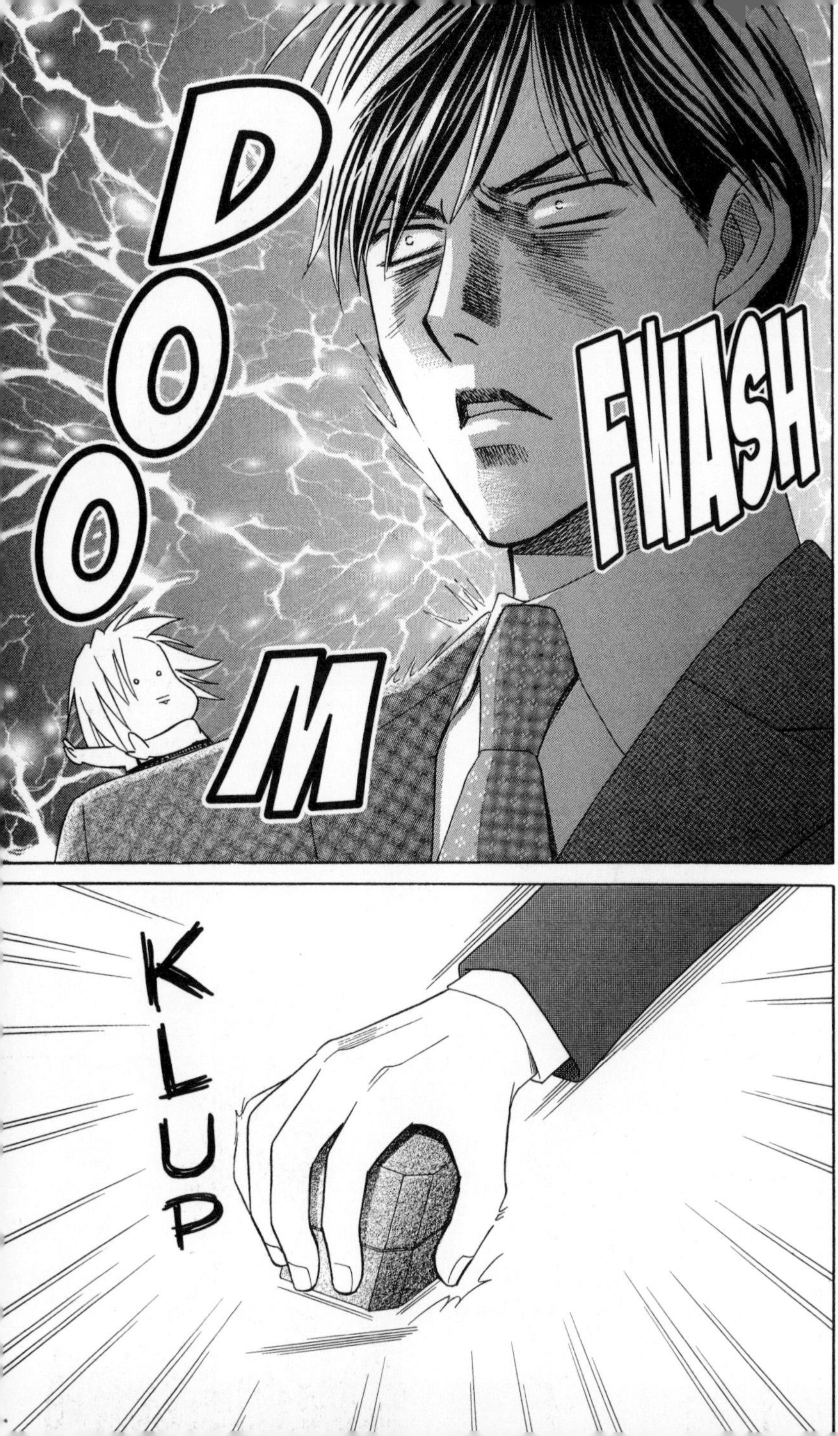
DOOOM
FWASH
KLUP

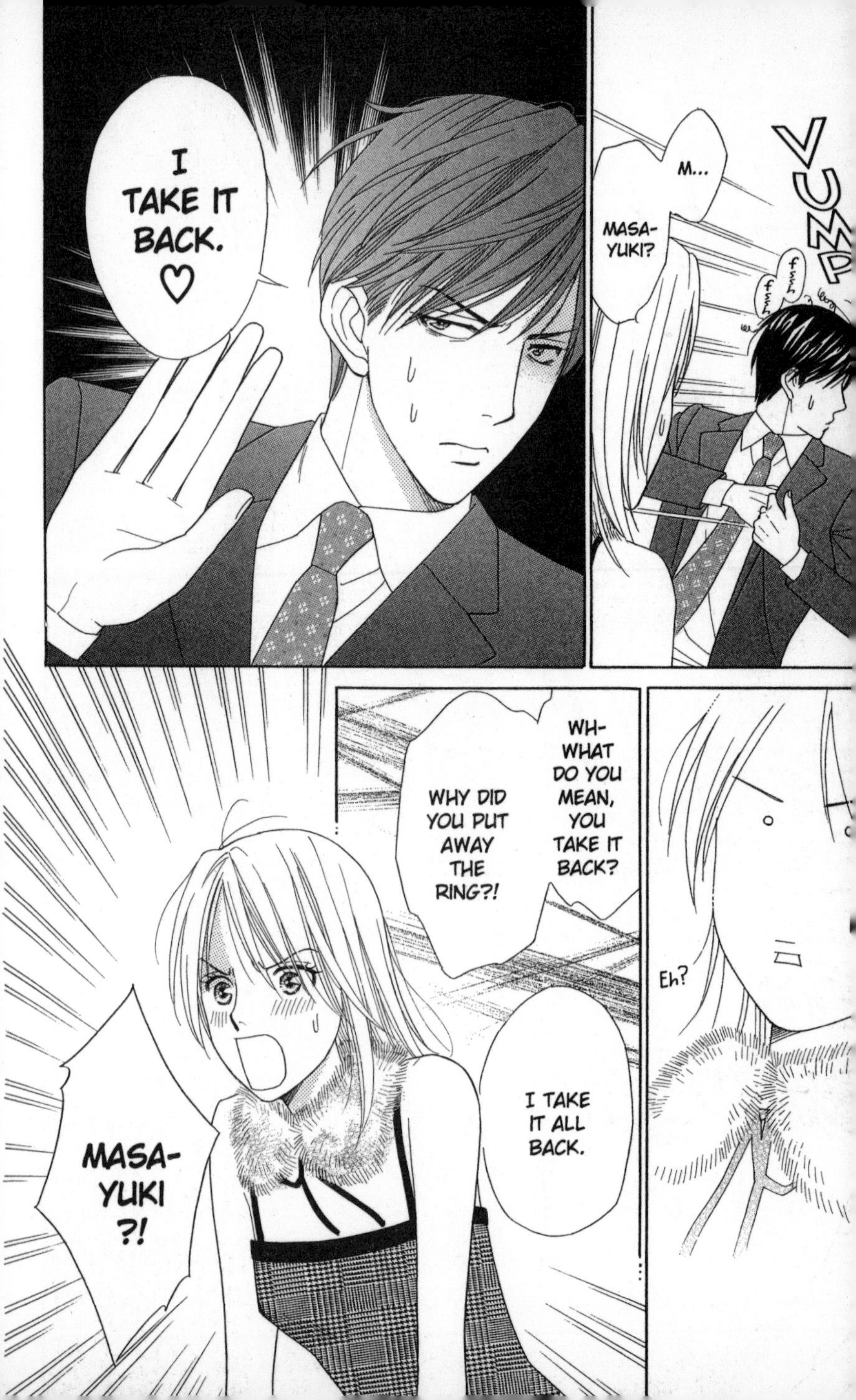
VUMP
M...
MASA-YUKI?
fwip
fwip
I TAKE IT BACK. ♡
Eh?
WH-WHAT DO YOU MEAN, YOU TAKE IT BACK?
WHY DID YOU PUT AWAY THE RING?!
I TAKE IT ALL BACK.
MASA-YUKI?!

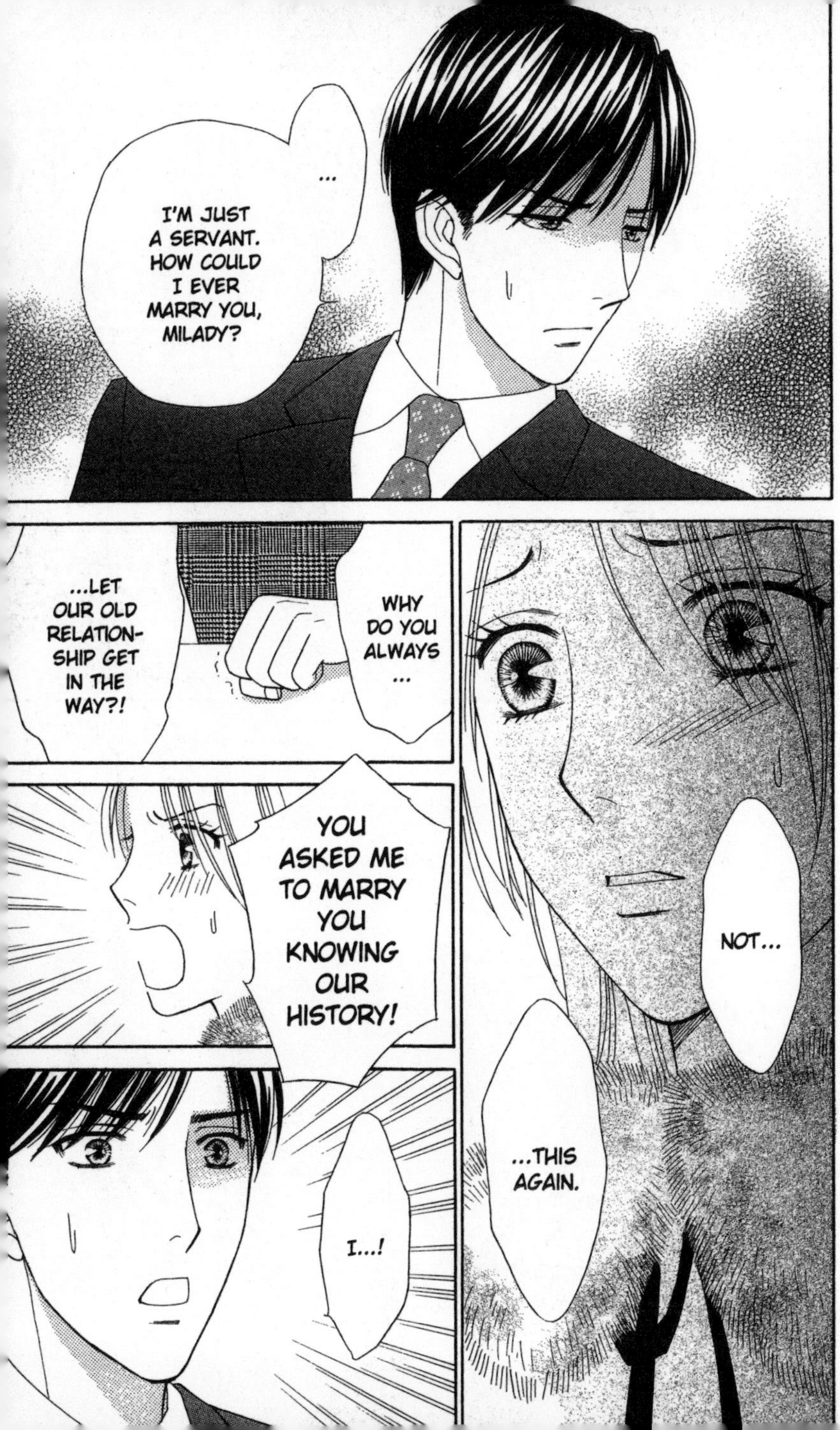
...
I'M JUST A SERVANT. HOW COULD I EVER MARRY YOU, MILADY?
NOT...
...THIS AGAIN.
WHY DO YOU ALWAYS ...
...LET OUR OLD RELATION-SHIP GET IN THE WAY?!
YOU ASKED ME TO MARRY YOU KNOWING OUR HISTORY!
I...!

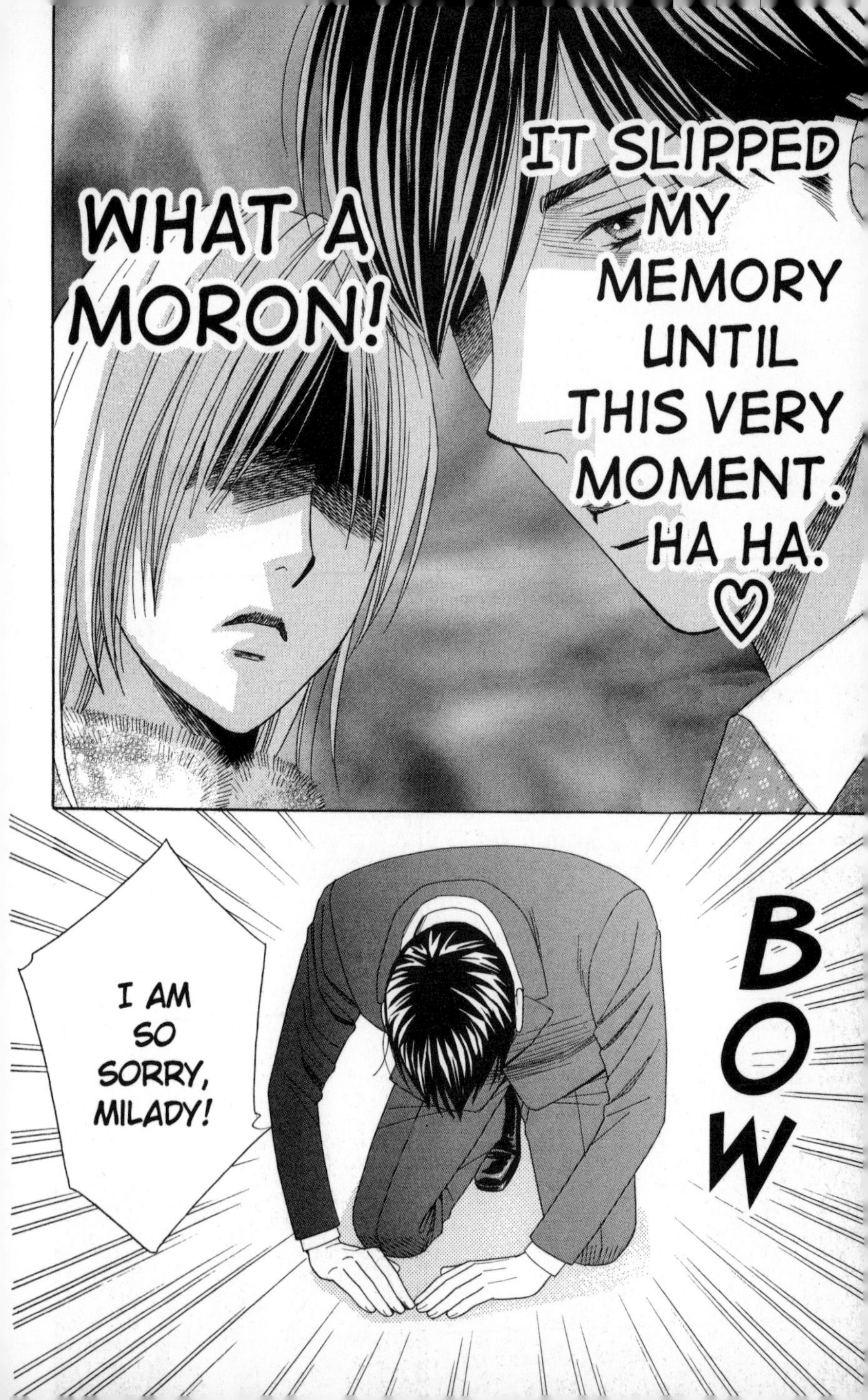
IT SLIPPED MY MEMORY UNTIL THIS VERY MOMENT. HA HA. ♡
WHAT A MORON!
BOW
I AM SO SORRY, MILADY!

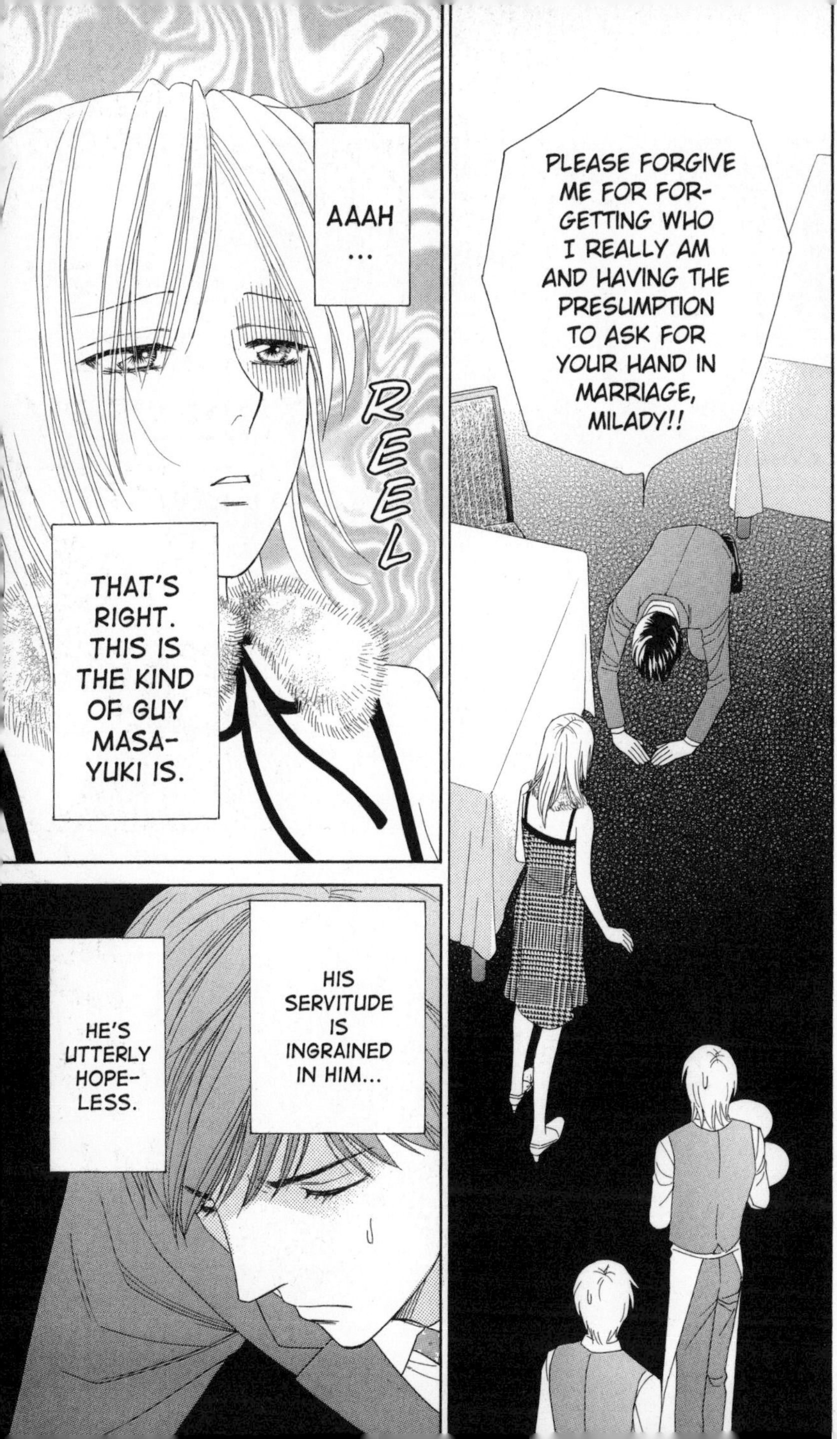
PLEASE FORGIVE ME FOR FORGETTING WHO I REALLY AM AND HAVING THE PRESUMPTION TO ASK FOR YOUR HAND IN MARRIAGE, MILADY!!
AAAH ...
REEL
THAT'S RIGHT. THIS IS THE KIND OF GUY MASAYUKI IS.
HIS SERVITUDE IS INGRAINED IN HIM...
HE'S UTTERLY HOPELESS.

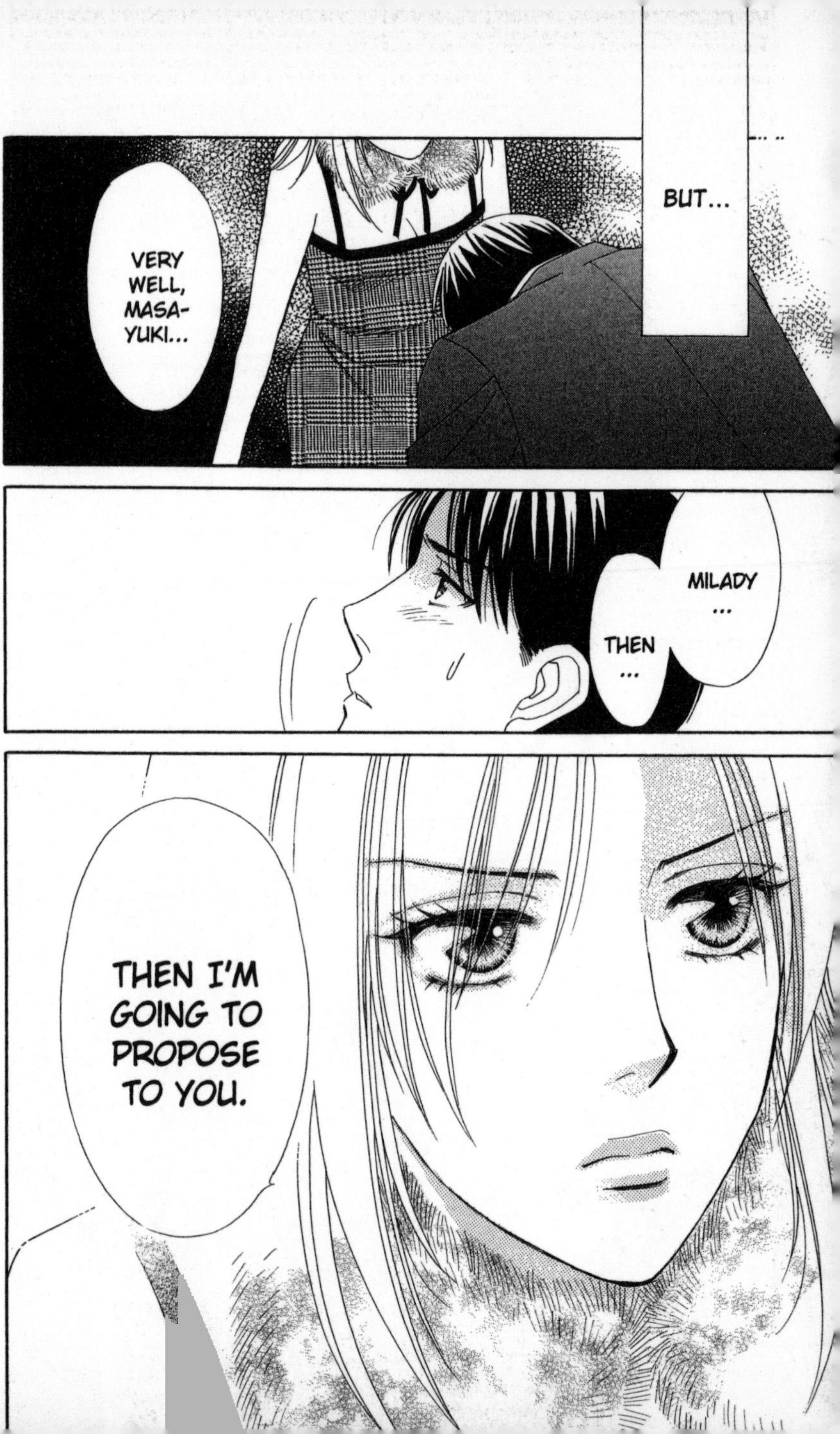
BUT...
VERY WELL, MASAYUKI...
MILADY ...
THEN ...
THEN I'M GOING TO PROPOSE TO YOU.

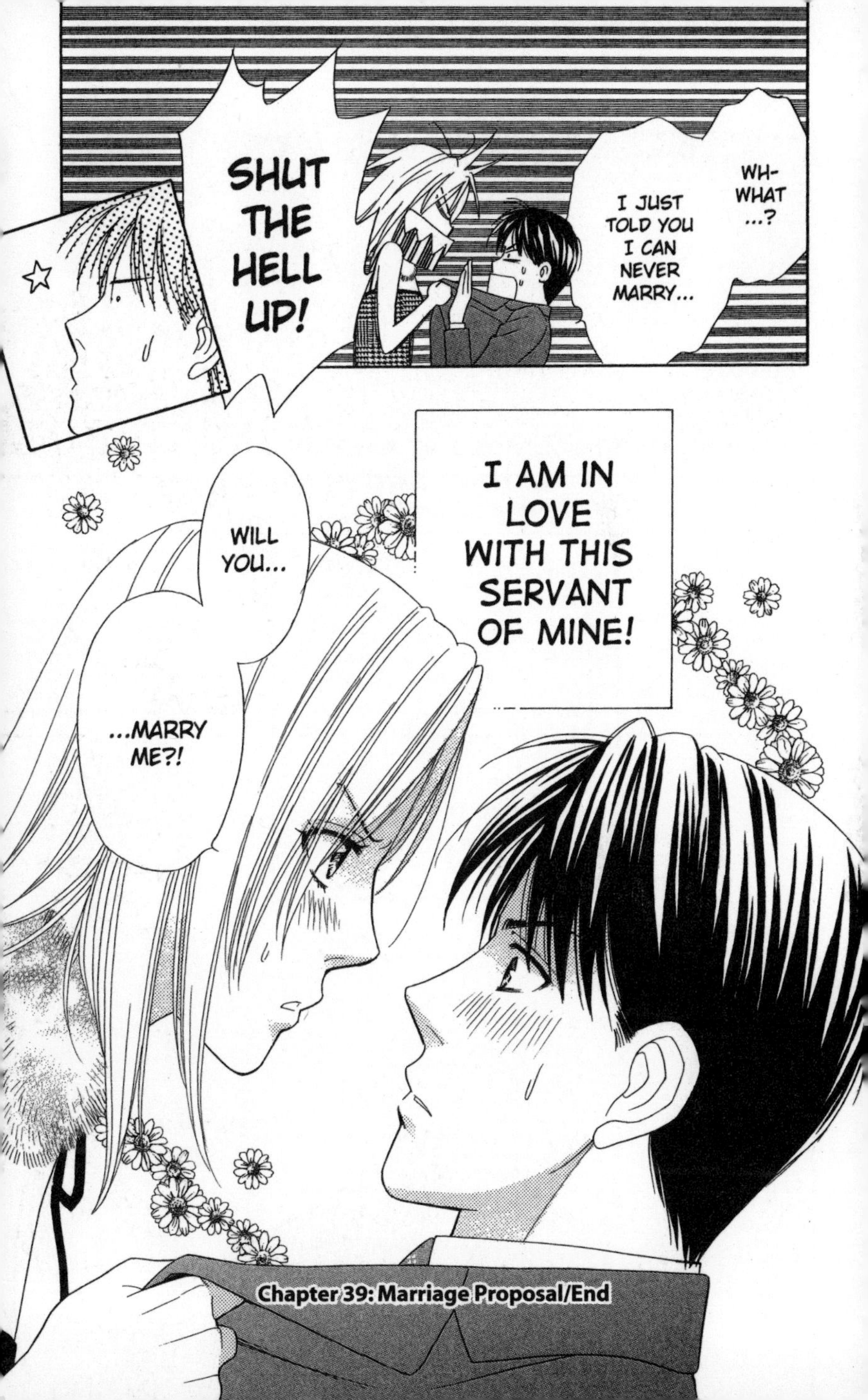
WH-WHAT ...?
I JUST TOLD YOU I CAN NEVER MARRY...
SHUT THE HELL UP!
I AM IN LOVE WITH THIS SERVANT OF MINE!
WILL YOU...
...MARRY ME?!
Chapter 39: Marriage Proposal/End

FINAL VOLUME SPECIAL
SOMETHING THAT'S NOT VERY IMPORTANT

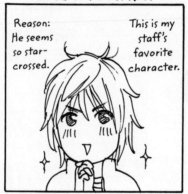

This is my staff's favorite character.
Reason: He seems so star-crossed.

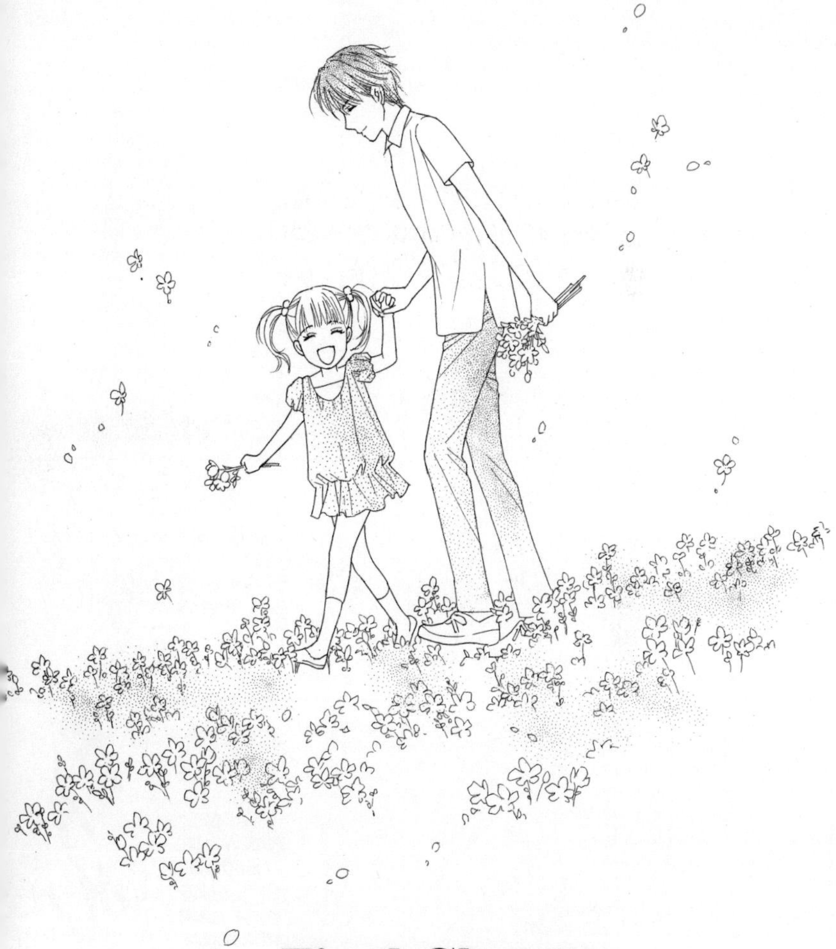

Final Chapter
Butterflies, Flowers

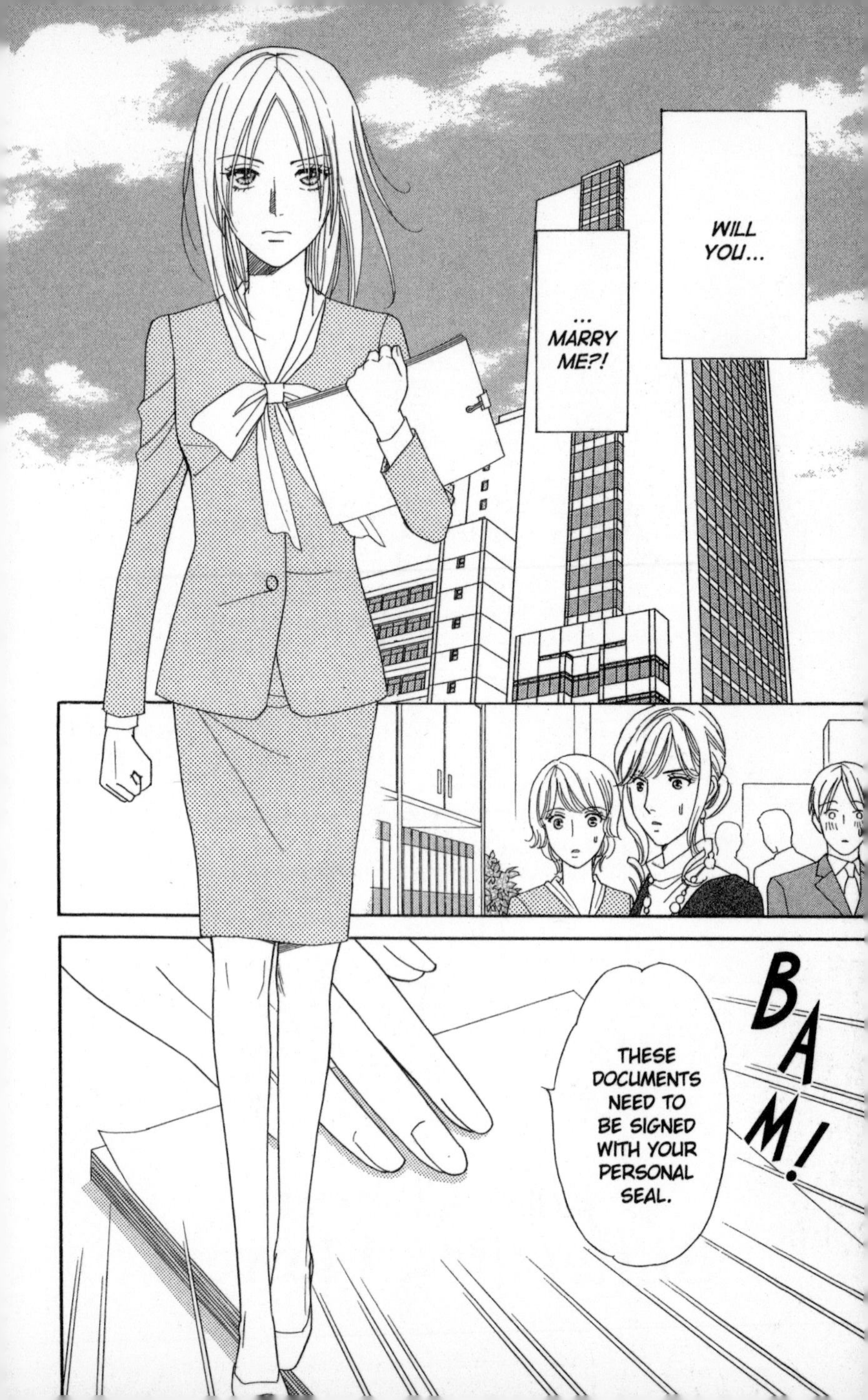
WILL YOU...
... MARRY ME?!
BAM!
THESE DOCUMENTS NEED TO BE SIGNED WITH YOUR PERSONAL SEAL.

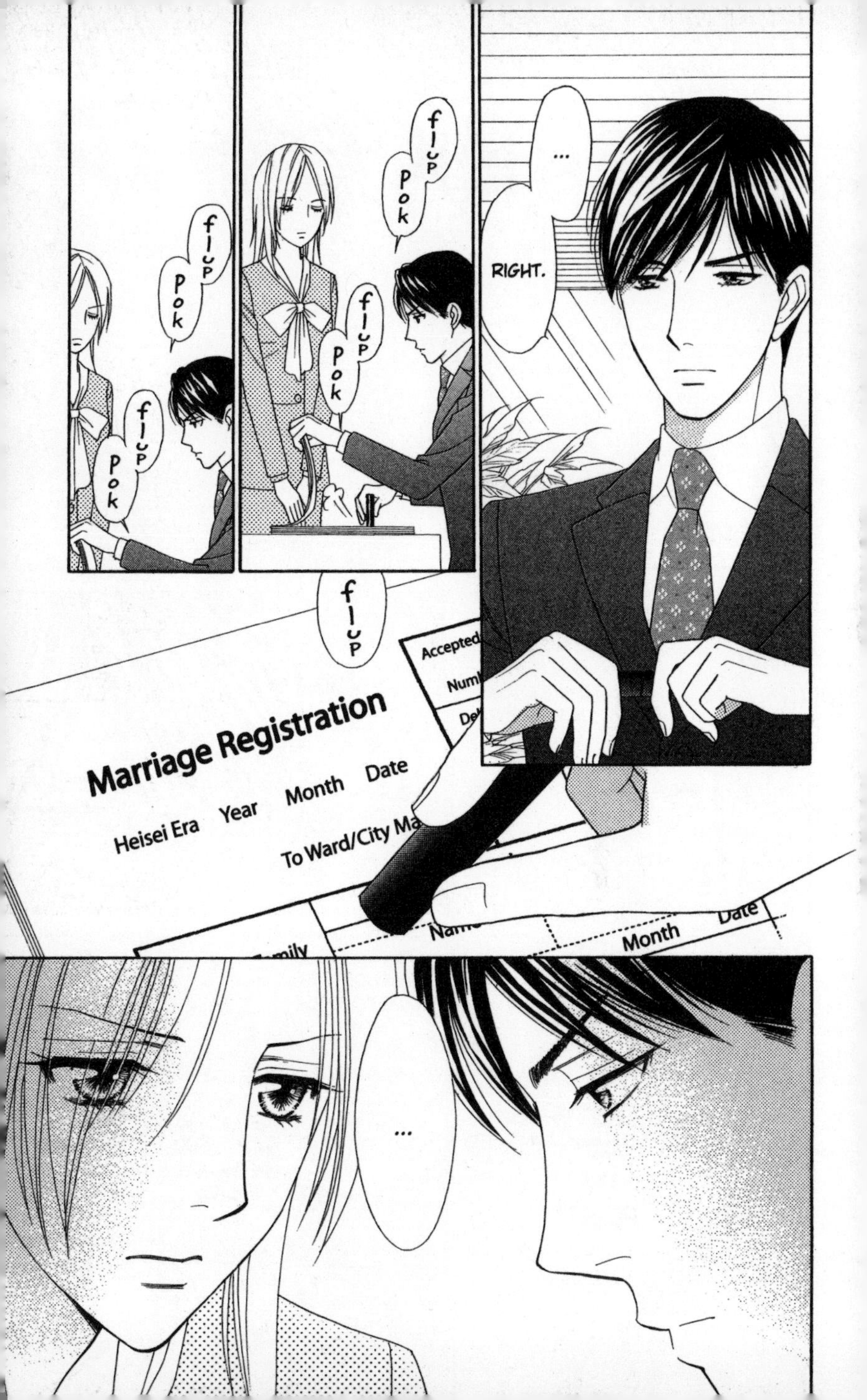
...
RIGHT.
flup
pok
flup
pok
flup
pok
flup
pok
flup
Accepted
Marriage Registration
Heisei Era Year Month Date
To Ward/City
Name
Month
Date
...

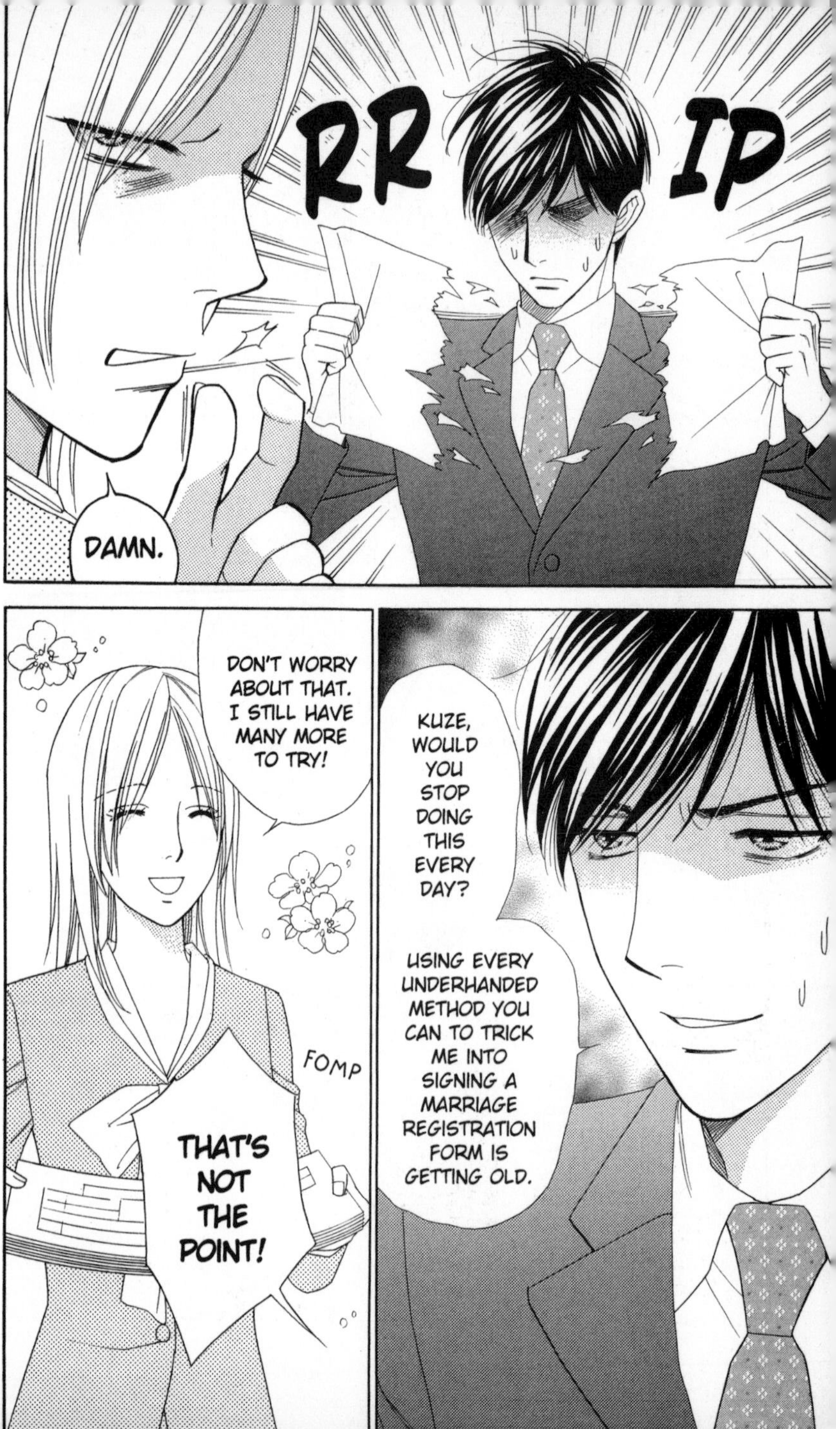
RR IP
DAMN.
KUZE, WOULD YOU STOP DOING THIS EVERY DAY?
USING EVERY UNDERHANDED METHOD YOU CAN TO TRICK ME INTO SIGNING A MARRIAGE REGISTRATION FORM IS GETTING OLD.
DON'T WORRY ABOUT THAT. I STILL HAVE MANY MORE TO TRY!
FOMP
THAT'S NOT THE POINT!

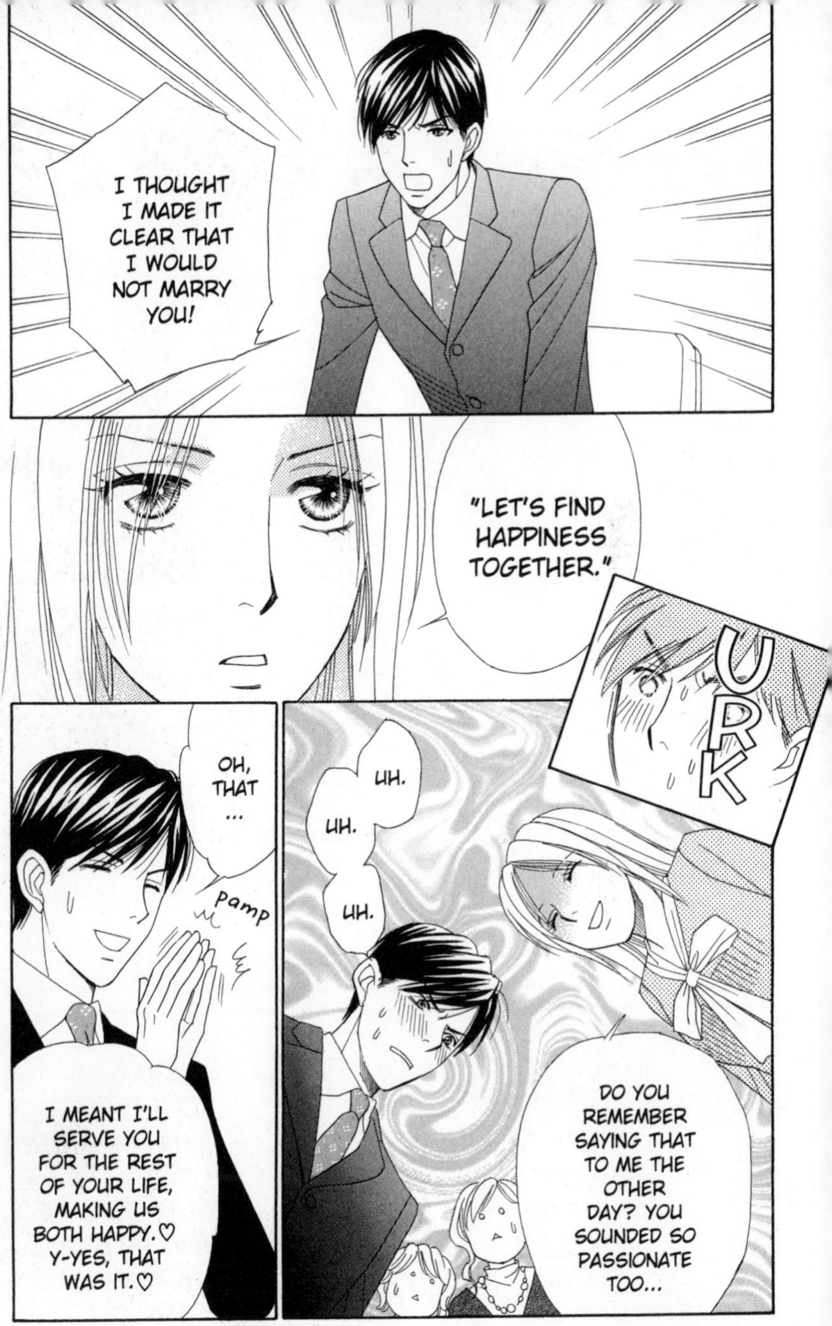
I THOUGHT I MADE IT CLEAR THAT I WOULD NOT MARRY YOU!
"LET'S FIND HAPPINESS TOGETHER."
URK
DO YOU REMEMBER SAYING THAT TO ME THE OTHER DAY? YOU SOUNDED SO PASSIONATE TOO...
UH.
UH.
UH.
OH, THAT ...
pamp
I MEANT I'LL SERVE YOU FOR THE REST OF YOUR LIFE, MAKING US BOTH HAPPY.♡ Y-YES, THAT WAS IT.♡

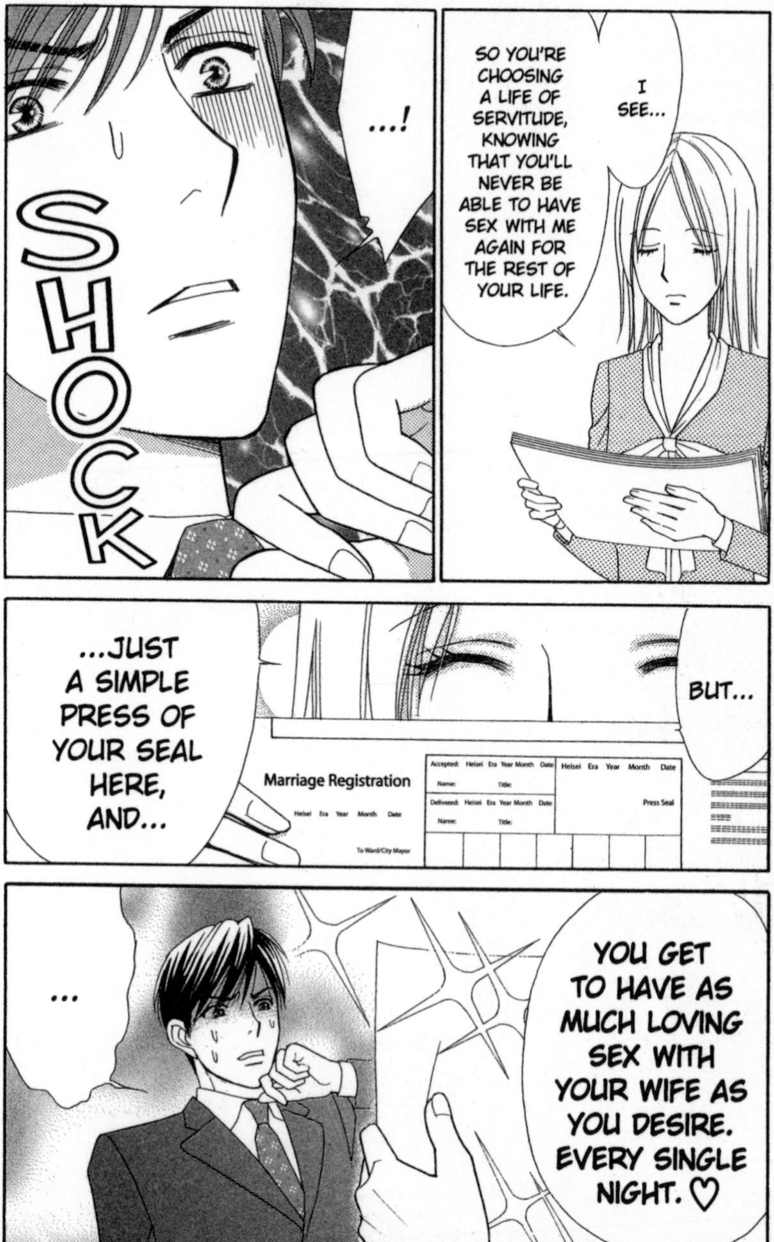
I SEE...
SO YOU'RE CHOOSING A LIFE OF SERVITUDE, KNOWING THAT YOU'LL NEVER BE ABLE TO HAVE SEX WITH ME AGAIN FOR THE REST OF YOUR LIFE.
...!
SHOCK
BUT...
...JUST A SIMPLE PRESS OF YOUR SEAL HERE, AND...
Accepted: Heisei Era Year Month Date
Name: Title:
Delivered: Heisei Era Year Month Date
Name: Title:
Heisei Era Year Month Date
Press Seal
Marriage Registration
Heisei Era Year Month Date
To Ward/City Mayor
YOU GET TO HAVE AS MUCH LOVING SEX WITH YOUR WIFE AS YOU DESIRE. EVERY SINGLE NIGHT. ♡
...

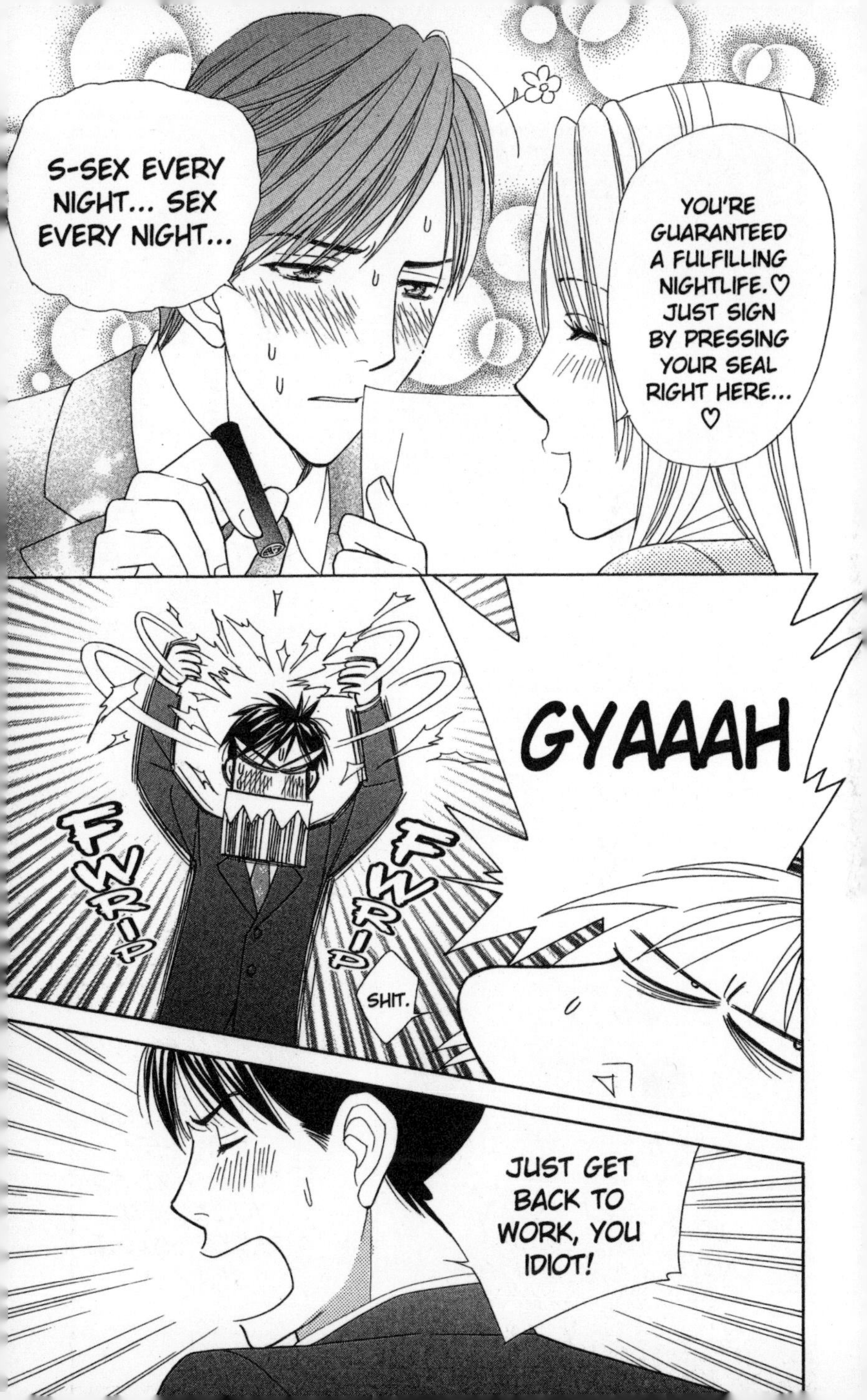
YOU'RE GUARANTEED A FULFILLING NIGHTLIFE.♡ JUST SIGN BY PRESSING YOUR SEAL RIGHT HERE... ♡
S-SEX EVERY NIGHT... SEX EVERY NIGHT...
GYAAAH
FWRIP
FWRIP
SHIT.
JUST GET BACK TO WORK, YOU IDIOT!

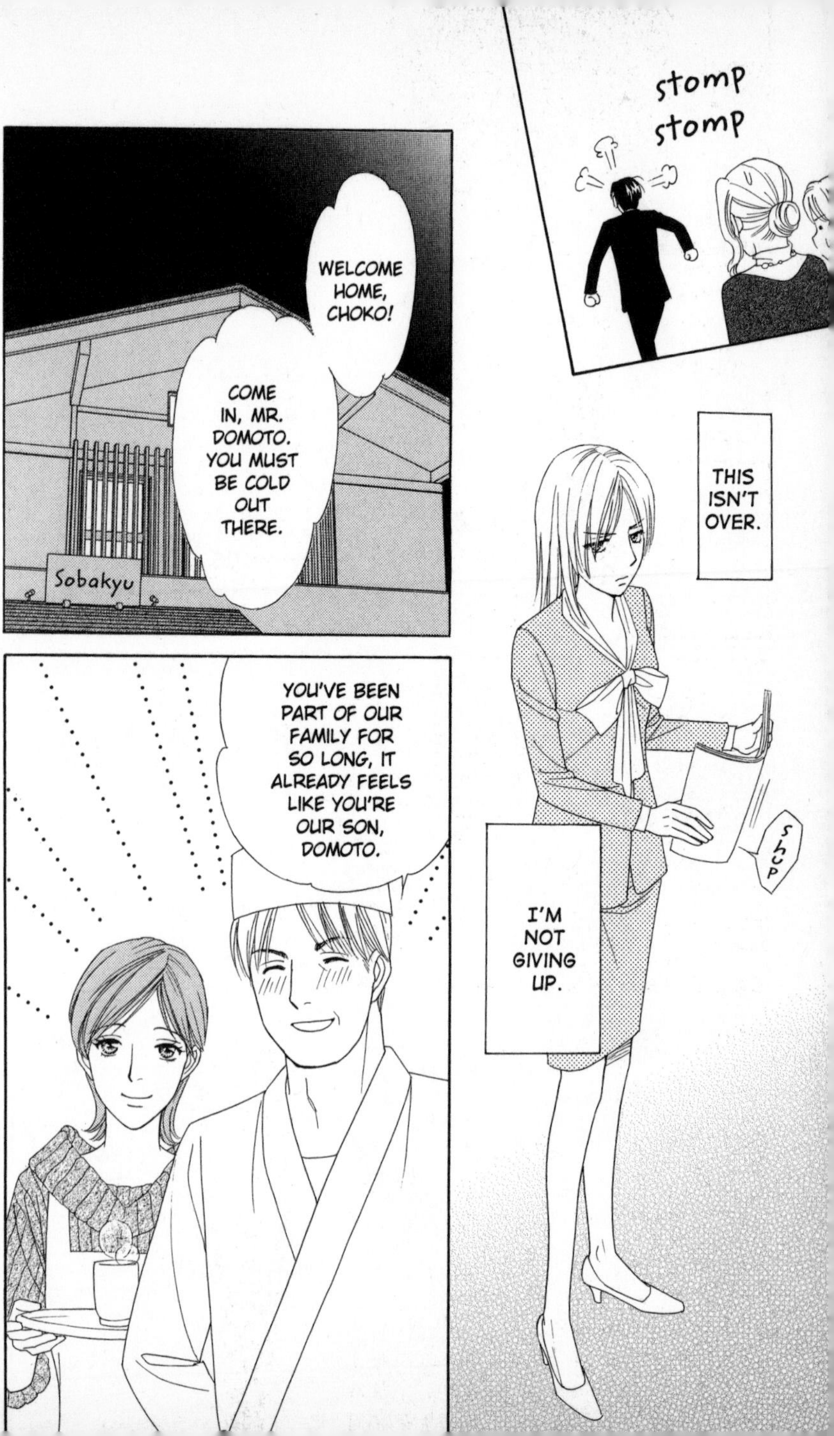
stomp
stomp
THIS ISN'T OVER.
SHUP
I'M NOT GIVING UP.
WELCOME HOME, CHOKO!
COME IN, MR. DOMOTO. YOU MUST BE COLD OUT THERE.
Sobakyu
YOU'VE BEEN PART OF OUR FAMILY FOR SO LONG, IT ALREADY FEELS LIKE YOU'RE OUR SON, DOMOTO.

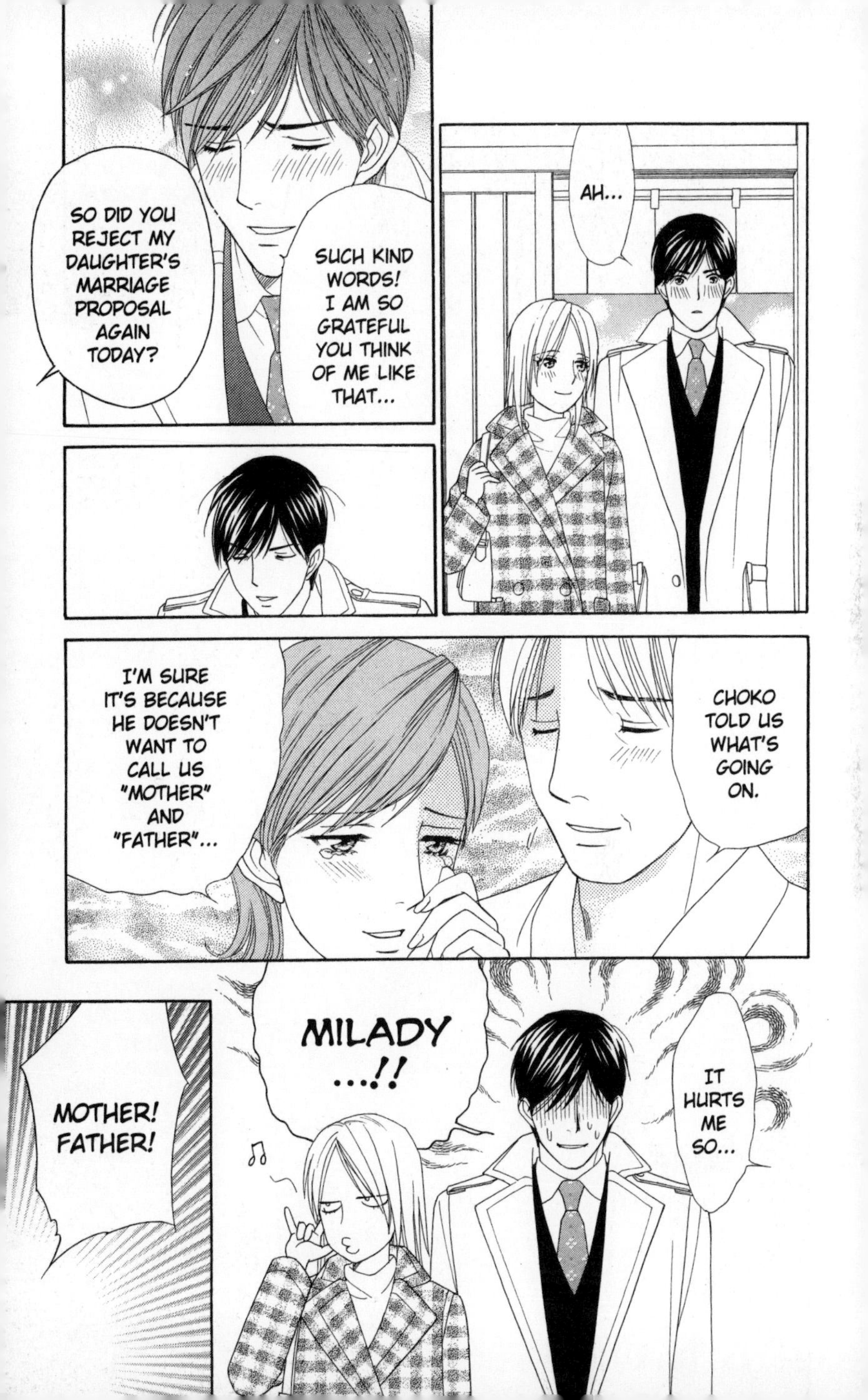
AH...
SUCH KIND WORDS! I AM SO GRATEFUL YOU THINK OF ME LIKE THAT...
SO DID YOU REJECT MY DAUGHTER'S MARRIAGE PROPOSAL AGAIN TODAY?
CHOKO TOLD US WHAT'S GOING ON.
I'M SURE IT'S BECAUSE HE DOESN'T WANT TO CALL US "MOTHER" AND "FATHER"...
IT HURTS ME SO...
MILADY ...!!
MOTHER! FATHER!

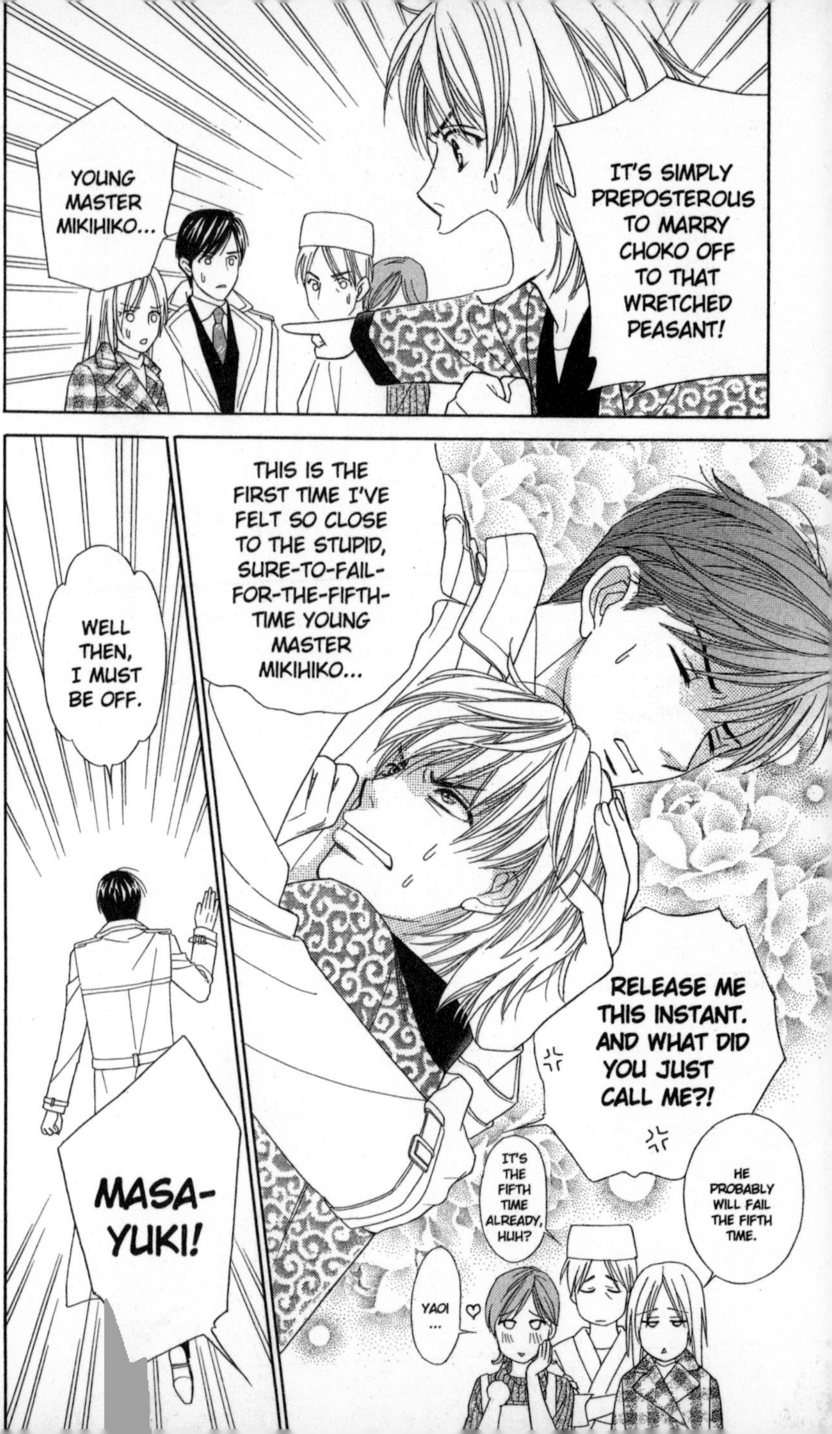
IT'S SIMPLY PREPOSTEROUS TO MARRY CHOKO OFF TO THAT WRETCHED PEASANT!
YOUNG MASTER MIKIHIKO...
THIS IS THE FIRST TIME I'VE FELT SO CLOSE TO THE STUPID, SURE-TO-FAIL-FOR-THE-FIFTH-TIME YOUNG MASTER MIKIHIKO...
RELEASE ME THIS INSTANT. AND WHAT DID YOU JUST CALL ME?!
HE PROBABLY WILL FAIL THE FIFTH TIME.
IT'S THE FIFTH TIME ALREADY, HUH?
YAOI ...
WELL THEN, I MUST BE OFF.
MASA-YUKI!

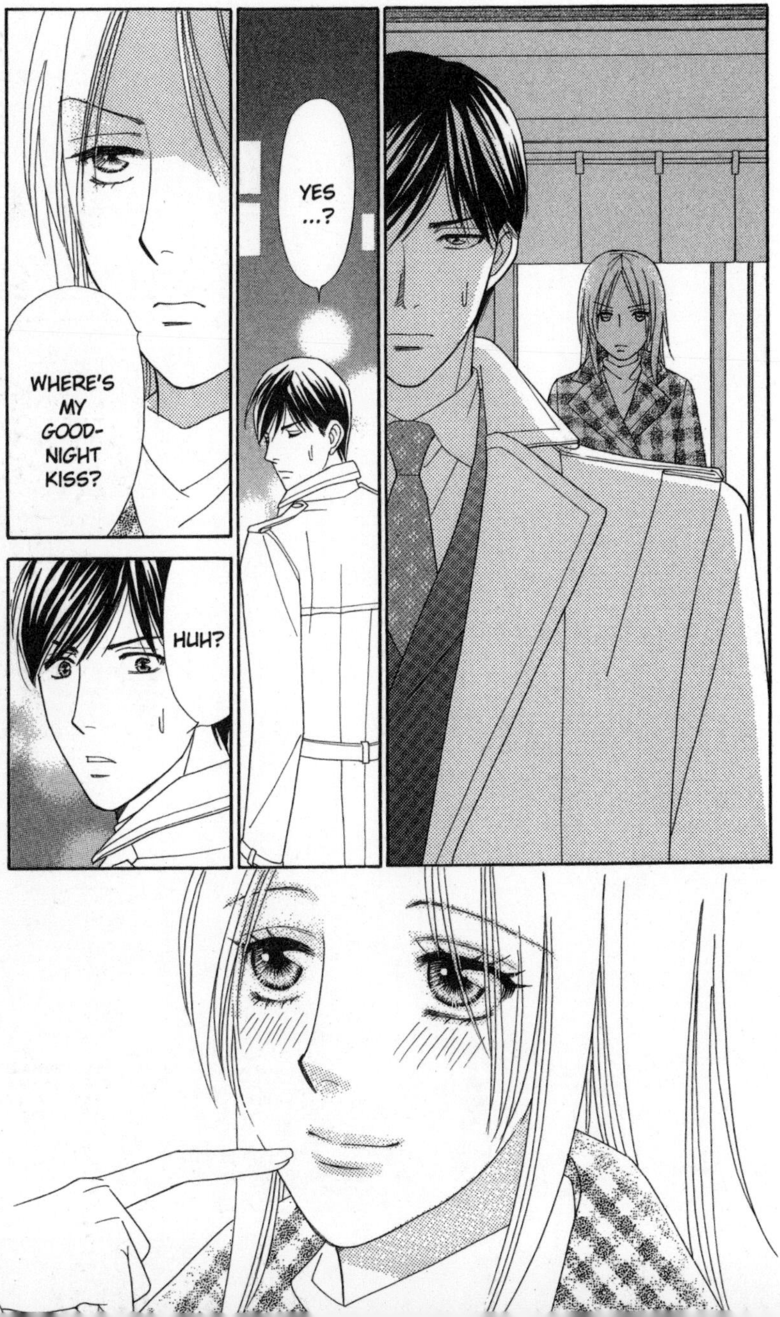
YES ...?
WHERE'S MY GOOD-NIGHT KISS?
HUH?

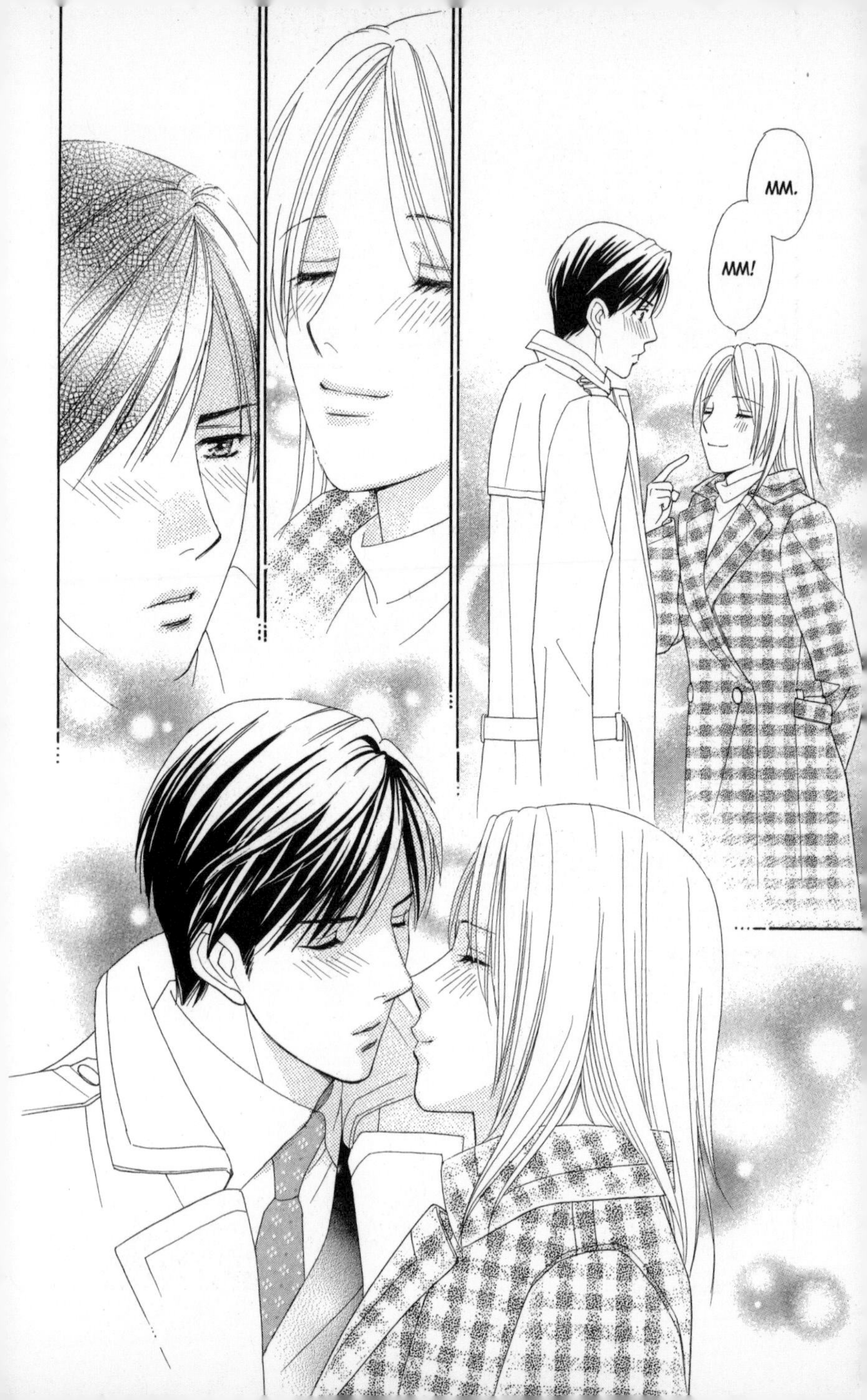
MM.
MM!

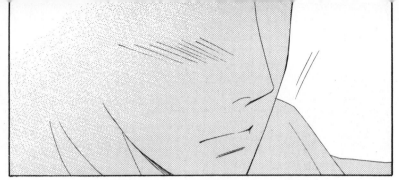

...

GOOD NIGHT, MILADY.

THAT'S OKAY.

WE'LL KISS EVERY DAY ONCE WE GET MARRIED ANYWAY.

GOOD NIGHT!

VROO

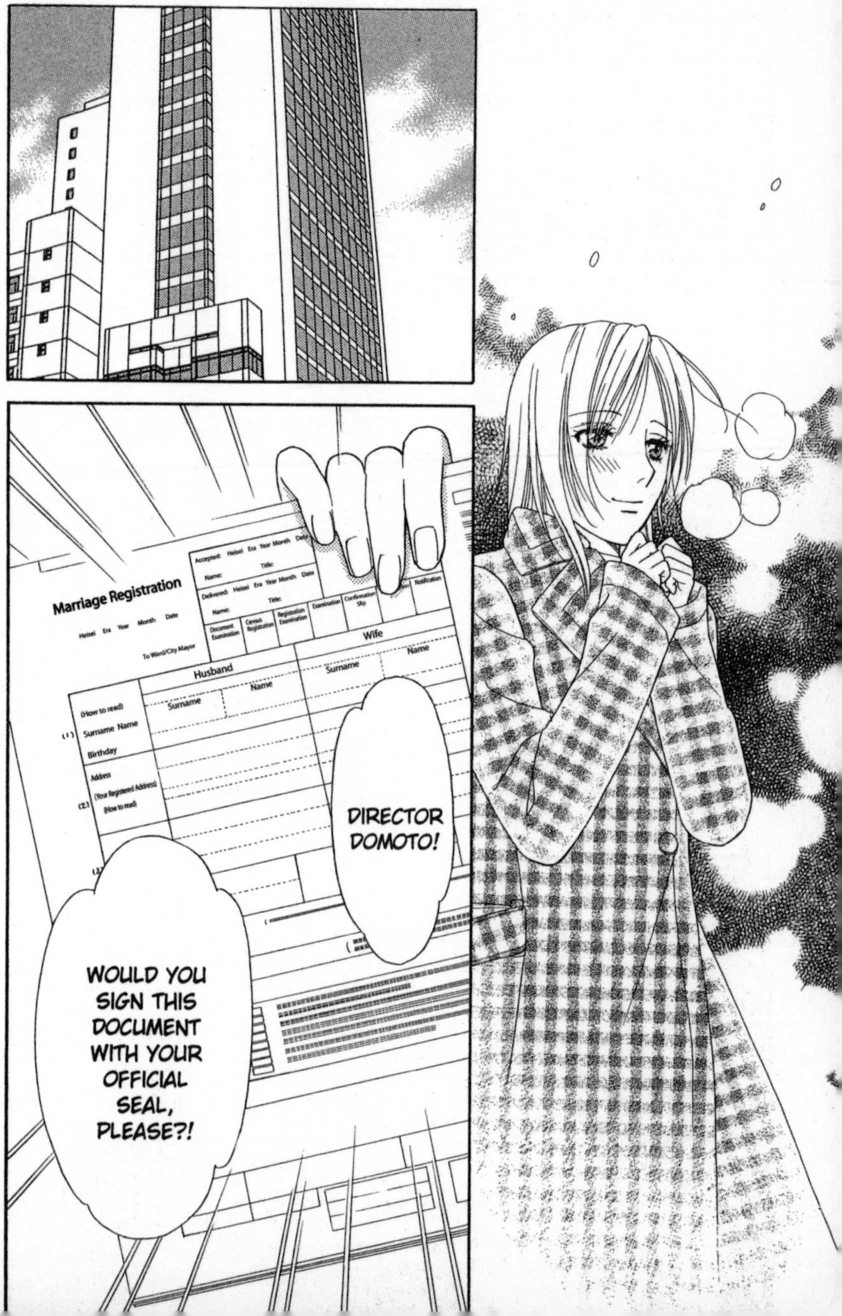
Marriage Registration
DIRECTOR DOMOTO!
WOULD YOU SIGN THIS DOCUMENT WITH YOUR OFFICIAL SEAL, PLEASE?!

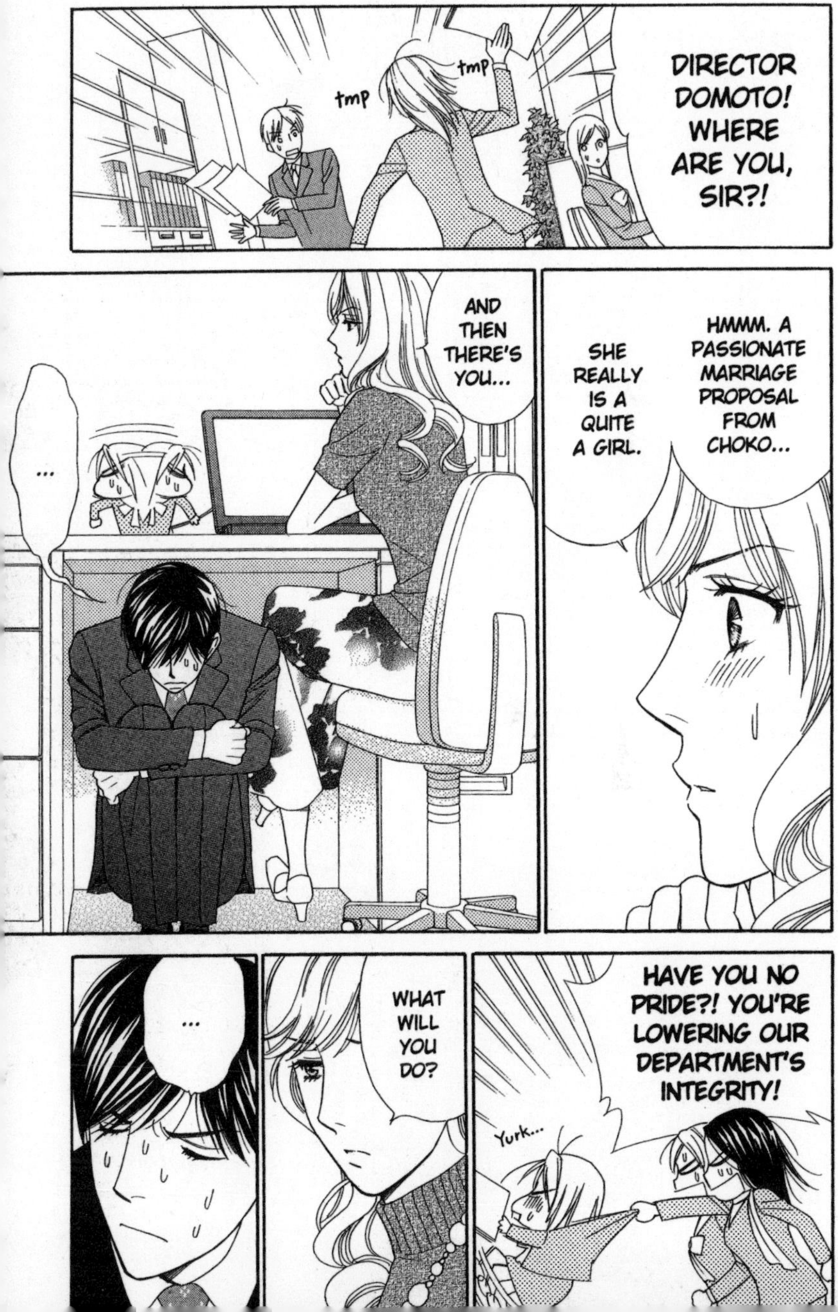
DIRECTOR DOMOTO! WHERE ARE YOU, SIR?!
tmp
tmp
HMMM. A PASSIONATE MARRIAGE PROPOSAL FROM CHOKO...
SHE REALLY IS A QUITE A GIRL.
AND THEN THERE'S YOU...
...
HAVE YOU NO PRIDE?! YOU'RE LOWERING OUR DEPARTMENT'S INTEGRITY!
Yurk...
WHAT WILL YOU DO?
...

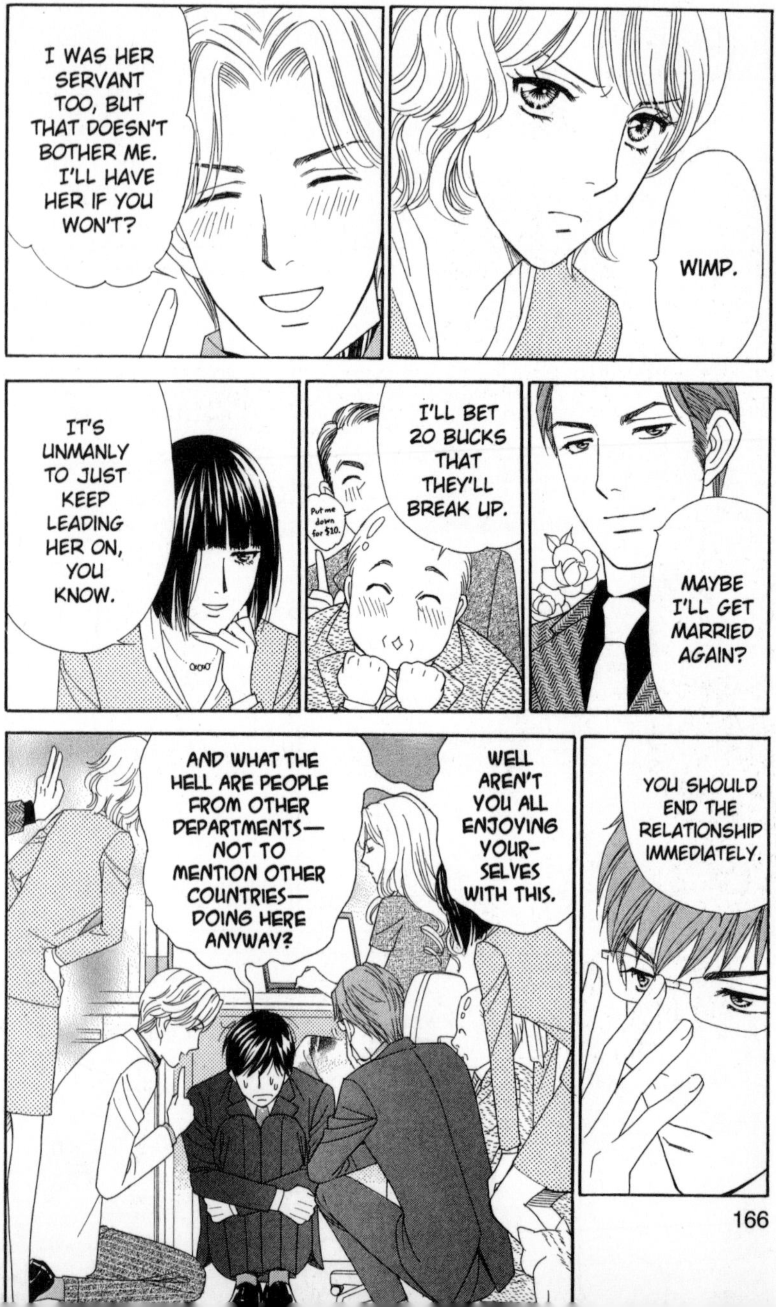
WIMP.
I WAS HER SERVANT TOO, BUT THAT DOESN'T BOTHER ME. I'LL HAVE HER IF YOU WON'T?
MAYBE I'LL GET MARRIED AGAIN?
I'LL BET 20 BUCKS THAT THEY'LL BREAK UP.
Put me down for $10.
IT'S UNMANLY TO JUST KEEP LEADING HER ON, YOU KNOW.
YOU SHOULD END THE RELATIONSHIP IMMEDIATELY.
WELL AREN'T YOU ALL ENJOYING YOURSELVES WITH THIS.
AND WHAT THE HELL ARE PEOPLE FROM OTHER DEPARTMENTS—NOT TO MENTION OTHER COUNTRIES—DOING HERE ANYWAY?

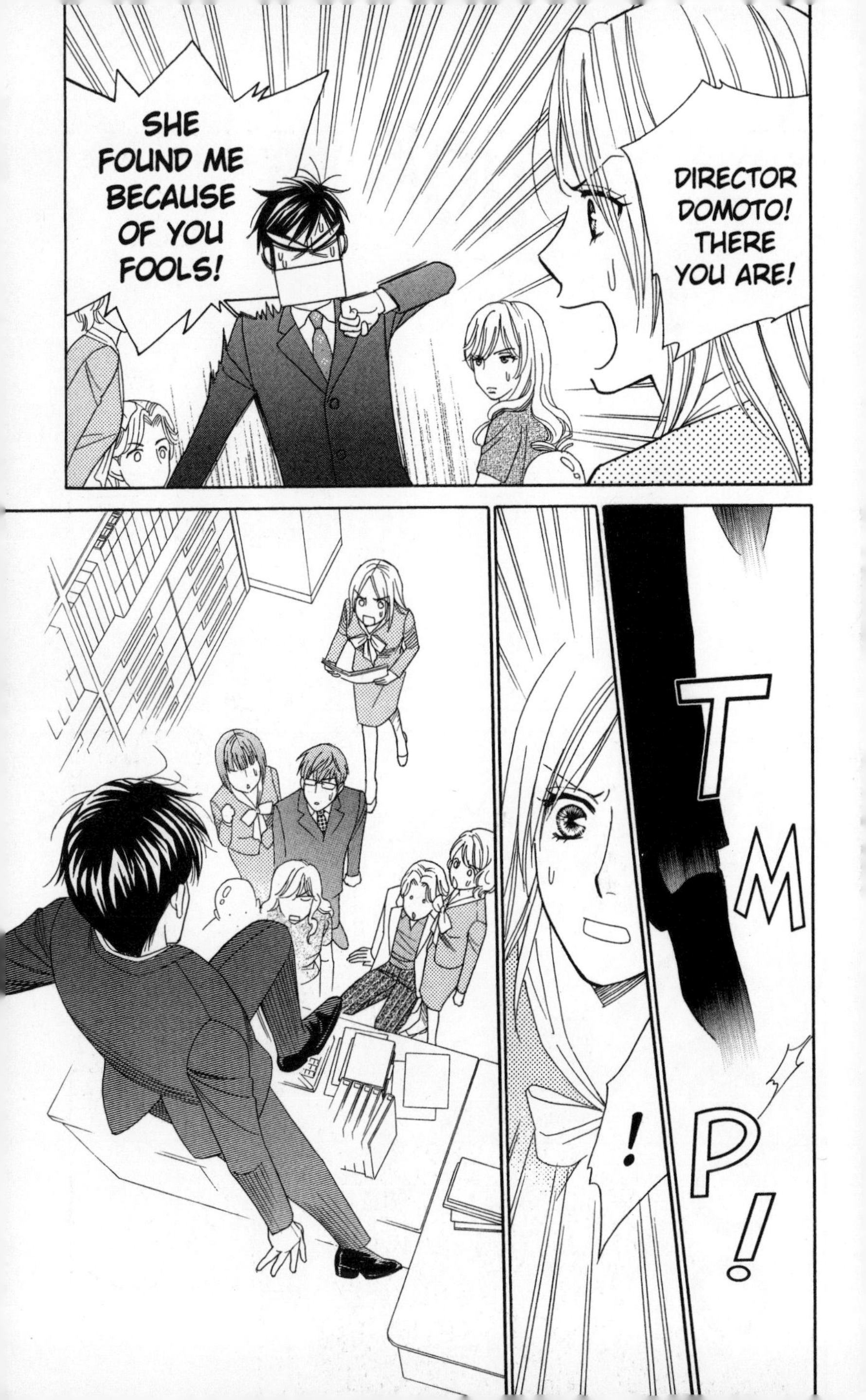
DIRECTOR DOMOTO! THERE YOU ARE!
SHE FOUND ME BECAUSE OF YOU FOOLS!
TMP!
!

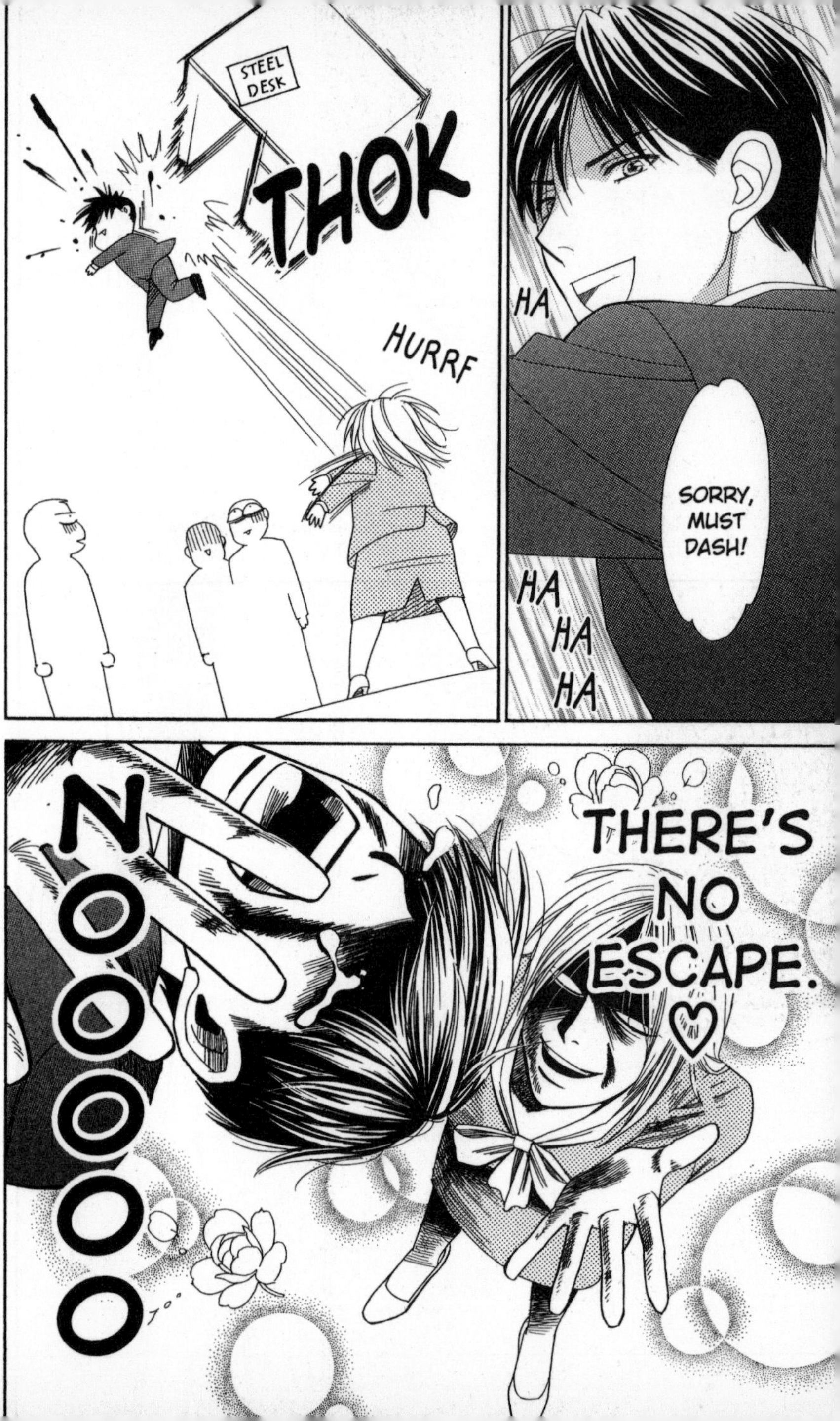
HA
SORRY, MUST DASH!
HA HA HA HA
STEEL DESK
THOK
HURRF
THERE'S NO ESCAPE. ♥
ZOOOOOO

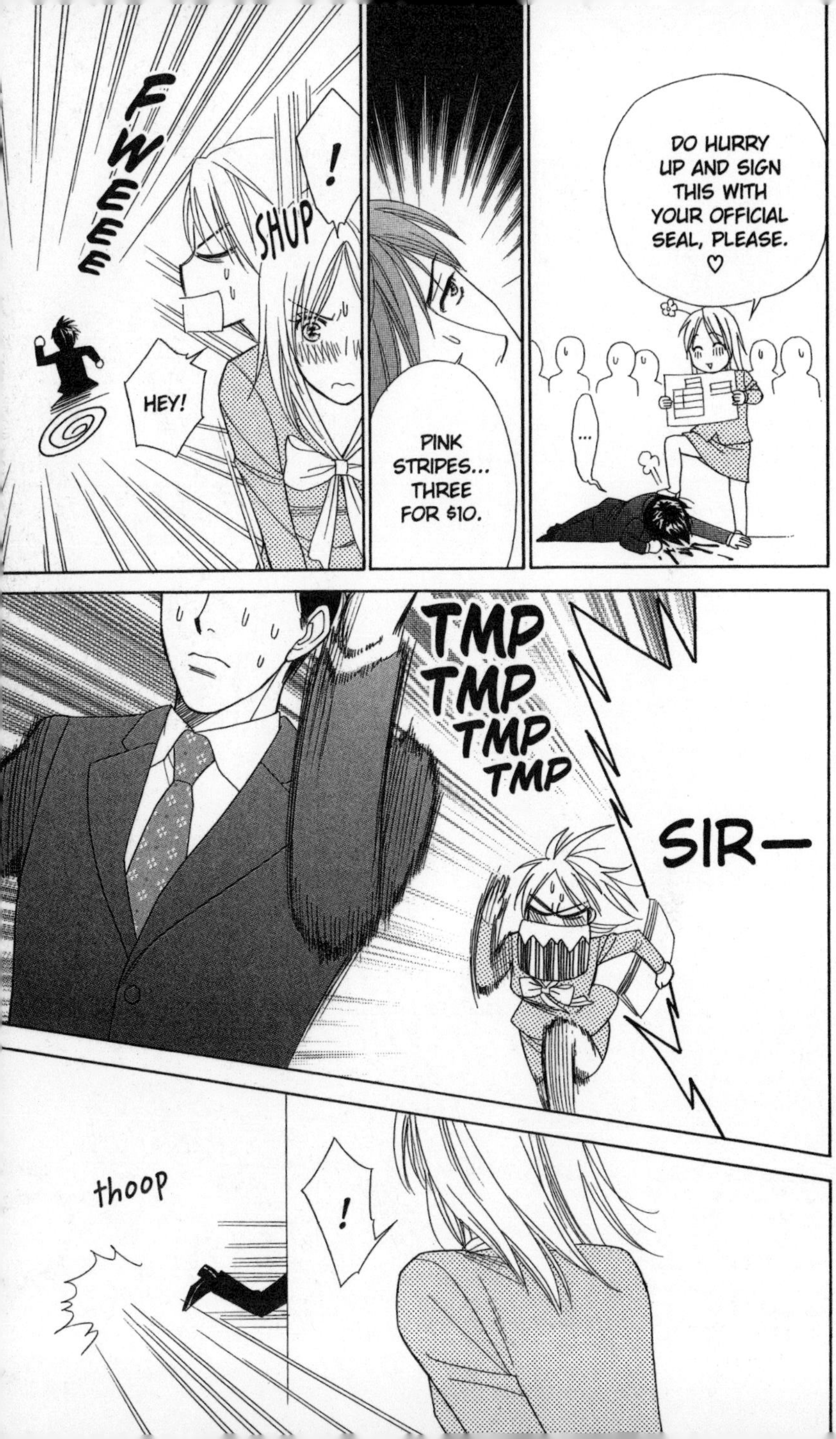

DO HURRY UP AND SIGN THIS WITH YOUR OFFICIAL SEAL, PLEASE. ♡
...
PINK STRIPES... THREE FOR $10.
!
SHUP
FWEEEE
HEY!
SIR—
TMP TMP TMP TMP
!
thoop

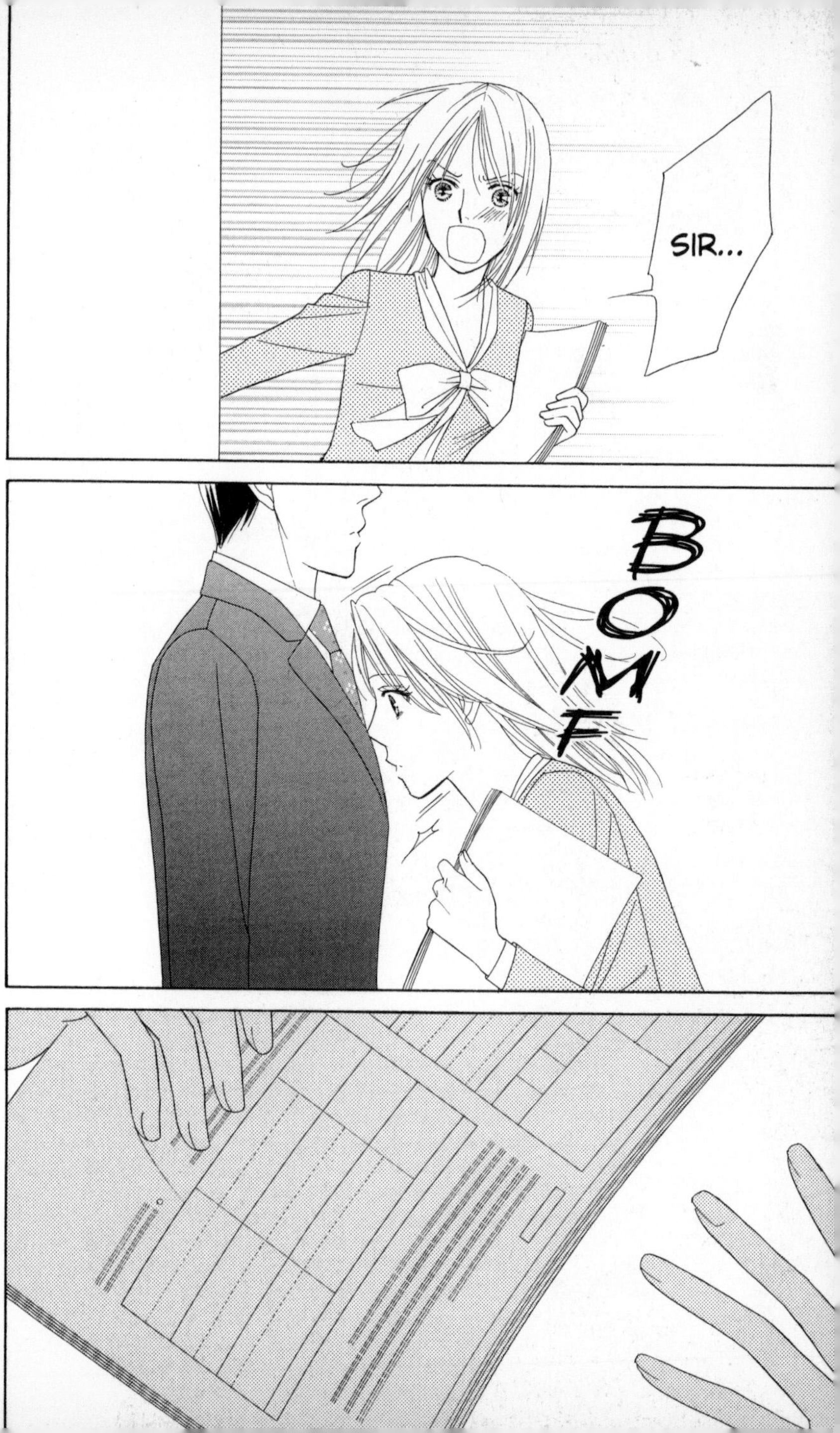
SIR...
BOMF

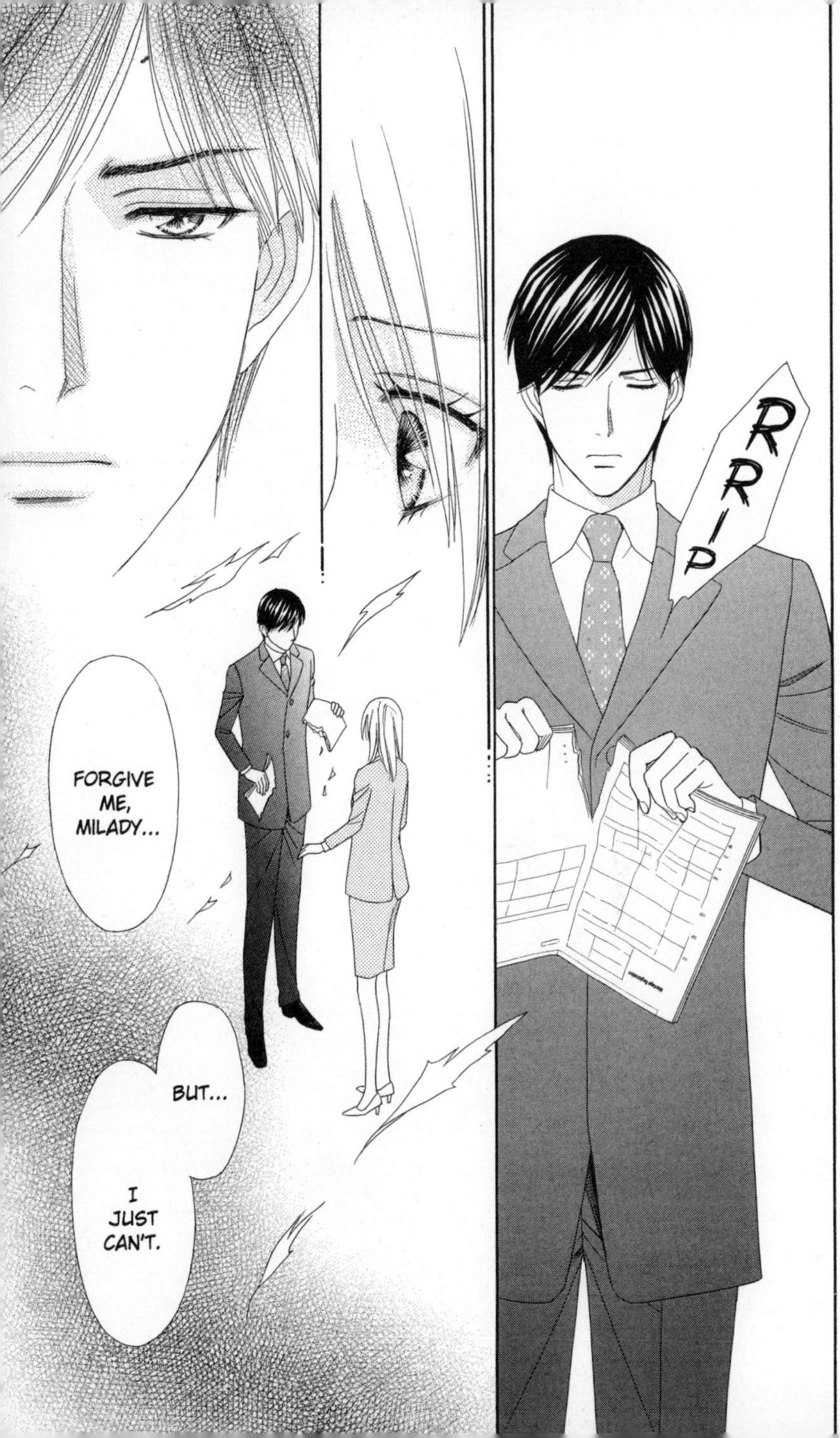
RRIP
FORGIVE ME, MILADY...
BUT...
I JUST CAN'T.

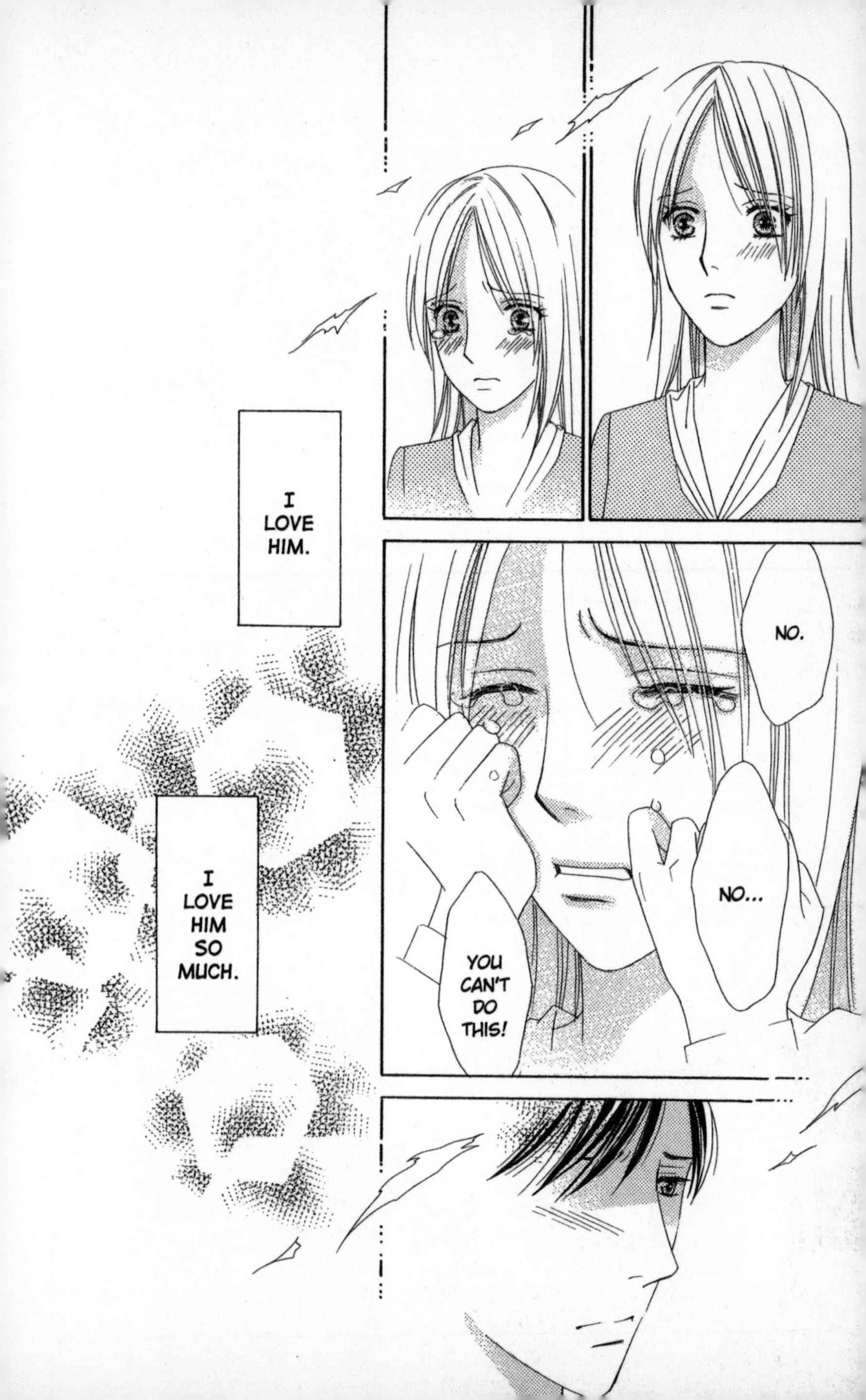
NO.
NO...
YOU CAN'T DO THIS!
I LOVE HIM.
I LOVE HIM SO MUCH.

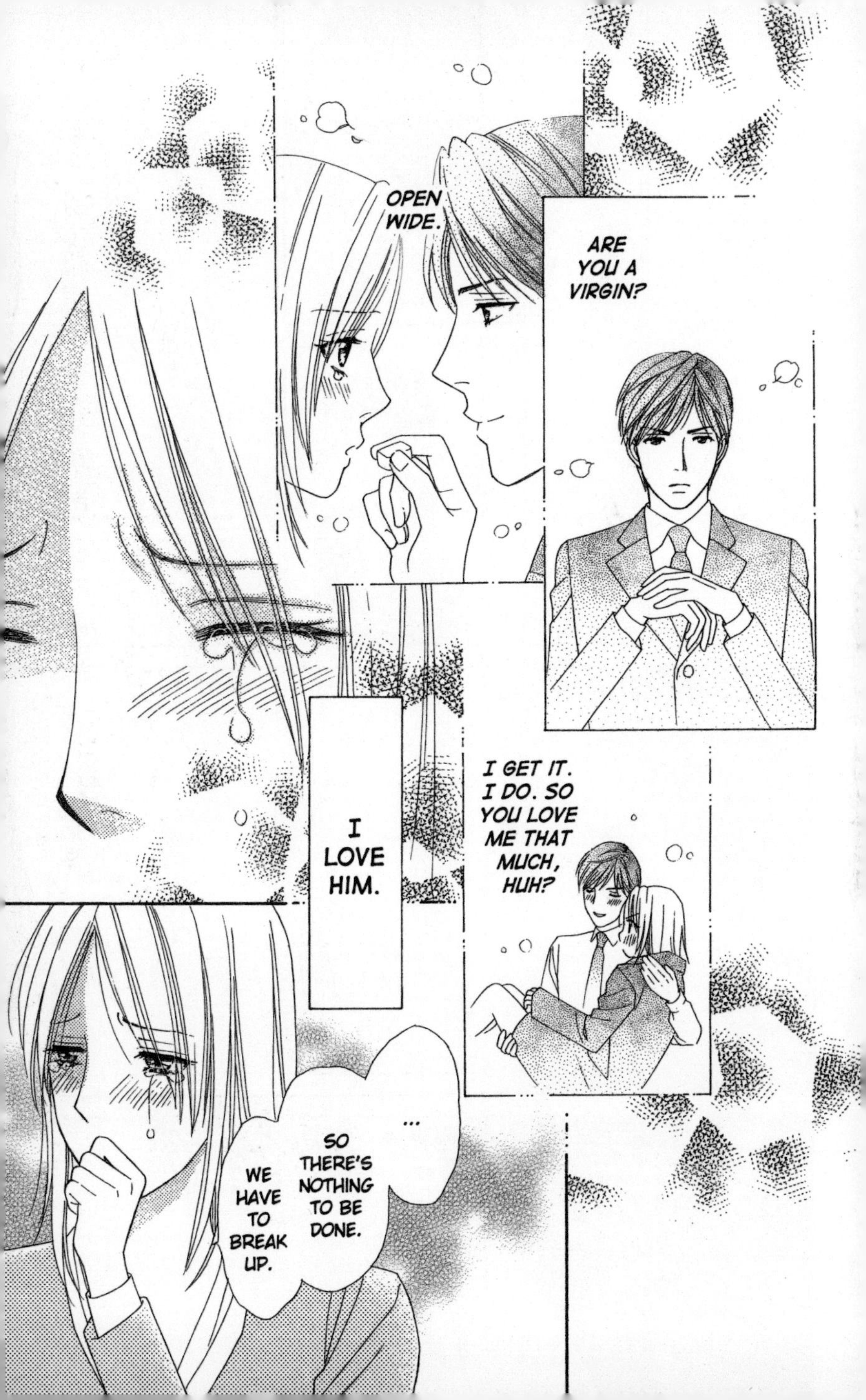
ARE YOU A VIRGIN?
OPEN WIDE.
I GET IT. I DO. SO YOU LOVE ME THAT MUCH, HUH?
I LOVE HIM.
...
SO THERE'S NOTHING TO BE DONE.
WE HAVE TO BREAK UP.

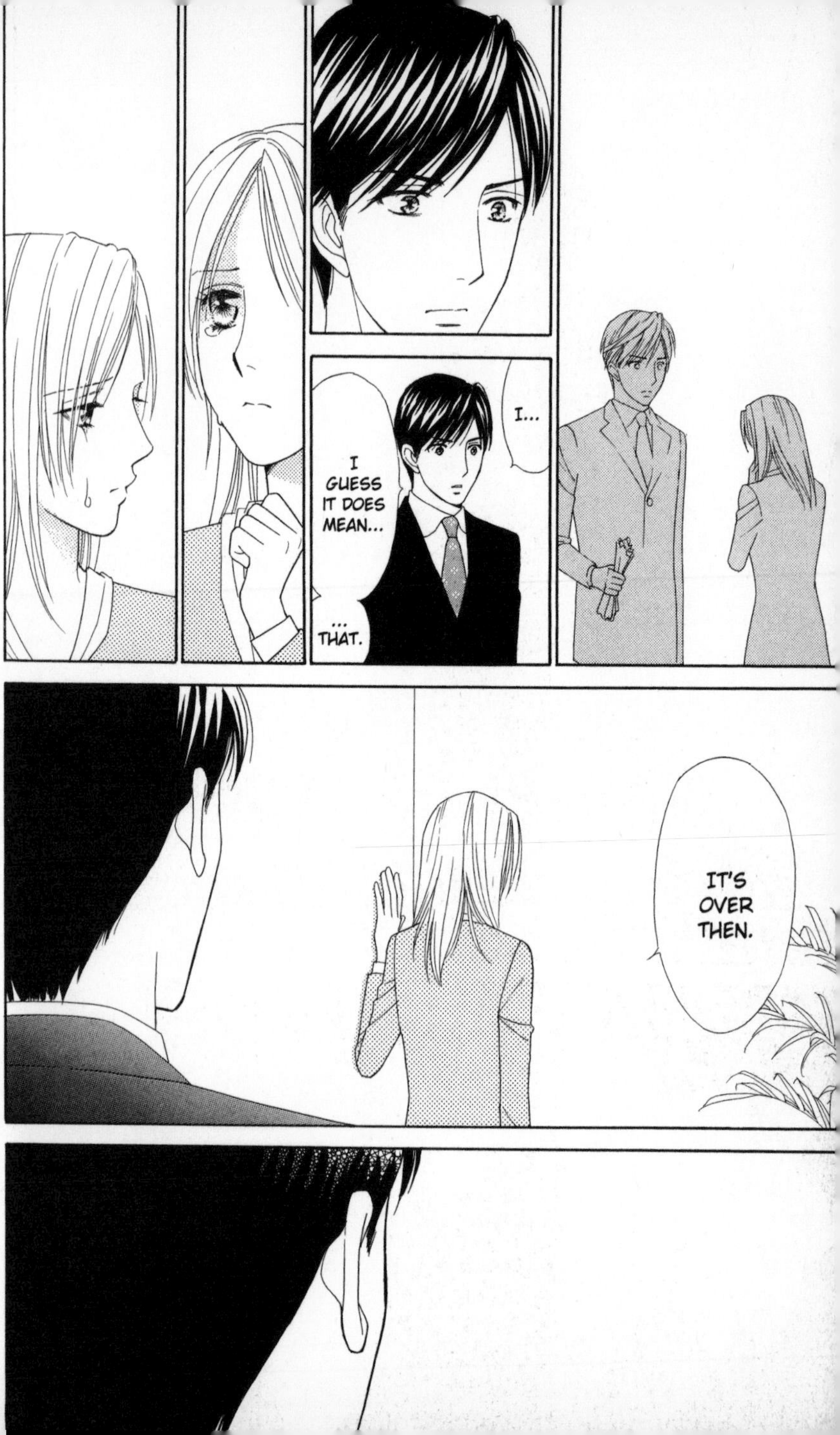
I...
I GUESS IT DOES MEAN...
... THAT.
IT'S OVER THEN.

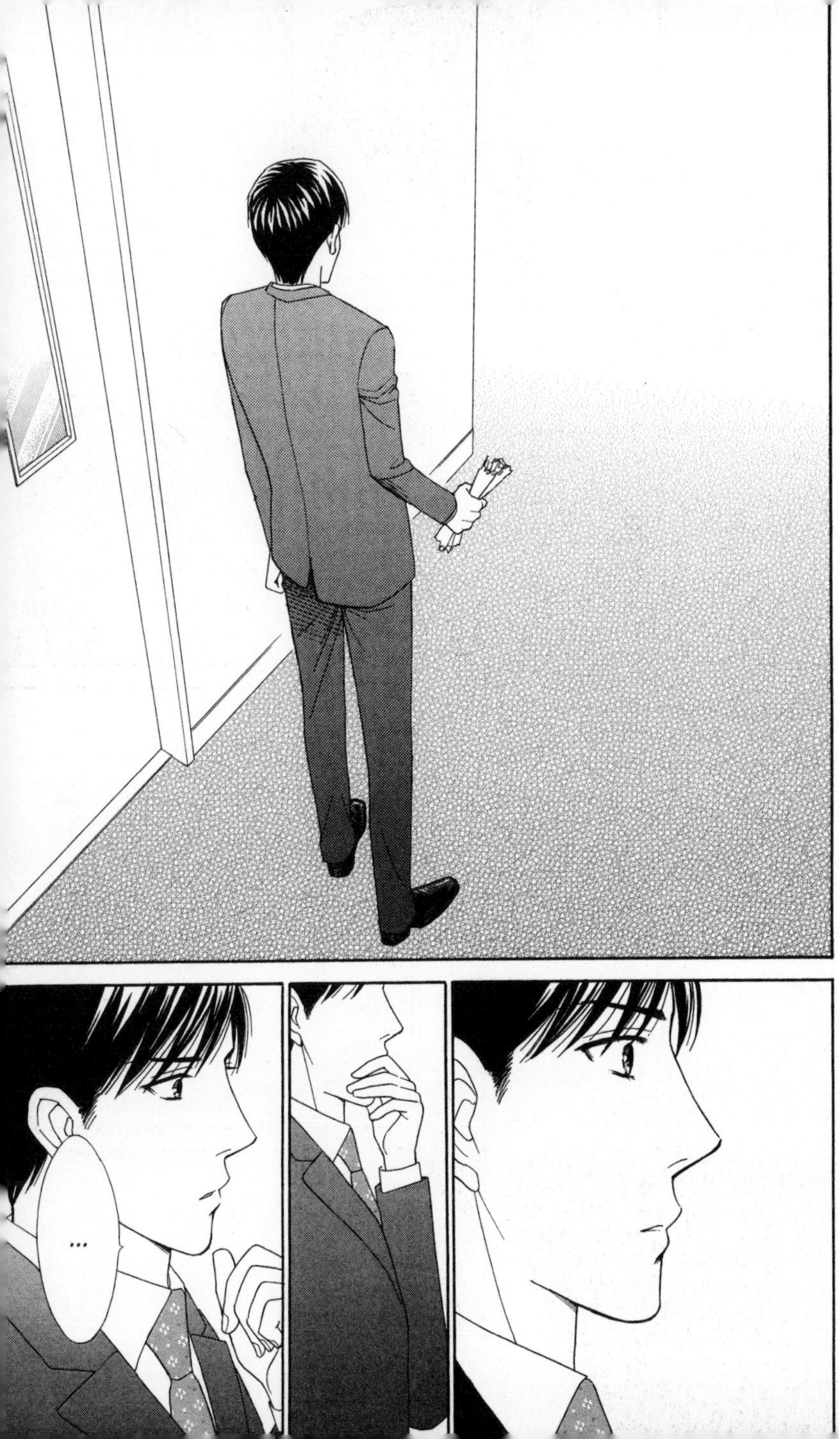
...

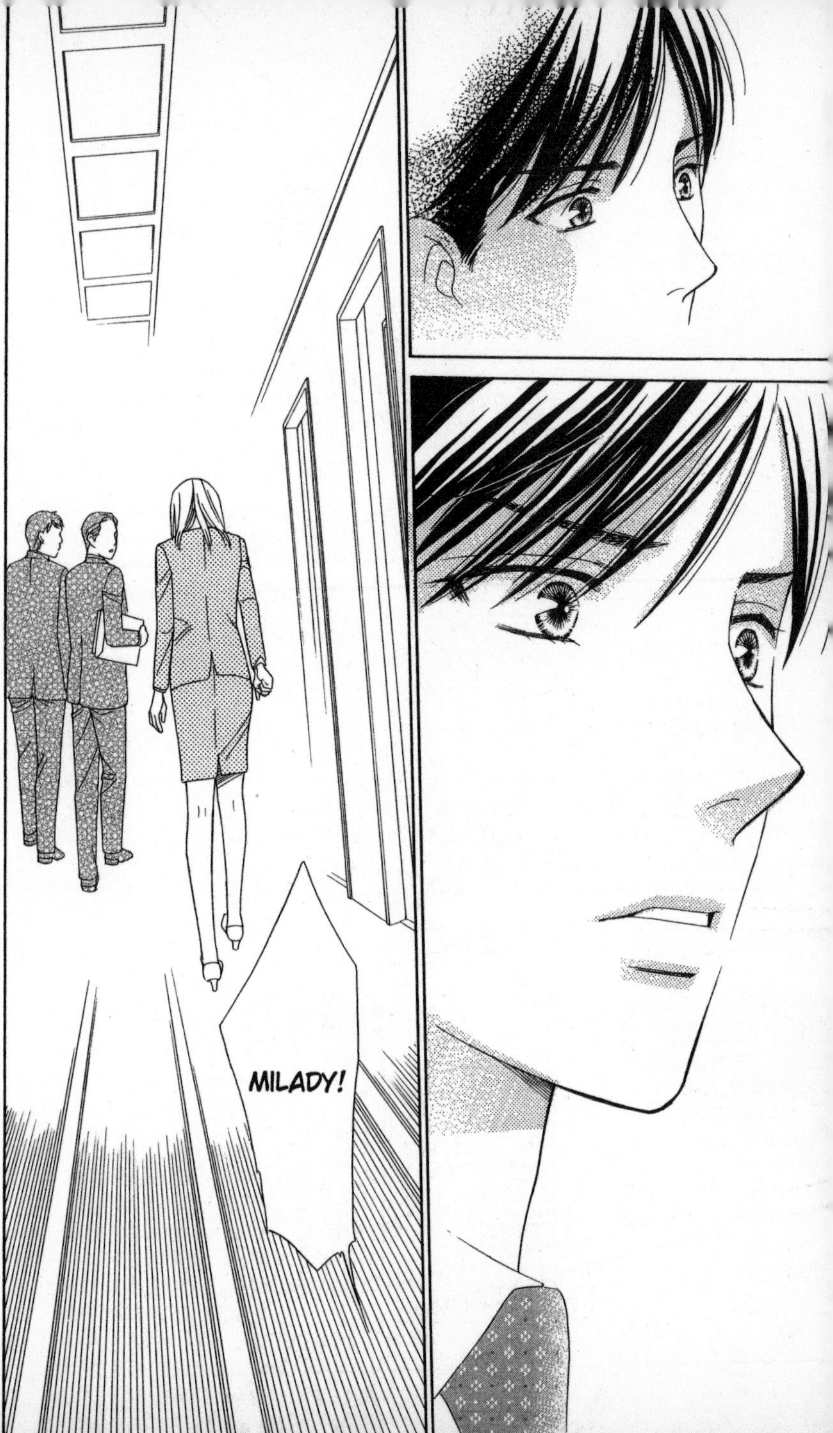
MILADY!

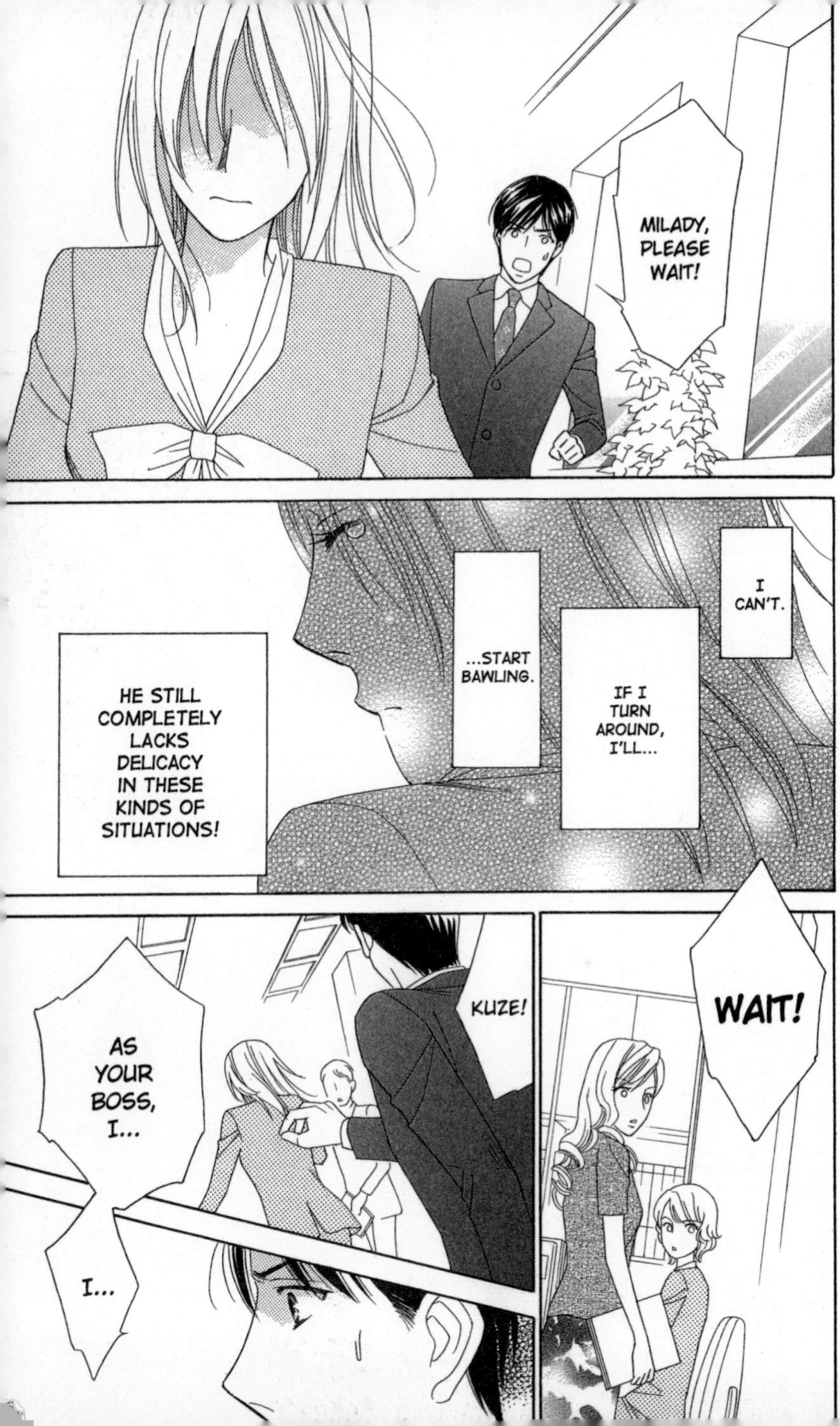
MILADY, PLEASE WAIT!
I CAN'T.
IF I TURN AROUND, I'LL...
...START BAWLING.
HE STILL COMPLETELY LACKS DELICACY IN THESE KINDS OF SITUATIONS!
WAIT!
KUZE!
AS YOUR BOSS, I...
I...

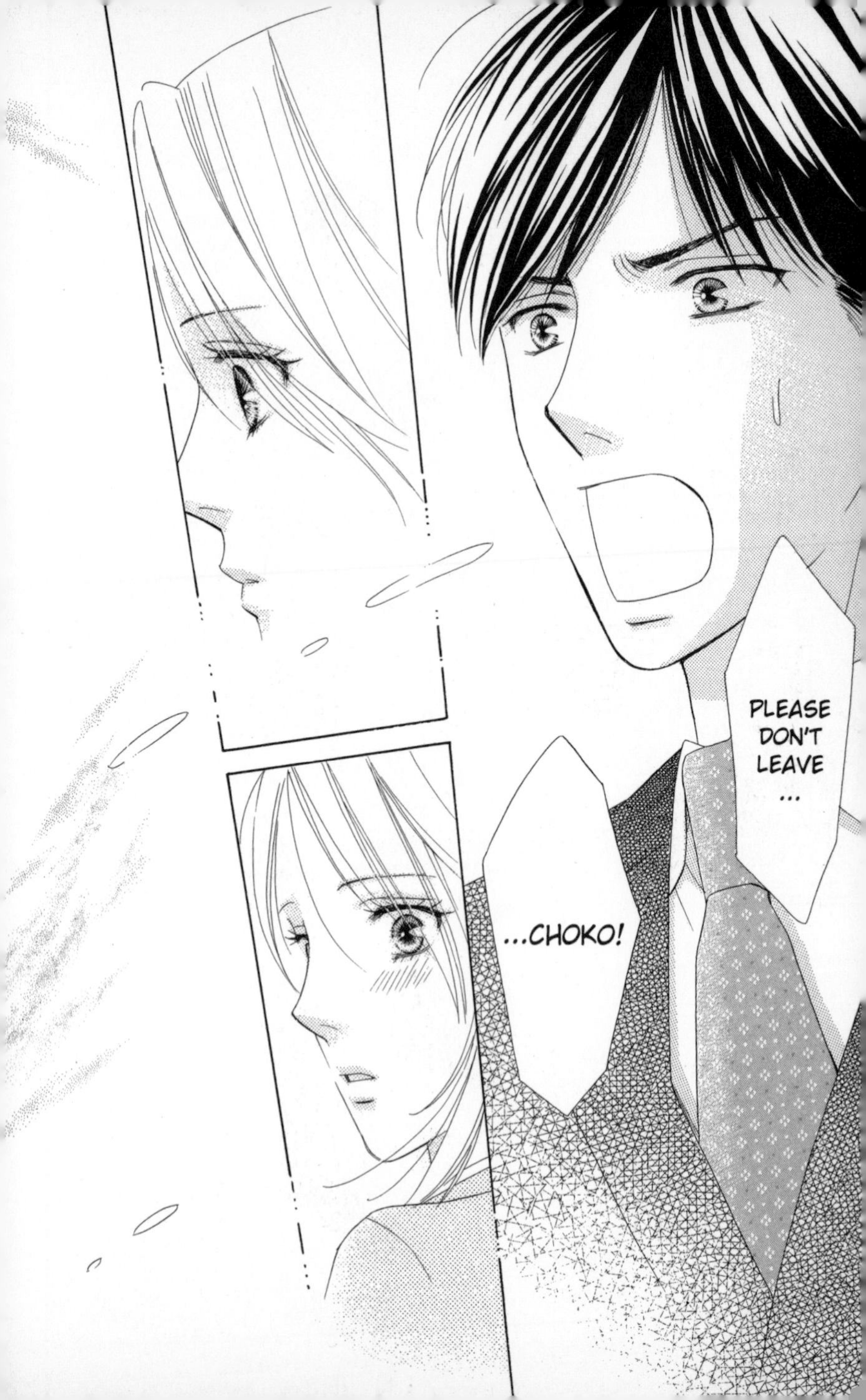
PLEASE DON'T LEAVE ...
...CHOKO!

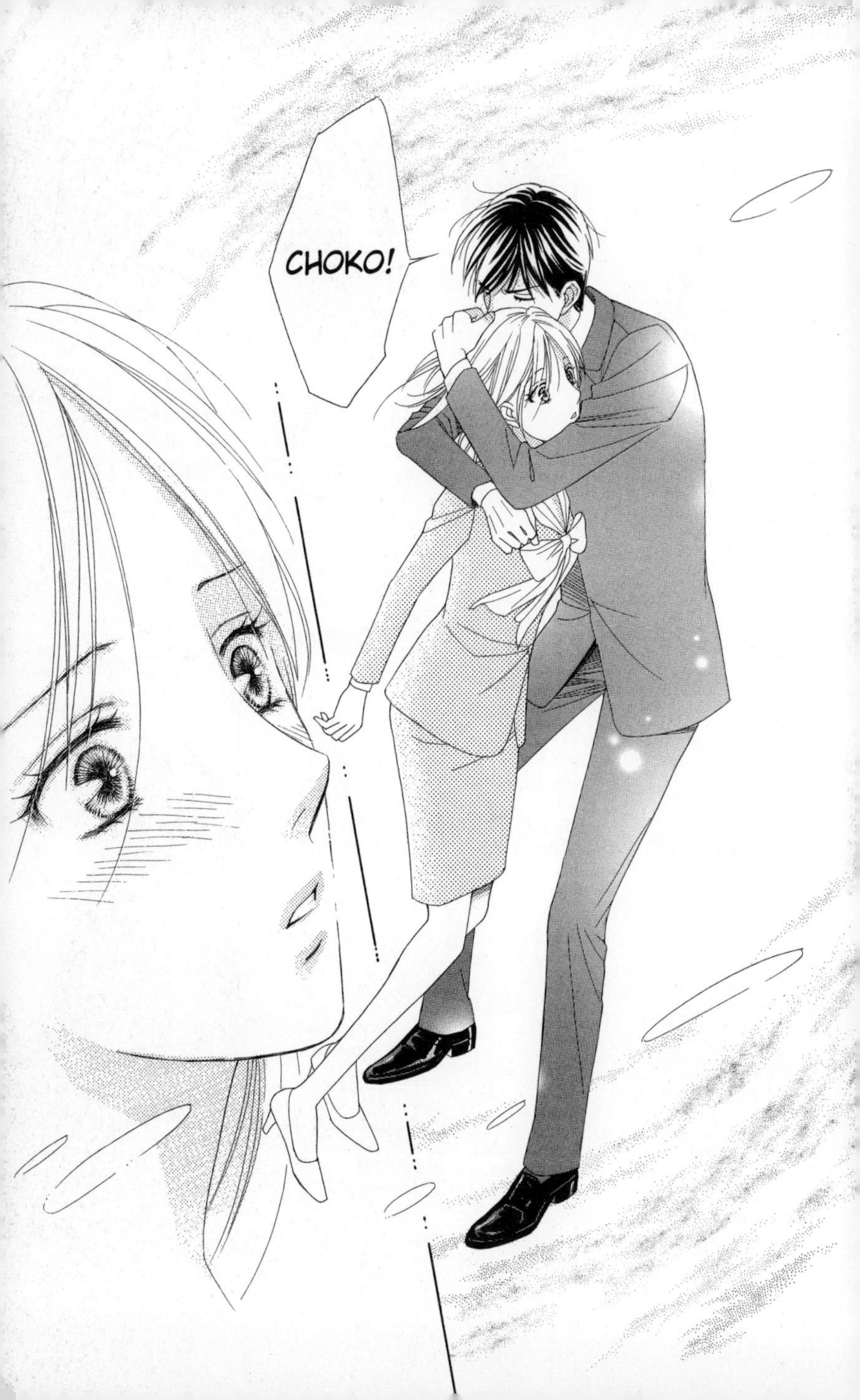
CHOKO!

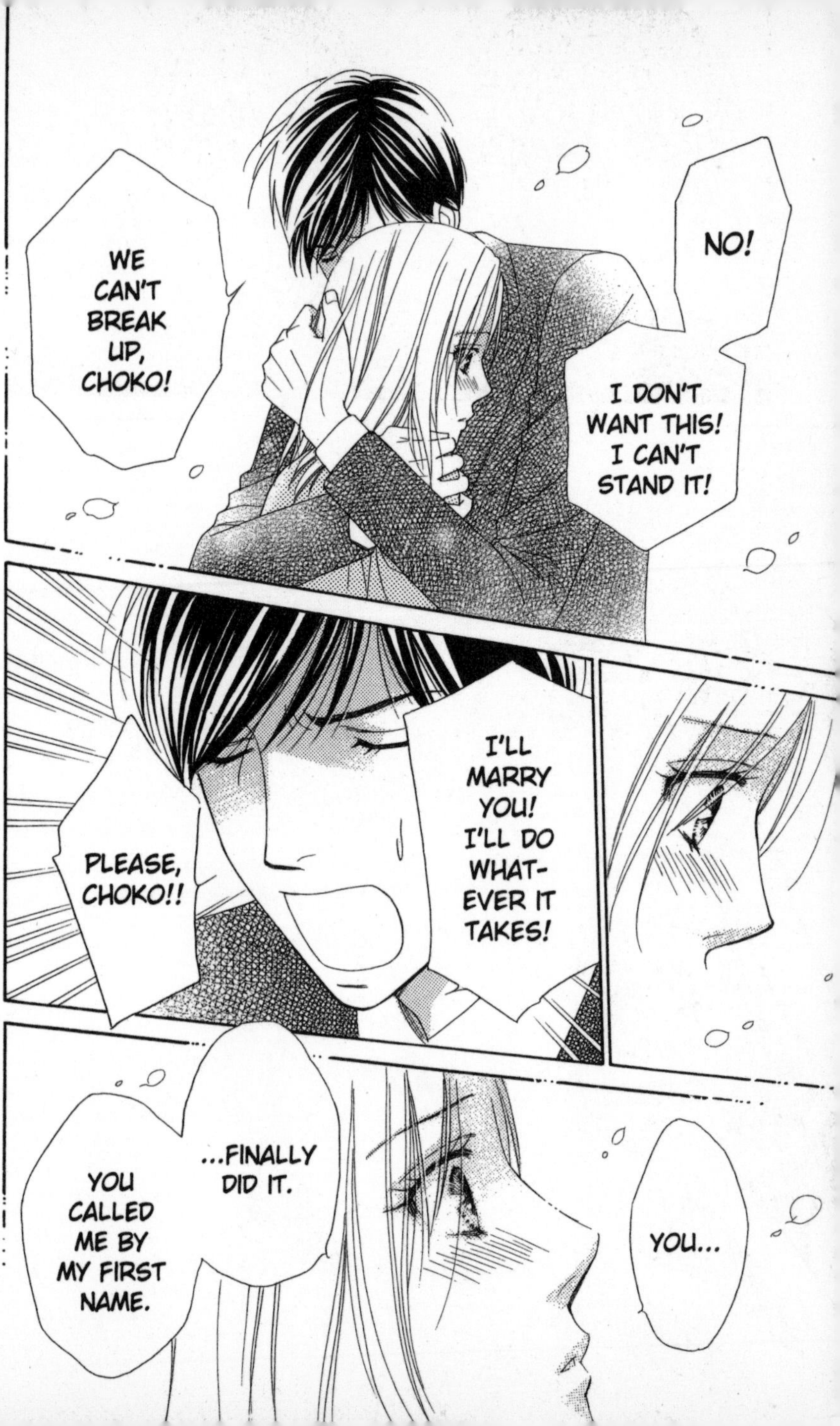
NO!
I DON'T WANT THIS! I CAN'T STAND IT!
WE CAN'T BREAK UP, CHOKO!
I'LL MARRY YOU! I'LL DO WHAT-EVER IT TAKES!
PLEASE, CHOKO!!
YOU...
...FINALLY DID IT.
YOU CALLED ME BY MY FIRST NAME.

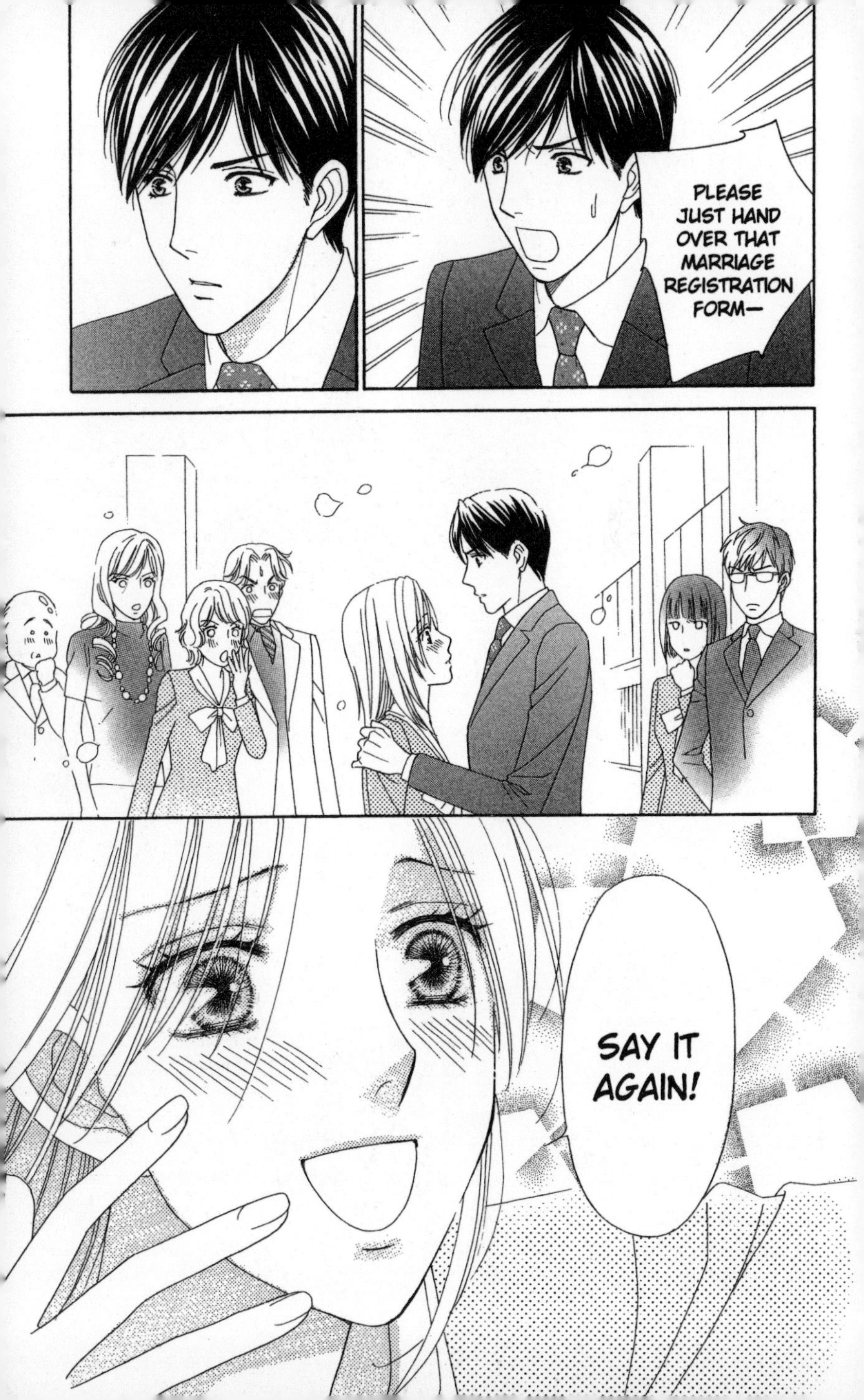
PLEASE JUST HAND OVER THAT MARRIAGE REGISTRATION FORM—
SAY IT AGAIN!

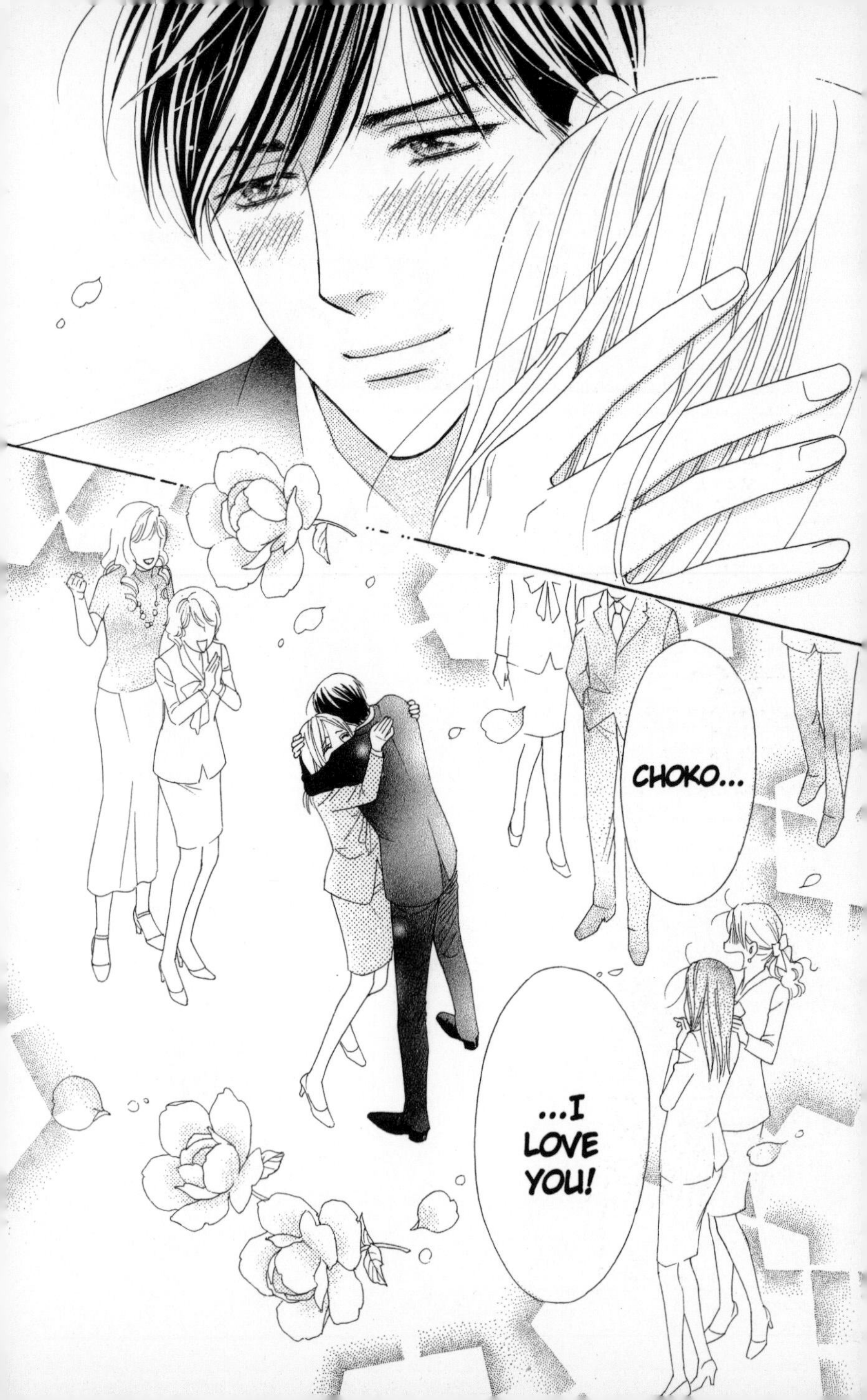
CHOKO...
...I LOVE YOU!

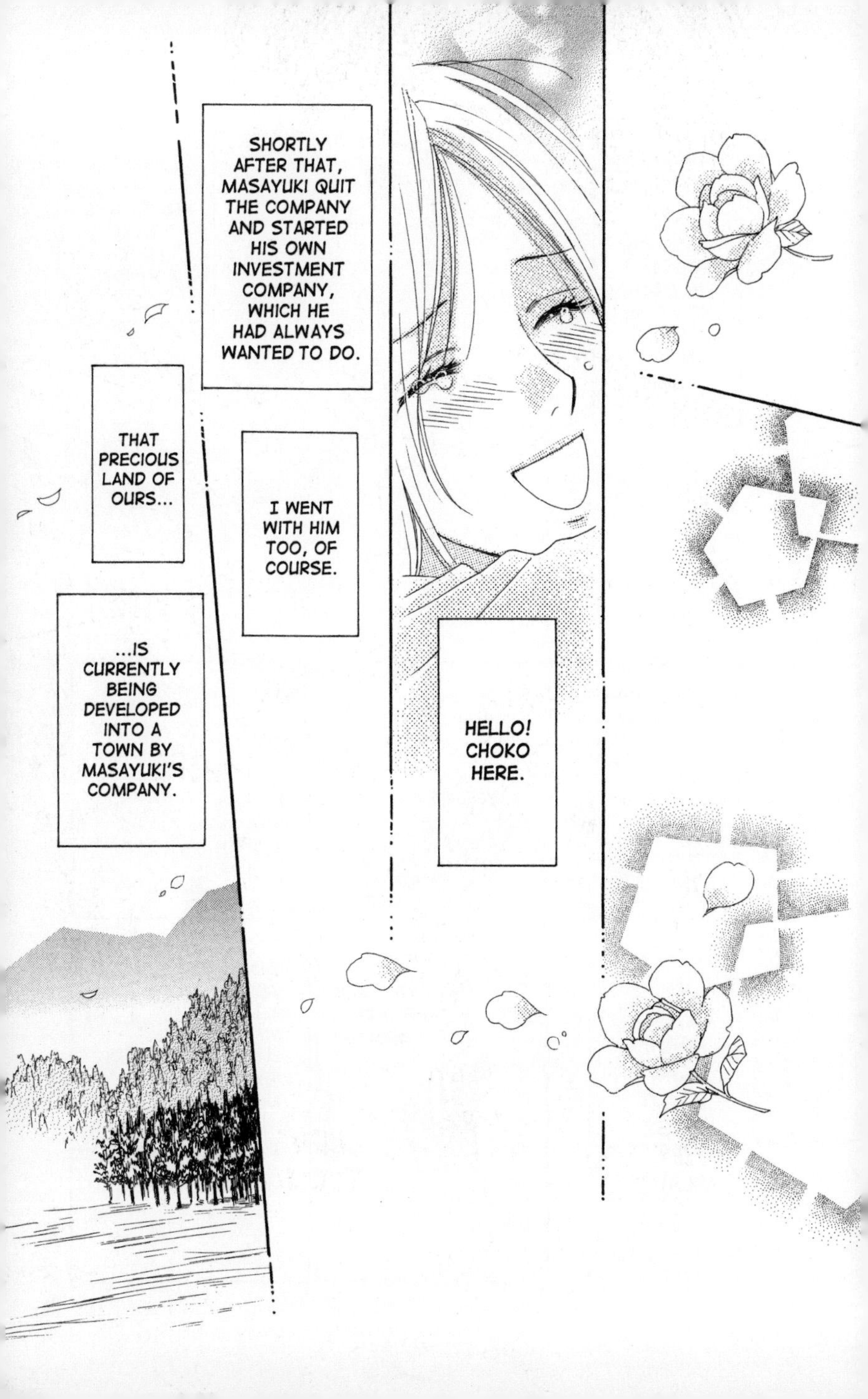
HELLO! CHOKO HERE.
SHORTLY AFTER THAT, MASAYUKI QUIT THE COMPANY AND STARTED HIS OWN INVESTMENT COMPANY, WHICH HE HAD ALWAYS WANTED TO DO.
I WENT WITH HIM TOO, OF COURSE.
THAT PRECIOUS LAND OF OURS...
...IS CURRENTLY BEING DEVELOPED INTO A TOWN BY MASAYUKI'S COMPANY.

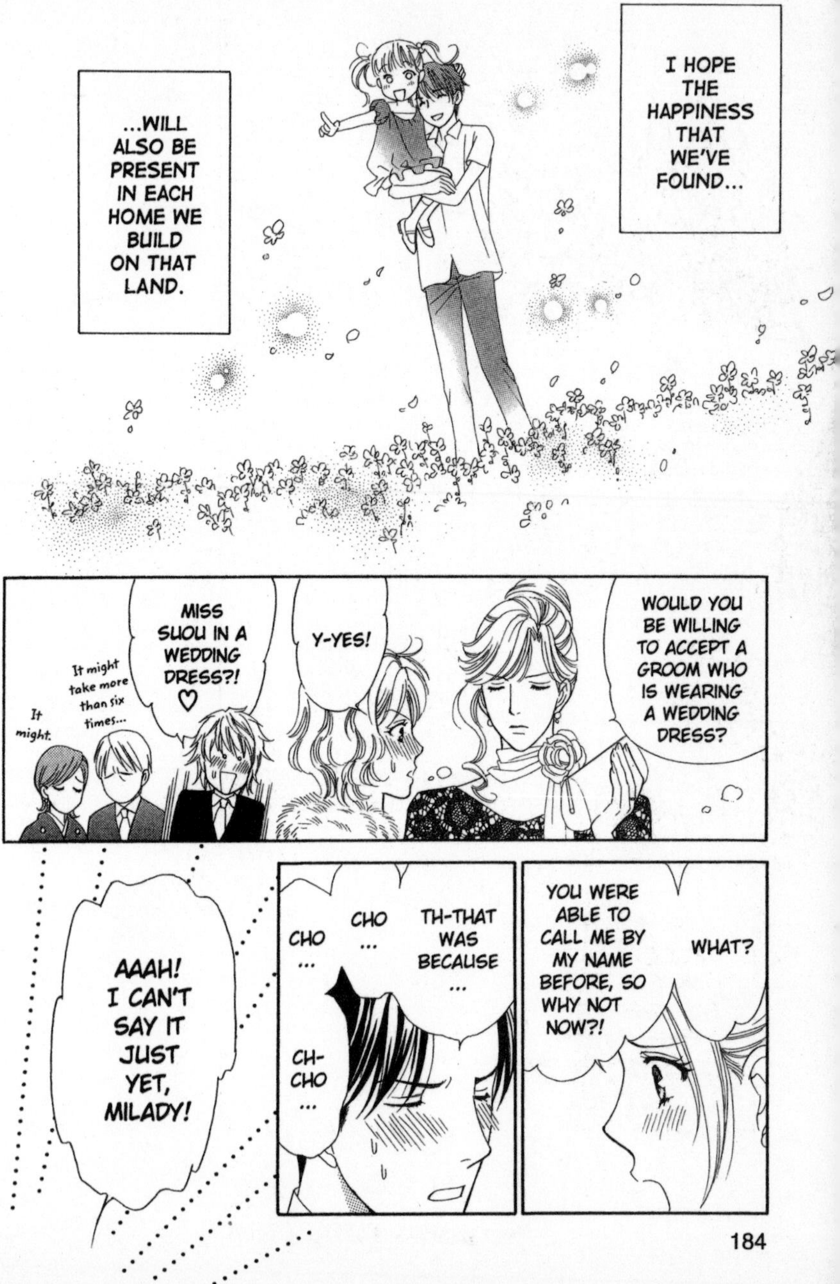
I HOPE THE HAPPINESS THAT WE'VE FOUND...
...WILL ALSO BE PRESENT IN EACH HOME WE BUILD ON THAT LAND.
WOULD YOU BE WILLING TO ACCEPT A GROOM WHO IS WEARING A WEDDING DRESS?
Y-YES!
MISS SUOU IN A WEDDING DRESS?! ♡
It might take more than six times...
It might.
WHAT?
YOU WERE ABLE TO CALL ME BY MY NAME BEFORE, SO WHY NOT NOW?!
TH-THAT WAS BECAUSE ...
CHO ...
CHO ...
CH-CHO ...
AAAH! I CAN'T SAY IT JUST YET, MILADY!

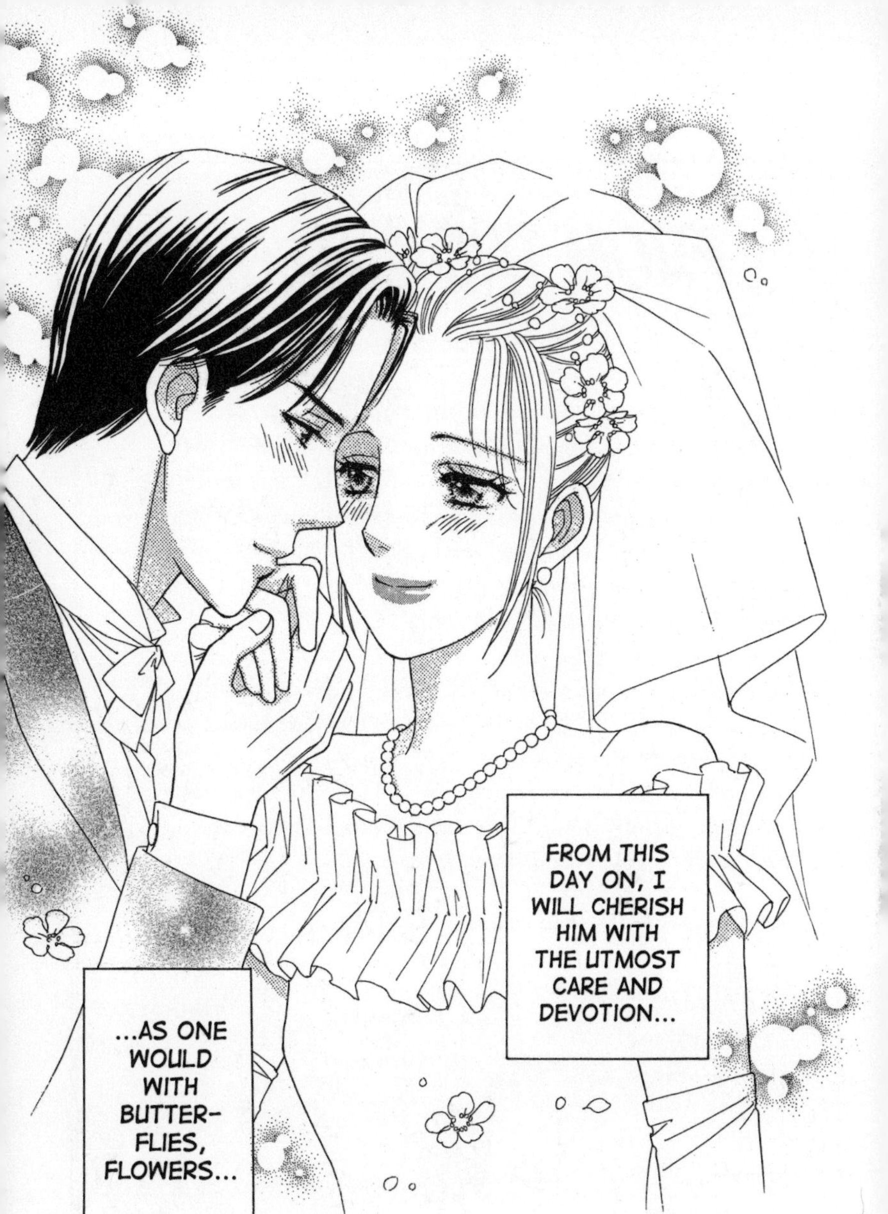
FROM THIS DAY ON, I WILL CHERISH HIM WITH THE UTMOST CARE AND DEVOTION...
...AS ONE WOULD WITH BUTTER-FLIES, FLOWERS...

Butterflies, Flowers/End

FROM THE AUTHOR

It's over...!! Thank you very much for reading *Butterflies, Flowers* to the very end, everyone...!! This is the first time in all my series that I had a **docile main character**, so I had to rely on the male character to move the story... but **this guy was**...!! Odd. When I started this series, he was a cool, calm guy who'd do what was needed when push came to shove, but before I noticed, he had turned into someone who speaks in hardcore otaku and **only thinks about having sex.**
I wasn't expecting this... UU
The two main characters pretty much had a split personality, so I had a very(x40) hard time moving them around...
It made me drink more...
I had a lot of fun these past three and a half years, and although this series made me drink more, I'd be more than grateful if you continued to enjoy it.

2009. 吉原.
Yoshihara

Send your remarks and reviews to...
Nancy Thistlethwaite, Editor
VIZ Media, LLC
295 Bay Street
San Francisco, CA 94133

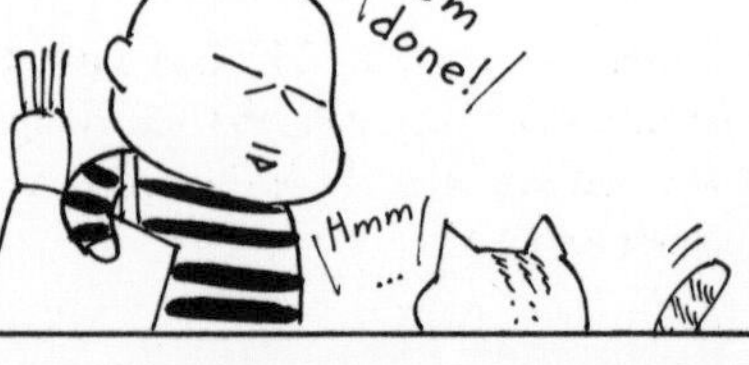
I'm done!
Hmm...

Butterflies, Flowers

Notes

Page 24: *Yokyoku* is the music of Noh theatre, a form of classical Japanese drama.

Page 44: "Masayuki Rising" is a play on the first episode title of *Mobile Suit Gundam* called "Gundam Rising." "Artesia" refers to Artesia Som Deikun, a character in the series. In the anime, the pilot Amuro is on the verge of a nervous breakdown, which is spoken of as "an illness rookie soldiers get."

Page 49: Shichi-Go-San is a rite of passage in celebration of girls who are 3 and 7 years old, and boys who are 3 and 5 years old. Children of these ages and their families visit Shinto shrines on November 15 to pray for their future and well-being.

Page 50: A *furisode* is a type of kimono with long augmented sleeves. This kind of kimono is worn by females who are not yet married. Girls often wear furisode to their Shichi-Go-San celebrations.

Page 103: *Chodenji Robo Combattler V* is a classic robot anime from the late 1970s.

Page 123: A *montsuki hakama* is a formal Japanese kimono with a family crest that is worn by men.

Pages 130 and 135: *Tentomushi no samba*, or "The Ladybird's Samba," and *Oyome Samba*, or "Bride Samba," are songs typically sung at weddings. They have the connotation of being old-fashioned.

About the Author

Yuki Yoshihara was born in Tokyo on February 11. She wanted to become a mangaka since elementary school and debuted in 1988 with *Chanel no Sasayaki*. She is the author of numerous series including *Darling wa Namamono ni Tsuki* and *Itadakimasu*. Yoshihara's favorite band is the Pet Shop Boys, and she keeps her TV tuned to the Mystery Channel.

BUTTERFLIES, FLOWERS
Vol. 8
Shojo Beat Edition

STORY AND ART BY
YUKI YOSHIHARA

© 2006 Yuki YOSHIHARA/Shogakukan
All rights reserved.
Original Japanese edition "CHOU YO HANA YO"
published by SHOGAKUKAN Inc.

Adaptation/Nancy Thistlethwaite
Translation/Tetsuichiro Miyaki
Touch-up Art & Lettering/Freeman Wong
Cover Design/Hidemi Dunn
Interior Design/Yuki Ameda
Editor/Nancy Thistlethwaite

Printed in the U.S.A.

Published by VIZ Media, LLC
P.O. Box 77010
San Francisco, CA 94107

10 9 8 7 6 5 4 3 2 1
First printing, September 2011

www.viz.com

www.shojobeat.com

Hot Gimmick

If you think being a teenager is hard, be glad your name isn't Hatsumi Narita

With scandals that would make any gossip girl blush and more triangles than you can throw a geometry book at, this girl may never figure out the game of love!